IRAN

IRAN

A People Interrupted

HAMID DABASHI

THE NEW PRESS

NEW YORK
LONDON

Requests for permission to reproduce selections from this book should be
mailed to: Permissions Department, The New Press, 38 Greene Street, New
York, NY 10013.

Published in the United States by The New Press, New York, 2007
Distributed by W. W. Norton & Company, Inc., New York

LIBRARY OF CONGRESS CATALOGING-IN-PUBLICATION DATA

Dabashi, Hamid, 1951–
   Iran : a people interrupted / Hamid Dabashi.
     p. cm.
   Includes bibliographical references and index.
   ISBN 978-1-59558-059-7 (hc.)
   1. Iran—History—20th century.   I. Title.
   DS316.3.D33 2007
   955.05—dc22   2006019250

The New Press was established in 1990 as a not-for-profit alternative to the
large, commercial publishing houses currently dominating the book publishing industry. The New Press operates in the public interest rather than
for private gain, and is committed to publishing, in innovative ways, works
of educational, cultural, and community value that are often deemed insuf-
ficiently profitable.

www.thenewpress.com

A Caravan book.
For more information, visit www.caravanbooks.org

Composition by NK Graphics, A Black Dot Group Company
This book was set in Warnock Pro

Printed in the United States of America

10 9 8 7 6 5 4 3 2 1

For

Golbarg Bashi

The green gaze of my assurances
At last:
My first love and final destination—
The meaning of all the poems
I ever read:
My Forough, Shamlu, Sepehri, and Akhavan
All in one
Shining interpretation—
The sigh of my relief
That all is well—
My Mayakovsky, Darwish, Nazem Hekmat,
Pablo Neruda and Faiz Ahmed Faiz—
All the love poems I ever read
In one
Gifted comrade
Coming to hold my hand:
My Christine de Pizan, Mary Wollstonecraft,
My Mother Jones, bell hooks, Angela Davis
(The nodding approval of my Brother Malcom smiling and)
Holding hands:
Gift of a Merciful fate—
The ray of hope,
Summer of my autumnal happiness,
The spring fate had hidden in all my winters—
Snowflakes of joy
Dancing:
The playful facts of reasons
To be—
The blissful fanfare
Of the shy shimmers
Of light—
The meaning of her own name—
The petals of my one and only rose
Everlasting.

Through the corridors of sleep
Past the shadows dark and deep
My mind dances and leaps. . . .

—Simon and Garfunkel

Contents

Acknowledgments

To Colin Robinson, who initially suggested this book; to Marc Favreau and Ellen Adler, who saw it through; to my copy editor, Adam Goldberger, who made my sentences behave; to my production editor, Sarah Fan, who chased after me around the globe, even in war-torn Beirut, to keep us on our scheduling toes; to Sara Bershtel for hearing me out loud; to Arien Mack for having always been there; to my comrades at Columbia—George Saliba, Joseph Massad, Gil Anidjar, Nicholas de Genova, Eric Foner, Kathryn Franke, Bruce Robbins, Richard Peña, Gayatri Spivak, and Manning Marable—and to our visionary provost Jonathan Cole for the ideal of academic freedom he upheld and exemplified; to Mariam Said and the grace with which she carries the memory of our fallen comrade Edward; to Eben Moglen, who knew exactly when to call; to Milton Butt Jr. for reminding me of our age of innocence in Philadelphia; to Amir Naderi, Nikzad Nodjoumi, Shirin Neshat, and Mohsen Makhmalbaf for correcting my vision and keeping my gaze on the sublime and the beautiful; to Mohammad and Najmieh Batmanglij for keeping the haven of their third floor and the generosity of their spirit always open to me; to Mahmoud Omidsalar for being the walking embodiment of our literary glory; to Said Amir Arjomand and Ervand Abrahamian for the model of scholarship and camaraderie they exemplify; to generations of my students holding our promises around the globe; to Shahla Talebi and Hamid Reza'i and the heroic deeds of their fallen comrades in Iran; to the light of my eyes, my children Kaveh and Pardis; and to the love of my life, the backbone of my moral and intellectual rectitude, Golbarg Bashi, goes my eternal gratitude for holding my hand and keeping me steady as I wrote this book.

I began writing this book during the darkest days of New York, in the aftermath of September 11, 2001, when villainous forces of fear and intimidation were reigning supreme, seeking to silence dissent and interrupting the course of uplifting thoughts, and I finished writing it convinced that the moral voice of defiance against tyranny and injustice must persist. All our mettle and determination was tested during those trying days, and only a few, a very happy few, passed the test of courage and imagination. I was lucky to have been surrounded by them.

Introduction

A few miles south of Ahvaz, the provincial capital of oil-rich Khuzestan in southern Iran, where I was born and raised, the Karun River bends slightly to the west before it flows quietly down, turns chocolaty brown and bright in the late-afternoon light, generously feeds patches of rich palm groves that have grown naturally on its banks, then ever so ponderously moves along to pour into the Persian Gulf, and from there runs into the Arabian Sea and ultimately the Indian Ocean—as if it had never existed. The water of this river bears graciously the pain it has suffered while passing through the mechanized trauma of the huge turbines of the massive dam that the last Pahlavi monarch had built on it to generate electricity, which is transmitted all over the country and feeds such appliances as refrigerators—quite a novelty in the mid-1950s, when the banks of the Karun River were the sites of my regular outings with my childhood friends.

Except for an occasional stray dog, a few frightened chickens and perhaps a cocky but quite useless rooster, a rare cat, or a tired and skinny horse wandering aimlessly, one never saw much animal life near the banks of the Karun. But if you were patient and paid closer attention to the base of the palm trees, the leafy crowns of their sculpted trunks dancing in the gentle breeze of the late afternoons and reaching proudly high and touching the grave gray sky, you would notice the busy comings and goings of a constellation of prosperous ant colonies. These ants were bigger, darker, fatter, and far more rowdy than our average city ants—which were a deeper brown in color, thin, and edgy, their flimsy legs showing far more agitation. The city ants always seemed to be running away from or toward something—one never knew exactly what. They always seemed so purposeful, determined, even frightened, chasing after something that always seemed out of their reach. If these city ants were theologians they would be defiant predestinationists. The rural ants, on the contrary, seemed to be theological free-willers, nourished by the bountiful agricultural life along the magnanimous Karun. They looked like affluent country cousins of their poor urban relatives. They always seemed to know what they were doing, never seemed to be in a hurry to perform their regular chores. They seemed to have an eternity to get where they were going. A more leisurely disposition distinguished these well-nourished and confident rural ants from their neurotic cousins, often swarming around a piece of bread or a discarded chicken bone in our city streets.

Something of those ants' patience and leisurely assumptions about space was also evident in the behavior of the farmers and inhabitants of the small villages built around those palm groves. I remember a characteristic of these farmers: their very generous notion of distance. If you asked them for directions to a village, for example, or where a particular grove was, they kept their hands clasped behind their backs or continued to finger their beads, and never pointed toward it and told you where it was. They would just look at you patiently, with a gentle smile on their sunburned faces, and then raise their head and just point with their chin in a particular direction and say, *"Hona, hona!"* ("There, there!") Maybe if you asked where Basra was, or Karbala, or Najaf, or Baghdad, or even Cairo, we used to joke, they might point with a finger and say, "Well, you have quite a long way to go in that direction."

I have often wondered about this generous, patient, leisurely conception of space and time. It must have been a manifestation of their adaptation to the climate and the rhythm of the days and seasons, I sometimes thought, or perhaps an indication of the long distances that they habitually walked, or the eternity of their unhurried patience. But what a great serenity of mind! Nirvana must be like that, sinking into silence the way a heavy and patient stone settles gently and deep into the memory of a distant pond.

Something of that sense of serenity, of time at once material and yet immemorial, of patience and perseverance through history, still shimmers and shies away under the thin skin of what today we claim and call "Iran."

Halfway around the globe and half a century later, and far from the joyous and generous wisdom of farmers and palm trees, Francis Fukuyama, then employed by the U.S. Department of State, expanded an article he had written in 1989 into a book, which was published in 1993 as *The End of History and the Last Man*. Soon after that, Samuel P. Huntington, a professor at Harvard University and a former White House coordinator of security planning, expanded an article he had written in 1993 into a book, *The Clash of Civilizations and the Remaking of World Order*. It was published in January 1998.[1]

In *The End of History and the Last Man*, Fukuyama argued that capitalist liberal democracy had finally succeeded in defeating all its ideological rivals, and that in the aftermath of the collapse of the Soviet Union, the fall of the Berlin wall, and the disappearance of the Eastern European bloc, "Western liberal democracy" had indeed prevailed over all its political alternatives. As a result, "history," as an ideological battlefield of contending ideas, had finally come to an end. Hegel, he said, had taught him that.

In *The Clash of Civilizations and the Remaking of World Order*, Samuel Huntington also assumed that the "Western liberal democracies" had won. But after decades of ideological struggle, the world had moved into an era of "civilizational" conflicts. People had run out of ideas about ways to oppose "Western" capitalist modernity and were resorting to their tribal affiliations in order to resist the march of "Western Civilization." Something, Huntington thought, ought to be done about this.

Fukuyama and Huntington complete and complement each other by linking a categorical cancellation of history and the unilateral pronouncement of "the West" as its victor to a mutation of that victory into a civilizational abstraction. While Fukuyama seeks to strike out all alternative historical narratives, for they give nations narrations with which to puncture the inflated hubris of empires and their bureaucratic functionaries, Huntington reduces the very same nations and their unpredictable revolts and resistances to a handful of fabricated civilizational categories in order better to manage their rebellions against globalized tyranny. They are both, something from the distant banks of the Karun assures me, self-delusional.

From somewhere in the space that marks the narrative distance between the serenity of a sense of history at once temporal and immemorial and a teleological finality that posits history at its thither, I have come to write this book on Iran.

How is it possible to tell the story of any nation, write any history at all, after "the end of history" has been proclaimed? This proclamation (to my mind a peculiarly North American intellectual banality) is really the end of moral imagination, commensurate with the rise of a self-congratulatory and triumphalist anti-historiography, of intentional amnesia, a refusal even to acknowledge, let alone relate to, any people's history. The telling of the history of Iran, or anywhere else, is a way morally and imaginatively to resist the presumptuous imperial hubris of a "superpower" that has convinced itself of its triumphant Christian finality, so it can confidently proclaim that history has come to an end. But history has ended nowhere except in the minds of bureaucratic strategists and imperial tacticians. For Hegel, history began with the Greeks and Romans and came to its height in Germany. For Fukuyama, history ended in the U.S. Department of State. The world begs to differ. Not having been permitted entry into history by Hegel, we are now told by Fukuyama, "Sorry, folks! History has ended." We, the people, subalterns rejecting all grand narratives, object.

There is a systematically nostalgic displacement between where people have been and the grand narratives of their whereabouts—as if the whole world has spent just one year in a forbidden domain and then been yanked away from it, and is now condemned and blessed to forget and remember that space at odd and unpredictable times, remembering it when it thinks it forgotten, forgetting it when it thinks it remembered.

The story of Iran over the last two hundred years is very much informed by that sense of displacement. Throughout the course of their encounter with colonial modernity, Iranians have experienced this sense of dislocation, assumed that their country has been dislodged from its rightful place, and thought that it has been geographically arrested in a place where it should not be, that it should be somewhere else. This explains why Iranians have a sense of impermanence about Iran as a nation, a people, a place. I wish to capture and convey that sense of displacement, of having been picked up and put somewhere you don't belong while things were happening elsewhere. Orientalists have told Iranians that they are Indo-European, but they are stuck in the Middle East, smack in the middle of Semites—Jews, Arabs, and such. People believe in the absolute validity of such arresting categories, as if they were divine revelations. Iranians fiercely insist that they are not Arabs, Indians, or Turks—yet they look very much like them and are often confused with them (which for some bizarre reason exceedingly aggravates them). Iranians believe they deserve to have had a democratic form of government generations ago. But today they are ruled by the most retrograde theocracy in the region, by the clerics of an Islamic republic. While sporting an Islamic republic, and in the neighborhood of a Jewish state and a Hindu fundamentalist movement, Iranians find themselves engaged in a belligerent conversation with a hubristic Christian empire. Somewhere in the middle of an Islamic republic, a Jewish state, a Hindu fundamentalism, and a Christian empire, history has still a lot to gather and fathom, to commence and conceive.

There is a sense of misplaced memory about modern Iranian history, a collectively repressed notion of temporary allocation of a spot in history, where one did not really belong. It is as if there is a communal consensus among Iranians that history is happening somewhere else, a place where we belong, while (in the meantime) we are stuck in the makeshift remissive space of somewhere else, somewhere we think we don't belong, we don't deserve. There is always a suspended sense of waiting for the other shoe to drop. Something traumatic happens—a military coup, a revolution, an earthquake, an invasion by another country—and we feel our memory is jogged, jump-started. We remember our historical misplacedness, our distant sweet memory of a place somewhere in time we so desperately tried to possess that it has turned around and possessed us—and we weren't even aware that this was happening. We remember moments of anxiety in those close and caring, near and dear to us—and then we have a collective habit of forgetting them, of not remembering what was once so peaceful and comforting, yet so alienating and temporary, about our place in the world.

It is that sense of having taken a momentary leave of absence from the normative course of history—and poof! history has left you behind—that I wish to capture and convey in this account of modern Iranian history, a narrative that is based on my conviction that no history has ended anywhere, that history has not in fact even started for us. From Hegel to Fukuyama we have been (placed) outside history. We sense that when history was about to start we were rounded up, marched away from where we were, and left somewhere else, somewhere we did not want to be—and thus we oscillate between the sweet memory of the "somewhere" we did not possess but that has forever possessed us, and the feeling that we belong elsewhere in history but have no clue where that "elsewhere" is. Our present history and our lived experiences are trapped and narrated between these two polar opposites of a temporarily borrowed past and a permanently postponed future. I wish to place modern Iranian history in between those two poles—where no history can even begin, let alone end.

My principal argument in this book is that "Iran" is a state of mind, systematically set to contradict itself. I wish to map out the contours of that contradiction, the paradoxes of its contemporary whereabouts. In this book you will read a history of Iran over the last two hundred years, but a history with a kick, with a point of view, with an ax to grind—a history bent on bringing up the unresolved questions raised in the course of Iranian encounters with colonial modernity. Almost seventy million Iranians living in their homeland, and millions more around the globe, as well as the rest of humanity, live with a deadly, spiraling cycle of violence, trapped between terrorism and the war on terrorism, which ultimately amounts to the same thing. Whether you believe in President Bush and Prime Minister Blair or in Osama bin Laden and Abu Musab al-Zarqawi (d. 2006) makes no difference when a bullet pierces your skull, or a suicidal bomber blows himself, herself, and everything in sight into smithereens.

Writing this book is an act of advocacy. In a public domain where thinking and writing about Iran are defined either by Azar Nafisi's *Reading Lolita in Tehran* (2003) or else by Kenneth Pollack's *The Persian Puzzle* (2004), all bets and gloves are off, and we all have stepped outside to settle our differences.[2] These two books share more than just their publisher. They complement each other in their organically linked services to the Project for the New American Century, and to the U.S. imperial design it projects. Nafisi portrays Iran as a land where crazed (clergy) men are abusing virgin houris who are impatiently reading *Lolita* while waiting to be liberated by George W. Bush and his Christian Crusaders; Pollack provides a strategic road map toward that liberation. Scandalously, after his previous book, *The Threatening Storm: The Case for Invading Iraq*,[3] helped pave the way for the illegal and immoral U.S.-led invasion of Iraq and the subsequent murder of tens of thousands of innocent people, Pollack was not taken to the International Court of Justice for his share in crimes against humanity; instead, he was given yet another lucrative contract by Nafisi's publisher to make the case (though this time a bit more circumspect) for attacking Iran. Pollack's imperial logic in his book on Iran remains the same, though his strategy is slightly different. I intend to take to task these warmongers— native informers and imperial strategists alike.

Writing this book on Iran is an act of restitution—of setting the record straight. I have a bone to pick with these people, and all the others like them, who have distorted the history of my people in order to belittle them and thus destroy their will to resist the regional domination of a predatory empire that these old and new con artists lucratively serve. I do not have a particularly rosy view of Iranian history or culture. I am ten times more critical of both the Pahlavi monarchy and the Islamic mullarchy than all of these people put together. But to me the story of modern Iran is one of defiance and rebellion against both domestic tyranny and globalized colonialism. In this book I intend to challenge and discard the image that has been presented by people like Azar Nafisi and Fouad Ajami—the image of a passive, corrupt, and malignant culture, a thoroughly malicious misrepresentation that they have manufactured and conveniently put at the disposal of their employers in the Pentagon. (Both have worked for former deputy secretary of defense Paul Wolfowitz and have been enthusiastically endorsed by old neocons like Bernard Lewis.)[4]

I write this book from a vantage point somewhere between the country I come from, where people are afflicted with too much history, and the country I now call home, where people are stricken with historical amnesia—where they are told history has ended. It is not only those like Fukuyama and Huntington who must be held accountable for such dangerous delusions; this amnesia, combined with ignorance (an almost deliberate blindness), is widespread, and part of the U.S. ideological machinery. I recently started reading a book edited by Thomas Cushman, *A Matter of Principle: Humanitarian Arguments for War in Iraq* (2005), in which a number of otherwise seemingly decent people attempt to make a "moral" case, as they say, for the U.S. invasion of Iraq.[5] What is astounding about this book is not its shameless defense of an immoral, unjust, and illegal war, a war responsible for the death and destruction, torture, and rape of an entire people, but the phenomenal ignorance of history displayed in it. I do not mean ancient, medieval, or even modern history—just a history as old as the two or three U.S. administrations that came before George W. Bush's presidency, a history that amounts to nothing more than the active memory of people still alive and in full control of their mental faculties. I cannot tell whether this bizarre historical ignorance is a product of deliberate ideological charlatanism intended to fool people and persuade them to support an immoral war, an innocent manifestation of a cultural leitmotif, or even worse, a sinister combination of both. But the result is the same and coterminous with Fukuyama's notion of "the end of history." Writing history is resisting power, particularly when eradicating history and cultivating a deliberate amnesia, in theory and practice, is the single most abiding manner of projecting the open-ended power of this empire and discrediting the necessary modes of contesting and resisting it. Iranians are still not over the fact that in 1953 the CIA toppled the democratically elected government of Muhammad Mosaddeq and installed a deposed monarch to serve the illegitimate interests of the United States more obediently, and now the United States is yet again up in arms against Iran. Someone ought to connect these dots, and a number of other dots, and put forward a historical account that will enable people, young people in particular, to speak truth to predatory warmongers.

Writing the history of a people is one way to persuade them to confront the internalized causes of their own historical failures (and cultural ailments), and thereby enable them to more effectively resist the predatory designs of a globalized empire, an empire that destroys, along with everything else—from common decency to the ozone layer—the history of any nation that might object to its global control of people's destiny.[6] Denying the very course and causal condition of history (beginning with the history of the beleaguered empire itself) is the first step in paving the way for this pernicious global domination. It is no coincidence that the thesis of "the end of history" was formulated by a bureaucratic functionary in the U.S. Department of State. Nor is it a coincidence that its complementary thesis, which consigns nations to their place in the spectrum of "civilization," was formulated first by Bernard Lewis and then by his kindred spirit Samuel Huntington, two tacticians who have faithfully served the U.S. military and intelligence community. Pointing out that the three of them are dead wrong in their respective theses is far less important than writing people back into the history of their regional and global resistance to such systemic mendacities. One must write the history of a people in a way that relates their struggles to the resistance of nations around the world against this amorphous and barbaric empire. This is the only way to dismantle the flimsy ideological structure founded on the pernicious maledictions of those who are part of this particular "axis of evil."

There is something not just regional but global about the Iranians' consistent struggle to overcome their colonial predicament in modernity—and the history of that defiance resonates with the struggles of other nations in Latin America, Asia, and Africa. I write this book on modern Iranian history in solidarity with the history of the struggle of people the world over, people whose history of resisting colonial and imperial domination of their homelands is at least as old as the entire history of the United

States, and as such a source of inspiration for the wretched of the earth. The story I tell has many variations on the same theme the world over, including the history of the most disenfranchised, impoverished, marginalized, and racialized Americans—the Native Americans, African Americans, Asian Americans, and Latino Americans. I write this book not just as an Iranian, but equally as an American, but an American of a different sort than the ones who seek to dominate the world, as indeed an Iranian of a different sort than those employed by the U.S. neocons to facilitate the realization of their hubristic imperial fantasies. The American empire and the European colonialism that came before it made deep and traumatic impressions on many countries, wounds that must not be forgotten, not consigned to oblivion at "the end of history."

I write this book to persuade people to discard the clichéd categorization of Iran as a country caught between a belligerent tradition and an alien modernity, and to adopt a more historically nuanced, culturally multifaceted, and materially grounded reading of Iran. I intend to demonstrate how Orientalists like Bernard Lewis have persistently and falsely asserted that there is a great and insurmountable divide between "Islam" and the "West" (or, more to the point, the "West" and the "Rest"), and to offer a more balanced reading of Iran and its discontents. "Tradition" is the greatest invention of "modernity," while this "modernity" itself went around the globe through the gun barrel of colonialism. I wish to dismantle that binary opposition between "tradition" and "modernity," and to overcome the paralyzing paradox of "colonial modernity."

I write this book as a testament to the hopes and aspirations of a people in pious search for the soul of a soulless world—the entry point of Iran in the curious course of modern history. Iranians have not found peace, nor has there been any indication that their hopes for peace will be fulfilled. This is the story of a people in search of their own identity, a nation looking for a sense of its own salvation, of its historic whereabouts, the global significance of its regional presence in its own native history. Iranians have been engaged in a long struggle in which victory has always seemed within reach, defeat pending, resurrection inevitable. Their story is the story of common and decent people all over the world. I wish to tell the story of their common humanity, their fragile hopes, and their tumultuous march toward freedom.

I plan to do all these things while giving you a straight history of Iran as well. I promise you that by the end of this book, you will know more about Iran than the U.S. Department of State, the CIA, the Pentagon, the Paul H. Nitze School of Advanced International Studies at the Johns Hopkins University, the Hoover Institution, the Heritage Foundation, and five other neocon think tanks—not to mention the Ministry of Islamic Guidance and Islamic Culture in the Islamic Republic of Iran—all put together. I know things they do not know, or do not care to know, or would rather forget, or never learned, or would not tell you.

On 116th Street where I live, between Broadway and Riverside Drive on the Upper West Side of Manhattan in New York, it is only a short walk to the Hudson River, mighty and seemingly mild, flowing as if it will flow through all eternity on its patient way toward the Atlantic. "That which is from the sea goes to the sea," says Rumi in a poem. Like the Karun and the Hudson, the two mighty rivers of my two hometowns, my past and present, history has the patience of an enduring wisdom, best conceived by Abu al-Fazl Beyhaqi (d. 1077), the most literate historian Iran has ever produced: "History follows a straight path," Beyhaqi said, "for in history it is not right to come short of truth, or to distort, or to dilute, or to be deceitful." And history wills and remembers us, just like the quiet certitude of the Hudson and Karun combined, on their separate but similar ways to the deepest oceans to embrace their differences, coming together just the way a heavy and patient stone settles gently and deep into the memory of a distant pond.

1

On Nations Without Borders

"Mother in need of Persian literature." The subject of the e-mail I received on May 18, 2005, from a young Iranian mother living in upstate New York was intriguing and unusual. "My son," the e-mail continued after a gracious salutation, "is going to have his Bar Mitzvah ceremony in October of this year. It is customary for parents to impart a word of wisdom and ethics and express their hopes and wishes for the Bar Mitzvah boy. On this meaningful occasion, I would like also to impart my Iranian heritage by tapping into our rich and exquisite Persian literature and grace my message to him with words of 'pand va andarz' [Persian for "advice and guidance"]. Unfortunately I have neither access to the appropriate Persian literature nor the training to do so."

The rest of the e-mail was as gracious as its opening. "By incorporating a Persian flavor to the ceremony," the young Iranian mother added, "I am hoping to reinforce his pride in his multifaceted 'asliat' [Persian for "cultural authenticity"] and also present our Iranian identity in a better light. After all he is also heir to the culture that can boast of Cyrus the Great and Anushiravan Dadgar, who possessed the same passion for justice as Torah insists to be everyone's religious obligation (Justice, Justice Shall Thou Pursue)."

I wrote back and said I would be happy to help, offered a few suggestions, and asked if she had access to any of the books I had recommended. "If not," I added, "let me think a bit further, and make copies of some appropriate passages and mail them to you." A few minutes after I sent my e-mail, I received another e-mail from the young mother in which she said she did not have access to those books, adding, "unfortunately, except for books of Forough Farrokhzad and a book of excerpts from *Golestan* of Sa'di I have no access to any other Persian literature. I would appreciate your offer of mailing me copies."

Iranians take poetry quite seriously—a habit that tends to lend a certain poetic diction to our historical recollections, the way we remember ourselves. If jazz is the cadence of American culture, as Robert O'Meally has put it recently in the title of his magnificent volume on the subject,[1] then Persian poetry is the pulse of Iranian culture, the rhyme and rhythm of its collective memory. It is said that what Muslims do is not memorize the Qur'an but Qur'anify their memory. If that is what Muslims do, then that must be what Iranians do too with their poetry, when they remember their past as the poetic resonance of their present—in fact, of their presence in history. The picture of a young Iranian woman packing her suitcase in Tehran and placing a copy of Sa'di's *Golestan* (1258) next to her collection of Forough Farrokhzad (1935–67) is a powerful example of this vital bond between Iranians and their poetry. In the judgment of this young Iranian mother, it was necessary to prepare her son's ritual entry into manhood by finding some appropriate selections from our literature that would give him some of the visions and words that are a vital part of his Iranian identity—placing Persian poetry right next to a Bible she holds sacred. It is not that surprising that she would have selections from the work of Sa'di at hand, but telling me that she had also brought Forough Farrokhzad along with her when she left Iran was a kind of message, a secret code through which she could create a bond with me even though we had never met. Without having laid eyes on that young mother from upstate New York, I could locate her emotive topography (as she could mine) fairly accurately, just by that subordinate clause, "except for books of Forough Farrokhzad and a book of excerpts from *Golestan*."

The young Iranian mother's copy of Sa'di's *Golestan* was not the first edition of the Persian literary masterpiece to have found its way to the New World. Nor indeed was she the first citizen of the United States who would link the words of the Persian sage with the Bible. Given the state of the world in which we live— President George W. Bush and Mr. Osama bin Laden having split all people's loyalties and leaving no room for maneuver—no one would believe that the first person on this continent to have read (and apparently liked) the legendary Persian poet was none other than a gentleman statesman, printer, inventor, publisher, fan of flying kites, and man of letters from Philadelphia (my own sweet hometown for many years, before I moved to New York), Mr. Benjamin Franklin himself! Chances are that if I were to say that when not busy flying a kite or helping build a nation, Benjamin Franklin (1706–90) sought (only in jest) to add a chapter to the book of Genesis in the Bible, and that this chapter was in fact a tale from a famous book of a very famous Persian poet—the self-same poet and the very book in possession of the young Iranian mother from upstate New York—you might consider this statement a prank of some Oriental sort and report me to the Department of Homeland Security. But I assure you, the prank is of an entirely different sort.

It is quite a strange story—but it's true.

The story does not begin in Philadelphia in the eighteenth century, but in Shiraz in the seventeenth century, where the mausoleum of the great Persian poet Sa'di (c. 1194–1292) was already a site that no visitor, particularly an adventurous European traveler, could miss. Among the notable companions of three legendary British travelers to Iran early in the seventeenth century—the indefatigable Shirley brothers—one Thomas Herbert had a rather refined taste for literature. In a very popular travelogue that he wrote and published, *Travels in Persia 1627–1629*, Thomas Herbert mentioned having visited the mausoleums of Sa'di and his fellow Shirazi poet Hafez. By the time that Herbert published his travelogue, Sa'di had already been translated into Latin and published in Amsterdam by the Dutch Orientalist George Gentius. In his travelogue, Herbert quotes a few of Sa'di's lines from this Latin translation. French and English translations of Sa'di were also published by the 1630s, and soon after that, German translations appeared as well. From then on, Sa'di became integral to the European Enlightenment and Romanticism alike. La Fontaine, Diderot, Voltaire, Hugo, and Balzac all knew of him and referred fondly to his poetry. Goethe adopted a few of Sa'di's poems in his own *West-Ostlicher Divan* (1814–18); while even before him Voltaire, in his "Epistle Dedicatory" to his satirical novel *Zadig* (1747), suggested in jest that he had translated it from its original Persian by Sa'di, without knowing a word of Persian—of course!

But how did Sa'di find his way to America? He died long before Christopher Columbus crossed the Atlantic. Sa'di was a favorite poet of American Transcendentalists. But did they gain access to his poetry through German Romanticism or directly through European Orientalism? This is one possible route: Gentius, who had done a Latin translation of *Golestan*, had written a book called *Historia Judaica* (1651), in which he had cited one of Sa'di's fables about how God admonished Abraham for refusing hospitality to a Zoroastrian. The English divine Jeremy Taylor (1613–67) had read this fable in Gentius's *Historia Judaica* and translated it into English in his own *Discourse of the Liberty of Prophesying* (1646)—a remarkable treatise on religious toleration. It is this text of Jeremy Taylor's that historians believe reached Franklin almost a hundred years after its publication, and he then "was able jocosely to pass it off among the English literati as a missing chapter of the Book of Genesis." Historians of both the French and American revolutions have not revealed that in 1789 certain literary worthies failed to appreciate Benjamin Franklin's little joke: when they noticed the similarity between his tale and that of Sa'di, they actually charged the prominent American statesman with plagiarism.[2]

Ralph Waldo Emerson (1803–82) had a far more detailed and intimate knowledge of Sa'di and his literary humanism. He greatly admired the Persian sage—as did other Transcendentalists, Whitman, and Melville. The legendary Henry David Thoreau (1817–62), whose idea of civil disobedience later influenced the anticolonial movement led by Mahatma Gandhi in India and the civil rights movement led by Martin Luther King Jr. in the United States, so thoroughly identified with Sa'di that at one point he declared (in a journal entry dated August 8, 1852), "I know . . . that Sadi entertained once identically the same thought that I do, and I can find no essential difference between Sadi and myself. He is not Persian, he is not ancient, he is not strange to me. By the identity of his thought with mine he will survive. . . . By sympathy with Sadi I have emboweled him."[3] Sa'di had found not only a new home in the New World but also a defiant writer and confident soul mate.

If the transcendental soul of Sa'di could migrate from across oceans and centuries and become "emboweled" in Thoreau, then why could not the defiant soul of Thoreau animate the civil disobedience of one or two Iranians when they march against the American empire in the streets of New York? From Sa'di to Thoreau to the young Iranian mother, now my friend in upstate New York, to the blank hope of these expectant pages—"There's a divinity that shapes our ends, rough-hew them how we will."

The copy of *Golestan* that the young Iranian mother had brought with her to America had gone through a very long and colorful cycle. But neither the moral nor the domain of the story is limited to upstate New York, New England Transcendentalism, Franklin and Philadelphia, the European Enlightenment, German Romanticism, European Orientalism, British travelers and colonial officers, or even illustrious Shirazi poets. The moral of the story begins with Sa'di himself, the principal medieval moralist of Iranian culture, the poet most definitive to classical Persian literature and paramount in the Iranian emotive universe. The itinerant disposition of Iranian culture, its restless character and syncretic fusion of ideas and sentiments, is already evident in Sa'di himself, the traveling troubadour, the visionary voyager who could not stay at home in his native Shiraz. He traveled all around the world, east and west, north and south, as far as to India, Arabia, central Asia, Asia Minor, and Palestine, and even managed to have himself captured by the Crusaders in Jerusalem.

If we take our cue from a poet like Sa'di, who remains definitive to the ancient disposition of even our most postmodern protestations, it is a useless task and entirely counterproductive to try to locate and define "Iranian culture." Sa'di is quintessential to Iranian culture because he was an itinerant poet, known for the mobility of his intelligence. Just like Sa'di, Iran can be identified only as a set of mobile, circumambulatory, projectile, and always impermanent propositions. Anytime anyone tries to capture, corner, or nail it, it loses its identity. It is like a butterfly. It can only be seen in motion, fluttering its inconsistencies around—just before it has been caught, trapped, and pinned in a box. All historians of Iran are (aren't all historians?) taxidermists. Understood according to its own miasmatic disposition and not cornered in one way or another, Iranian culture has been formed *centripetally*—tending toward a center that exists only by a collective will, by an imaginative osmosis. This formation is like that of the city squares in every major Iranian urban setting; no monument marks the center, and yet that collectively willed and evidently emptied center is the defining locus of the city, a place marked only by the space created by the surrounding buildings that architecturally point to it, a presence defined by an absence.

Iran is a cozy quilt, not a fluttering flag. There are too many conflicting claims to its colorful culture for it to rise triumphantly above any singular nascent nation-state. Iran, Afghanistan, Tajikistan—from central to southern Asia, from Kashmir to Asia Minor—all have legitimate claims on it. One of our major literary figures, the poet Rumi, was born in Afghanistan, fled the Mongol invasion of central Asia, shook hands with Attar in Nishapur on his way to live in contemporary Turkey, and then wrote in Persian. He alone constitutes and contradicts, at one and the same time, this thing called "Iran." We claim Rumi because he wrote in Persian, and we disregard the fact that he never lived within the current borders of Iran. We also claim Avicenna because he lived in Iran, and we disregard the fact that he wrote almost all his important books in Arabic. The logic of the nation-state discards the best we ever produced. In order to be "Iranian," we have to be illogical. "When there was Sufism there was no name for it, and when there was a name for it there was no Sufism"—that's what the early Sufis said about Sufism, and that is also true about Iran. The instant we call ourselves Iranians we cease to be Iranian. Inside that paradox we live—as Iranians.[4]

There is a reason why Iranians adore their poets—even though at times they may not be quite sure why. Take, for example, Forough Farrokhzad, the other poet whose book the young Iranian mother from upstate New York took along with her when leaving Iran. Farrokhzad wrote a satirical poem called "O Bejeweled Land!" It scandalized those engaged in Persian nationalism and Iranian identity politics, smack in the middle of the second and final Pahlavi king's megalomaniac monarchy and his stupendous claim to a 2,500-year-old civilization. "I succeeded," Farrokhzad declares in this poem,

> *I registered myself:*
> *I adorned my name in a Birth Certificate,*
> *And my Existence is now marked*
> *By a number—Thus:*
> *Long Live Number 678,*
> *Issued in the Fifth District,*
> *Residence of Tehran!*
>
> *I can now rest assured for good:*
> *The kind bosom of the Motherland,*
> *The Pacifier of our Glorious Historical Past,*
> *The Lullaby of Civilization and Culture*
> *And the gobbledygook mumbo jumbo*
> *Of the Tintinnabulu of Law . . .*
> *Oh, yes—*
> *I can now rest assured for good.*[5]

Farrokhzad then lists a litany of horrors afflicting her homeland: the polluted air she breathes, the debts she has accumulated trying to make a half-decent living, the useless job applications she keeps sending out, the versifying charlatans dominating the literary scene, the ceaseless plasticization of daily life, intellectual bankruptcy, commercialism, corruption, stupidity, glossy magazines, and the myriad inanities of urban life. It is here, in the dismantling of the very notion of any culture, let alone a civilization, that Farrokhzad becomes most "Iranian," drawing on the humor of a culture always busy with the paradoxical undoing of its own claim to longevity and authenticity, roaming freely around the periphery of its own centripetal imagination.

Like Sa'di and Farrokhzad, two poets embracing the medieval and modern history of a people, the actual lived experiences of Iranians have been impossible to cast and characterize in one dominant domain or another. Ancient, medieval, or modern;

Persian, Iranian, or Muslim; traditional, modern, or Westernized: these and all other manufactured categories fail to grasp the factual evidence and actual experiences of a people caught and then let go in the crisscrossing crosscurrents of cultures, the clamorous crossroads of history. Greek, Roman, Arab, Mongol, Turkish, and European invasions; Zoroastrian, Manichaean, Mazdakian, Buddhist, Jewish, Christian, and Islamic religions; Asian, African, and European traders—they have all come and they have all gone and left their passing or pressing marks on the body and soul of a culture that is syncretic and hybrid to the very bone of its character, in the nooks and crannies of the collective consciousness it has engendered and sustained—to this day.

Iranians are Zoroastrian, Jewish, Catholic, Armenian, Muslim, Sunni, Shi'i, and Baha'i, and there are also many blessed atheists among them. Iranians are Arabs, Azaris, Baluchis, Kurds, Persians, Turkmans, and (illegal) immigrants to countries all over the globe. Iranians are socialist, nationalist, Islamist, nativist, internationalist, liberal, radical, and conservative, and a few of their topnotch intellectuals have even joined the Oriental regiment of the U.S. neocons—Iranians cannot be cornered—they run away from all their stereotypes as a rabbit flees a fox. When I was a young student activist in Tehran, my Stalinist classmates would not have anything to do with me, for they believed I was a Trotskyist. Trotskyists wouldn't talk to me, for they believed I was a Maoist. Maoists said no, you can have him, he is an anarchist. Anarchists said no way—he is a Shi'i. To this day, I have no clue what in the world they were talking about.

"Iran" is a fusion of conflicting "facts" stuffed under the artificial and meaningless construct called a "nation." What prompted that young Iranian mother from upstate New York to send me that e-mail was our common language and culture, a binding force despite all our other possible and presumed, actual and potential, differences, which (on that particular occasion) remained unarticulated and irrelevant. I, for example, have no rosy conception of two first-class imperialists like Cyrus and Anushiravan and what they have had to say for themselves, but that diversity is narrated within the common vocabulary of our shared history. That common language and culture is predicated on the body of a vast and diversified *literary humanism* (*adab*, as we call it in Persian) from which she wanted a sacred sample that would grace her son's ritual passage to manhood.

That literary humanism is produced by men and women of all religions, of all ethnicities, of all thriving provinces and ruined capitals, of communities living and sentiments dead, of hopes rising and fears rampant—all narrated centripetally around an imaginative center, at once vacant and energetic, present and absent, collectively code-named "Iran." What holds Iranians together is a literary humanism that by its very nature is diffused, disperse, disparate, and itinerant. The common denominator of Iranians is the literary sublimation of their deepest political differences. This aesthetic mutation of violent history into beautiful poetry is what has canonized the masterpieces of Persian literature, long before any European Orientalist, halfway through college, picked up a Persian dictionary and began to learn the Persian equivalent of a sentence as simple as "This is my hand," or as laden as "Iran is a country with vast underground reservoir of oil and crucial strategic significance for our empire."

Shahla Haeri,[6] a distinguished Iranian anthropologist and a good friend of mine, told me once that when she was doing fieldwork in a remote village in Iran, she told one of the villagers, "Next time I come to Iran, I will bring you" one thing or another. "Where is Iran?" the villager asked. "I don't know that village. Is it near here?" Understanding the contemporary history of Iran requires a categorical reconsideration of the validity and the imaginative boundaries of the very notion of the "nation." No longer is it possible (if it ever was) to talk about any nation—Iran or otherwise—in the hermetic seal of its presumed national boundaries.[7] There has never been a national destiny either above and beyond its subnational categories, or insulated from and immune to its supranational—regional and global—contexts. The production of national narratives is a very recent phenomenon throughout the world. The manufacturing of "Iran" as a singular cultural identity, set up against the factual evidence of its subnational, multicultural, multiethnic, multifaceted, syncretic, and hybrid fusion of divergent traits, is rooted in the rise of colonial modernity, the European formation of national economies, national polities, and ultimately national cultures. All anticolonial movements that have sought to reverse colonial domination have effectively (and paradoxically) corroborated national identities.

The disciplinary formation of "Iranian studies" as a particularly potent component of "Middle Eastern" and "area studies" projects was a crucial factor in the narrative manufacturing of "Iran." If Orientalism, as Edward Said has persuasively demonstrated in his magisterial work *Orientalism*,[8] was a manner of knowledge production conducive to the European colonial domination over its "Oriental" territories, the nationalist mode of knowledge production is equally instrumental in an illusively stabilized and historically fixated conception of a nation and its sealed boundaries. The forceful nationalization of a polyfocal culture is no less colonial in its epistemic disposition and racial in its analytics. Orientalism manufactured an "Orient" to authenticate the primacy of "the West,"[9] precisely in the same manner that Iranian studies subnationalized Kurdish or Azari cultures in order to corroborate the manufactured primacy of "Iran." The field of Iranian studies—best represented today by the monumental body of scholarship of the *Encyclopedia Iranica* and journals such as *Iranian Studies* and *Studia Iranica*—is a direct descendent of old-fashioned Orientalism, through the intermediary of Cold War–initiated area studies, albeit now mostly inhabited by native scholars, a nativist disposition, and cast in entirely domesticated and (ultra) nationalistic terms.

Promoting a categorical conception of Iran, as it has been formed by European Orientalists and now continued by Iranian studies scholars, not only glosses over its subnationalized categories and components, but also systematically distorts the historical integration of Iran into its larger regional geopolitics—from southern Asia to North Africa, from central Asia to sub-Saharan Africa—including Indian, Arab, Turkish, and many other cultural elements as the active ingredients of its syncretic disposition. Iranists—native and foreigners alike—have at times opted for a fictive imperium called "the greater Iran," taking their clues from the imperial heritage of the Achaemenids (550–330 B.C.) and the Sassanids (A.D. 226–650). In its imperial proclivities, this pan-Iranism (or pan-Arabism and pan-Turkism for that matter) has produced a mode of knowledge that is inimical to historical experiences of people in the cosmopolitan and multicultural crosscurrents of their lived and narrated experiences.

The idea of Iran is contingent on the narration of a sustained and uninterrupted national history for it—mostly a project of European Orientalists and on the model of other European national historiography and at the expense of subnational and cross-national facts compromising the very idea of the nation-state. The Iranian national and nationalist historiography falls on the fault line of "Islam" and is divided into a pre-Islamic and an Islamic period. The breaking point is the mid-seventh century on the Christian calendar, when in 658 the reigning Sassanid dynasty was defeated by the invading Muslim army. The pre-Islamic period extends all the way back to the centralized polities of the Medes and the Elamites in the northern and southern regions, respectively, of present-day Iran, both succeeded by the first Persian and world empire, the Achaemenid (550–330 B.C.). The Achaemenids ruled over a vast empire that extended from the Indus Valley to North Africa and Asia Minor. When it finally overextended itself, it was defeated by Alexander the Great. Then followed a Hellenic period when what today we call Iran was ruled by Alexander's surviving generals, who came to be known as the Seleucids (312–247 B.C.). The Seleucids were followed by the Parthians (247 B.C.–A.D. 226) and the Sassanids (A.D. 226–650). Much of the evidence of what happened in this period is either from Greek sources, from Zoroastrian sacred texts, from what later survived in Ferdowsi's rendition of the *Shahnameh*, or else of an entirely archaeological and numismatic nature. No art, no literature, no philosophy that in one way or another did not relate to the idea and practice of "the Persian Empire" was anywhere in sight. At a time when the Greeks were busy reading Plato and Aristotle, "the Persians," as the Greeks called them, were up in arms invading other people's lands, occupying their territories, and forming a vast, useless, shapeless, and embarrassing empire. There is scarcely anything in the pre-Islamic history of Iran, as we know it, that serves as a free and democratic, just and inspiring, ideal for a contemporary nation-state. The Achaemenid kings coroneted themselves repeatedly and through the local rituals of the peoples they conquered, and the nationalist

Iranian historiography interprets this political practice to manufacture consent and legitimize domination as "respect for other cultures." The assumption that Cyrus the Great promoted "human rights" wherever he went or that he freed Jews from slavery is very much on the model of George W. Bush's promotion of democracy in Iraq.[10]

Much of this ancient history, and particularly the laudatory Orientalist language in which it has been narrated, is of an entirely antiquarian, nostalgic, and imperial disposition, with very little to offer toward the ideals and aspirations of a people struggling toward a free and democratic nation-state. What is particularly traumatic for this jingoistic historiography of "ancient Persia" is the fact that after the Muslim invasion of Iranian territories in the mid-seventh century, what today we call Iran became part of Islamic history, placing Iranians next to Arabs, Turks, Indians, and other Muslim people, all governed by yet another succession of globalizing empires: first the Umayyads (651–750) and then the Abbasids (750–1258). Local dynasties began emerging soon after the formation of the Abbasids all over the Islamic world, including in Iranian territories. The reigns of such warlords as the Tahirids (821–73), the Saffarids (867–1163), and the Samanids (829–999) were very limited in their territorial claims, mostly paralyzed by internecine wars and invasions, and above all by incessant revolts by the urban poor and the peasantry. The two major dynasties that ruled Iran throughout the medieval period were the two Turkish dynasties of the Ghaznavids (997—1186) and the Seljuqids (1040–1220). The Seljuqids in particular curtailed the central authority of the Abbasid caliphs and formed an empire of their own. The intermediary period that links the Seljuqids to the modern history is the Mongol invasion of Islamic territories (1219–58), the succession of their descendants as Ilkhanids in Iran (1256–1336), and then the reign of three almost simultaneous empires: the Ottomans in Asia Minor, Eastern Europe, and North Africa (1453–1922); the Safavids in Iran (1500–1722); and the Mughals in India (1526–1707). These three empires ultimately fell under the mightier power of European colonialism that gained momentum early in the sixteenth century, and in the form of three competing colonialisms—Russian, British, and French—finally reached Iran early in the nineteenth century during the reign of the Qajars (1789–1926). Thus between the Arab conquest of the mid-seventh century and the colonial conquests of the early nineteenth century, Iran was integral to the rest of Arab and Muslim history, and from then on it shared the history of other colonized peoples, though it was never officially colonized.

The manufacturing of a solitary national and nationalist historiography for Iran has been a principal product of a colonial and colonized imagination, falsely resting the pride of a people's place exclusively in the fabricated idea of a prolonged, uninterrupted, consistent, and above all monarchic nation-state. There is no pride in such a false premise. As a people, Iranians have a world of shared memory to honor and celebrate, a collective resistance to tyranny, an uninterrupted struggle for freedom, decency, and justice. Their history is to be found in their poets and philosophers, their artists, artisans, and architects; in the masterpieces of their literary, visual, and performing arts; in the beauty of their landscape and the abundance of their natural resources; and in the fact that unlike other people in the region, their homeland is not based on the broken back of another people—they did not steal their country from someone else. Above all, if they need to boost their pride, it is in remembering, honoring, and partaking in the struggles of their mothers, sisters, and daughters defying their fate and demanding justice, freedom, and equality. Written into the very fabric of Iranian (and all other) national and nationalist historiography is a horrid patriarchal misogyny. There is no pride in a masculinist history that deprives half of humanity a pride of place, the dignity of who and what they are. If they are Arab, Azari, Baluchi, Kurd, Persian, Turkmen, or otherwise, they are all Iranian by virtue of their millennial struggle for women's rights, human rights, civil rights, for freedom and democracy, for decency, and for an abiding sense of justice. No dynastic history gave them that thriving and legitimate sense of dignity, no monarchy was needed to sustain it, and certainly no colonial or imperial hubris can take it away. Ideologues of colonial plundering of countries like Iran, senile Orientalists such as Bernard Lewis who have forgotten how we came about, are now fond of saying that if countries like Iran were left to their own devices they would disintegrate and collapse into their tribal and ethnic components. They are dead wrong. A creative cosmopolitanism of unsurpassed energy and elegance holds the shared history of countries like Iran together. We have become a nation not by virtue of European colonizing or Orientalists writing about us, but by virtue of resisting colonialism, talking back to senile Orientalists, reminding them of where we come from, striking back at the imperial hubris that has denied us agency. We are a nation by virtue of our collective will to resist power, and we are a modern nation by virtue of an anticolonial modernity that locates us in the defiant disposition of our current history.

The breakdown of regional geopolitics into national categories, and the concomitant production of an exclusively nationalist historiography, is not reducible to but is nevertheless integral to an old colonial game ("Divide and rule!"), now functioning as a device to serve the U.S. imperial designs for the globe at large. Up until the publication of Edward Said's groundbreaking *Orientalism* in 1978, the terms of the debate were still the colonial connection and the concomitant epistemic assumptions of Orientalism as a mode of knowledge production. From the immediate aftermath of World War II, however, classical European Orientalism gave way to the episode of area studies specialists providing intelligence in the global confrontation between the United States and the USSR.[11] With the collapse of the Soviet Union in the late 1980s, and the rise of the USA as the solitary global empire, neither classical European Orientalists nor American-style area studies specialists were of any use to the emerging predatory empire. "The New World Order," as President George H. W. Bush declared it, required a new mode of knowledge production for the United States better to rule it. What is crucial in the current production of national histories (Iran's included) is that at the beginning of the twenty-first century, research universities and other academic institutions, even with all their flawed and epistemically challenged assumptions and operations, are no longer the exclusive or even privileged site of knowledge production about nations and their histories. After the collapse of the Soviet Union, and certainly since the cataclysmic events of September 11, 2001, the politically consequential production of knowledge about countries like Iran is no longer the prerogative of academic disciplines and research universities—which are increasingly under attack for presumably harboring radical thinkers.[12] Instead we see the monumental rise of right-wing think tanks and research centers (such as the Hoover Institution and the Heritage Foundation) that bypass the cumbersome requirements of an old-fashioned university (such as high standards of research and integrity in teaching) and simply hire local aye-sayers and expatriate native informers, as the late Edward Said called them, to do the legwork of manufacturing a form of knowledge that is conducive to the project of the U.S. empire.[13]

Opposing this outpouring of politically expedient forms of knowledge production, squarely at the service of manufacturing domestic and global consent and providing ideological legitimacy for an otherwise ideologically bankrupt and predatory empire, requires a critical reading of Iranian history that is neither nativist nor internationalist, neither pro–Islamic Republic nor Islamophobic; neither illiterate dilettantism nor secluded scholasticism. Such a reading would prevent the ideologues of a Christian empire, the advocates of a Jewish state, or the theologians of an Islamic republic from determining the terms of critical engagement with our collective fate. Seeking instead to envision Iran from a perspective at once local and global, regional and cross-cultural, critical and intimate, we must out-imagine and outmaneuver this banal band of morally depraved and intellectually bankrupt powermongers. The collective destiny of Iranians as a people (like that of any other) is today more than ever integral to rethinking them outside their post/colonial predicament by positing them within their shifting regional and global configurations. As Fukuyama tells the world that history has ended in order to dismantle people's resistance to a predatory empire, we need to produce even more enabling histories, "one thousand histories," as Che would say, a free-floating guerrilla tactic of ceaselessly writing varied histories so that the Fukuyamas and Huntingtons of the world get dizzy and have no blessed clue from which way they are being hit.[14]

*　　*　　*

Between a traveling troubadour like Sa'di and a visionary icono-clast like Forough Farrokhzad, both bearing witness to the reali-ties of a turbulent and unruly culture on one side, and mercenary Orientalism and outdated Iranism on the other, thrives the lived experiences of people defiant in their determination to make sense of their lives and secure a pride of place for who and what and where they are.

My central proposition in this book is that both as an idea and as historical reality contemporary Iran is the dialectical outcome of two diametrically opposed forces—one centrifugal and the other centripetal, one pulling Iran asunder from the edges of its communal fears and the other focusing it on an imaginary cen-ter, a wishful gathering of its collective hopes. While its racialized minorities (who are the majority of Iranians) and varied ethnici-ties are pulling it asunder, its drive toward an anticolonial mo-dernity with which it has been blessed and afflicted pulls it together. What we witness today in Iran is a political culture that over the last two hundred years has been in a continuous crisis—a crisis that has extended to its economy and polity alike, from the symbolics of its relations of power to the institutions of what it holds to be legitimate authority. This crisis originated in the early nineteenth century (where I will begin my story in the next chapter), with the commencement of a central paradox in the Iranian encounter with colonial modernity—a project that at once ushered it into the modern world and yet denied it histori-cal agency. Iranians became colonized and exposed to European modernity at one and the same time; thus, they can be modern only in a colonial sense, and they cannot be decolonized without simultaneously losing a presiding sense of how to live with the modernity of their own history. The root of the paradox is not just the fact that we (like pretty much the rest of the world) re-ceived Enlightenment modernity through the gun barrels of Eu-ropean colonialism, but also that in the very pronouncements of the principal theorists of the Enlightenment we were cast as the negational shadows of people othered from us: "If the Arabs are, so to speak, the Spaniards of the Orient, similarly the Persians are the French of Asia. They are good poets, courteous and of fairly fine taste. They are not such strict followers of Islam, and they permit to their pleasure-prone disposition a tolerably mild interpretation of the Koran." Such was the view of (then) "Persia" advanced by Immanuel Kant, the founding father of European Enlightenment modernity.[15] Suppose Iranians were to remain Iranian and not "the French of Asia." What then? Iranians could be modern only despite themselves. They had to be less Muslim and more French to remain in Asia and have a claim on "the feeling of the beautiful and sublime"—which for Immanuel Kant was not merely a matter of aesthetics, but far more importantly a question of agency: moral, normative, and historical.

The only way out of this paralyzing paradox is narratively to emancipate Iranians from this false and falsifying paradox between "tradition" and "modernity" by recasting Iran back to its regional geopolitics and the crosscurrent of cultures that have historically informed and dialectically sustained it. Caught in the snare of that paradox, the cul-de-sac of colonial modernity, of being either modern in the indignity of colonial terms or else decolonized with the delusions of cultural authenticity, which is itself the worst kind of "Westoxication,"[16] Iranians (like all other people around the world marginalized around the imaginary center of "the West") have fended for themselves by oscillating among nationalist, socialist, and Islamist terms of their struggles for freedom and democracy.[17] Through these struggles, and in whatever self-contradictory terms they have been articulated, Iranians have managed a modicum of survival in terms domestic to their own predicament. But whenever they have fought their battles in nationalist, in socialist, or especially in Islamist terms, they have paradoxically corroborated the centrality of that paralyzing center called "the West," globally imagined at the heart of history— first by Europeans themselves and then by their admirers and detractors alike. Now under the heightened shadow of globalization, "the West" has self-destructed, and the terms of a universal emancipation from its terror are in sight. In Iran in particular, the only way out of this dead end, out of this debilitating and futile swinging between the two fictive poles of "Islam" and the "West," the "East" and the "West," or "tradition and modernity," is to rescue Iran from its false claims to cultural authenticity and relocate it back in the regional geopolitics of its presence in history, in the cosmopolitan disposition of its syncretic culture—multifaceted, polyvocal, a festive carnival of incongruities.[18]

The idea I propose here is not such a historical oddity. What today we call "Iran" has always been integral to far wider frames of political and cultural references. Mapped out within three concurrent empires (the Ottomans, the Safavids, and the Mughals) and coveted by three competing colonial powers (the Russians, the British, and the French), Iran entered its modern history divided in its political disposition and fragmented in its cultural identities. Its premodern history is almost entirely set in the context of Islamic civilization at large, ranging from southern Asia to North Africa, from central Asia to the Indian Ocean. The pre-Islamic history of Iran is equally assayed in successive imperial domains of its own, ranging from the Achaemenids in the fifth century B.C. to the Sassanids in the seventh century A.D. Thus, recasting Iran in its contemporary regional and global geopolitics—completely against the grain of Iranian national/ist historiography—is not entirely new, but is in fact a revisiting of Iran's historical disposition, the return of its nationalized repressed. Iranian history of the last two hundred years can be told only in terms at once domestic to its internal developments and yet regional and global in their causes and consequences.

From the politics of its despair to the poetics of its emancipation, from ideologies that have sought to liberate it to the arts and literature that have envisioned the terms of that freedom, the domestic affairs of Iran have always been intertwined with their regional and global contexts and configurations—in ways that preclude forcing the country into a metaphysically sealed space in an East–West, a North–South, or any other such warped axis. Persian prose and poetry was nourished from its rich roots in Arabic and Indian literatures, before Iranian poets and prose writers spread their green and fruitful branches as far east as India, Nepal, and China; north into central Asia and Caucasia; south to the coasts of the Indian Ocean; and west as far as the Ottoman territories could reach. In its most recent globally celebrated artistic adventure, Iranian cinema is thoroughly grounded in the best of world cinema. This is not just an Iranian artifact that people around the globe are celebrating. This is the mirror of their own dreams—of ordinary people from Japan to India, from Europe to the Americas, from Asia to Africa, as depicted in the masterpieces of their own cinema. Iranian cinema is the result of the grateful apprenticeship of Iranian filmmakers at the feet of their masters from all over the world. They have learned from Russian formalism, Italian neorealism, French new wave, and German new cinema, and studied American masters like John Ford, Howard Hawks, Elia Kazan, George Stevens, and Stanley Kubrick, as well as master filmmakers from around the globe— Akira Kurosawa, Satyajit Ray, Alfred Hitchcock, and Ingmar Bergman. Iranian cinema has consistently benefited from a sustained and creative conversation with the best of world cinema. Abbas Kiarostami is as much indebted to the Japanese master Yasujiro Ozu as he is to his fellow Iranian poet Sohrab Sepehri. Amir Naderi is more indebted to Akira Kurosawa and John Ford than to the entire pantheon of Persian poets and literati put together.[19] The same is true of modernist Persian literature. Masterpieces of Russian, European, and American literature were translated and widely read in Iran as if they were part of Persian literature and without the slightest attention paid to a categorical inanity called "Western literature," which for generations of Iranian literati meant absolutely nothing. To this day, I cannot tell if Dostoyevsky and Steinbeck—two writers closest to the heart, and confident companions of both the darkest and the happiest days of my generation of Iranians—are Western, Eastern, Northern, Southern, or lived in igloos in Alaska. One was Russian and the other was American, and they carried their respective universes within their visions—which had no conception of where this "West" was. I, along with generations of other Iranians, read them in Persian translation (by exceedingly competent translators—no neocon English professor with a degree from the University of Kalamazoo was needed or was in sight) as if they were written originally in Persian. The poetry we read was no less wideranging in its cosmopolitan embrace of an emancipated world. Without losing sight of their individual visions, we read Ahmad Shamlu, Mahmoud Darwish, Bertolt Brecht, Nazim Hikmat, Faiz Ahmad Faiz, Vladimir Mayakovsky, Langston Hughes, and Pablo Neruda, as if they were all close or distant cousins of Sa'di and Hafez, born and raised in the same neighborhood in downtown Tehran.

*   *   *

The story of Iran that I am about to tell is based on these convictions, informed by these contentions, and seen through the critical angle of this vision—a perspective after all *Persian*, outside any qualifying quotation marks marking that language. There is an enduring perseverance about the prose that that Persian speaks. Among the passages I photocopied to send to that young Iranian mother from upstate New York were the opening lines of the first chapter of Sa'di's *Bustan* (1256), "On Justice, Wisdom, and Prudence":

> *I have heard that as he was about to die,*
> *Anushirvan gave his son Hormuz the following advice:*
> *Attend to the needs of the needy,*
> *For your own comfort do not be greedy.*
> *No one will rest in your kingdom and domain,*
> *If all you do is avoid your own discomfort and pain.*
> *No wise man will approve of a shepherd falling fast asleep,*
> *While the wolf is roaming amongst the sheep.*

Katrina had just hit New Orleans, and President Bush was sending troops to shoot any poor person left stranded and daring to approach a supermarket to find something to eat, when I received the following e-mail from the young Iranian mother in upstate New York. After customary salutations,

> Many thanks for the material you sent me. Unfortunately the protocol of the Synagogue that we go to does not accommodate personal handout for Bar Mitzvah. However, I am taking your advice and asking my son to recite in Persian at least the first verse of Sa'di's poem during his Bar Mitzvah speech. I would be honored if you would grace our celebrations with your presence. Regards . . .

2

The Dawn of Colonial Modernity

Bright and early on Wednesday morning, May 10, 1815, a nervous, rather formally dressed young man walked swiftly through the empty streets and fragrant back alleys of Tabriz in the northwestern province of Azerbaijan. He needed to be sharp for a very important meeting. The spring air of the provincial capital was crisp, cool, and gently bright, soothing the aroma of fresh acacias that was rushing to mix with the smell of freshly baked bread. The handsomely groomed Mohammad Saleh, son of the late Hajj Baqer Khan Shirazi, known as Kazeruni, was anxious to meet Major Joseph D'Arcy, a British colonial officer, whom our Mirza Saleh, like all his compatriots, called "Mr. Colonel."

The quiet early-morning streets of Tabriz could not quite hide either the nervous expectations of the young Mirza Saleh or the obvious tensions of the state of war the city had experienced over the last decade. Less than two years before this meeting between Mirza Saleh Shirazi and Major D'Arcy, the Qajars and the Russians had concluded the Golestan Treaty on October 24, 1813, ending what would later be known as the First Russo-Persian War, which had lasted almost a decade (1804–13). The Qajars had relinquished the northern, most fertile, provinces of their kingdom in Transcaucasia to the Russians. The French and British colonial officers were now in the Qajar court, competing against each other in their efforts to convince the benighted monarch, Fath Ali Shah (1762–1834), to accept their respective governments' assistance in resisting further Russian incursions—assistance that would be given, of course, in exchange for advancing their own colonial and imperial designs in the region.

The interest of Napoleon (1769–1821) in the Qajar court was primarily due to his strategy of finding a logistical ally against Russia while threatening the British Indian possession via a pact with Fath Ali Shah. Napoleon had met with the Qajar envoy, Mirza Mohammad Reza, in April 1807 in the castle of Finkenstein, in the vicinity of Osterode in East Prussia; after asking a few questions about Persian literature, and learning about an extensive body of Alexander romances in Persian and ordering one translated into French, he concluded with the Qajars what was later referred to as the Finkenstein Treaty. Soon after this treaty, Napoleon dispatched his aide-de-camp, General Claude-Mathieu de Gardane, to Iran to help the Qajars carry out their campaign against the Russians in exchange for a pact to facilitate Napoleon's passage to India. Among a series of military and diplomatic arrangements that General Gardane had made with Abbas Mirza, the valiant Qajar prince ruling the border province of Azerbaijan and holding the fort against the Russian incursions, was one to dispatch a group of Iranian students to Paris every year to learn contemporary European military sciences.[1]

The British were aware of this French move and concerned about its outcome. By April 1808, the British had already sent one of their most prominent colonial officers in India, Brigadier General Sir John Malcolm (1769–1833), to the Qajar court to counter the French initiative. Sir John was not successful, so the British dispatched yet another experienced colonial envoy, Sir Hartfort Brydges Jones (1764–1847), who had extensive experience in Basra and Baghdad and an elaborate set of connections to the Qajar royal court (he reportedly spoke fluent Persian). Sir Hartfort arrived in Iran in March 1809 and managed, by hook and by crook (including a handsome amount of bribes he paid to the Qajar royalty) to convince Fath Ali Shah to send General Gardane packing.[2]

Among the things that Abbas Mirza, perhaps the sole Qajar prince with a modicum of decency, discussed with the British envoys was his wish to send a group of Iranian students to London to master modern arts and sciences. (The group's previous arrangements for travel to France were, of course, now canceled.) Sir Hartfort agreed to this request and on his way back to England in 1811 took two Iranian students, Muhammad Kazem, the son of the royal painter at Abbas Mirza's court, and Mirza Haji Baba Afshar, another courtier, to England. Poor Muhammad Kazem died about eighteen months after he arrived in London, but Haji Baba Afshar continued with his studies of modern medicine for six years and returned to his homeland to practice his profession.[3]

Since the end of April 1815, the young Mirza Saleh had been feeling nervous and conflicted, though thoroughly excited too, about the possibility of a second group of Iranian students being sent to England. Rumor had it that he was a candidate for this privilege. Mirza Saleh knew some English, quite a bit of French, some Russian, and of course Persian and Turkish. The colonial languages he had learned by virtue of the comings and goings of the British and French officers in the region because of the extended war with the Russians. Mirza Saleh had spoken with his friends, soliciting their advice, which was mostly negative. They warned him that he should not go to England, for fear that he might lose his religion, become alienated from his culture, and indeed die in obscurity and ignominy. In his previous meetings with Major D'Arcy he had shared his reservations about going to England. Major D'Arcy had repeatedly appealed to Mirza Saleh's sense of loyalty to his king, to the crown prince, and above all to his country—he had, the major insisted, a duty to go abroad and return as a more useful subject of the kingdom. "I will think it through tonight," he had finally told Major D'Arcy on Tuesday, May 9, and then he had gone home to make his decision in peace.[4]

This is an extraordinary period in the history of Mirza Saleh's homeland. A medieval monarchy, deeply corrupt and incompetent at the very core of its opiate existence, was now threatened by three simultaneous colonial incursions into its territories: the Russians, the French, and the British, caught in the snare of their own colonial rivalries, were using Iran as a site for their strategic contests. The Qajars (1789–1926) had come to power exactly at the time of the French Revolution, and as Europe was rising in its military might, economic prowess, and invigorating social and intellectual upheavals, Iran was ruled by an exceptionally demented, inept, and indigent dynasty, presiding over a feudal economy, with medieval forms of social stratification; the sedate and disembodied moral and intellectual debates were of concern to no one except to those in the scholastic circles in which these debates took place. The Qajar dynasty was founded by Agha Muhammad Khan Qajar (reigned 1779–97), an exceedingly cruel psychopath who was castrated in his youth and spent the rest of his days taking his revenge upon the world that had so violated him so early in his life, until he met his death at the hands of three servants who murdered him because he had condemned them to death. The mutilated figure of Agha Muhammad Khan Qajar, his balls cut off at the moment that he entered adulthood, and then his throat slit open when he was dispatched to kingdom come, sums up the history of Iran under the reign of the Qajar dynasty and the fateful entry of Iranians into colonial modernity.

The reign of Fath Ali Shah (reigned 1797–1834), Agha Muhammad Khan's nephew and successor, and an equally decadent and depraved monarch under whose sovereignty our young Mirza Saleh was now contemplating a trip to Europe, coincided with the Napoleonic Wars (1799–1815); the British loss of their American colonies (1776) and assumption of direct colonial control of India after the East India Act (1784); and Russian colonial expansion into Crimea, Poland, Ukraine, Belarus, Moldova, and Georgia (1772–1814), and then the further involvement of Russia in the Napoleonic Wars, culminating in Napoleon's defeat in 1812. By 1799, Fath Ali Shah's kingdom was drawn into Britain's "sphere of influence" because of Iran's importance to the advancement of British colonial interests in India. When in 1798 Zaman Shah of Afghanistan intended to invade India and threaten the British colonial interests, the British, already preoccupied with the uprisings of Marathas and Tippu Sultan of Mysore, appealed to Fath Ali Shah to engage Zaman Shah militarily and thus prevent his incursion into India. For the duration of his reign, Fath Ali Shah was besieged by three colonial powers; he endured two Russian incursions into his northern territories (resulting in the ignominious treaties of Golestan in 1813 and Turkamanchai in 1828); he had no visionary or even competent statesman to help him repel these onslaughts (with the exception of Qaem Maqam Farahani, whom his grandson will soon murder); and could rely on only Abbas Mirza, his son and the crown prince, to try to defend the territorial integrity of the kingdom.[5]

None of these overwhelming realities could have been far from Mirza Saleh's mind when he arrived for his meeting with Major D'Arcy early in the morning of May 10, 1815—just about a month before Napoleon was to be defeated at the battle of Waterloo on June, 18, 1815. The British had outmaneuvered the French in Iran and had the Qajar court serving them as an acquiescent client. When Mirza Saleh arrived at Major D'Arcy's office, he noted that His Royal Highness Mirza Mas'ud, a confidant of Crown Prince Abbas Mirza, was already there. "Someone has to go with this group of students," Mirza Saleh overheard Mirza Mas'ud tell Major D'Arcy, "and study French, English, Latin, and natural philosophy." Major D'Arcy immediately turned to Mirza Saleh and asked, "Would you allow me to write down your name?" "Write down my name," Mirza Saleh responded instantly, against the advice of practically all his friends and acquaintances.

"Write down my name!" What kind of diction is that? There is a mechanical crudity to Mirza Saleh's Persian prose, something exceedingly Latinate, cumbrous, and even ham-handed, which almost cries out for an explanation. Reading Mirza Saleh's prose almost two centuries after he wrote it, one cannot help noticing his awkward, strange, and tentative language and above all his utterly infelicitous diction. There is a telegraphic brevity and a literary clumsiness about his prose that speaks of generations of stolid and court-corrupted diction in Persian prose and, by extension, poetry, both in a deplorable state when Mirza Saleh was writing early in the nineteenth century. What happened to the glory and grace of Persian language that Ferdowsi, Nezami, Rumi, Sa'di, and Hafez wrote and that Abu al-Fazl Beyhaqi put to use so gloriously in historical prose and a deeply ennobling narrative? Well, the Safavids happened. Since the time of the Safavid dynasty (1501–1732) the grace of Persian literature in Iran had been steadily fading as Shi'i scholastic learning had become the modus operandi (and the dominant ideology) of the state. As the Persian literati escaped from the Safavid courts and sought refuge with Indian princes, Shi'i theologians from southern Lebanon mounted their mules and headed east toward Isfahan. This was an intellectual migration driven by the changing apparatus of state ideologies: Shi'ism transplanted Persian literature in Safavid Iran, while Persian literature succeeded in India—only to be defeated by the English language of British colonialism. The Safavids fabricated a lineage linking themselves directly to Shi'i imams (they were of course lying) and established Shi'ism as the state religion, and the glorious days of Persian literature between the tenth and the thirteenth centuries became only a dim memory. Beginning with the rise of the Safavids in the sixteenth century, Persian poetry became a ludicrously self-indulgent plaything of the rich and the powerful at the courts of the Ottomans and the Mughals, where expatriate Persians wrote useless and wretched verses that pandered to the turgid daydreams of kings, queens, and princes. By the time it reached Mirza Saleh Shirazi early in the nineteenth century, the Persian language was sapped of all its living and robust energy, and it would be another half century—in preparation for the Constitutional Revolution of 1906–11—before life, power, passion, and political purpose would come back to inhabit and reanimate the language of Sa'di.[6]

Under the reign of Fath Ali Shah, the opium-infested air and the jaundiced disposition of the Qajar court had infiltrated Persian prose to its core. It had absolutely nothing to say and nothing to offer real people and their lived experiences. It had become a decorous shell, devoid even of its formal grace. The best poet that the period produced was Fath Ali Khan Kashani (1796–1822), known as Saba, whose claim to fame is *Shahanshah-namah*, which he composed daydreaming about the majesty of Ferdowsi's *Shahnameh* and, fool that he was, thinking he had matched or even surpassed it. In reading this work of astounding vanity, one searches in vain to find a single line worthy of comparison to the miracle that is Ferdowsi's *Shahnameh*. But no one cared, and Saba was paid lucratively for his inane glorification of the corrupt king he obsequiously served. He was given the governorship of certain provinces, which he ruled without even poetic justice. Poets as governors—that was the state of affairs under the Qajars. A similar state of insane verbosity fatally infected the prose of the period. There is a letter a Qajar courtier named Mirza Abd ol-Wahab Neshat composed on behalf of Fath Ali Shah and sent to Napoleon on the occasion of the Finkenstein Treaty. One is dumbfounded today by its unsurpassed imbecility and its servile tone; it is full of empty praise, an effusion that had no other purpose than to acknowledge the utter submission of the Qajar king to his French counterpart. This is how the letter starts:

> After the necessary Praise and grateful Appreciation to our Lord—Oh You Magnanimous King, Great Monarch, Noble Master, Magnificent Emperor, Owner of the countries of France and Italy: May your Soul be in everlasting Joy, and May this world be always solicitous to your wishes! O Monarch! O He whose wishes are always granted! Ever since in between our two everlasting states, a treaty of alliance is signed, and our flower-covered branches of solidarity have embraced each other, to this very moment, there has not been a single day, all thanks to the good fortune of our victorious destiny, that the bonds of friendship have not been turned in the capable hands of our friendship, nor indeed has the flowerbed of solidarity wasted a day without being watered from the fountain of everlasting freshness.[7]

"I saw the Persian ambassador this morning," Napoleon wrote to his minister Talleyrand after meeting with Mirza Muhammad Reza, Fath Ali Shah's ambassador to Finkenstein, and reading this inanity. "I cut short all his Oriental phrases and asked him bluntly how things stood, making him understand that I was well informed about his country and that business has to be treated as business."[8]

Only in the singular figure of Qaem Maqam Farahani (1779–1835) and the nobility of his literary diction does one come close to a person writing prose that is infused with life, moral rectitude, courageous audacity, caring intellect, and necessary confidence. Qaem Maqam was a visionary statesman at the service of Abbas Mirza while he was fighting the Russians, and much of the vigor and power of his prose comes from his political integrity. Qaem Maqam was no sycophantic courtier and would take issue with decisions of Abbas Mirza and Fath Ali Shah. This cost him dearly. He was repeatedly suspended from his service to the Qajars because he did not concur with the servile and self-serving consent of other courtiers, who were encouraging the monarch to fight with the Russians (while safely tucked away in their own private quarters with their countless concubines). Qaem Maqam played a critical role in initiating the dispatch of Iranian students like Mirza Saleh Shirazi to Europe, for he was among the very few who were aware of the fundamental backwardness of Iran in economic, social, political, and (more to the point) military matters. He also was key to getting the British and French colonial officers in Azerbaijan to modernize the Iranian army. Fath Ali Shah would wage wars with the Russians following the recommendation of his corrupt courtiers, and then, after he lost every battle with the Russians, he would call on Qaem Maqam to come and negotiate the terms of his shameful surrenders. The Turkamanchai Treaty of 1828 was drafted by Qaem Maqam, and if not for him, the treaty would have been even more damaging to the territorial integrity of Iran. (It was signed when the Russian army was already in Tabriz.) Qaem Maqam was instrumental too in keeping Abbas Mirza and, after he died, his son Muhammad Mirza in power as crown prince, holding the myriad other Qajar contenders at bay (for Fath Ali Shah had lost count of how many wives and concubines he had and how many "princes" and "princesses"—as these useless creatures still like to refer to themselves—he had procreated). When Muhammad Shah (reigned 1834–48), Abbas Mirza's son, succeeded his grandfather Fath Ali Shah, he appointed Qaem Maqam as his prime minister. But within a year after this appointment, corrupt Qajar courtiers conspired with their colonial officer supporters and persuaded Muhammad Shah to issue an order for the murder of Qaem Maqam on June 27, 1835. What has remained from Qaem Maqam, in addition to some exquisite poetry, is the collection of letters that he wrote in his official capacities and privately. These letters are the very definition of political vision and moral imagination, written with a solid and simple command of the best that Persian prose could offer during this transitional period.[9]

What Qaem Maqam Farahani did not know as he wrote his letters, with a rare combination of literary grace and political purpose, was that he was laying down the very foundation of Persian literary modernity. His prose was written when Iran was in the throes of a colonial modernity he was destined to confront and come to terms with: British and French colonial officers were negotiating the terms of their imperial designs on the region and seeking to oppose the equally voracious stratagems of Russian imperialism. Farahani's prose is robust, vigorous, and engaging not by virtue of any deliberate or formal literary trope, but because he had to comprehend and navigate European colonialism. That critical encounter with colonial modernity would remain definitive to the rise of Persian literary modernity.

None of Farahani's literary grace is evident in the prose of Mirza Saleh, and yet, however awkward and hesitant his prose might be, his memoir and travelogue gradually begins to come alive as he tells himself and his readers about what he still does not recognize are exceedingly crucial days in the life of his nation. After his meeting with Major D'Arcy, Mirza Saleh's doubts persisted, but he managed to overcome them. Finally, on Thursday May 11, 1815, he had an audience with Crown Prince Abbas Mirza.

"Congratulations!" said Abbas Mirza, evidently happy to give the good news to Mirza Saleh himself. "You are leaving with Mr. Colonel."

Mirza Saleh summoned his courage and said, "I am not leaving because of him. I leave because I want to pursue my studies."

"What sort of science do you wish to study?" Abbas Mirza asked.

"I am not interested in sciences," Mirza Saleh declared. Then he listed the names of his fellow students who were going to study various sciences.

"So what is it that you will study?" Abbas Mirza asked the nervous Mirza Saleh. "English, French, Latin, and natural philosophy. But no science." That said, Mirza Saleh finally received his sovereign's gracious permission to proceed, went home to collect his wits, and avoided the company of his friends and acquaintances. He was afraid they would persuade him to change his mind.

On Friday May 19, 1815, Mirza Saleh Shirazi got up bright and early and went and paid his respects to the crown prince one last time, and at about 11:30 A.M. he and his group of fellow students left Tabriz for England. He immediately began writing in his diary on this auspicious occasion. He was so nervous that he confused the Islamic and Christian calendars. The day that he left Tabriz was Friday, Jumada II 10, 1230, which is May 19, 1815. Mirza Saleh thought it was April 19—he miscalculated the Christian calendar by exactly a month, or else he was narratively repressing his experiences during the anxiety-ridden month before his departure for England.

After all these stressful preparations and hopeful expectations, the journey of Mirza Saleh and his friends to England turned out to be a disaster. They had scarcely left Iranian territory and were still in Russia when the treachery of the British envoy in charge of taking them to England (and by extension the bad faith and true intentions of the British government) became evident. As soon as they arrived in Moscow they learned that Napoleon had been defeated at Waterloo. In the face of this momentous event, the British government completely lost interest in this helpless group of students and began rethinking its policies toward the Qajars. The initial interest of the British in making clients of the Qajars (and thus the idea that it would be useful to have these Iranian students come to England) arose from their determination to prevent the French from establishing relations with Iran and thereby threatening Britain's Indian possessions. This colonial objective had also made Russia a natural ally for the British. The British did not mind antagonizing the French, but not at the expense of alienating the Russians. As early as 1813, two years before this journey started, the Russians were already complaining to the British about their support of the Qajar campaign while Russia was allied with them in the war against Napoleon. It was in this context that Robert Gordon, a secretary at the British embassy, had written to his brother in a letter complaining about the British putting weapons, as he put it quite succinctly, "in the hands of these barbarous Mussulmans and even fighting their battles against our brothers in Christianity."[10]

The five students proceeded to England, but every day the treacheries of Major D'Arcy became more evident. D'Arcy was, like all other colonial officers, an opportunistic thief. He pocketed the money that Abbas Mirza had given him to cover the expenses of these students. On a number of occasions, Mirza Saleh caught D'Arcy red-handed; he discovered a striking discrepancy between D'Arcy's accounting of expenses and Mirza

Saleh's calculations. This made D'Arcy exceedingly angry (for he had not known that Mirza Saleh was keeping a record of their expenses). When they finally reached England, D'Arcy refused to pay for the expenses of the students or even to give them letters sent to them from Iran, and he made their lives in London miserable. While his fellow travelers endured the anxiety of uncertainty about what would happen to them in England, Mirza Saleh began selling a couple of paisley shawls he had wisely brought along from Iran to pay for a teacher to teach him and his friends English. (The name of this teacher was "Mr. Shakespeare," or perhaps in jest Mirza Saleh refers to him as such!) Mirza Saleh also found a priest to teach him Latin and English history. Later he also found an old physician who agreed to rent him a room, teach him English, Latin, and natural philosophy, and charge him 190 pounds a year, for which he had to sell yet another paisley shawl.

D'Arcy's main problem was that he was not satisfied with all the money he had already stolen from these students and wanted the Iranian or the British authorities to pay him more money to supervise them. He soon began circulating a rumor that these students were not pursuing their studies and were in fact wasting their time frolicking in London, which at some point resulted in Abbas Mirza asking them to go back to Iran. Mirza Saleh and his friends now had to go around London collecting testimony from their teachers and acquaintances that they were indeed busy with their studies.

Despite the contemptible double-dealing of D'Arcy and the British colonialism he represented, Mirza Saleh and his friends persisted and survived; they lived and learned whatever they could for about two years, and then returned to their homeland (one of them, Muhammad Ali Chakhmaq Saz, with his British wife). While the other four students had studied either medical or military sciences, Mirza Saleh had learned other things and had a distinctly different agenda.

It can hardly be overstated how crucial this initial group of Iranian students, and Mirza Saleh in particular, were to the course of modern Iranian history. From the awkward beginning of its narrative, Mirza Saleh's travelogue gradually picks up speed, tenacity, verve, and even audacity as he travels to and in England, then goes to Europe and begins to record his meticulous observations. His prose gradually becomes simpler and more direct, ushering in a whole phase of simplified Persian diction, stripped of its languorous courtly decorum and suffocating formality. The rapid simplification of Persian prose from the early nineteenth century onward, exemplified in Mirza Saleh's travelogue, becomes a crucial factor in the production of a public discourse suitable for radical and revolutionary changes to come.

The role of Mirza Saleh's travelogue in this simplification of Persian prose was the least of his contributions. Immediately connected to the creation of a politically potent prose for wide public circulation was the introduction of the printing press in Iran. During the last six months of his stay in London, Mirza Saleh apprenticed at a printing house. Then, on his way back from England in 1819, he purchased (probably after selling yet another paisley shawl) a printing press. The use of printing technology in Iran dated back to the middle of the seventeenth century, when Christian missionaries printed and distributed Persian translations of the Bible. But the printing machine that Mirza Saleh brought back from England was to be used for more secular purposes and on far wider and more public domains.

After his arrival in Iran, Mirza Saleh established the first Persian newspaper published in his homeland. He named it *Kaghaz-e Akhbar*, a literal translation of "Newspaper." The newspaper that Mirza Saleh founded became the first in which a simplified prose was effectively put to immediate public use, opening up a wide range of discussions of emerging public concerns. The publication of this newspaper is a landmark in the formation of Iranian civil society and the carving out of a public domain within which issues of immediate political consequences were discussed.

Equally important in Mirza Saleh's travelogue is the commencement of a translation movement beginning in the early nineteenth century, in which European literary and historical sources were made available in Persian. Mirza Saleh's travelogue is full of such translations, which either he made himself or others did for him and he included in his travelogue. These translations were helping Mirza Saleh understand the European history of his time, and he recorded, in extensive detail, what he had learned, with an eye to reaching an emerging reading public. Following the instructions of Abbas Mirza, one of Mirza Saleh's fellow students on this trip, Mirza Reza Mohanddes, translated into Persian Voltaire's historical novel on Charles XII and Edward Gibbon's *The History of the Decline and Fall of the Roman Empire*. This translation movement continued well into the latter part of the nineteenth century, and helped the emerging Iranian reading public to continue to cultivate a simplified Persian prose and to get acquainted with the tumultuous history of Europe; it inaugurated a critical process of comparing Iran's state of drift and stagnation with groundbreaking events around the globe; and it helped expand the emotive and thematic domains of emerging Persian literary modernity.

Mirza Saleh's travelogue also marks the dawn of awareness of current European and world political and cultural developments. While Mirza Saleh and his friends were in Moscow, they heard the news of the defeat of Napoleon at Waterloo. This was the first time that a major historical event in Europe was the subject of immediate reflections and commentaries among a small group of Iranians, who would later reach out to their fellow citizens, discussing how this affected their lives and soliciting their reactions. This takes Iranians into the mainstream of world historical events.

There was also a cultural and artistic aspect to this historical self-awareness. Starting in Russia and continuing in England, Mirza Saleh regularly attended operatic and theatrical productions (as well as a few church services that included choral music), and he wrote in some detail about what he had seen. His accounts are among the first occasions when Iranians become aware of the European cultural scene, and have something (positive or negative) to say about their experiences. These pages of Mirza Saleh's travelogue might in fact be considered the commencement of modern literary and art criticism in Iran—and, as such, instrumental in cultivating a more global dimension to Iranian cultural modernity. In his discussions of everything from politics to aesthetics, Mirza Saleh's language and scope become increasingly global. This is no longer the language of that obsequious courtier who wrote that nauseating letter to Napoleon, not even the noble but limited language of Qaem Maqam Farahani. Halfway through his travelogue, the vibrant reality of a wider world is resonating in Mirza Saleh's prose.

Perhaps the most significant aspect of Mirza Saleh's travelogue was the space that it provided him to compare (however tacitly) the backward state of his own homeland to the far more advanced institutional achievements of Europe in democratic rule at home (predicated, of course, on the predatory exploitation of other people through global colonial expansion and the associated support of tyranny that was integral to it). Mirza Saleh used every opportunity to reflect on topics such as the rule of law, parliamentary democracy, freedom of expression, freedom of assembly, the institutional autonomy of civil society, and the safety and security of highways. Mirza Saleh was using England as a manufactured utopia, a model of freedom. He compiled a checklist for Iran, enumerated things—institutions, laws, practices—he wished he could purchase, put in his suitcase, and bring back with him (just like that printing machine) to his own country. Mirza Saleh's travelogue can indeed be read as a foundational narrative, a kind of Persian version of Plato's *Republic* in which he wishfully narrates the future of his own homeland.

Practically all these groundbreaking events early in the nineteenth century—simplification of Persian prose, importing of a printing machine, the first newspaper, the translation movement, direct exposure to global geopolitics and European bourgeois art scenes, and above all a firsthand account of European parliamentary democracy—all gradually came together to become the foundation of both radical and liberal movements in Iran that would carry on a struggle for freedom, democracy, and the rule of law. The only drawback of all these pioneering institutional breakthroughs in the course of modern Iranian history, however, was the effective formation of a set of phantom liberties, all dreamed and interpreted in the active imagination of a small band of inorganic intellectuals and their disembodied critical consciousness. This ghostly liberation was rooted in the quintessential paradox of the Iranian encounter with colonial modernity: the European Enlightenment modernity that was meant to liberate Iranians from darkness and set them free into *"Sapere Aude,"* as Kant put it in "What Is Enlightenment," and encourage them to "have the courage to use their own intelligence," denied them that very agency by bringing the Enlightenment message to them through the gun barrel of colonialism.[11]

The problem was not with the message Europe sent around the world, but with the messenger it chose to bring the message— a colonial officer with a long gun in one hand and a Bible in the other. The face of modernity for Iranians was the revolting countenance of the rapacious Major Joseph D'Arcy. To this day, and as myriads of bewildered, inorganic, and disembodied Iranian intellectuals in or out of their homeland write one book after another on "modernity," the very same paradox blinds their insights and dulls their wits. The fundamental fact, utterly lost to these intellectuals, is that we, like the rest of the world, were ushered into European modernity via European colonialism (I repeat the adjective *European* intentionally, for modernity and colonialism are two sides of the same European coin)—this is the quintessential fact of our modern history. We became modernized and colonized at one and the same time. We cannot be modern without speaking through a colonized mind, and we have not learned how to decolonize our minds without abandoning what Jürgen Habermas still insists on calling "the unfinished" project of modernity. The proverbial baby and bathwater have long since lost their referential significance for us. Without a systematic critique of modernity (but not from the mind-numbingly depoliticized, absurd perspective of American postmodernism, which has sapped every ounce of political energy from this critique while producing an astoundingly supercilious, convoluted, and useless language), we cannot achieve that radical decolonization of the mind.

A significant assortment of contemporary Iranian public intellectuals (Daryush Ashuri and Daryush Shayegan chief among them) have embarked on a wild-goose chase, seeking ways to catch up with modernity, effectively chasing after their own tails for decades.[12] The project of radically decolonizing the analytical frame of our references must begin with a criticism of modernity from the site of the colonial occupation of consciousness, and the first fact to consider is that Kant and Hegel, the forefathers of European Enlightenment modernity, deliberately, consciously, systematically, and pointedly wrote us and the rest of what they called "the Oriental world," which means the entirety of humanity minus Western Europe, out of their project.[13]

Iranians (like the rest of the world) received the universal promises of Enlightenment modernity through the gun barrel of European colonialism. Constitutional to the predicament of Iran in modernity, that paradox is written all over its modern history and evident in the quintessentially extraterritorial constitution of Iran as a nation-state—evident not only in successive colonial incursions, foreign occupations, and travel narratives by Europeans and Iranians alike but also in the thoughts and deeds of successive groups of Iranian students who were sent abroad to master contemporary sciences in order to help defend their country against foreign aggression and transform it into a modern nation-state. These students in effect became (against all good intentions and entirely despite themselves) the very first generation of a body of inorganic intellectuals daydreaming phantom liberties entirely disconnected from the factual evidence of their homeland—predicated on the colonial economy at the basis of their nation-state.

The formative period of modern Iranian political culture is thus rooted in the exposure of Iranians to colonial modernity and the development of the modern nation-state and civil society, while a robust and critical literary and artistic imagination highlighted the promises and warned against the pitfalls of the modern age. A disembodied and inorganic group of intellectuals was chiefly responsible for redrafting the idea of "Iran" as a nation-state out of a multifaceted reality and reinventing it in the mirror of colonial modernity. The result was a bizarre, counterintuitive, yet enduring manner of imagining a nation: though as a territorial domain Iran was populated and inhabited by people native to its land since time immemorial, Iran (or Persia, as the Europeans called it) as a modern nation-state was actively imagined and creatively conceived in absentia and from angles peripheral to its geographical location—by imperial envoys, colonial officers, missionary Orientalists, superpower interventionists, expatriate intellectuals, and exilic communities, as well as by travel writers, separatists, and nativist conspiratorial theorists fearful and suspicious of foreign interventions. What remained constant at the center of all these spiraling circulations of ideas and sentiments, designs and depictions, visions and wishes, phantom liberties and phantasmagoric dreams, was called "Iran."

Reflecting the same set of anxieties, the Iranian land has been consistently fetishized, and its current map (in the shape of a sitting cat) treated with talismanic tenderness. The symbolic, almost sacred, significance of land for Iranians (manifested in countless poems, films, and photographs) is not accidental to Iranians' collective consciousness and reflects a territorial trauma at the heart of a people repeatedly subjected to foreign intervention—and above all their birth into modernity via colonial occupation. This territorial trauma is rooted in an even deeper layer of a collective anxiety. Historically, Iranians have been the exact opposite of Jews. Jews held on to their book and were forced out of their ancestral land, and from then on it did not matter where in the world the Jewish diaspora was, for their book was the focal point of their definition as a people. Iranians, on the contrary, held on to their land, and kept changing their books. Zoroastrianism, Manichaeism, Zurvanism, Mithraism, Mazdakism, Islam and the myriad revolutionary sects and opposing schools it generated to support or subvert it, and now Shi'ism in particular, have all kept providing Iranians with a different book by which to regulate their lives. They did so. But they kept their land as the constant frame of their metaphysical references, the source of their self-definition, of who and what they are. No matter what measure of time and distance defines the *place* called "Iran," Iranians are those who live in Iran. But Iran, or the land on which they live, is a place more in the realm of imagination than geography. Iranians in places like Los Angeles have created a little Iran for themselves, as have others in Toronto, in London, in places as close to Iran as Istanbul and Dubai, as far as Japan and Denmark, Malaysia and Australia. When Reza Shah and after him Muhammad Reza Shah were forced to leave Iran for good, they took a fistful of Iranian soil with them. The endemic fetishization of Iranian land, treating its patches as if they were pages of their sacred book, is the sign of the sacrilegious anxieties of a people fearful of ritual desecration of their most sacred sign of peoplehood. The current practice of Iranian Shi'is prostrating five times a day and placing their forehead reverentially on a piece of clay brought from Karbala is the substitutional extension of their sacrosanct treatment of their own land into their most pious ritual exercises.

The principal task of this body of inorganic—and more than often expatriate—intellectuals who have thus envisioned "Iran" extemporaneously and extraterritorially has been to provide Iranians at large with a quintessentially disembodied national narrative. Having come to creative and critical fruition mostly outside their own homeland, these expatriate intellectuals, and their extraterritorial visions of their homeland, have had a lasting influence on Iranian political culture. Leaving Iran, residing in foreign countries, thinking and writing about a homeland in which they no longer live (whether temporarily or permanently), has been definitive not just to the rise of a group of disembodied and expatriate intellectuals but also, by extension, to their notion of "Iran" as a nation-state. There is a short story by the founding father of modern Persian fiction, Mohammad Ali Jamalzadeh (1895–1997), himself a prototypical example of an expatriate Iranian intellectual who lived most of his life in Europe, in his first collection of short stories, called *Yeki Bud Yeki Nabud (Once Upon a Time)*, published in Berlin in 1921. In this short story, called "Farsi Shekar ast" ("Persian Is Like Sugar"), an ordinary Iranian peasant ends up in a jail with a French-educated Iranian and a Shi'i cleric. While the latter two try to convey their sense of their predicament to their fellow Iranian in their French-infested and Arabic-dominated languages, respectively, the poor native Iranian is left entirely bewildered about what in the world they are trying to say. In the midst of that misunderstanding dwells the paradoxical formation of Iran as a nation-state.

One of the most enduring consequences of the paradox of colonial modernity in Iran has been the prolific gathering of generations of mostly expatriate intellectuals, producing a disembodied vision of their country extraterritorially, while envisioning for it phantom liberties. The result is the emergence of vast and widening discrepancies between the material basis of Iranian society at large and the intellectual disembodiment of ideas and aspirations—one slumbering with a jaundiced bourgeoisie, a weakened labor class, and an impoverished peasantry, the other dreaming ever more glorious illusions of freedom and democracy. Only in the course of revolutionary upheavals, from the Babi movement of the mid-nineteenth century, to the Constitutional Revolution of the early twentieth century, to the national liberation movement led by Muhammad Mosaddeq in the middle of the twentieth century to the Islamic revolution led by Ayatollah Ruhollah Khomeini in the late twentieth century—do these two diametrically opposed facts of Iranian political culture come into conflict and temporary resolution. In the paradox of that encounter, and the historical agency it generates and sustains for Iranians as a people, the paradox of colonial modernity can be resolved for good.

In the decades following the return of Mirza Saleh Shirazi to his homeland, many other Iranians traveled abroad and came back home with ideas and helped in the formation of a succession of liberal and radical thinkers,[14] as well as a series of reformist and revolutionary movements, that gradually but inexorably pulled Iran out of its medieval slumber and pushed it into further engagement with the political and economic consequences of colonial modernity and the entrenched institutional persistence of a hitherto medieval and recalcitrant society.

Following Abbas Mirza's, Qaem Maqam Farahani's, and Mirza Saleh Shirazi's examples, a significant portion of these reforms were in fact court affiliated. By far the most consequential reformist figure of the nineteenth century was Mirza Taqi Khan Amir Kabir (1807–52), a prime minister of uncommon integrity and unsurpassed commitment to transforming Iran into a modern nation-state. After the death of Fath Ali Shah in 1834 and the premature death of Crown Prince Abbas Mirza a year earlier, Abbas Mirza's son Muhammad Shah succeeded to the throne and ruled for fourteen useless and entirely catastrophic years. The sole worthy statesman in Muhammad Shah's court was Qaem Maqam Farahani, whom the shah had ordered murdered in 1835 because his reformist polices and administrative intelligence did not please His Majesty and his corrupt courtiers. Next Muhammad Shah engaged in an entirely futile and ill-fated invasion of Afghanistan in 1837.

Upon Muhammad Shah's death on September 4, 1848, his sixteen-year-old son Naser al-Din Shah succeeded him and ruled over the Qajar realm for almost half a century (1848–96). From 1848, when Naser al-Din Shah ascended the Peacock Throne, to

1852, when he treacherously had Amir Kabir murdered, the wise and visionary prime minister served his king and country as a farsighted statesman who was the source of enduring and unprecedented reform in Qajar administration. Amir Kabir began his career as a diplomat, performing miraculously well in defending Qajar territorial integrity against both the Russians and the Ottomans. He was solely responsible for reforming the administrative apparatus of Qajar rule; systematizing the collection of taxes, the distribution of income, and the administration of law; and cutting off the abusive access of a myriad of Qajar princes to unearned income and undeserved power. Amir Kabir created and systematized a centralized budget for the administration. He encouraged domestic production and foreign trade. He radically modernized the Iranian army and seriously curtailed the influence of foreign embassies in Iran, while initiating a major urban development of Tehran and (following Mirza Saleh's initiative) establishing the first nationwide newspaper (the first issue of which was published on February 6, 1851).

Perhaps the most significant institutional achievement of Amir Kabir was the establishment in 1851 of Dar al-Fonun, a modern college that he founded on the model of a European *polytechnique*, in which Iranian and European faculty taught social and scientific subjects in what must be considered the first modern college in Iranian history. Of course, none of these good deeds would remain unpunished by the corrupt Qajar aristocracy, and Nasir al-Din Shah had Amir Kabir murdered on Saturday, January 10, 1852.[15]

Those like Amir Kabir who dared to initiate wide-ranging reforms at the court put their lives at risk. Quieter but more enduring initiatives were equally instrumental in opening up the moral and intellectual horizons of Iranians at large. The treachery of murdering Amir Kabir and putting incompetent reactionaries in charge of the national destiny failed to prevent the ensuing struggle of those who had a vision of the outside world and its earth-shattering events. By 1853, René Descartes's *Discourse on the Method of Rightly Conducting the Reason, and Seeking Truth in the Sciences* (1637) was translated into Persian. The enemies of reason burned this translation, but in 1862 another translation of the *Discourse* appeared. Nothing would stop the courageous efforts of learned Iranians to open up their society to fresh ideas. In 1870 a Persian translation of Charles Darwin's *The Origin of Species* (1859) appeared in Tehran; the translator was Mirza Taqi Khan Ansari, a practicing physician and a member of the Dar al-Fonun faculty.[16]

Almost two decades after Naser al-Din Shah had Amir Kabir murdered in 1852, another major reformist minister came to power in his court. Mirza Hasan Khan Sepahsalar (1827–80) was instrumental in initiating some crucial administrative changes, taking on the unfinished work of Amir Kabir. In 1872, for example, he tried to systematize and incorporate into a central administrative apparatus the appointment of high-ranking clerics, which of course deeply angered the corrupt elements within the Shi'i establishment.[17] Sepahsalar proceeded, however, to establish a cabinet in Naser al-Din Shah's court, appointing competent people to crucial administrative posts. Sepahsalar's attempt to reform the Iranian judicial system also deeply angered and antagonized the Shi'i clerical establishment. Crucial to the clerical opposition to Sepahsalar's reforms were of course their vested economic interests. During the famine of 1871, Hajji Mulla Ali Kani, the chief nemesis of Sepahsalar, made millions, as did many other high-ranking Shi'i *ulama* (the collective term for the most learned and powerful among the Shi'a clerics). The opposition of Kani and other like-minded clerics to Sepahsalar taking Naser al-Din Shah to Europe in 1873 in order to encourage the monarch to undertake reforms was equally informed by their fear that such reforms would put their economic and political power in danger. Kani's opposition to such trips, however, did not mean that such ventures into European capitals did not result in lucrative deals for European companies and the furthering of European colonial investments in Iran. The situation finally culminated in the aggressive assault of the clerical class against Sepahsalar while he accompanied the monarch on his trip to Europe. The concession that the Qajar court had made to Baron Julius Reuter in 1872 for the exploitation of minerals and forests as well as the construction of a railroad triggered the consolidation of opposition from the Shi'i *ulama*. The opposition was strong enough to force Naser al-Din Shah, who had no will or vision of his own, to summarily dismiss Sepahsalar in 1873. When analyzing these developments it is crucial to distinguish between the revolutionary role that lower-ranking Shi'i clerics play in anticolonial movements and the treachery of the high-ranking clerics in protecting their own lucrative interests—always coterminous with those of the Qajar aristocracy; it is equally important to distinguish between the reformist policies of visionary courtiers like Sepahsalar and their at time obsequious and entirely uncritical stands vis-à-vis European colonialism.[18]

Other court-affiliated reformists followed Sepahsalar, courageous visionaries such as Mirza Ali Khan Amin al-Dowleh (1844–1904), who accompanied Nasir al-Din Shah on his European trips to encourage him to sponsor reforms. Amin al-Dowleh wrote pioneering treatises on the rule of law (very much influenced by Montesquieu's *The Spirit of the Laws*), thoroughly reformed the Iranian postal system, assumed a variety of administrative posts, and ultimately played a pivotal role in curtailing the reigning monarch's power and paving the way for the Constitutional Revolution of 1906–11.[19]

Reformist ideas and practices were not limited to the Qajar court. A number of leading liberal and radical intellectuals appeared in the course of the nineteenth century and in a variety of crucial ways contributed to changing the disposition of the emerging nation. Mirza Fath Ali Akhondzadeh (1813–78), one of the most influential Iranian literati of this period, was a public intellectual of great vision and tenacity. Born and bred in Azerbaijan, Akhondzadeh was familiar with the Russian intellectual scene of the nineteenth century, and through his command of Turkish and Russian, he was equally familiar with French and English liberal and radical thoughts. Akhondzadeh was a liberal reformist and a literary humanist who believed in constitutional democracy, the rule of law, and a free and democratic state apparatus. His political thoughts were deeply influenced by his reading of Plato, Aristotle, Jean-Jacques Rousseau, and John Stuart Mill. Akhondzadeh's staunch nationalism crossed into anti-Arab racism—a malady that persisted in Iran through the twentieth century. Nevertheless, Akhondzadeh revolutionized the critical discourse of his age. He wrote extensively against classical and contemporary Persian historiography and expounded persuasively on what he believed was a more critical mode of writing history. Akhondzadeh had similar ideas about changing the Persian alphabet in order to make it easier to learn to read and write—with an eye toward expanding the public domain of literacy and making it more socially significant. He wrote pathbreaking essays on literary criticism, informed by his readings of such Russian novelists as Gogol, Tolstoy, Turgenev, and Dostoyevsky. Akhondzadeh was among the first Iranian literary humanists to radically rethink Persian poetics, criticizing classical prosody and suggesting liberating reforms. He wrote some of the first Persian novels and plays, using these genres as vehicles to engage others and share his views of contemporary politics. He was a trailblazing intellectual of high-voltage vision and conviction—writing not only literary criticism but also social and economic treatises, creative prose, and commentaries on poetry, all in a highly cultivated language. Amid Russian, French, and British colonial designs on the region, Akhondzadeh used the literary humanism of these very nations to help craft a Persian literary modernity that would articulate the terms of an emancipatory agency for his own nation.[20]

There were other highly influential reformist intellectuals in this period, such as Hajj Muhammad Ali Sayyah Mahallati (1837–1925), who traveled extensively around the world and used his travelogue as a medium of critical conversation with the world around him; Abd al-Rahim Talebof (1834–1911), who opted for a simple pedagogical narrative to address the most crucial issues of the time; Jalal al-Din Mirza (1830–72)—a rare bird among the Qajar princes—who became thoroughly engaged with ancient Iranian history, wrote a major book, *Nameh-ye Khosrowan*, on the subject, and corresponded extensively with Mirza Fath Ali Akhondzadeh; and Mirza Yusuf Khan Mostashar al-Dowleh Tabrizi (d. 1895), whose "A Treatise on One Word" (that word being *law*) was among the most important reformist statements of his time.

But the most extraordinary revolutionary character of the nineteenth century was Mirza Aqa Khan Kermani (1853–96); he and his lifetime friend and devoted comrade Sheykh Ahmad Ruhi (1855–96) became the exemplary models of radical activists and intellectual beacons of hope in their age. What was most extraordinary about Mirza Aqa Khan Kermani was his unusual command of medieval scholastic learning (that of Islamic philosophy in particular), coupled with his wide range of exposure to contemporary European thoughts and movements. He was born and raised in Kerman (central Iran), where he mastered Islamic scholastic learning; then he went to Isfahan, where, at a Jesuit school, he learned French; then he spent time in Tehran, Mashhad, and Rasht, until he finally escaped to Istanbul. He lived there for about a decade, writing extensively on political, historical, and literary issues while making a living by teaching Persian and Arabic. In Istanbul he had direct access to contemporary Russian and Western European thought and wrote extensively against the endemic tyrannies of the Qajars. The radical activities of Mirza Aqa Khan Kermani and his two closest comrades, Sheykh Ahmad Ruhi and Mirza Hasan Khan Khabir al-Molk, finally resulted in their arrest and extradition to Iran, where on the evening of Friday, July 17, 1896, they were all beheaded. Mirza Aqa Khan was a socialist revolutionary who paid close attention to the crucial role of the peasantry in revolutionary movements. Despite, or perhaps because of, his detailed knowledge of Islamic intellectual history, Mirza Aqa Khan ultimately opted for a radically secular worldview with unflinching conviction of the necessity and justice of social revolutions. He wrote a succession of highly erudite treatises that made him a founding figure of modernist philosophical thinking in Iran. He seriously considered social and economic forces in the course of history and wrote extensively on the philosophy of history (dismantling generations of useless court-affiliated historiography). He was a gifted poet, a deeply learned literary comparatist and theorist, a staunch nationalist, and a powerful critic of European colonialism.[21]

A combination of liberal and radical thinkers, ranging from Sepahsalar (cozily nested in the lucrative Qajar court) to Mirza Aqa Khan Kermani (suffering the indignities of exile), generated and sustained the intellectual consequences of colonial modernity in Iran in terms of phantom liberties they collectively dreamed but failed to institutionalize in any meaningful or enduring way. Something else was needed to jolt the corrupt Qajar court.

*   *   *

While highly cultivated but entirely uprooted, expatriate, and in-organic intellectuals from Mirza Saleh Shirazi to Mirza Aqa Khan Kermani were busy recasting the critical vision of the emerging nation-state, the fate of revolutionary movements challenging the criminal atrocities of the Qajars was cast by an entirely different event. By far the most radical revolutionary movement of the nineteenth century in Iran had absolutely nothing to do with any one of these groundbreaking ideas, but was squarely rooted in medieval scholastic Shi'ism. What was later known as the Babi movement shook the foundation of the Qajar dynasty for about a decade (1843–52) and all but delegitimized its tyrannical reign. A succession of rural and urban revolts began to shake the Qajars' confidence in their medieval tyranny. In 1851 in Rasht, in 1869 in Talesh, and in 1874 in Gilan, the impoverished peasantry and the disenfranchised poor in the major urban centers rose in armed revolt and challenged the Qajar authorities. But all of these scattered revolts fade in comparison with the widespread revolutionary movement of Babism that spread like a brushfire throughout the Qajar realm.[22]

The ideological banner under which Babism began to gather momentum was the millenarian doctrine of Shi'ism, which throughout its history has always catalyzed urban and rural revolts. The "disappearance" (*ghaybah*) of the twelfth Shi'i imam in the third century A.H. (ninth century A.D.) has given Shi'ism a permanently revolutionary disposition, for the expectation of his return has always given members of Shi'i communities a sense that they must be prepared to expedite his "second coming."[23] A central figure in retheorizing this radical dimension of Shi'ism in the nineteenth century was Sheykh Ahmad Ahsa'i (1753–1826), whose denial of the Islamic doctrinal mandate of bodily resurrection (*ma'ad jesmani*) particularly angered orthodox clerics. After the death of Sheykh Ahmad Ahsa'i, his student Seyyed Kazem Rashti (d. 1843) picked up on his teacher's idea of proposing a link between the Hidden Imam and his community of believers and promised that soon the embodiment of such a human connection would appear to lead Muslims to worldly victory over injustice. Among Seyyed Kazem Rashti's students and followers, a certain Seyyed Ali Muhammad (d. 1850) took that idea, carried it to its logical conclusion, and suddenly declared that he in fact was that human link between the Hidden Imam and the masses of Shi'i believers.

From an obscure theological doctrine, this idea suddenly exploded among the masses of impoverished peasantry in rural areas and the disenfranchised poor in the cities. A revolutionary movement of unsurpassed tenacity and power ensued, ultimately named after the name that Ali Muhammad had given to himself—"Bab," meaning "the Gate" or "the Door" between the Hidden Imam and the Shi'i community. As Qajar officials and their clerical supporters began the persecution and public trial of Bab, his appeal grew among his supporters, and noting his popularity, Bab began to up the ante and suddenly called himself "the Promised One," or the expected Mahdi, and announced that his book *Bayan* had surpassed and annulled the Qur'an. On July 7, 1850, Qajar officials, thinking they had heard enough of Ali Muhammad Bab, secured the endorsement of their clerical supporters, put the revolutionary leader in front of a firing squad, and executed him.

After the death of Bab, one of his followers, Mulla Husayn Boshruyeh, took up the leadership and wreaked havoc on the Qajar dynasty and its meager military might. As soon as one Babi rebellion was quelled in Mazandaran, another gathered momentum in Zanjan, and soon after that yet another broke out in the Fars province. On August 4, 1852, the Babis tried to assassinate Nasir al-Din Shah himself but failed. The massive grassroots basis of the Babi movement began with the urban poor and professionals and gradually extended into the impoverished peasantry. A few prominent merchants and a number of leading intellectuals (including Mirza Aqa Khan Kermani) at one point or another identified with Babism—if not with its ideological foundation, then certainly with its massive popular appeal. Perhaps the most spectacular figure among the Babis was Tahereh Qorrat al-Ayn (1817–52), a revolutionary woman of unsurpassed courage, intelligence, and imagination. She was a learned theologian, a gifted poet, and a courageous revolutionary leader—the Rosa Luxemburg of nineteenth-century Iran. There are historical reports that in the course of their revolutionary uprisings, the Babis practiced a rudimentary form of socialism.

The reformist and radical ideas of learned but inorganic intellectuals such as Mirza Aqa Khan Kermani and Mirza Fath Ali Akhondzadeh were also inconsequential in the next rebellion, which gathered momentum around the so-called Tobacco Revolt of 1890–92. Among the state-sponsored reforms of the post–Amir Kabir period was the systematization of a taxation program that had sought to increase state revenues. In 1886, Nasir al-Din Shah issued an edict in which he sought to create a tobacco régie to generate income for the state. In 1890, the Qajar monarch granted a British colonial officer, Major Gerald F. Talbot (whom he had met while vacationing in England), a monopoly over the production and sale of tobacco in Iran. The tobacco concession became a major bone of contention between the Qajar court and some members of the Shi'i clerical establishment, particularly those who had a vested interest in tobacco production. But soon the conflict assumed unanticipated proportions when radical clerics turned it into a major anticolonial movement and forced Nasir al-Din Shah to rescind the concession. Like Gandhi's boycott of imported British cloth in favor of homespun cotton half a century later, the clerical banning of the use of tobacco until and unless the concession was rescinded symbolically assumed a larger anticolonial character and became a dress rehearsal, if not in ideological articulation then certainly in popular mobilization, for the Constitutional Revolution.[24]

"The insertion of India into colonialism," Gayatri Chakravorty Spivak once said, "is generally defined as a change from semifeudalism into capitalist subjection. Such a definition theorizes the change within the great narrative of the modes of production and, by uneasy implication, within the narrative of the transition from feudalism to capitalism."[25] That "uneasy implication" can be made far easier if the act of "insertion" of India, or Iran, or any other hidden history of capitalist modernity, altogether abandons the grand narrative of a singular world history, centered in Europe, and locates its point of departure in the predicament and paradox of *colonial modernity* itself, which is not just colonial but also modern, which is not just modern but also colonial, and which by virtue of that paradox dismantles that Eurocentric grand narrative altogether, while leaving room for a global history that remains true to its regional lived experiences. The discrepancy I here outline between the phantom liberties articulated by revolutionary activists like Mirza Aqa Khan Kermani and revolutionary movements like Babism or the Tobacco Revolt require no "strategic essentialism" to understand them, as Gayatri Spivak would say. Manners of disruptive modernities that I wish to articulate in this book generate as much historical agency on the part of the colonial subject (on the battlefields of anticolonialism) as they puncture the Eurocentricity of any grand narrative of modernity that cannot but make any re/entry of the post/colonial into the paradoxical disposition of modernity "uneasy."

While radical Islamists like Seyyed Jamal al-Din al-Afghani (1838–97) took the political implications of the Babi movement and the Tobacco Revolt in Iran to their revolutionary conclusions and wed them to larger regional uprisings against European colonialism, the succession of these homegrown uprisings in Iran proper points to the political inefficacy of inorganic intellectuals, while marking the integral link of Shi'i millenarian doctrines and the clerical establishment to grassroots movements, a characteristic of Iranian political culture that remains definitive to its periodic outbursts to this day. The significance of inorganic intellectuals and their disembodied ideas, however, becomes far more evident and socially consequential if we link them to the rise of Persian literary modernity, the *condito sine qua non* of Iranian cultural modernity.

After a period of astounding mediocrity at the service of the Qajar court, Persian literature of the nineteenth century gradually yielded to the rise of a literary modernity deeply rooted in the ideals and aspirations of the emerging nation-state. What effectively rescued Persian literature of this period from its suffocating dungeons in the Qajar court was a small band of expatriate intellectuals who had fled the tyranny of the Qajars and sought refuge in adjacent countries, to the Ottoman territories in particular. It is exceedingly important to keep in mind that the most radical and groundbreaking ideas in nineteenth-century Iran were in fact produced by a very small band of expatriate intellectuals with very limited (at times almost nonexistent) organic links to their homeland—except when they were yanked from their exilic conditions and extradited to Iran, where Qajar officials cold-bloodedly murdered them.

The extraordinary achievement of Mirza Habib Isfahani (d. 1893), one of the most distinguished literary figures of the late nineteenth century, is representative of this expatriate band of intellectuals who, at great cost, created Persian literary modernity. Mirza Habib was born in Chahar Mahal, educated in Isfahan and Tehran, spent a few years in Baghdad, and upon his return to Tehran was accused of having composed a satirical poem that attacked Mirza Hasan Khan Sepahsalar. In 1866, Mirza Habib escaped the tyrannical reign of the Qajars altogether and sought refuge in Istanbul, where he worked as a teacher, a translator, a manuscript copyist, and a bureaucratic functionary, earned a meager living to support himself and his family, and commenced a reading and writing career that, before his death in 1893, revolutionized Persian literary modernity. One of the principal achievements of Mirza Habib was the writing of a number of books about Persian grammar, based on an entirely new and systematic model. Literary historians propose that the very grammatical foundation of modernist Persian prose is almost entirely indebted to Mirza Habib's groundbreaking work on Persian grammar in the 1870s. The literary output of Mirza Habib between his arrival in Istanbul in 1866 and his death in 1893 laid the foundation of modernist Persian literature.[26]

Mirza Habib had a solid command of French, and among his major achievements while in Istanbul was his translation of Alain-René Lesage's *Gil Blas*, the novel that was instrumental in making the picaresque form a major European literary sensation. By far the most spectacular achievement of Mirza Habib Isfahani was his Persian rendition of James Morier's *The Adventures of Hajji Baba of Ispahan*. The publication of both the English version of the novel by James Morier in 1824 and its Persian version by Mirza Habib Isfahani in 1892 provoked considerable discussion and controversy. At the beginning of his *Adventures of Hajji*

Baba of Ispahan, James Morier writes that he in fact translated it from the original Persian. Was that only a literary trope or did he mean it literally? Morier was a bureaucratic functionary and a colonial officer with a modest and clumsy command of Persian. His English edition of *The Adventures of Hajji Baba of Ispahan* is full of verbatim and entirely ludicrous translations of Persian phrases. How could a bureaucratic functionary with a meager command of Persian and a very limited exposure to Iranians during his short diplomatic sojourns in Iran have written such a book? Some believe that Morier's book is really a translation of a Persian novel and not an original work. Others wonder how a text of such astounding colonial racism in its English original could become, in its Persian translation, so seminal a text in the course of the Constitutional Revolution.[27]

Much of this controversy surrounds a single and singularly baffling fact: while James Morier's original is a horrid Orientalist and racist farce, Mirza Habib's Persian version is an absolute literary gem of unsurpassed beauty, grace, and elegance, and is both foundational to Persian literary modernity and a preparatory text in the course of the Constitutional Revolution of 1906–11. How could an Orientalist novel of the worst kind in its English version become in its Persian translation a definitive text of the moral imagination at the core of the Constitutional Revolution? Abbas Amanat, a distinguished Qajar historian, rightly characterizes James Morier's text as "an Orientalist project *par excellence. Hajji Baba* lampoons Persians as rascals, cowards, puerile villains, and downright fools, depicting their culture as scandalously dishonest and decadent, and their society as violent." Baffled by the positive and laudatory reception of Mirza Habib's Persian rendition of this book, Amanat resorts to the following rather outlandish explanation:

> Yet Mirza Habib, a sophisticated Persian intellectual of his time, was in heart an early example of the masochistic Persian modernists who were fascinated with everything Western, even to the extent of deprecating their own culture. This internalization of Orientalist stereotypes found resonance especially among the intelligentsia of the Constitutional Revolution and thereafter.[28]

This ludicrous explanation stems from a factual confusion rooted in a failure to understand how a literary work of art is written and received (here is a good example of what bizarre explanations emerge when positivist historians lack literary training). The laudatory reception of Mirza Habib's version, however, is due to two fundamental facts: Mirza Habib's Persian version radically domesticates the diction of the novel with such astounding literary felicity that it transmutes the Orientalist piece of nonsense into a literary masterpiece; and, of equal importance, it is the presumed authorship and thus reception of the text by the leading Iranian revolutionaries that reconfigured the text into a radical tract for revolutionary mobilization. Mirza Habib was not an ordinary "translator." He was a close friend and a comrade of the two leading revolutionary activists living in exile in Istanbul— Mirza Aqa Khan Kermani and Sheykh Ahmad Ruhi (the Iranian Marx and Engels of the time). These three comrades collaborated with each other, read each other's work, and copyedited each other's writings. The first copy of Mirza Habib's translation of *The Adventures of Hajji Baba of Ispahan* that reached Iran was in fact in Sheykh Ahmad Ruhi's handwriting; people thought it was his book, and its first published version was misattributed to him. Sheykh Ahmad Ruhi was no run-of-the-mill activist. A year after the publication of *The Adventures of Hajji Baba of Ispahan* in Persian, he and his comrades were cold-bloodedly murdered by the Qajar executioners. It was thus the presumed authorship of that novel, and the radical condition of its revolutionary reception, that turned it into a defining text in both the rise of literary modernity in Iran and its role in the Constitutional Revolution, not a nonsensical notion about "the masochistic Persian modernists." Morier's text characterizes an entire nation as deceitful and thus in need of political domination and colonial control. In his translation, Mirza Habib turns the text into a sociological examination of clerical and courtly corruption. These are two vastly different readings of the same reality, predicated on the same text.[29]

The literary modernity that Mirza Habib Isfahani initiated in Istanbul was soon matched by the equally important work of his close friend and comrade Mirza Aqa Khan Kermani, and that not merely as a radical thinker and revolutionary activist but also as a literary modernist. *Ridwan* (1886), which he wrote on the model of Sa'di's *Golestan*, is an exemplary model of updating the graceful Persian prose of the thirteenth century for effective use in the tumultuous period of Kermani's activism. In a subsequent work, *Reyhan* (1895), on which he was working when he was arrested and executed, Kermani pushed the boundaries of literary modernity even further. He severely criticized the literary stagnation of his time, including his own *Ridwan*, and demonstrated a thorough familiarity with European literary traditions, citing them as a model for the literary renaissance badly needed in Iran. In *A'in Sokhanvari* (1889), he provides a literary history of Iran, while in *Nameh Bastan* (1895), which he modeled on Ferdowsi's *Shahnameh*, he introduced contemporary historical criticism to pre-Islamic Iranian history. At the end of this book, Kermani included a critical essay on poetry and poetics, plus a number of poems on more contemporary political issues.

Paramount in Kermani's literary prose, evident for example in his *Ayeneh Eskandari* (1891), a book he wrote on the history of Iran, is his elegant fusion of a graceful Persian prose and poetry with a radically critical and deeply cultivated contemporary criticism. Kermani put his prose to good historical use and wrote extensively on medieval and modern Iranian history. The point of all his historical writing was to diagnose the maladies of tyranny and find a way out of the historical predicament of Iranians. Such titles as *The History of the Qajars and the Causes of the Rise and Fall of the Iranian Nation and State* (1893) and *On the Civic Duties of a Nation* (1893) clearly indicate what sort of historiography engaged and preoccupied Kermani.[30] What we witness in all these writings is a relentless mind systematically tackling every aspect of his country's cultural stagnation and systematically seeking to remedy its diverse aspects. Kermani wrote on music, painting, sculpture, and dance. He theorized about aesthetics, speculated on the nature of musical composition, and wrote a comprehensive theory of poetics. Having mastered the classics of Persian prose and poetry to a degree rare for his time, he proceeded to make groundbreaking innovations in prose and poetry, both in his own work and in theorizing about what he thought Persian literature needed to experience. What is paramount in Mirza Aqa Khan Kermani's literary modernism is his infuriated fusion of radical ideas and formal innovations. Kermani's radical and progressive political argument is the rising flame that glows through his prose and poetry.

Istanbul was not the only location where expatriate Iranian intellectuals cultivated Persian literary modernity. Central Asia and Caucasia were equally important. Chief among the literary achievements of this period, following the exposure of Iranians to European drama in the pages of Mirza Saleh Shirazi's travelogue, was Mirza Fath Ali Akhondzadeh's residence between 1834 and 1850 in Tbilisi, where he was heavily exposed to Russian literary and intellectual giants—particularly Aleksandr Pushkin, Mikhail Lermontov, Nikolay Gogol, Vissarion Belinsky, and Nikolay Chernyshevsky. Soon after his exposure to Russian (and by extension French and English) literature, Akhondzadeh wrote six plays and one novella between 1850 and 1857. Akhondzadeh wrote these plays originally in Turkish and then translated them into Russian himself. They were all staged in Tbilisi, and some of them in Moscow and St. Petersburg as well. Mirza Ja'far Qaracheh Daghi, a friend of Mirza Fath Ali's, translated all these works into Persian, and then from Persian they were translated into a number of European languages. Practically all of Akhondzadeh's plays, such as *Mulla Ibrahim Khalil the Alchemist* and *The Miser*, are in fact literary devices for articulating his social and political ideas, and a budding social realism is evident in most of them. Soon after Akhondzadeh, a follower and admirer of his named Mirza Aqa Tabrizi wrote the first modern plays in Persian. The title of one of them is so long it reads like the summary of the whole play: *The Story of Ashraf Khan the Governor of Arabia Who While in Tehran in the Year 1816 Was Summoned to the Capital Where He Pays the Three-year Tax of the Province, Receives a Receipt, and After Much Hardship Is Again the Recipient of the Robe of Governorship and Returns, Which Story Is Completed in Four Acts, God Willing*. In his politics, Akhondzadeh was an anticolonial nationalist; in his economics, a solid socialist; and he had a widely critical perspective at once deeply historical and global.[31]

The peripheral vision of an expatriate Iranian intellectual either looking back at his homeland or else traveling to his country to find it in ruins and in dire need of reform soon came to define the emerging literary imagination of the period. By far the best example of this vision is by Hajj Zeyn al-Abedin Maraghe'i (1839–1910), *Seyahat-nameh Ebrahim Beik* (*The Travelogue of Ibrahim Beik*, 1894). Zeyn al-Abedin Maraghe'i was born and raised in Iran, but he soon left his native land and traveled to central Asia and then into Ottoman territories, where he became a successful merchant. He finally settled in Crimea for a while and formed a family, and then as a successful businessman he was invited to become a Russian citizen, which he accepted. But soon he developed a deep sense of regret and remorse, rescinded his Russian citizenship, and retrieved his Iranian credentials. In Tbilisi, Maraghe'i was exposed to the progressive ideas of Russian revolutionaries; it was under their influence that he wrote his *Seyahat-nameh Ebrahim Beik*. The central figure of *Seyahat-nameh* is Ibrahim Beik, the son of an expatriate Iranian merchant living in Egypt, who, after his father's death, and following his wishes, decides to make a trip to his homeland. This narrative ploy then sets the stage for Zeyn al-Abedin Maraghe'i's scathing attack against the tyrannical reign of the Qajars and the horrid condition of decay and disarray they had created in Ibrahim Beik's homeland.[32]

The development of Persian literary modernism in this period, mostly by a group of dispersed and inorganic expatriate intellectuals, posits the creative act of the *literary* as the emancipating domain of the anticolonial imagination. "As we look back at the cultural archive," Edward Said observes in his *Culture and Imperialism* (1993), "we begin to reread it not univocally but *contrapuntally*, with a simultaneous awareness both of the metropolitan history that is narrated and of those other histories against which (and together with which) the dominating discourse acts."[33] The dialectics that Edward Said systematically sought to articulate, here and elsewhere, between the metropolitan center and the colonized periphery, and to theorize contrapuntally— his signature hermeneutic principle—is in fact always already evident in the foregrounding of literature produced on the site of colonial modernity, which operates through a will to resist power and domination. Literary modernists from Akhondzadeh to Kermani were let loose on a creative encounter with colonial modernity that, by virtue of the defiant subject informing their historical agency, constituted an autonomous authorship for the colonized subject otherwise made impossible by the very fact of colonialism. That liberating agency, definitive to Persian literary modernism, became the fertile ground of much revolutionary disposition—in both literary and political terms (to the point that the binary corners collapsed into each other)—for generations to come.

At the close of the century in which Mirza Saleh had introduced Iranians to the outside world, Iran remained quintessentially the same in terms of its recalcitrant feudal economy and its intractable medieval social structure, both presided over by a decadent aristocracy, a by and large corrupt clergy, and a variegated body of landlords ruthlessly ruling their peasants. A massive revolutionary movement (the Babi uprising of the 1840s) and a major anticolonial resistance (the Tobacco Revolt of the 1890s) shook the foundations of the medieval aristocracy and revealed the vulnerability of its corrupt and decadent foundations. Meanwhile the Iranian colonial encounter with modernity had given rise to a body of inorganic, mostly expatriate, intellectuals who revolutionized the discursive disposition of the emerging nation-state. Between Mirza Saleh Shirazi's travelogue early in the nineteenth century and a range of spectacular literary and intellectual masterpieces that were created by expatriate intellectuals later in the same century, a literary imagination, a critical consciousness, and a cultural modernity of unprecedented dimensions and tenacity took shape and defined the terms of Iranian resistance to colonial modernity. All these entrenched forces, from feudal and medieval to reformist and radical, had a fateful rendezvous with history at the opening decade of the twentieth century.

3
A Constitutional Revolution

Early in the morning of Friday, April 30, 1896, Mirza Reza Kermani quietly maneuvered his thin, clerically clad body into the inner sanctum of the Shah Abd al-Azim shrine near Tehran and waited for the right moment. Sultan Sahib Qiran, the Most Auspicious Monarch, Nasir al-Din Shah Qajar, just about ready to celebrate the golden anniversary of his reign, was scheduled to come and pay His Most Humble and Royal respects in this historic Shi'i shrine. As he sat quietly in a corner, Mirza Reza reached under his cloak, searched for his Russian five-shooter, and curled his finger around the trigger. He closed his eyes.

> *Q: When did you leave Istanbul?*
> *A: I departed on 11th January 1896.*
> *Q: When did you arrive in Shah Abd al-Azim shrine?*
> *A: On 16th March 1896.*

Mirza Reza Kermani was born and raised in Kerman and in his youth became a devotee of Seyyed Jamal al-Din al-Afghani, the most celebrated Muslim revolutionary of his age. When al-Afghani was expelled from Iran, Mirza Reza openly and adamantly supported al-Afghani and his outspoken criticism of the Qajar dynasty.

> *Q: Why did you decide to kill His Majesty?*
> *A: What do you mean why? I decided to do so because of*
> *all the incarcerations I endured, all the beatings I took, to*
> *the point of picking up a knife and tearing open my own*

stomach, because of all the calamities I have suffered. . . .
I was incarcerated for four years and four months, while in
my own judgment all I wanted was in fact the best for the
state and for the nation. I was serving my people, long
before the Tobacco Revolt.

Mirza Reza's open criticism of the Qajar officials and his devotion to al-Afghani finally landed him in jail. When he was released from prison he found that his wife had divorced him, his
eight-year-old son had been put to work as a servant in someone's house, and that his other son, a mere toddler, had been
given to an orphanage. He left Iran and found his way to Istanbul,
where he visited al-Afghani again and told him about the hard-
ships he had endured. "You should not tolerate such tyranny,"
al-Afghani told him casually. Mirza Reza took that advice literally, and said to al-Afghani, "Let me rest here for a while, I will go
back and take my revenge."

Q: Who were the people who were harassing you?
A: The horrid, disgusting, abominable, detestable bastards
like Vakil al-Dowleh, and the unbelievable love that His
Royal Highness the Crown Prince has for him. . . .
Q: If so . . . what had the Martyred Monarch done? You
should have revenged yourself against those who had
harmed you and not orphaned an entire nation.
A: When a king has ruled for fifty years and still receives
false reports and does not ascertain the truth, and when
after so many years of ruling, the fruit of his tree are such
good-for-nothing aristocratic bastards and thugs, plaguing
the lives of Muslims at large, then such a tree ought to be
cut down so it won't give any more fruits like that. When a
fish rots it rots from its head. Tyranny begins from the top.

Mirza Reza returned from Istanbul to Iran, buying a Russian
five-shot revolver on his way. He secured a residence in the Shah
Abd al-Azim shrine and bided his time. He would occasionally go
to Tehran and visit with al-Afghani's supporters and sympathiz-
ers. He also arranged for his eldest son to be brought to Shah
Abd al-Azim so he could see him for a few days. Finally, on the

evening of Thursday, April 29, 1896, he heard that Nasir al-Din Shah was scheduled to come to the shrine and pay his respects. The following day Mirza Reza went to the main mausoleum and located the exact spot where years earlier his revolutionary hero, al-Afghani, had been dragged out of the shrine and publicly humiliated before being expelled from Iran. Now Mirza Reza was sitting there, waiting.

> Q: *If you really care about the country and as you say you wished to protect the dignity of the nation, then how come you did not worry about creating chaos and anarchy?*
> A: *You are right. But if you look at the history of European countries, you'll see that there is no great purpose that is not achieved through bloodshed.*

Mirza Reza finally heard the commotion caused by the shah's entourage approaching the mausoleum. Just before Nasir al-Din Shah entered the sanctuary, Mirza Reza got up and sneaked in from the Imamzadeh Hamzeh gate of the shrine. Nasir al-Din Shah entered—royal, majestic, heavy, and yet humble for the occasion—with his entourage right behind him and began to pay his most humble respects and say his prayers reverently. "Peace and Benediction be upon Thee, You the Sacred Descendent of our Revered Prophet!" As soon as the king finished his prayer, he turned around and headed toward the Imamzadeh Hamzeh mausoleum, adjacent to the Shah Abd al-Azim shrine, and "just about one step before he was about to enter Imamzadeh Hamzeh, I fired my pistol."

> Q: *Do you really have no idea what happened to the pistol? They say there was a woman there who picked up the gun and ran away.*
> A: *No. There was no woman involved. This is all gibberish. Where do you think we live? Do you think Iran has suddenly become Nihilist, and that such courageous women are to be found amongst us?*
> Q: *Did you have any accomplice or did you kill the king all by yourself?*
> A: *I had five accomplices.*

Q: Tell me their names. You can trust me.
A: It was me, myself, my shadow, and my two balls.[1]

The shot with which Mirza Reza Kermani killed Nasir al-Din Shah on Friday, April 30, 1896, has reverberated throughout Iranian history.[2] After Mirza Reza was further interrogated and tortured, he was hanged publicly, early in the morning of Thursday, August 10, 1896, to make an example of him. He was indeed made an example of—but in exactly the opposite way that the Qajar dynasty and its clerical supporters had intended. That bullet passed through Nasir al-Din Shah's body and ricocheted to the rest of the corrupt Qajar dynasty a decade after the aging patriarch—heavy, huge, languorous, indolent, and lazy—fell down in the Shah Abd al-Azim shrine and soon after that rushed to meet his maker.

The patricidal shot with which Mirza Reza Kermani killed Naser al-Din Shah liberated an entire nation from historical bondage and thrust it into the modern world—the world as Iranians in and out of their homeland recognize it today. Mirza Reza Kermani was a simple-minded man driven to extreme measures by a combination of political convictions and personal grievances against the Qajar dynasty. In his political convictions, he represented a creative combination of Islamist, nationalist, socialist, and above all anticolonial ideas prevalent in late-nineteenth-century Iran, as indeed in much of the rest of the colonized world; in his personal grievances, he represented the ordinary people at the receiving end of the brutalities of the Qajar dynasty. This combination of forces ultimately led to a massive, prolonged, and bloody uprising that today we identify as the Constitutional Revolution of 1906–11—a revolution through which the absolutist monarchy of the Qajars was forcefully, by the collective will of a nation that picked up arms and opposed tyranny, transformed into a constitutional monarchy.

The constitution itself, which Mirza Reza Kermani and his radical comrades were not alive to see ratified by the reigning monarch officially on August 5, 1906, was the result of over one hundred years of anticolonial struggles (against the Russians, the French, and the British), as well as prolonged exposure to the ideals and aspiration of communities and societies the world over, themselves rebelling against domestic tyranny and European imperialism. In the letter and spirit of its aspirations, the constitution posited a radical departure from premodern Iranian and Islamic political thought, in which the rule of the monarch, the sultan, or the caliph was deemed divinely ordained. In this constitution, the power of the monarch was severely limited, subject to the collective will of his subjects (now dubbed "citizens"), and the body of the government was divided into three branches, the executive, the legislative, and the judiciary. In the body and soul of this constitution, nationalist ideals of a liberal democracy, socialist aspirations to justice and equanimity, and Islamist doctrines as interpreted by a supervisory clerical class all found an uneasy and problematic coexistence; a hundred years after the Constitutional Revolution, that unease has yet to resolve itself.

The Constitutional Revolution, which gained political momentum in 1906 and finally came to institutional fruition in 1911, was the birth channel of Iran into its contemporary history. In its origins and aspirations, goals and projects, achievements and failures, it was a revolution very much similar to other "Third World," anticolonial movements that defined much of the twentieth century. "If colonialism was a system," Edward Said proposes in his *Culture and Imperialism,* paraphrasing Jean-Paul Sartre, "then resistance began to feel systematic too."[3] What Sartre and Said, both following Frantz Fanon, observed about Asian, African, and Latin American anticolonial movements of the latter part of the twentieth century was of course evident in Iran and much of the rest of the world about half a century earlier— with a strong socialist element agitating the bourgeois dimensions of the revolution. Following a century of anticolonial struggles—from the Qajars' feeble attempt to safeguard the territorial integrity of their realm against the bloated Russian imperialism, to the French and British colonial overtures to offset, check, and balance each other—the Constitutional Revolution finally targeted the local venue of European colonialism and severely limited the damages initiated and sustained at the Qajar court. Throughout the nineteenth century, the Qajar court was the principal vehicle through which European colonialism sought to incorporate Iran into a global capitalist economy. Iran would offer its raw material, cheap labor, and strategic location, and in return (or rather in addition) would provide an expanding market for finished goods; it would also subject its national economy, polity, and culture to colonial mandates. The deadly combination of European colonialism and Qajar monarchical corruption amounted to a systematic surrender of Iran to a global capitalist economy beyond its control and detrimental to its interests.

Three major ideological formations and their corresponding politics emerged out of the anticolonial struggles of Iranians throughout the nineteenth century: liberal democratic *nationalism*, social democratic *socialism*, and theocratic *Islamism*.[4] Both the pages of the constitution of 1906 and the tumultuous streets of major Iranian cities early in the twenty-first century are the battlefields where these three ideologies contest these claims on the future of the Iranian national economy, polity, and culture. The unresolved predicament of Iranians for the last one hundred years, trapped inside the mutually exclusive paradoxes of these three concurrent ideologies, is deeply rooted in their more fundamental entrapment in a colonial modernity that has granted them historical agency precisely at the moment that it has denied them the political foregrounding of that agency.

As Frantz Fanon noted, and Edward Said later explained, anticolonial movements the world over set the historical record straight: "the West" did not give modernity to the rest of the world; rather, the rest of the (colonized) world made "Europe" possible. "Europe is literally the creation of the Third World," Fanon asserted; "the well-being and the progress of Europe [were] . . . built up with the sweat and dead bodies of Negroes, Arabs, Indians, and the yellow races."[5] Thus exposing the paradox of colonial modernity reverses the power-based metanarrative in which "the West" is assumed to liberate the rest of the world ("the white man's burden"), and grants historical agency to the world at large. Based on the cumulative arguments of Fanon and Said, we can thus argue that the entire canon of modernization (aka Westernization) theories, and with it the bogus dichotomy of tradition versus modernity, is in fact the precise opposite of what has happened in world history, where a white supremacist fiction was manufactured on the broken back of the colonized people and code-named either "Europe" or "the West."

The narrative assumption of the centrality of "Europe"—thus casting the rest of the world as peripheral—was predicated on the abusive relation of power between capital and labor, in terms both domestic to European capitalism and external (colonial) to it. As the Constitutional Revolution took shape and momentum, Iran's national economy was fundamentally compromised by a place in the world economy that denied it the necessary moral and material condition to achieve its political and cultural agency. As flawed, contradictory, and contested a text as the constitution of 1906 was, in terms of its political and cultural aspirations it provided the birth channel of a defiant anticolonial agency, as articulated from within the three simultaneous narratives of emancipation that it at once engendered, legitimized, and set in motion.

Upon Nasir al-Din Shah's death, his crown prince, Mozaffar al-Din Shah (reigned 1896–1906), succeeded him. Mozaffar al-Din Shah had spent forty useless and pathetic years as crown prince, tucked away in the province of Azerbaijan, where the shadow of mighty Russia had made him and his corrupt entourage obsequiously pro-Russian in their fearful and treacherous politics. Nevertheless, soon after he ascended the Peacock Throne, Mozaffar al-Din Shah had the decency to dismiss Amin al-Sultan, a fraudulent courtier he had inherited as prime minister from his royal father, and appoint Mirza Ali Khan Amin al-Dowleh, a reform-minded statesman who managed to resume some of the administrative initiatives of Amir Kabir and Sepahsalar and brought a modicum of order to the Qajar house. Because of a fundamental lack of local expertise in advanced administrative skills, Amin al-Dowleh employed a number of European technocrats, Belgians in particular, to help him reform the Qajar administration. (These Belgian technocrats turned out to be lackeys of the Russians and facilitated the czar's colonial intrigues in Iran.) As the examples of Qaem Maqam Farahani and Amir Kabir clearly indicate, initiating such reforms has always been dangerous to the health of the reformer. Corrupt Qajar courtiers were the immediate targets of these reforms, for they had become wealthy by looting the national treasury to finance their luxurious habits. The progressively minded Amin al-Dowleh was soon dismissed by

Mozaffar al-Din Shah, and the chief robber, Amin al-Sultan, was put back in power, with the full, enthusiastic, and well-paid support of key clerical operators.[6]

Between 1898 and 1903, Amin al-Sultan continued to divert money from the treasury for his own uses and borrowed money from the Russians to finance Mozaffar al-Din Shah's two pleasure trips to Europe, one in 1900 (to see the Paris Expo among other tourist attractions), and another junket in 1903, to visit European spas. The proceeds of northern Iran's customs tariffs were given to the Russians as collateral, principal, and interest on these loans. The Russians now effectively controlled the economic (and by extension political) affairs of northern Iran. Meanwhile, the British had southern Iran at their economic (and thus political) disposal: by 1900 yet another catastrophic loan, from the British, had been secured to finance the shah's royal visit to Europe. In exchange for this loan, the British were given the income of the fishing industry in the Caspian Sea, the royal mail and telegraph, and the customs revenues of Fars province and the Persian Gulf. Directly disenfranchised by all these concessions were, of course, the Iranian merchant class, the budding Iranian petite bourgeoisie, and their clerical supporters. By 1903, the rebellious voices of these groups and their moral and economic constituencies were heard at the Qajar court. The king dismissed Amin al-Sultan and appointed Ayn al-Dowleh, yet another opportunistic courtier, as his prime minister. The ground under the Qajar dynasty was now trembling, but the court was too drunk and opium-sedated to notice it.[7]

The rivalry between the dismissed Amin al-Sultan and the appointed Ayn al-Dowleh catalyzed further agitation in the Qajar realm. Ayn al-Dowleh put Sheykh Fazl Allah Nuri, a reactionary monarchist and antireformist cleric of unusual oratorical power, in charge of religious matters. The appointment deeply angered two diametrically opposed groups of clerics: those who coveted that position, and those who had opted to oppose the Qajars and their foreign supporters in favor of the Iranian merchant class, which was directly affected by economic concessions to foreigners. The appointment of Sheykh Fazl Allah Nuri to a key political position in these preparatory stages of the Constitutional Revolution, and the rise of active opposition to revolutionary clerics by the monarchist and conservative clerics, marked the emergence of the Shi'i *ulama* as a major force on both sides of the political divide.[8] The groundbreaking events happening in Iranian social and economic formations were now affecting the medieval institution of the Shi'i clerical establishment, which fragmented along the emerging class lines. Based in Qom and Najaf and widely spread throughout Iran, Iraq, Syria, and Palestine, the Shi'i clerical establishment assumed an increasing political power that has remained unabated to this day. The Constitutional Revolution in Iran was the crucible of these institutional changes.

The economic underpinning of this particular alignment of forces between the Shi'i clergy and the merchants was that in the course of the Constitutional Revolution, the Qajar court and its clerical supporters were the direct beneficiaries of British and Russian investments in the active exploitation of Iranian raw material and cheap labor, which effectively kept Iran a colonial economic subsidiary of European manufacturing and distribution interests. As was evident during the Tobacco Revolt, Iranian domestic agricultural products were now coveted by British and Russian merchants. "An increase in private landholding and the production of cash crops," as an economic historian of nineteenth-century Iran has pointed out,

> benefited the big merchants . . . while the lives of the great numbers of small merchants, artisans, and peasants deteriorated. . . . A combination of factors in the second half of the nineteenth century pushed the merchant class into investing in private landholdings. As foreign competition increased and European companies established trade centers in the country, merchants sought new sources of revenue and turned toward agricultural land. Many become full-time landlords. As a result, the foreign demand for raw materials, and the profitable market for opium and other cash crops, transformed the country's economy. It now depended upon a much larger export of raw materials together with a significantly reduced trade in manufactured goods, except for carpets.[9]

Historians agree that "nineteenth-century development in Iran should be characterized as colonial and dependent, serving the best interests of foreign merchants rather than the native community. The greater consumption of sugar and tea in the nineteenth century indicated a significant increase in the use of 'colonial goods' similar to that experienced by other Middle Eastern societies."[10] The Iranian merchant class and the emerging bourgeoisie were hurt by these developments. As a result, they actively recruited their own radical and moderate clergy to back their protests against the Qajar court, its clerical beneficiaries, and its foreign supporters. The hostility between anti-Constitutionalist clerics such as Sheykh Fazl Allah Nuri and pro-Constitutionalist clerics such as Seyyed Muhammad Tabataba'i and Seyyed Abdullah Behbahani was representative of a wider, entirely class-based, opposition between the entrenched aristocracy and its recalcitrant landed gentry and its feudal economy on one side, and the merchant class and the growing modern bourgeoisie on the other. European colonial investors in Iran at this point sided with the feudal aristocracy, bribing it heavily so its members could smoke opium and live in total indolence while Europeans robbed the nascent nation-state blind. The emerging alliance between the Iranian merchant class and the more radical forces among the clergy was thus in principal opposition to the Qajar court—which accounts for the anticolonial posture of this alliance.[11]

The economic concessions that Europeans, especially the British and the Russians, were receiving marked the beginning of appropriating an outrageous share of the wealth generated by the Iranian economy through a variety of commercial arrangements, the abuse of its raw materials and cheap labor in particular, as well as its expanding market, into the global operation of capital. Thus Iran was robbed of its natural resources; more important, this exploitation inhibited the growth of Iran's GNP, which would facilitate the formation of the Iranian national bourgeoisie and its contingent labor class, the contradictory interests of which would in turn create a robust economy, an expansive civil society, and bona fide democratic institutions. The decadent Qajar aristocracy would thus be forced to yield and not stand in the way of these developments by the material forces of a wholesome economy. The Constitutional Revolution was the revolt of the budding Iranian bourgeoisie against these foreign investors and those members of the Qajar aristocracy and Shi'i clergy who were the immediate and direct beneficiaries of these investments. The oppositional members of the Shi'i clergy were thus "revolutionary" or "progressive" not by virtue of any innate or institutional attribute, but because they allied themselves with the emerging Iranian bourgeoisie rather than with a dying Iranian aristocracy.[12] Meanwhile, the court-initiated reforms of Amin al-Dowleh in effect unified both factions (the reactionaries and the progressives) of the Shi'i clergy, for his reforms jeopardized the interests of both. In the tradition of Qaem Maqam Farahani, Amir Kabir, and Sepahsalar, Amin al-Dowleh wished to initiate state-sponsored reform, which included forming a constitutional assembly and eliminating the influence of high-ranking clerics on state affairs. The radical elements opposed the reforms because the monarchy's endorsement of them effectively legitimized Qajar rule and delayed more radical and enduring changes.

At the time of the Constitutional Revolution, the domestic Iranian productive machinery was not significant enough to generate a sizable working class, and the principal objective of the nascent Iranian bourgeoisie was to curtail foreign investments in order to safeguard their own interests. They sought to prevent the integration of the weak Iranian economy into the global productive machinery that had already generated major bourgeois and working classes in the main industrial zones while preventing the robust formation of these classes in the rest of the world. As the unholy alliance between neoliberal economics and neoconservative politics clearly indicates, liberal democracy is nothing more than the bourgeois social demand for the political apparatus necessary to the unfettered formation of its economic interests. At this juncture in Iranian history, late in the nineteenth and early in the twentieth century, the inevitable formation of an economically invested and politically vocal working class that would have resisted its economic exploitation by the bourgeoisie would have in turn resulted in a contingent class conflict. In a social democratic context, these contending interests would ultimately have resulted in the formation of an organically rooted democracy—a free, democratic, and robust civil society and the political apparatus to sustain it. In both political and economic terms, colonialism sustains democratic institutions at its European home while withholding the capital generated by industrial growth from the rest of the world. The presence of democratic institutions in the cosmopolitan heart of the capital and their absence at its colonial edges are thus the two sides of the same coin and as such the central paradox of global capitalism. In other words, the democratic institutions in the heart of capitalist machinery are made possible by, and thus stand on, their denial in the rest of the world. In the United States and Western Europe, these democratic institutions developed not because they had more eloquent theorists articulating the rationale for instituting and maintaining them, but because the productive machinery had generated and sustained a robust and regenerative class conflict that is definitive to the formation of democratic institutions. On the colonial edge of the capital, the ideological argument for such institutions is far more eloquent and vociferous precisely because the economic energy required to demand and exact them is so weak.

To prevent the belligerent clergy from opposing its lucrative deals with Russia and Britain, the Qajars were ready to do anything, including conducting a systematic campaign of appeasing and bribing the Shi'i *ulama*. This was made evident by the Qajar court participation in a barbaric persecution of Iranian Baha'is (a later and pacifist offshoot of the Babis), particularly in Isfahan. Mozaffar al-Din Shah was ready to do anything to appease both belligerent and reactionary forces within the Shi'i clergy who were demanding such persecutions. But none of these treacheries seemed to slow down the revolutionary momentum. In September 1905, as Mozaffar al-Din Shah returned to Iran from yet another trip to Europe, the Constitutional uprising was spreading throughout the country. By October the opposition had squarely focused on Prime Minister Ayn al-Dowleh and his hostile and vindictive policies against the revolutionaries. By December 13, leading Shi'i clerics had sought "defiant refuge" (*bast*) in the Shah Abd al-Azim shrine, and the open uprising against Qajar rule was now in full swing. *Bast* was an old strategic practice, whereby political dissidents would seek refuge in the sacred precinct of a mosque, a shrine, or a mausoleum where they could air their grievances with impunity. By the time of the Constitutional Revolution, foreign embassies had been added to the list of these sites of refuge.

About a month after the leading clerics had their *bast* in the Shah Abd al-Azim shrine, on January 11, 1906, the monarch requested their return to Tehran, agreed to curtail the power of Ayn al-Dowleh, and consented to the establishment of a parliament. The *ulama* returned, but Ayn al-Dowleh did not yield and instead arrested the leading revolutionaries. The king was now mortally ill. The leading *ulama* soon left Tehran and had their *bast* in the holy city of Qom, while the leading merchants of the capital did the same in the British embassy in Tehran. Finally the king dismissed Ayn al-Dowleh, appointed a reformist technocrat, Moshir al-Dowleh, as his successor, and signed an edict on August 5, 1906, granting his permission for the formation of a constitutional assembly. By October 7 the constitution was drafted, and on December 30, 1906, the king signed it. Five days later the Qajars were *checkmated* and the king was dead.

There was yet another king waiting for his father to die—and thus the bloodiest days of the Constitutional Revolution were still ahead. Muhammad Ali Shah (reigned 1906–9) succeeded his father, Mozaffar al-Din Shah. Initially Muhammad Ali Shah promised to honor his father's signature and uphold the constitution. But soon he changed his mind. In April 1907 he dismissed Moshir al-Dowleh and reinstated the diabolical Amin al-Sultan—an open declaration of war against the Constitutional revolutionaries. The first thing that Amin al-Sultan wanted to do was to get yet another loan from the Russians and send the king to Europe. (This is not a joke. Iranian prime ministers of this period seem to have been more like travel agents than statesmen.) In August 1907 a revolutionary activist named Abbas Aqa had finally had enough of Amin al-Sultan and killed him at the parliament. By November of that year, the king came to the parliament and swore on the Qur'an that he would honor the constitution. He was lying. The capital was now in complete chaos. By July 1908, the king feared for his life and escaped to Bagh Shah, a royal residence in the suburbs of Tehran. On June 22 he ordered Colonel Vladimir Liakhov, the commander of the Russian Cossack brigade at his disposal, to bombard the parliament. Scores of MPs were murdered. The short-lived constitutional period had lasted only from August 5,

1906, to June 22, 1908. What followed, the so-called *istibdad-e saqir*, or the "Minidictatorship" (or "lesser autocracy,") lasted just over a year.

Despite the attack on the parliament, the revolutionaries would not be silenced. As soon as Tehran was taken over by the absolutist monarchists through an effective military coup and fully endorsed by reactionary monarchist mullahs like Sheykh Fazl Allah Nuri, Tabriz rose in revolutionary defiance. As Sattar Khan and Baqer Khan, two revolutionary leaders, led the rebellious uprising from Azerbaijan, other cities joined forces with them, including a contingent of Armenian Iranians, led by Yephrem Khan, from Gilan, and the Bakhtiyari nomads, led by Sardar As'ad Bakhtiyari. Isfahan soon joined the revolutionaries as well, and a unified army marched toward Tehran; after facing a meager resistance by the Russian Cossacks protecting the Qajar king near Karaj, they entered the capital triumphantly on July 15, 1909. Muhammad Ali Shah fled the wrath of the revolutionaries, sought refuge in the Russian embassy, and resigned from his royal post. But there was yet another useless king waiting in line. Ahmad Shah (reigned 1909–25) succeeded his father and proclaimed himself king on July 16. He was only twelve years old. On July 31 Sheykh Fazl Allah Nuri, the most virulent anti-Constitutionalist cleric of his time, was publicly hanged.[13]

The Constitutional Revolution once again placed Iran squarely in the global geopolitics of the region—though this time with a new, mighty force with which all parties had to contend: the collective will of the nation. The two global superpowers at the time of the Constitutional Revolution in Iran, the Russians and the British (half a century later they would be replaced by the USSR and the USA), were not pleased with the rise of a revolutionary nation in the region and did all they could to thwart it, dampen the people's enthusiasm, and, in the middle of the mayhem, try to reap their own benefits.

As Fanon recognized, the "fight for democracy against the oppression of mankind will slowly leave the confusion of neo-liberal universalism to emerge, sometimes laboriously, as a claim to nationhood."[14] This claim to "nationhood," as Fanon realized on the anticolonial battlefield of Algeria, and as was later corroborated by similar events from Vietnam to Palestine, and as indeed was already evident from India to Africa to Latin America, is squarely limited by a global geopolitics that warrants a national economy and a corresponding national polity only to the degree that its inner logic of political power and economic interest allows or tolerates. The overwhelming power of the British and the lesser power of the Russians in revolutionary Iran early in the twentieth century did not compromise the rise of the Iranian national interest so much as systematically implicate it in a global capitalism entirely detrimental to Iran's very existence as a nation—from its economy and polity to its culture and character.

From the middle of the nineteenth century forward, Russia had massively expanded in the region. The 1861 Emancipation Edict had freed the Russian serfs; the new, modernizing spirit in Russia drove increasing industrialization, witnessed a monumental increase in the Russian working class, and added significantly to Russia's need for raw materials, cheap labor, and an expanded market. The Russian expansion into Manchuria in 1904 had resulted in a major war with Japan, a war that in conjunction with the Crimean War (1853–57), the Caucasian War (1856–64), the annexation of Central Asia (1864–65), the Russian-Turkish War (1877–78), and the Russian-Austrian rivalries in the Balkans (which finally led to the outbreak of World War I in 1914) points to the incessant imperial energy of Russia and its insatiable desire for territorial expansionism. The same Emancipation Edict of 1861 had of course also created a huge labor class, and along with it ushered in the rise of new and revolutionary ideas. The Russian Revolution of 1905, the drafting of a constitution, and the establishment of a parliament (Duma) were the immediate (but penultimate) results of these groundbreaking developments. By 1903, the Russian Social Democratic Party (founded in 1897) had split into Bolshevik and Menshevik factions and would soon wreak havoc on the House of the Romanovs.

Equally trapped in the hubris of their own imperial power were the British. From the middle of the nineteenth century forward a succession of regional uprisings had marked the challenge that various colonized nations posed to the global domination of the British Empire. Beginning with the Second Sikh War

(1848–49), the British were relentlessly at war with the peoples they had sought to dominate, rob of their natural resources, and impoverish and neutralize. The Second Anglo-Burmese War (1852–55) had not quite ended when the Indian Mutiny (1857–58) broke out. The British purchase of the Suez Canal (1875) had just been completed, in order to further facilitate their thieveries in Arabia and Africa, when the Second Afghan War (1878–80) was upon them, and soon after that came the Zulu War (1879), the First Boer War (1880–81), and the Mahdi War (1881–98). The British occupation of Egypt (1882) had barely taken place when the Sudan War (1896–99) broke out, and after that the brutally repressed Matabele Revolt (1896–97), followed by the Second Boer War (1899–1902). The sun indeed was not setting on the British flag, but under that flag the carnage and catastrophe necessary for maintaining a great empire were staggering.[15]

The revolutionary Constitutionalists in Iran were scarcely aware of these events, which had a distant but substantial effect on their predicament. But in the heat of the Constitutional uprising, the British and the Russians had every reason—ranging from economic to strategic—to come to an agreement over how to divide the Iranian domain. They thus signed a treaty on August 30, 1908, dividing Iran into three sections: the north under Russian influence, the south under British, and the center open for competition between the two of them. By 1915 the two imperial powers had concluded that the third zone was unnecessary, and so revised the terms of their earlier agreement and divided all of Iran between the two of them. It was not until the Russian Revolution of 1917 that the 1915 colonial agreement between the Russians and the British finally collapsed. Now the British went for the whole of Iran, and in 1919 they imposed on the fragile constitutional government a treaty forcing it to accept the effective colonial domination of their homeland by the superior British army. Meanwhile, William Knox D'Arcy (1849–1917), a gold and oil tycoon who in 1901 had secured an oil concession from the Qajars for sixty years, had struck oil in Iran (1908). By April 1909, the Anglo-Persian Oil Company was established and thus the British had far more at stake in Iran than Rafsanjani pistachios, Kermani carpets, and Oriental poetry.

It is instructive to compare the destructive role of Russian and

British imperialism in the region with the almost complete absence of the United States, nowhere near a global superpower at this time, in the course of the Constitutional Revolution. In the middle of the nineteenth century, when Iranian internal affairs were negotiated between Russian and British imperialisms, the United States was still confined to the Western Hemisphere and busily acquiring fertile new territories, particularly from 1846 to 1848, when it annexed California and New Mexico during the Mexican War. Soon after that the United States was engulfed in the Civil War (1861–65), and even after that it was preoccupied with quelling the rebellious Native Americans. Between 1876, when the Oglala defeated the U.S. Army at Little Big Horn, and 1890, when U.S. troops massacred them at Wounded Knee, the United States was largely focused on internal expansion. Then it acquired Puerto Rico, Guam, Hawaii, the Philippines, and Cuba in the aftermath of the Spanish-American War (1898).

The absence of U.S. influence in Iran in this period is accentuated by the presence of two extraordinary American citizens who were instrumental in the success of the Constitutional Revolution and are still honored in the collective memory of a thankful nation and the unending annals of their struggles for freedom. One was a Christian missionary turned revolutionary activist named Howard Conklin Baskerville, who in 1909 led a regiment of Iranian fighters (most of them his students) in a crucial battle in the Tabriz uprising; the other was a financial adviser named William Morgan Shuster, who in 1911 revolutionized the Iranian Ministry of Finance and sought to rid Iran of the monstrous colonial thieveries of the British and the Russians. The images of these two legendary Americans shine luminously in Iranians' collective memory of the birth of their nation into global modernity. To this day Iranians are grateful for the courageous sacrifice that these two foreigners made and for the services they performed.

The significance of Howard Baskerville (1885–1909), a Princeton graduate and a Presbyterian missionary to Tabriz, to the Iranian Constitutional Revolution has been (with a bit of exaggeration) compared to that of the Marquis de Lafayette to the American Revolution. Soon after the fall of Tehran under Muhammad Ali Shah and the rise of revolutionary Tabriz in 1909, Baskerville abandoned his teaching position at the Presbyterian mission school there and served directly under the command of Sattar Khan, the legendary revolutionary leader (the Emiliano Zapata of the Constitutional Revolution). Before he was killed on April 19, 1909, just eight days after his twenty-fourth birthday, Baskerville led a small band of student revolutionaries in a crucial battle against Ayn al-Dowleh's forces, who had besieged Tabriz. Baskerville's mission was to break this siege and facilitate the transport of food to the trapped inhabitants of the rebellious city. But he was shot and killed in the course of this mission. There is a beautiful letter written by Annie Rhea Wilson, wife of the principal of the Memorial Training and Theological School in Tabriz, on the occasion of Baskerville's death and addressed to his parents in Minnesota. Fearing for Baskerville's life when he resigned his post and joined the revolution, Annie Rhea Wilson told Baskerville on one occasion to look after himself and added, "You know you are not your own." "No," Baskerville responded, "I am Persia's."[16]

William Morgan Shuster (1877–1960) was an American lawyer and civil servant who became the treasurer-general of revolutionary Iran by appointment of the newly founded parliament, serving from May to December 1911. Despite extraordinary pressure from the Russians and their Belgian employees (for he had stopped their colonial thievery), Schuster managed to put the finances of the revolutionary parliament in order. The Russians were furious about Iran's revolution and encouraged the deposed monarch to mobilize his forces and reclaim his throne. At the time, Russia effectively ruled Iran's northern provinces up to and including the capital. The opposition of the British and the Russians to Shuster finally forced him out of Iran. Upon his arrival in the United States he wrote *The Strangling of Persia* (1912), a scathing attack on colonial intervention in Iran. "Only the pen of Macaulay and the brush of a Verestchagin," he wrote early in his book, "could adequately portray the rapidly shifting scenes attending the downfall of this ancient nation—scenes in which two powerful and presumably enlightened Christian countries [Russia and Great Britain] played fast and loose with truth, honor, decency and law, one, at least, hesitating not even at the most barbarous cruelties to accomplish its political designs and to put Persia beyond hope of self-regeneration." At the height of the

Constitutional Revolution, and in grateful acknowledgment of Shuster's services to Iran, the legendary poet, musician, singer, and songwriter Aref Qazvini composed a beautiful song about Shuster. He must be the only American celebrated in the crowning achievement of Constitutional poetry.[17]

At the end of her extraordinary study of the domestic and foreign aspects of the rise of the United States as a global empire, *The Anarchy of Empire in the Making of U.S. Culture*, Amy Kaplan concludes that "the anarchy of empire in its convulsive reach across the globe both erects and destabilizes the geopolitical boundaries of nation-states and colonies and the conceptual borders between the domestic and the foreign."[18] Perhaps paramount exceptions that prove the role, the figures of Baskerville and Shuster posit the alterity of a global empire—the equal globality of kindred souls to resist it.

The Constitutional Revolution of 1906–11 was the most significant event in the course of the Iranian encounter with colonial modernity—perforce narrated in nationalist terms and launched against domestic tyranny and foreign occupation and influence alike. Anticolonial nationalism, however, was not the only ideological force driving the Constitutionalists. A militant form of Islamism also inspired the leaders of the Constitutional Revolution. And a number of the most prominent revolutionaries were equally influenced by social democratic ideas filtering down to Iran from the tumultuous events in Russia—from Baku, Azerbaijan, in particular. The three ideological formations—nationalism, socialism, and Islamism—had a catalytic impact on each other and thus remained definitive to the rest of modern Iranian history, down to the present time. Once a constitution was drafted and ratified, and the skeletal structure of a modern democracy was established, Iran entered the realm of modern global geopolitics. In the course of this revolution, oil was discovered in 1908. This intensified the European colonial powers' resolve to exploit not only Iran's oil but also its other natural resources and ensure that they would have a dominant position in its expanding commercial markets.

The emergence of Iran into global capitalism, however, was

neither full and productive nor predicated on a robust economic infrastructure. A weak bourgeoisie, an equally feeble and anemic working class, an increasingly dislocated and impoverished peasantry drawn to a rapid but artificial process of urbanization, and abusive foreign investments detrimental to the Iranian national economy all amounted to an almost complete absence of powerful class interests and their contingent conflicts, which are preconditions for the formation of democratic institutions. Though the skeletal simulacra of these institutions did emerge in the course of the Constitutional Revolution and were indeed articulated in the letter and spirit of the constitution itself, the phantom liberties they guaranteed were in fact the wishful illusions of a weak and inorganic body of reformists and radicals. Iran thus emerged as a nation-state in the extended colonial shadow of capitalist modernity, increasingly robbed of its natural resources, and permanently located at the receiving end of a rapidly globalized capital. "Iran's growing participation in the world market," according to the distinguished economic and social historian Willem Floor, "was mainly as supplier of raw materials, chiefly agricultural products."[19]

Despite this fundamental weakness in the Iranian political economy, a wide range of new social classes began to emerge and expand the normative domains of both the civil society and its contingent political community. As the Qajar aristocracy lost its grip on a feudal society, the clerical class began to fragment into opposing forces, reflecting the fundamental divisions of the society along actual and potential class interests. The opposition of the merchant class to colonial contracts and foreign investments increased their class consciousness, and thus a new (but structurally weak) bourgeoisie began to exercise increasing power in the domestic economy. Though still economically weak and structurally inconsequential, the emerging working class employed in small-scale factories led to the gradual formation of labor unions and artisan guilds. As the impoverished peasantry became aware of the political role it could play, tribal communities such as the Bakhtiyaris and the Qashqa'is also entered the political process in earnest, as is evident in the leading role that Sardar As'ad Bakhtiyari played in the immediate aftermath of the Constitutional Revolution.

As the clerical class fragmented, the globally conscious urban intellectuals entered the political scene, banking on more than a century of social and intellectual activism. Soon the leading public intellectuals were segmented into radical and liberal forces, taking part in the groundbreaking political movements that were shaking Europe and Russia to their foundations. At this point, Iranian women entered the political process in full self-conscious confidence, as did religious minorities (Armenians in particular).[20] With the entrance of women and religious minorities into the scene we are witnessing the birth and nascent formation (however fragile) of citizenship in Iran in the context of a modern nation-state—a citizenry independent of rural or urban, clerical or secular, gender or ethnic identities.

Coterminous with the revolutionary formation of democratic institutions were the rise of a free and boisterous press and the emergence of key public intellectuals and revolutionary leaders. On the surface of the society the most elemental ingredients of a liberal democracy were now in place, but all in the absence of a robust economic structure that would sustain, animate, and invigorate them.[21]

As Iran was incorporated into global capitalism, the struggles of people for freedom around the world had a lasting influence on the prevailing ideological disposition, as well as on the ideals and aspirations of the Constitutional Revolution at its various stages. The cumulative effects of these revolutionary movements were formulated in specifically liberal democratic ideals, with solid socialist aspirations at the roots of the revolutionary uprising. In conjunction with the ideals and aspirations of a liberal and/or social democratic program informing much of these revolts, the global expansion of European colonialism had given rise to regional movements: pan-Islamism, pan-Arabism, pan-Iranism, pan-Turkism, and pan-Slavism.

Before his death on March 9, 1897, Seyyed Jamal al-Din al-Afghani was the principal architect of pan-Islamism. He argued that since all Muslim countries were under European colonial influence in one way or another, then a united front had to be formed to oppose it. Pan-Islamism, however, was not the only ideological outcome of hostility to European colonialism in and around Iran. Similar ideas had developed among Arabs, Iranians, and Turks entirely independent of their Islamic identities. The emerging aspirations of the Iranian national bourgeoisie ultimately worked against Iranian acceptance of any form of pan-Islamism, particularly that form that advocated religious rapprochement between the Sunnis and the Shi'is and the associated proposal to recognize the Ottoman sultan Abd al-Hamid II (reigned 1876–1909) as the new caliph of the Muslim world, an idea that some Turks obviously found quite attractive, for it offered a cover for their own emerging pan-Turkism. None of these racialized and/or sanctified anticolonial initiatives received much support from the Iranian bourgeoisie struggling for the formation of a national polity, a national society, a national economy, and their concomitant engineering of a national culture. Only those Shi'i clerics with organic connections to the merchant class and who were anti-Qajar, anti-Ottoman, and anticolonialist acquired real political influence during the Constitutional Revolution. Whether they took these positions because of their own vested interest, or ideological anticolonialism, or doctrinal commitments to Shi'ism became historically a moot and entirely academic question.

"An immense wave of anti-colonial and ultimately anti-imperial activity, thought, and revision," wrote Edward Said, summarizing his observations concerning the resistance of people the world over to European incursions into their lives, "has overtaken the massive edifice of Western empire, challenging it, to use Gramsci's vivid metaphor, in a mutual siege. For the first time westerners have been required to confront themselves not simply as the Raj but as representatives of a culture and even of races accused of crimes—crimes of violence, crimes of suppression, crimes of conscience."[22] Ever since the height of the Constitutional Revolution, Iran as a nation-state has been integral to that Gramscian "mutual siege," a dialectic of emancipation with "Islam and the West" as the principal (false) binary opposition at once distorting its lived experiences and yet pushing it forward toward liberation from tyranny. The location of Iran on the map of the global geopolitics at this point fundamentally compromised its national interests and made them vicarious and contingent on unpredictable colonial variables, and yet at the same time tested Iran's mettle and assured its survival, for if facing the colonial monstrosities of the age did not kill Iran, then it made the nation stronger.

*   *   *

At the threshold of the twentieth century and at the inaugural moment of its entry into global geopolitics, Iran thus suffered from a weak, colonized economy dominated by two superpowers, driven by grand and absolutist ideologies, and marked by the skeletal simulacrum of a constitutional democracy that looked perfect on paper but had very little economic fire in its expanding political belly.

The Constitutional Revolution in Iran was much more than a mere political upheaval and a collective uprising of unprecedented dimension in Iranian history. It was a revolution in the very moral fabric of a nation, in its collective self-imagination, in its introduction of Iranians into a turbulent modernity as a bona fide nation-state. The moral core of the revolution was an all-out revolt against past centuries dominated by a medieval and decadent monarchy and the cultural ossification that resulted from its tenure. Nowhere is that all-out rebellion more evident than in the tsunamilike upsurge in creative imagination that wreaked havoc on the received Persian literary formalism. This became the basis of almost everything else creative and imaginative that happened in Iran in the course of the twentieth century. The entire medieval history of Persian literary imagination was subjected to close examination, and thus the springboard of a massive cultural revolution was set solidly in place for the next century. The very language and diction of Persian prose and poetry, film and fiction, drama and satire, literary journalism and critical historiography that learned Iranians speak and write today evolved during the Constitutional Revolution.

In the making of the radical literary humanism of the Constitutional period, Iranian factors and foreign influences mixed to produce a unique and unprecedented cultural force—literary in its disposition, humanist in its global reach, and radically transformative in its formal ambitions. Edward Said has already in his *Culture and Imperialism* fully argued the instrumental organicity of European literature in making possible the European imperial imaginary—without being reductionist, pedantic, or mechanically causal.[23] In her extraordinary book *Masks of Conquest*, Gauri Viswanathan has also documented the extent to which the use of English literature in particular was instrumental in the making of a colonial subject.[24] What still remains to be fully understood and theorized, however, is the extent to which foreign literatures, English and otherwise—and without their being straitjacketed into an inanity called "Western literature"— were read contrapuntally, counterintuitively, and against the grain of their intended audiences, and thus produced an effect precisely the opposite of compliance with European imperialism. Perhaps the best example would be Mirza Habib Isfahani's Persian translation of James Morier's *The Adventures of Hajji Baba of Ispahan*, in which a horrid colonial piece of racism was turned around and read as an emancipatory text charged against both domestic tyranny and foreign domination.[25] In addition to this counterintuitive reading of foreign (mostly colonial) literature, Iranian literati gradually produced a vast body of literature in Persian that was conducive to a cumulative culture of resistance against imperialism. The predicament and paradox of colonial modernity could be resolved and outimagined only through this particular constellation of literary and cultural movements, in which the battle-tested and creative fusion of the foreign and familiar produced a unique and robust body of literary humanism, in which the Iranian subject found her or his historical agency. Thus, as on the battlefield of political resistances to colonialism multiple ideologies combated foreign domination while fighting against each other, a far more enduring battle ensued whereby poets and novelists, the intelligentsia and the literati, artists and filmmakers, began imagining their nation out of its colonial predicament.

To make that groundbreaking literary humanism and its radical social implications possible, some fundamental steps needed to be taken. Instrumental in the continued rise and the radical momentum of Persian literary modernity was the establishment of secular schools, free of clerical influence, that began with the establishment of Dar al-Fonun by Amir Kabir in the middle of the nineteenth century and continued into the Constitutional period. Amin al-Dowleh, the reform-minded prime minister of Mozaffar al-Din Shah, was instrumental in the establishment of a series of secular schools under the visionary leadership of Mirza

Hasan Rushdiyyeh, the most farsighted educational reformist of his time. Of course, this initiative deeply angered the reactionary (not the progressive) clerics, and in return they incited their seminary students to go and destroy these schools, having already declared Rushdiyyeh an infidel. The illegitimate opposition of the Shi'i clerics to these secular schools should not, however, be conflated with the opposition to European missionary schools, which at times (not always) facilitated the moral and imaginative colonization of countries like Iran. To be sure, Christian missionary schools did play a crucial emancipatory role in modern Iranian history (particularly in the education of Iranian women) despite their evangelical/colonial missions. Baskerville is a salient example. But the reactionary opposition of the Shi'i clerics to the secular schools that Rushdiyyeh had courageously envisioned must always be put in the colonial context of the time. What the establishment of secular schools achieved was the elementary constitution of a literary humanism at a public and politically consequential level, something that neither Muslim seminaries nor Christian missionary schools did, and in fact sought to undermine. (Both failed to do so.)

The movement to establish secular schools was accompanied by the rise of a free and outspoken press. It is impossible to exaggerate the impact of the volcanic eruption of radical and reformist periodicals in the course of the Constitutional Revolution. In the run-up to the ratification of the Constitution between August 1906 and June 1908, temporarily halted after Muhammad Ali Shah's military coup in June 1908, and resumed soon after the abdication and escape of Muhammad Ali Shah in July 1909, Tehran and other major cities were the site of an astounding growth of radical and reformist papers, including an avalanche of periodicals committed to the cause of women's emancipation. Because of the state monopoly over both papers and printing machines, the reformists and revolutionaries had to resort to the most elementary forms of producing their periodicals and distributing them as widely as possible. In Tehran, Rasht, and Tabriz, chief among the major cosmopolitan centers of revolutionary activism, literally hundreds of papers sprouted like mushrooms grown on a fertile but inconspicuous land. The events of the Constitutional Revolution came so rapidly that dailies and weeklies were the only way that the revolutionaries could catch up with those events and mobilize their constituencies. As a result, the best in social and cultural commentaries, political criticism, poetry and satire, global issues, and particularly matters of women's rights and education were all addressed in the pages of these exceedingly popular newspapers. The illiteracy of a majority of the population was entirely irrelevant to the significance of these papers because all it took was one literate person to come to a teahouse or even a street corner and read the papers for a large audience. The language of these periodicals was often simple, straightforward, and even colloquial, easily accessible to many people. The revolution in Persian prosody and poetry that would take place soon after the Constitutional period was rooted in the radical agenda of periodicals in this period.[26]

Such legendary periodicals as *Habl al-Matin*, *Sur-e Israfil*, and *Bahar* in Tehran; *Nasim Shomal* in Rasht; and *Mulla Nasr al-Din*, which was published in Azari in the Caucasus and distributed widely in Azerbaijan and read in many other parts of Iran as well, revolutionized Persian literary journalism. *Sur-e Israfil*, which commenced publication on April 30, 1907, was a weekly magazine edited by Mirza Jahangir Khan Shirazi (d. 1908) with the collaboration of his friend and comrade Mirza Ali Akbar Dehkhoda (1879–1956). In the course of its publication, *Sur-e Israfil* scandalized the treacherous Qajar court, its clerical supporters, and the Russian and British colonial envoys. Soon after the military coup of Muhammad Ali Shah in 1908, Mirza Jahangir Khan Shirazi was arrested and savagely murdered. One of the most beautiful poems of the Constitutional period *("Yad ar ze sham'-e mordeh yad ar"/"Remember the Blown-Out Candle, Remember!")* is by Mirza Ali Akbar Khan Dehkhoda in memory of his fallen friend.[27] After the execution of Mirza Jahangir Khan Shirazi on June 24, 1908, Dehkhoda fled to Switzerland and resumed the publication of *Sur-e Israfil* from Yverdon.[28]

Equally important in the course of the Constitutional Revolution was the gem of a paper called *Nasim Shomal* (which means "the Northern Breeze") that Seyyed Ashraf al-Din Qazvini, known as Gilani (1870–1934), began to publish initially in Rasht in 1906, and then from 1914 in Tehran—after a hiatus when it was banned soon after the military coup in 1908. Gilani was a poet of ingenious felicity: "I want to establish a newspaper," he said, "in which I will speak to people in a sweet and simple poetic language. I want to sell every issue of this paper for a pittance on ordinary people, for I believe that simple poetry, whether sad or happy, is the only language that can speak to the masses, especially if they can sing it too."[29] There are eyewitness accounts of the amazing popularity of *Nasim Shomal*, and how small kids would take bundles of the paper and run along to sell it for a pittance on street corners, where poor and ordinary people, whether they could read or not, would buy it (perhaps as a simple talismanic sign of their freedom), and then all gather around a literate person who would read Gilani's poems for them. Like the writings of Mirza Jahangir Khan Shirazi and Mirza Ali Akbar Dehkhoda, Gilani's poems were all dedicated to a scathing satirical attack on the decadent monarchy and its clerical and colonial supporters, encouraging people first to get to know who these corrupt tyrants were and then to rise against them.

Another extraordinary periodical, *Mulla Nasr al-Din*, founded in the Caucasus by Jalil Muhammad Qoli Zadeh (1869–1932) in 1906, was equally crucial in the rise of Iranian anticolonial modernity. Published in Azari and read widely throughout Iran, *Mulla Nasr al-Din* was a social democratic organ that gave a voice to the most progressive forces in the course of the Constitutional Revolution. It openly advocated a social system in which

masters and slaves, the wealthy and the poor, would be equal in their rights and abilities, where a government would come to power that would clearly declare democratic principles, and that instead of imposing laws of torture and execution . . . would distribute the land among the peasants, and would involve workers and peasants in matters of governance, and manage the affairs of the state via consultation and discussion.[30]

What is remarkable about the public intellectuals who published these papers is that they were usually known not by their last names but by the name of the paper they published. What more fitting tribute—when mere mortals become their immortal words!

"The post-imperial writers of the Third World," Edward Said summarized his observations about the themes of resistance cultures that emerge against imperialism and colonialism, "bear their past within them—as scars of humiliating wounds, as instigation for different practices, as potentially revised visions of the past tending toward a post-colonial future, as urgently reinterpretable and redeployable experiences, in which the formerly silent native speaks and acts on territory reclaimed as part of a general movement of resistance, from the colonist."[31] Before Edward Said, both Frantz Fanon and Antonio Gramsci had noted the necessity of what Gramsci had rather indexically called the "Sorelian spirit of cleavage" that must move the subaltern cause.[32] But it was Said who more than any other postcolonial theorist underscored and theorized the significance of culture in general and literature in particular as acts of (material) resistance to domination. "As scars of humiliating wounds [and] as instigation for different practices," the literary humanism that later in his life became the defining preoccupation of Said must creatively combine the spontaneity of the present with a recast configuration of a radically revised past in order to generate and sustain revolutionary momentum for emancipation.[33] In the course of the Constitutional Revolution, the creative core of that literary humanism effectively reversed the predicament of colonial modernity into the theoretical foundation of its resolution and mutation into an anticolonial modernity. The devil of this emancipatory reversal, as always, was in its details. A critical example of this liberating literary humanism, recasting the wounds of a nation into the site of its emancipation, was in the rise of satirical prose and poetry.

The defining moment of the prose and poetry of the Constitutional period was in the central significance of satire in political mobilization. Mirza Ali Akbar Taher Zadeh Saber (1862–1911) is one of the shining examples of satirical poetry in this period. Although he composed his poetry mainly in Azari and published in *Mulla Nasr al-Din* in the Caucasus, he had a universal appeal and was read and admired widely throughout revolutionary Iran. The example of Saber is perhaps the best indication of the extraordinary significance of Greater Azerbaijan in not just the Constitutional Revolution in Iran, but the Russian revolutions of 1905 and 1917, as well as reformist and radical movements in the Ottoman territories. Azerbaijan, in and out of the territorial boundaries of Iran proper, was a hotbed of revolutionary activism, and Saber's satirical poetry is a good example of the exquisite literary taste and the extraordinary revolutionary significance of this region for progressive movements beyond the borders of Azerbaijan proper. In the aftermath of the Russian-Japanese war of 1904–5, the revolutionary ideas that swept across central Asia and the Caucasus had Baku, Azerbaijan, as the major intellectual center of its activities. Those who have been pushing an entirely Eurocentric set of "modernization" theories that kept generations of American political scientists in business will find it a nightmare trying to account for Azerbaijan as the principal site of progressive ideas and liberating monuments in the region.

Saber's collaboration with *Mulla Nasr al-Din* was the direct result of these progressive movements in literary and cultural modernity that were coterminous with the revolutionary momentum sweeping throughout the region. The reigns of terror and tyranny in Russian, Ottoman, and Iranian domains were the principal targets of these progressive movements. Saber was deeply influenced by the Russian Revolution of 1905. "The poetry of Saber," as one literary historian of the period puts it, "is the ballad of happiness and light, the song of a free, honorable, and dignified life."[34] Saber's very existence and significance demand a radical reconsideration of literary, and by extension political and cultural (all anticolonial), modernity, in the region in which he was born and grew up, namely in the Russian, Ottoman, and Iranian territories. Self-delusional speculations about "Westernization" have been a lucrative pastime for generations of American political scientists who have no blessed clue who people like Saber were and what revolutionary ideas they articulated for their own people—and from the midst of battlegrounds against colonialism. Azari intellectuals such as Saber were deeply committed to the cause of freedom in not just their own immediate domain but in fact in the entire region, particularly for Persian-speaking

Iranians, with whom they had a deeply historical connection. As Janet Afary, the distinguished historian of the Constitutional period, rightly notes and documents, the Constitutional Revolution was a deeply multicultural and pluralist movement in which Iranians, Azaris, Turks, and Armenians (men and women) were unified in the making of a glorious uprising against tyranny—domestic and foreign.[35]

What is astonishing about Saber's satirical poetry is that because Russian censorship did not allow him to speak directly about the Russian situation, he effectively used the Iranian and Ottoman context as a metaphor for his criticism of Russia.[36] The converse is also true: some of Dehkhoda's poetry was written in a mixture of Persian and Azari, published in *Mulla Nasr al-Din*, and used the condition of the Caucasus as a metaphor for revolutionary Iran.[37] The Russian censors were deeply disturbed by Saber's and his comrades' devotion to the cause of the Constitutional Revolution in Iran. As a biographer of Saber has put it, "Saber's poetry was more important in the success of the Constitutional Revolution in Iran than a platoon of soldiers."[38] It is a curse of national (and nationalist) historiography of Persian literary history and the jingoistic racialization of "Persians" by Orientalist-identified and mentally colonized Iranian historians that many of these profoundly important events are neglected in Iranian literary historiography, simply because they are written in Azari and not in Persian, the fetishized language of state-sponsored and colonially conditioned nationalism of the worst kind.[39] Advocating the cause of the Constitutional Revolution, informed and fortified by a superior intelligence and a vastly learned and cultivated literacy, was the principle that inspired Saber's poetry of this period.

The two counterparts of Saber in Iran were Seyyed Ashraf al-Din Qazvini of *Nasim Shomal* and Mirza Ali Akbar Dehkhoda of *Sur-e Israfil*, who in poetry and prose perfected Persian satire with unprecedented daring and imagination. Gilani was deeply influenced by Saber and freely adapted and translated many of his Azari poems into Persian, so much so that some literary historians have in fact accused him of plagiarism.[40] But in the political context of a revolutionary condition in which most poets and activists were in fact using various, and deliberately confusing, pseudonyms to escape censorship and imprisonment, such notions of authorship are really of interest only to subsequent historians, far distant in time and understanding from that turbulent era, who express historiographical concerns that are founded on irrelevant ideas about the definition of authorship. In his translations and adaptations of Saber's poetry, Gilani made them pertinent to his immediate Iranian conditions. One example is a powerful poem that he translated from Saber and applied to the notorious counterrevolutionary cleric Sheykh Fazl Allah Nuri.[41] In many of his "translations," as a result, Gilani extensively expanded on the original Azari and gracefully appropriated it for his Persian-speaking audience. The problem is not really what these poets did in translation (or as the poet Robert Lowell would term it, "imitation") but with bourgeois-nationalist historiography that fails to comprehend and thus misrepresents the actual situation and context of the time in the interest of nationalizing literature.

In prose the absolute masterpieces of Constitutional satire belong to Mirza Ali Akbar Dehkhoda and his *Charand-o-Parand* (*Gibberish*), a series of satirical columns he wrote and published in *Sur-e Israfil*.[42] In *Charand-o-Parand*, Dehkhoda defied the literary arrogance of formal Persian prose and developed its colloquial properties to perfection. Dehkhoda later emerged as a folklorist and encyclopedist of extraordinary significance whose two monumental works, *Amthal-o-Hikam* and *Loghat-nameh*, were the most important sources of both colloquial and formal Persian literary lexicography. But the roots of his fascination with colloquial Persian were in the satirical prose of the Constitutional period, which he helped to establish. When, decades later, one of the greatest modernist Persian poets, Ahmad Shamlu (1925–2000), carried on Dehkhoda's project in his *Farhang-e Kucheh* and continued to collect, catalog, and document Persian colloquialisms, the initial efforts of Dehkhoda were wedded to the next generation of revolutionary poets and activists with a systematic and radical fascination with the capabilities of Persian colloquialism. Shamlu's other major achievement was to extend Dehkhoda and his generation's introduction of Persian colloquialism into engagé poetry; in one poem after another he navigated the uncharted realms of Persian folklore and folktales and thus established the genre as a bona fide mode of poetics that soon attracted many other poets of his generation.

Perhaps the most important aspect of this generation of satirists is the spontaneity of their utterances, the swiftness of their biting criticism, and above all the detection of frivolity as a literary trope best suited for the tumultuous period. That spirit of spontaneity is also evident in eyewitness accounts of the Constitutional Revolution, perhaps best exemplified in Nazem al-Islam Kermani's *Tarikh-e Bidari Iranian* (*The History of Iranian Awakening*). Nazem al-Islam Kermani (1863–1918) both participated in and observed the Constitutional Revolution, and with a single book he consigned the languorous verbosity of the court-affiliated and opium-addicted chroniclers to the dust heap of history and effectively brought Iranian historiography into the streets and squares, where history was taking place.[43]

If we abandon the Eurocentricity of a singular idea of modernity, which privileged a white band of predatory colonialists in Europe and disenfranchised the rest of humanity (including the disenfranchised classes inside Europe), and posit the very site of anticolonial resistances as the modus operandi of a different kind of (emancipatory and universal) modernity, then the literary modernity that flowered during the Constitutional period in Iran and its regional context have a theoretical implication far beyond their own historical vicinity. The significance of *anticolonial modernity* is that it not only speaks to the lived experiences of myriads of colonized territories the world over but also includes the so-called West (the ideological mutation of Western European colonialism) within the domain of its criticism, does not hold it as the overriding measure of truth and emancipation, and can in fact include the disenfranchised and racialized minorities within the West as part and parcel of its emancipatory project.

Like any other nation facing the predicament of colonial modernity, Iran was not trapped between two false and debilitating binary opposition of "tradition" and "modernity." Iranians practiced a defiant historical agency by collectively resisting the colonial powers that had come to dominate in the name of liberating them. They did not buy into that fabricated paradox, and by opposing colonialism they did not just end it but also cultivated the terms of their own modernity—a modernity defined and articulated in the robust battlefields of struggling against colonialism, and not just obsequiously analyzed by a band of useless and inorganic intellectuals constantly toggling between "tradition" and "modernity."

"As potentially revised visions of the past tending toward a post-colonial future," as Edward Said put it, and "as urgently reinterpretable and redeployable experiences," the defiant nation finds in the prose and poetry of its emancipation the terms of its future history—its modernity. Here, "the formerly silent native speaks and acts on territory reclaimed as part of a general movement of resistance, from the colonist," and precisely here, the collective significance of momentous events in Iranian literary modernity ultimately came to a crescendo in the principal site of resistance in the course of the Constitutional Revolution: Persian poetry, a creative domain that has much to offer in articulating further the cultural characteristics of anticolonial modernity. Paving the way and mapping out the contours of this literary (dimension of an anticolonial) modernity, Persian poetry of the Constitutional period emerged as the moral conscience of the revolution, its political claims sublated in poetic truth, the mirror of its immediate visions and distant hopes. The movement toward literary modernity was gradual and organic, formal and factual, in both the manner of Persian poetic diction and the matter of its claims against colonialism.

A key transitional figure in the poetic revolution that happened in this period was Adib al-Mamalek Farahani (1860–1916), who was a staunch classicist and wrote extensive panegyrics for useless Qajar princes; yet, when the Constitutional Revolution was about to happen, signs of an internal struggle became evident in his work. With Malek al-Sho'ara Bahar (1886–1951) the revolutionary spirit of the time began to infiltrate the poetic disposition of Persian classicism, for Bahar did his utmost to facilitate a graceful entry of contemporary concerns into classical Persian prosody. Thematically, Bahar did wonders in speaking to matters immediately relevant to his time. But when it came to the structural edifice of Persian prosody he took one step back in reverence and hesitated. The audacious defiance required to break through classical Persian prosody was found in Taqi Raf'at (1889–1920), who, as a revolutionary poet-activist, insisted on breaking loose from the tyrannical reign of Persian classicism. The feisty debate between Bahar and Raf'at remained quintessential to the revolutionary disposition of Persian poetry at this stage, one insisting on salvaging Persian classical formalism, the other proceeding to dismantle it.[44]

However, such theoretical and scholastic debates were too abstruse for the time, particularly when we look at the ground-breaking work of poets such as Mohammad-Reza Mirzadeh Eshqi (1894–1924) and Iraj Mirza (1874–1926). Eshqi and Iraj Mirza applied their gifted poetic language to contemporary social and cultural issues, without giving much theoretical consideration to what walls and citadels had to be brought down. Their poetry was, in fact, actually breaking down these walls and obstacles. The same is true of the widely popular poetry of Ali Akbar Dehkhoda, and perhaps even more poignantly the poetry of two extraordinary women of this period, Parvin E'tesami (1906–41) and Shams Kasma'i (d. 1961). Parvin E'tesami took the world of male-dominated Constitutional poetry by storm and suddenly reminded the patriarchal clique (including the leading revolutionaries) of the neglected half of the Iranian population. She was not an outspoken feminist or even someone who wrote from a feminine perspective. Perhaps that was the most powerful aspect of her poetry—that she took Persian poetry of the Constitutional period to unsurpassed thematic and stylistic heights and then simply put her name under it. The impact was so powerful that for years the demented patriarchal culture she had thus taken to task refused to believe that the author of these exquisite, timely, and powerful poems was actually a woman. Because she had a progressive and dedicated father who also happened to be a leading literary figure of his time, they said these were her father's poems. Parvin E'tesami survived the banalities of her culture and remained a shining example of Constitutional poetry, as did Shams Kasma'i, who despite her small body of work has the singular privilege of having been the first modernist poet to break down the formal tyranny of classical Persian prosody and experiment with free verse. It would be false, however, to dismiss all the revolutionary male poets as indifferent to the question of women's emancipation, for many of them were in fact among the leading advocates of women's liberation from their medieval bondage. Under the pseudonym "Femina," Taqi Raf'at wrote many of his poems in defense of women's liberation, as did another poet, Rafi' Khan Amin, who signed his poems "Feminist."[45]

By the time Constitutional poetry had produced a figure like Abolqasem Lahuti (1887–1957) or a committed revolutionary like Muhammad Farrokhi Yazdi (1889–1939), it was way ahead of any scholastic theoretical debate, for it had moved right into the heart of a rebellious uprising against Persian prosody and monarchical patriarchy alike. Lahuti was a revolutionary poet of uncommon brilliance and courage who put his gifted command of the Persian language at the service of his socialist ideals. In Tehran he published his subversive poems clandestinely. In Rasht he fought with other revolutionaries against the Qajars and received a medal of valor from Sattar Khan. He was soon arrested on charges of "terrorism." But he escaped to the Ottoman territories and lived in dire circumstances until he immigrated to the Soviet Union in 1922. Lahuti was indispensable to the formation of a poetry totally dedicated to the cause of the working class. Next to Lahuti stands the rebellious figure of Farrokhi Yazdi, the wholeheartedly committed socialist poet of the period. Farrokhi Yazdi has rightly been compared to the great Turkish poet Nazim Hikmat (1902–63) in the sweep of his political and poetic imagination. When he angered a provincial governor in a poem, the angry tyrant ordered Farrokhi Yazdi's lips sewn with a needle and thread. His devotion to the Constitutional cause finally took him from his native Yazd to Tehran, where he established a newspaper called *Tufan* (*Storm*). He endured the initial phases of Reza Shah's dictatorship, but was forced to close down his newspaper and escape to the Soviet Union, where he became disgusted with Stalin's opportunistic abandonment of Iranian Communists in exchange for lucrative business contracts with the Pahlavi monarch. (This marked the commencement of Soviet imperialism and the end of independent socialism in the region.) From Moscow, Farrokhi Yazdi went to Berlin. But he could not endure the poverty and indignity of exile and returned to Iran, knowing full well that Reza Shah would have him killed. And so he did. In the evening of Monday, October 16, 1939, Reza Shah had Farrokhi Yazdi murdered in his cell. He was almost naked when he was killed by injection of air into his veins. The four walls of his cell were covered with his poems.

> *For a lifetime in search of Freedom and Justice*
> *We have rushed towards our own annihilation.*
> *Look at the masthead of our Newspaper*
> *To see the Red Flag of Equality.*[46]

Among the poets of the Constitutional period, Aref Qazvini (1882–1934) was a breed apart. His significance is not limited to a collection of astoundingly beautiful poems he wrote and his impeccable record as a revolutionary activist devoted to the ideals and aspirations of his friends and comrades. He was, above all, a gifted musician, a singer, and a popular songwriter. His songs and ballads were definitive to the Constitutional period; every line of his poetry is a graceful and moving record of the hopes and aspirations, trials and tribulations, of his nation. When the malevolent Sheykh Fazl Allah Nuri was hanged by the revolutionaries, Aref was there to commemorate the event with an emancipatory ode. When Muhammad Ali Shah's military coup failed to overturn the achievement of the Constitutionalists, Aref was there to sing his people's song of freedom. When the deposed shah collected a pathetic army (with the help of Russians) and sought to regain his lost throne, Aref was there to compose one of his most beautiful, moving, and memorable songs. When Russian colonialists conspired to force Morgan Shuster out of Iran, Aref was there to immortalize the caring American adviser to the revolutionaries in one of his most beautiful odes. When the revolutionary leaders were weary, Aref was there to lift their spirits with a timely and stunningly composed and performed song. With its origins in classical and perhaps even ancient Iranian melodic composition, the Persian songs (or *tasnifs*) that Aref brought to melodic perfection in his time were impeccably suited for the popular and revolutionary uses to which they were put during the Constitutional period. The melodic beauty of these songs made them particularly suitable for public gatherings and revolutionary mobilization. They were easy to recite and memorize, and harmonically compatible with classical melodies in Persian music, which made them instantly and intuitively appealing to Iranians.[47]

Just about a generation before Aref, a singer and songwriter named Mirza Ali Akbar Sheyda, whose unrequited love for a Jewish girl later became legendary and perhaps helps account for the intense passion of his songs, had made important headway in integrating this long tradition with his contemporary taste and aesthetic disposition. But historians of Persian literature agree that what Aref did to *tasnif* was nothing short of a revolution in its thematic range and social consequences. As Yahya Aryanpour, the most distinguished literary historian of the nineteenth century, puts it, "the crucial significance of Aref is that he was a poet, a musician, and a singer, and he used the form of *tasnif* with astounding virtuosity in order to express nationalist ideals and themes. In other words, he borrowed the limited framework of popular songs and gave it a nationalist significance."[48] Aref himself was quite conscious of the fact that the rise of Iranian nationalism, and the very notion of "nation," were made possible in Iran largely because of his songs: "If I have done nothing else," he said once, "for Persian music and literature, I composed nationalist songs at a time that one out of ten thousand Iranians had no clue what a 'nation' was."[49] Indeed, to this day, Aref's memorable song that begins *"Az khun e javanan-e vatan laleh damideh / v-az matam sarv-e qadeshan sarv khamideh"* ("From the blood of young people of this nation tulips have grown / In mourning for their fallen figures, cypress is bended") is something of a national anthem for Iranian revolutionary nationalists at the purest and most noble moments of their idealism. Aref was angered and frustrated by the absence of musical notation in Iranian music, and his aspiration was to compose operatic music using folkloric melodies, an ambition that he took to his grave.

The domain of anticolonial cultural modernity of the Constitutional period was of course not limited to poetry. Entirely overshadowed by the overwhelming public presence and political consequence of poetry, modernist Persian fiction and drama are equally rooted in this period. The earliest attempts at writing novels date from the later decades of the nineteenth century, leading up to the revolution, as is the case with modernist drama.

Literary circles emerged, and with them began spirited debates about the nature of literary modernity. Equally rooted in the Constitutional period is the rise of Iranian cinema. Perhaps the only benefit of Mozaffar al-Din Shah's trip to Europe in 1900, when he visited the Paris Expo, was that he brought back a Gaumont camera. (He had himself filmed by his court photographer, Akkasbashi).[50]

The lasting significance of the Constitutional Revolution was in its unleashing of a cultural effervescence that overcompensated for the absence of economic vigor with an overwhelmingly creative literary imagination. Persian poetry of the Constitutional period—perhaps best represented in Aref's songs, poems, and music—exudes a peculiarly powerful fusion of eroticism and politics, of earthly and material love injecting beauty and passion into the subversive violence at the root of all collective defiance of tyranny. This has, perhaps, something to do with the youth of the revolutionaries; they were mostly young people who were simultaneously falling in love and becoming political. There was an erotic aspect to the revolution's violence against decadence, a poetry at the heart of its politics, which translated into an impatience with injustice, a beautiful irritation at the sight of ugliness. Be that as it may, the radical agenda that these poets and songwriters, revolutionaries and rabble-rousers, outlined and executed in the span of less than a decade determined the fate of an entire nation for a century to come.

4

The Pahlavis

Late in August 1970, when I had just turned nineteen, I took an overnight bus ride from my hometown of Ahvaz in southern Iran and the following day arrived at a bus terminal in downtown Tehran, where I had just been admitted to college. I still feel lurking in my bones the joy and ecstasy, mixed with an inexplicable sense of fear and uncertainty, that I had on that gorgeous summer day, with a small suitcase in my hand and all my monetary claim to financial security for about six months sewed into the seat of my pants (for my mother was absolutely convinced that it was the safest place, with all the thieves running loose in our imperial capital). Was it because of that overwhelming sense of triumphant uncertainty, of what was ahead of and what behind me, that to this day and for the life of me I cannot remember how I ended up with a folded, crumpled-up piece of paper in my hand, right there in the middle of that bus terminal. On the paper was a heading of a cautionary nature: "List-e Kutub-e Zalleh" ("The List of Books That Will Misguide You!").

Ever since that day, that strange title at the center of that piece of paper stands out in my memories of my undergraduate years in Tehran. The list of books, I later learned, had been prepared by the shah's secret police, the dreaded SAVAK (which I had learned the hard way to fear and loathe), and distributed to bookstores across the country. No books on that list were to be sold, or even found, in any bookstore. That list became my core curriculum, as it were, the map of my liberal education into a defiant politics, for the next four years. To this day, I first remember the Persian titles of the non-Persian books on that page: Jack London's *Ava-ye*

Vahsh (*The Call of the Wild*), Ethel Lillian Voynich's *Kharmagas* (*Gadfly*), John Steinbeck's *Khusheh-ha-ye Khasham* (*The Grapes of Wrath*), Bertolt Brecht's *Naneh Delavar* (*Mother Courage*) and *Dayereh-ye Gachi Qafqazi* (*The Caucasian Chalk Circle*), Emile Zola's *Zherminaal* (*Germinal*), Ignazio Silone's *Nan-o-Sharab* (*Bread and Wine*), Maxim Gorky's *Daneshkadeh-ha-ye Man* (*My Universities*), Stendhal's *Sorkh-o-Siah* (*The Red and the Black*), Pearl Buck's *Khak-e Khub* (*The Good Earth*), Shakespeare's *Haamlet* (*Hamlet*). Yes, Shakespeare's *Hamlet*, where the king is killed by a student. We might get ideas!

Suppose you had that precious list in your hand: how in the world would you find these banned books to read them? I remember that during one of my regular visits to a series of bookstores lining up in front of Tehran University along what used to be called Shah Reza Avenue, I was having tea with a bookseller friend of mine when a strange-looking fellow walked into the bookstore and shouted at the top of his voice, "Do you have Steinbeck's *Grapes of Wrath*?"

No, said my bookseller friend hurriedly.

"What about Ignazio Silone's *Bread and Wine*?" the disheveled man shouted back.

"No!" my frightened friend cried out loud, "we have no such books here" (he was stretching the truth).

"What about Ahmad Shamlu's *Ayda, Khanjar, va Khatereh*?" This was a recently published collection of our glorious rebel poet.

"Any one of these books you mention," my bookseller friend shouted as he went to the door, "lands you in jail for five years, and I have none of them. Now get lost."

The man left, and left the two of us with two theories of what it had all been about. My bookseller friend was convinced that he was a SAVAK agent. I thought he was an idiot savant.

A subversive pleasure in reading (forbidden) books has always been definitive to my generation of Iranians, who are constitutionally suspicious of books that are readily available for sale. I remember when I came to the United States in 1976 and went to Philadelphia for my graduate studies at the University of Pennsylvania, for almost a year I used to walk around the university bookstore at the corner of Thirty-sixth and Locust and look at the shelves full of Marx's books, but I would not dare go near them, for I was absolutely convinced that the CIA (or some other secret agency) was keeping track of those who bought these subversive works. I would stare at the three magnificent volumes of *Capital* from a distance, pretending I was looking at Joseph Conrad's books on a nearby shelf, looking anxiously at the store's surveillance cameras installed to prevent shoplifting (or so "these simple-minded Americans were led to believe," I thought). Only someone with my superior (conspiratorially alert) intelligence knew that the pictures obtained by those cameras went straight to the Philadelphia office of the CIA, where (I was absolutely convinced in my nightmares) a SAVAK agent was sitting, sipping his coffee and watching me buy a book by our great brother, Comrade Karl! What terrors and what overwhelming joy I had watching those beautiful copies of Marx for weeks and months, before I finally collected my courage and dared to pick one of them up (*The German Ideology*, I remember it was), hide it in between plenty of Conrad and Hemingway, and take it to a corner in the stationery department of the bookstore, where I pretended I was thumbing through *Heart of Darkness* while furtively reading Marx. It took me a whole semester (maybe two) to muster my resolve and take a few books, including the three volumes of *Capital*, to the cashiers and actually pay for them and go home. Many times I was indeed tempted just to hide Marx inside my shirt and steal the precious thing out of the bookstore.

But back in Tehran in the early 1970s, how would you get hold of banned books of this sort? Well, this is how we did it. An enterprising comrade of ours—his name was Ali, and he was a very learned young man from Tabriz (to this day I remember hearing him expound on Marx in Persian with a splendid Turkish accent, and with far more courage and imagination than I could muster at the Penn bookstore in 1976)—was connected to a collection of banned books stolen (or "confiscated," as we used to say, and then add, "via revolutionary appropriation," *mosadereh enqelabi*) from the School of Engineering at Tehran University. (For some bizarre reason, unlike comparable schools and departments at American universities, the School of Engineering at Iranian universities was always filled with the most progressive and radical students.) The ingenious comrade to whom my friend Ali was connected had then created what would amount to an invisible circulating library, through which we would get books from one friend and pass them on to another. This way these books were always in circulation in many places, so it would have been difficult for the SAVAK to come and round us up.

All Third World literature, the distinguished American literary critic Fredric Jameson has said, is allegories of nationalism.[1] This indeed might be the case. But the literature my generation of Iranians read did not allude to a chimerical construct called the Third or the First World. To this day I have no clue if Dostoyevsky is "Western literature" or not, or Steinbeck, or Turgenev, or Melville. For us literature was no allegory, and it was certainly not divided along any power-basing axis of East and West, or First World and Third. In what we read we thought ourselves connected, emancipated, admitted to a world beyond our material limitations, into what we dreamed possible, in the company of humanity at large. Literature for us was the material metaphor on which we based our historical agency—who we were, what we were up to, and what constituted our moral and normative principles. The fear and the ecstasy of being handed a list of forbidden books to read, as soon as I landed in the tumultuous capital of my country, are definitive to a dynasty that represented us in a larger world beyond our control and yet made our place in that very world so unbearably untenable. That impossible paradox, definitive to colonial modernity at large and constitutional to all our failed revolutions, was the Pahlavi regime in a nutshell.

The history of Iran under the Pahlavis was acted out and narrated in a miasmatic space navigated creatively between the facts of our tyrannous predicament and the fantasy of our wish for freedom—one more materially evident and politically potent than the other, and we could never quite tell (isn't that strange) which was which. Where exactly the debilitating political facts of our entrapment in a tyrannous polity ended, and where our emancipatory poetic fantasies began to tickle our defiant fancies, was terra incognita, a porous puzzle, a condition at one and the same time the curse and the cure of our political ailments, the material premise of our failures and the moral parameter of our victory. "The slow and often bitterly disputed recovery of geographical territory which is at the heart of decolonization," Edward Said proposes in *Culture and Imperialism*, "is preceded—as empire had been—by the charting of cultural territory. After the period of 'primary resistance,' literally fighting against outside intrusion, there comes the period of secondary, that is, ideological resistance, when efforts are made to reconstitute a 'shattered community, to save or restore the sense and fact of community against all the pressures of the colonial system.'"[2] I am not sure if the teleology that Said suggests here works that mechanically—first this and then the other. From the Iranian experience of the last two hundred years, it seems to me that the reverse is true—that people first begin to dream the otherwise and then engage in an unending battle to achieve it. But one might perhaps better abandon all such primary and secondary teleologies and recognize the dialectical interplay between what people dream in their fictions and fantasies, arts and ideologies, and the better life they then seek to secure for themselves from the very heart of those revolutionary reveries. Forbidden books are the navigational charts of daydreaming their emancipatory illusions.

For my generation of Iranians, the Pahlavi regime is not a historical abstraction. It is written and carved on the tablet of our biographical memories. I was born in the provincial capital of Ahvaz in the oil-rich province of Khuzestan, the year that Prime Minister Mosaddeq had nationalized Iranian oil, just about two years before the CIA-engineered coup of 1953 toppled him. I have a vague memory (corroborated by my late parents' accounts) of crossing a street in Ahvaz in my mother's arms when suddenly a military personnel carrier whirred past and hit my mother and a few other passersby. I have vivid memories of the early anniversaries of the CIA coup, when hired hoodlums would march through the streets of my hometown and scream rhythmically, *"Shahanshah piruzeh, Mosaddeq dayyuseh!"* (The King of Kings is victorious, Mosaddeq is a pimp!") I can close my eyes and remember a very early morning when I must have been eight or nine years old when the late Muhammad Reza Shah Pahlavi came to my hometown for a visit, and I and thousands of other schoolchildren were told to report to school very early in the morning. Then we were taken to the airport to welcome him. One of our classmates, sleepy and bewildered in the early hours of the morning, was run over and maimed for life by a police motorcycle in His Majesty's motorcade. I clearly remember the day soon after that when Reza Pahlavi, then our crown prince, was born, on October 31, 1960. I was nine years old and on my way to buy fresh bread around lunchtime, when suddenly cars started honking and turning their headlights on in celebration of the royal nativity. Less than three years later, in June 1963, when I had just turned twelve, I remember the very same cars giving way to street demonstrations in support of Ayatollah Khomeini.

Instead of repressing the reality of these recollections and feigning value-neutrality, it is imperative for my generation of Iranians to think the Pahlavi history not despite but through these memories. I remember the late shah's coronation in 1968, when the rumor in our city was that if we did not raise our imperial flag over our home and decorate the house with the shah's picture, SAVAK would come and question our loyalties. I remember the exact moment when I was a junior in high school and told our school principal I refused to go to the airport for yet another royal visit to Ahvaz. I remember the exact police station on Baharestan Square in Tehran that urban guerrillas blew up during the 1971 celebration of 2,500 years of Persian monarchy. Among the most precious memories of my life are my four years of college in Tehran, which began in 1971 with high hopes that the Pahlavi monarchy was about to fall any minute, and ended in 1975 with the utterly desolate feeling that it would last forever.

The enduring power of these memories spells out the terms of what Hans-Georg Gadamer calls an "effective history." "The very idea of a situation," Gadamer observes in his monumental work on hermeneutics, *Truth and Method*, "means that we are not standing outside it and hence are unable to have any objective knowledge of it. We always find ourselves within a situation, and throwing light on it is a task that is never entirely finished."[3] That unending task is made plausible not despite our presence in it but because of it, and because denying it is a disingenuous act that dismantles any claim to any insight about matters that have changed the course not just of our own lives but of the world at large, of history. I still remember the exact location where I was sitting and sipping from a cup of coffee on November 15, 1977, when I saw on television in the lobby of the Holiday Inn on the corner of Thirty-sixth and Chestnut Street in Philadelphia how the shah of Iran and President Carter began wiping their eyes— during a welcoming ceremony on the White House lawn— because they were streaming from the tear gas the police had used to break up an anti-shah demonstration in Washington. I vividly recall the electrical-appliances shop in a King of Prussia shopping mall near Philadelphia where I went to buy a shortwave radio to try to listen to the Iranian National Radio broadcast when the revolution took place.

"The illumination of this situation—reflection on effective history," Gadamer continues, "can never be completely achieved; yet the fact that it cannot be completed is due not to a deficiency in reflection but to the essence of the historical being that we are."[4] Our understanding of history must be informed through the contingency of that presence and not by pretending to have overcome it. I can close my eyes and once again walk through the crowded and excited streets of Tehran in July and August 1979, when, during the summer break from Penn, I had gone back to Iran and joined anti-shah and anti–Islamic Republic demonstrations. I remember the sense of bewilderment I had, with an uncanny twist of sadness (how strange), the day the shah died in Egypt. When I was in Egypt in May 2001, I went to ar-Rifa'i Mosque in Cairo and visited the shah's grave and recited my prayers—and I have no idea why. For all my life I detested (feared and loathed) the man and everything he did and everything he represented—and here I was praying on his grave, asking his God to forgive his sins. Maybe I thought he needed my prayers, and I a sense of cleansing, a reconciliation between a dead king and one of his unruly subjects. Maybe I just wanted to see a dead king, resting in peace in the proximity of all those mummified pharaohs, and achieve a sense of closure—and my prayers were perhaps just some talismanic whispers that the king was indeed dead and done for, and that there was no more kingdom to come. "Moses once saw a man murdered and left by a road"—I stood on the shah's grave and remembered this poem of our great poet Naser Khosrow—

He pondered in bewilderment and waited in woe.
He wondered, "Whom did you kill, so you too were murdered?
And when will he be killed who murdered thee?"
Do not harass anyone—knocking at his door with your fingers,
So no one may bother you—banging on your door with his fist.

Carved on the collective memory of an entire nation, the Pahlavi monarchy was the summation of two words: *fear* and *ecstasy*—fear of the tyranny that ruled a people with systemic mendacity, and the ecstasy of dreaming what was possible beyond it. It is imperative to suspend (just for a heuristic moment) describing the terror that came after the Islamic Revolution and imagine ourselves sometime after the Constitutional Revolution of 1906–11, and before the Islamic Revolution of 1977–79, for with that cataclysmic event, the whole collective disposition of the nation changed. During the Pahlavi period, hardly anyone was dreaming of what turned into the nightmare of an Islamic Republic—not even Ayatollah Khomeini himself, who long after his exile in 1963 in Iraq had given up all hope of toppling the Pahlavis.[5] The period between the Constitutional Revolution and what turned out to be the Islamic Revolution was mapped out by the topography of an entirely different disposition—the fear and ecstasy of a radically different politics.

The collective memory had century-and-half-long recollections. If early in the nineteenth century, Iran was forced to open its windows to the world, and then by the mid-nineteenth century tried to come to grips with what it saw, and then early in the twentieth century rose up in arms to claim a share of democratic dreams it saw through those windows, then during the reign of the Pahlavis the emotive geography of the entire nation exploded into new planes and momentous proportions, entirely unprecedented in its modern history. The world changed in 1935, when Reza Shah altered the official name of the country from " Persia" to "Iran." Persia was flat, dead, bogus, imperial, Oriental, phantasmagoric—full of useless cats, expensive carpets, and these strange things rich foreigners liked to eat and called caviar. Persia? We had no blasted clue where that flat-footed kingdom was. In Iran we saw how the world was actually quite round, and where on the global curvature of things we stood.

The globality of our Iranian whereabouts at the time of the Pahlavis was held together by two giant claims on our fears and hopes. The period of the Pahlavis witnessed the waning of Russia and England as two colonial competitors plundering the world, and the waxing of the Soviet Union and the USA as two planetary superpowers determined to divide the globe into their respective spheres of influence. The USSR stood for a global socialist revolution under its imperial control, and the USA stood for the freedom of predatory capitalism to wreak havoc on the world. Between the two of them the USSR and the USA ravaged the earth, each in the name of saving it from the other's evil. They were both right, because they were both wrong.

The Pahlavi dynasty came to power through a military coup that was launched on February 22, 1921, and concluded successfully on April 25, 1926, when Reza Shah, the military might behind this coup, crowned himself as the first Pahlavi monarch and designated his eldest son, Muhammad Reza, as the crown prince. The cause of the coup was rooted in the conflict between the two major superpowers of the time, Russia and Britain. After the October 1917 revolution, the Russians were preoccupied with their internal affairs and rapidly disengaging from the rest of the world. Vladimir Lenin was so anxious to end Russian participation in World War I that on March 3, 1918, after months of negotiations, he ordered Leon Trotsky to sign the Brest-Litovsk Treaty with the Germans and the Austrians, which put an end to Russian control of Ukraine, Finland, Poland, the Baltic provinces, and the Caucasus. Taking advantage of Russia's preoccupation, the British moved in quickly. In 1919, the British sought to achieve effective control over Iran's entire economic and political infrastructure. When the illegitimate reign of Ahmad Shah Qajar showed no sign of stability, the British decided that a strong military man should be put in power. Reza Shah was that man—a skilled military leader who finally succeeded in outmaneuvering his co-conspirators in the military coup to become the next king of all kings, and the first monarch of the Pahlavi dynasty.[6]

The commencement of the Pahlavi dynasty (and thus the enabling paradox of fear and ecstasy, politics and poetry) coincided with the rise of a new literary movement that banked on the glorious achievements of the Constitutional period and expanded its horizons into far more ambitious terrains. The rise of modernist Persian fiction, drama, poetry, and cinema—all crucial indices of major cultural, social, and political shifts in the nation at large—took place exactly at this period. The publication in Berlin in 1921 of Mohammad Ali Jamalzadeh's *Yeki Bud Yeki Nabud* (*Once Upon a Time*), the first modern Persian novel and one that initiated a strong (and politically significant) literary tradition, was a hallmark of Persian literary modernity. The almost simultaneous publication by Nima Yushij (1895–1960) of *Afsaneh* (*Myth*) (1922) initiated a radical new phase in modernist Persian poetry, seeking to break up the tyrannical reign of classical prosody. It was precisely at this time also that the prominent British Orientalist E.G. Browne completed and published his monumental work, *A Literary History of Persia* (1902–24), perhaps the most significant event in the process of the nationalization of Persian literature as a major nation-building project. Meanwhile the return of Sadeq Hedayat (1903–51) from Paris to Iran in 1930 and the commencement of his illustrious literary career, culminating in the publication in 1937 of his literary masterpiece, *Buf-e Kur* (*The Blind Owl*), marked the rise of a literary movement that outmaneuvered the attempts of a medieval monarchy to clothe itself in a sham "modernization" project.

Iranian cinema also originated in the earliest years of the Pahlavi period, when a young Armenian Iranian named Ovanes Oganians (1900–1961) made the first feature (silent) film, called *Abi and Rabi* (premiered on Friday, January 2, 1931). On Tuesday, November 21, 1933, the first Iranian feature talkie, Ardeshir Irani's *Lor Girl*, premiered in Tehran. It had been filmed in the Imperial Studios in India, in collaboration with Abd al-Hossein Sepanta, an emerging Iranian intellectual who was fascinated with pre-Islamic Iranian heritage and had studied Zoroastrianism in India (where a sizable Zoroastrian community still lives). *The Lor Girl*, subtitled *Iran of Yesterday and Iran of Today*, premiered in Tehran and was accorded an unprecedented and overwhelmingly favorable reception from the critics and the public. A few months earlier, in May 1933, Abd al-Hossein Sepanta, who was well connected with leading Indian intellectuals, had taken the legendary Bengali poet Rabindranath Tagore (1861–1941) to meet with Aref Qazvini, the equally legendry poet-songwriter-singer of the Constitutional period. In that barely noted meeting, one of the most distinguished Iranian poets of his time, the representative of the budding Iranian cinema, the revolutionary aspirations of the Constitutional Revolution, the formative period of Iranian visual modernity, and two shining stars in the Iranian and Indian literary firmament had all come together.[7]

Many of these developments in Iranian cultural modernity were related to global events beyond its political borders. But these were not the only indices of the rapid Iranian incorporation into ever-larger frames of global references. The period of the Pahlavis (1926–79) witnessed the accelerated integration of Iran into the geopolitics of its region, as its expanding economy became increasingly interwoven into the global operation of trans-national capitalism, which assigned to Iran the role of producing oil (first discovered in 1908) in exchange for imported manufactured goods for its emerging market. This role made the wobbly Iranian bourgeoisie almost entirely compradorial, the Iranian labor class systematically weak, and the whole economy subject to the whims of global capitalism. The increasing contingency of Iran on an oil-based economy denied it any possibility of a sustained and progressive class formation to support its domestic economic interests and all its contingent social consequences, chief among them the formation of democratic institutions. The result was the organic absorption of the Iranian bourgeoisie into the Bourgeois International (in moral and material culture), and the equally catastrophic exposure of the Iranian working class, the urban poor, and the impoverished peasantry to the clerical class and its populist propensities and religious sentiments.[8] One particularly daunting consequence of this condition has been the continued and endemic problem of colonial modernity in Iran being successfully camouflaged and falsely split into two opposing domains, one called "Western modernity," increasingly identified with the state-sponsored modernization projects of the Pahlavis, and the other "Islamic tradition," the exclusive domain of the belligerent clerical class. This false dichotomy, glossing over underlying geopolitics of classical or neocolonial modernity, has plagued Iranian intellectuals ever since, forcing them to choose between their inherited "tradition" and imported "modernity." That the dichotomy is false, and the choice irrelevant, has completely evaded generations of Iranian public intellectuals.[9]

During the reign of Reza Shah (reigned 1921–41), a series of infrastructural reforms gradually changed the institutional basis of the state from a medieval monarchy into a modern nation-state, with sizable demographic changes, expanded exploration of natural resources for raw materials, rapid urbanization, and the rise of a national oil industry. The modernization policies of Reza Shah were directly influenced by his fascination with the Young Turk Movement (1895–1914) in Turkey. Mustafa Kemal Ataturk (1881–1938) became an exemplary model for the first Pahlavi monarch, particularly after his visit to Turkey in 1934. Chief among these infrastructural developments was the construction of a national railroad and an interstate network of highways that marked the territorial connectedness of the new nation-state. The modernization of the army, the formation of a centralized administrative bureaucracy, the establishment of a far-reaching public health system, the creation of a modern judiciary and educational system, and above all the incorporation of women into the workforce were the crucial developments in this period—all of them necessary to make Iran's economy, society, and polity compatible with its subservient role as a *locus desideratus* for global capitalism.[10]

The first decade of Reza Shah's reign coincided with the rise of Sadeq Hedayat as the founding figure of modernist Persian fiction. It is not possible to understand the military violence of the early Pahlavi period without reading the phantasmagoric fiction of the early Hedayat, as indeed Hedayat's violent metaphysics of self-annihilation makes little sense unless one understands how it fit into the delusional "reality" created during Reza Shah's reign. Hedayat was born to an aristocratic family, went to Europe during his formative years, and became fascinated with the works of Kafka, Poe, Dostoyevsky, and Rilke. In 1930, at the height of Reza Shah's reign, Hedayat returned to Iran and began publishing his pathbreaking short stories and novellas. In his masterpiece, *The Blind Owl* (1937), to this day the finest work that modernist Persian fiction has produced, Hedayat tapped into the farthest reaches of a collective terror at the heart of a people perpetually condemned to remember its past but never allowed to learn what its future would be. Dwelling on the miasmatic delusions of a narrator lost in the phantasmagoric memories of a life that he may or may not have ever lived, Hedayat navigated through the collective subconscious of Iranians. *The Blind Owl* reads like the collective history of a culture unable to recognize what its senses and perceptions were telling it about the reality of its situation and trapped in a quagmire of narcotic delirium—all made of self-indulgent, self-pitying, vile, violent, and false memories of things that could or should have happened. *The Blind Owl* is the repressed monstrosity underlying the Pahlavi modernization schemes, a mockery of their purposefulness, the mad cousin of the upwardly mobile nouveau riche who is kept chained in the basement for fear of embarrassment. Here is fiction hallucinating troubling truths and daydreaming forgotten facts. There is a lyrical violence about Hedayat's prose in *The Blind Owl* that would remain characteristic of Persian literary modernity throughout the twentieth century.[11]

The metaphysical subversiveness of Hedayat's fiction escaped his contemporaries and remained merely as a testimonial of his time—a time now overwhelmed in its public domains by grand designs and rebellious uprisings. The gradual transformation of Russia into the Soviet Union (and its role in the vanguard of world socialist aspirations); the increasing colonial belligerence of Britain in the region (beginning in 1920, Mahatma Gandhi launched his anti-British civil disobedience campaign); the emergence of the United States as a global superpower (in the aftermath of World War I); and the increasing centralization of power under the Reza Shah dictatorship were all commensurate with the rise of secular leftist movements in Iran. Initially independent and later under the direct influence of the Russian Revolution of 1917, these movements led to the establishment in 1921 of the Iranian Communist Party, which remained active until 1931, when Reza Shah banned it. The brutal murder of the Communist poet Muhammad Farrokhi Yazdi while he was incarcerated in Reza Shah's dungeons marked the severity with which the Persian patriarch sought to destroy leftist movements in Iran, a repressive policy that was disrupted only after the Allied occupation of Iran and the abdication of Reza Shah in 1941. It was during the Allied occupation that the Iranian Tudeh (Communist) Party was established in 1941. The twelve-year period of freedom that ensued, between the abdication of Reza Shah in 1941 and the CIA-sponsored coup of 1953, is one of the most significant periods of political freedom and secular leftist activism in modern Iranian history. An assassination attempt against Muhammad Reza Shah in 1949, for which the Tudeh Party was blamed, resulted in a temporary banning of the party, which remained active underground until the coup of 1953, when it was altogether outlawed.[12]

The presence of radical ideas and leftist institutions such as the Iranian Communist Party in this period coincided with a number of revolutionary uprisings challenging both the central administration of power and the territorial integrity of the country. The end of the Qajar dynasty and the gradual commencement of Reza Shah's reign were marked by a succession of radical movements, a trend that continued well after his abdication during the Allied occupation of Iran in 1941. Mirza Kuchak Khan Jangali in Gilan, Colonel Muhammad Taqi Khan Pessyan in Khurasan, and Sheykh Muhammad Khiyabani in Azerbaijan launched perhaps the most challenging socialist and/or separatist movements of the early Reza Shah period, proposing to turn Iran into one or more Soviet-style socialist republics. Despite the ardent support of the British, who were eager to create a buffer zone around revolutionary Russia, all these movements were ultimately defeated.

Undefeated and undaunted, however, was one tiny, determined man named Nima Yushij, who was destined to alter the classical course of Persian poetry and launch the most radical movement in poetic modernity in his nation. All the radical ideas and revolutionary movements of the early Reza Shah period pale in comparison with Nima's theories of poetics and the corresponding poetry he wrote, which was distinguished by a graceful audacity and formal authority unprecedented in the long and illustrious history of his nation and culture. Building on the radical ideas of poetic modernity in the creative disposition of the Constitutional Revolution, Nima patiently and persistently developed an entire theory of aesthetic emancipation from the confining formalist rules and suffocating grip of classical Persian/Arabic prosody and worked out a manner of poetic expression that he believed was closer to the "natural music of speech," and as such truer to life and all its moral and imaginative imperatives. The formal destruction of Persian prosody was an iconoclastic task that contemporaries of Nima, magnificent poets such as Malek al-Sho'ara Bahar, had bashfully and obediently shied away from, remaining faithful to the outworn classical forms. Nima opened up unprecedented possibilities within Persian poetic diction. His objective was primarily to transform the worn-out poetics that underlay Persian classical poetry, but he did not fail to pay attention to the political dimensions of his time. While in most of his work he is after the poetic disclosure of Being beyond its formal bondage in the political prosody of everydayness, in "Morgh-e Amin" ("The Aye-saying Bird") his more formalistic aspirations and a radically emancipatory politics come powerfully together to create one of the greatest political poems of all time.

For about four decades, but particularly during the formative decades of the 1920s and 1930s, as his nation was engulfed in the most tumultuous political transformations of the century, Nima retreated to his native Caspian woods and mountains and concentrated on one and only one task—destroy and throw away the heavy, rusting, and overbearing shackles of formal prosody that had for millennia framed and formed Persian poetry. To accomplish this he conceived a new poetics, a carefully articulated poetic emancipation within which new life and new hopes could be detected and probed. It would not be an exaggeration to suggest that Nima was as significant in the formation of a defiant Iranian subject (and an agential autonomy that was contingent on it) as the entire course of the Constitutional Revolution was for societal formations within the Iranian nation-state. Judging by Nima's success and the devotion of generations of poets to his ideals and aspirations, nothing happened in Persian poetry of the twentieth century after Nima that did not bear his unmistakable mark— while the emancipated defiance of Nimaic poetry also turned out to be the defining moment for the leading public intellectuals of their time. Mehdi Akhavan Sales, Ahmad Shamlu, Forough Farrokhzad, Sohrab Sepehri, and Ismail Khoi, chief among myriads of others, took Nima's prophetic vision and read the emancipation proclamation of their people in a poetic diction that was true to the classical centrality of poetry in Iranian creative consciousness yet exuded a graceful and ennobling elegance that was worldly and wise, assuredly defiant and morally binding. No Iranian could read that poetry and still take no for an answer from a tyrant at home or a colonial officer from abroad. It is the supreme sign of his success that not a single European or American Orientalist could make heads or tails of his poetry, and just like their counterparts among the Iranian classicist professors of literature, despised the Nimaic poetry, for they had no clue about what the man was up to. Nima restored in his people the joyous confidence that there was a hidden treasure in their defiant and indomitable soul.[13]

Nima's poetic defiance and formal destruction of Persian prosody (and along with it the Iranian patrimonial claim to invulnerability) was taking place during the same period that the Shi'i leadership was taking its own position of defiance. Reza Shah's banning of *Ta'ziyeh* (*Persian Passion Play*) performances in 1931 marked the adoption of a critical anticlerical and anti-Shi'i policy as he sought to shift the political culture of Iran away from its Islamic disposition and tilt it toward an Ataturk-inspired secular nationalism. A significant uprising in Mashhad in 1935, which was brutally suppressed by Reza Shah's army, was the most obvious indication of a religious revolutionary disposition in this period, brewing under the banner of disaffected and disenfranchised Shi'i clergy. The assassination of the secular reformist Ahmad Kasravi (1890–1946) by a member of the Fada'ian-e Islam (Devotees of Islam) became an equally important indication of the rise of religious political activism during the immediate aftermath of the abdication of Reza Shah and the Allied occupation of Iran. A few years later, the assassination of Prime Minister Ali Razm Ara in 1951 by the very same Islamist group showed the range and intensity of its political influence in contemporary affairs. As a political ideology, Islamism was now in full swing in Iran, partaking in a larger pan-Islamism that was emerging in the region in the aftermath of the establishment of a Jewish state in Palestine and the partition of India along sectarian (Hindu-Muslim) lines, both in 1948. The banning of women's veiling in public in 1936 was yet another blow to clerical sensitivities. In the same year, the public screening of *The Lor Girl* (1933) projected the image of an unveiled rural young woman as the precursor of women's urban unveiling, sponsored by the royal palace.[14] The clergy was disaffected but compliant. At a time that Reza Shah was contemplating replacing the Qajar monarchy with a republic, the leading Shi'i authorities insisted on preserving Persian monarchy.[15]

Perhaps the greatest challenge to the institutional authority of the Shi'i clerical clique was the establishment of Tehran University in 1934, which marked the most significant academic event of the century, for the foundation of a modern, secular university institutionalized an autonomous sphere of operation for the production and dissemination of modernist knowledge. Not since the establishment of Dar al-Fonun by Amir Kabir in the mid-nineteenth century had an educational institution provided such a profound and far-reaching impact on the moral and intellectual disposition of the nation. Tehran University gradually emerged not only as the central site of the most progressive scholarship and scientific research and discovery for decades to come but also as the principal pedagogical location for the education of generations of intellectuals—ranging in their political sentiments from nationalist to socialist to Islamist. Tehran University would of course also function as the secular counterpart of religious seminaries in Qom and Mashhad—thus there were now two, diametrically opposed, educational systems, one almost exclusively under the control of the Pahlavi government, while the other thrived under a more or less autonomous clerical establishment. Student activism that traces its origin to the venerable campus of Tehran University, soon replicated in all other major Iranian cities, has consistently played a critical role in the destiny of the nation, a task shared equally by the seminary students in Qom (and to a lesser degree in Mashhad). But Qom and Tehran became two distinct modes of moral and intellectual imagination, embracing the political consciousness of Iranians but channeling it into diametrically opposed, yet politically catalytic, emotive energies.

The reign of the first Pahlavi monarch began and ended by positing Iran as the locus classicus of a post/colonial nation, saved from the fate of an overtly colonized country, yet afflicted with its most dire consequences—a weak and contingent economy and a social formation that matched its vulnerable economic pathologies, but corresponding to an anticolonial modernity that in its varied cultural projects cultivated the terms of a universal emancipation from tyranny and colonialism alike. The *antico-lonial modernity* that was now socially evident and culturally articulated—from the rebellious uprisings of Mirza Kuchak Khan Jangali and Mohammad Taqi Khan Pessyan to the emancipatory prose and poetry of Sadeq Hedayat and Nima Yushij—effectively dismantled and surpassed the fictive centrality of "the West" as the defining moment of world history—a fact perceived and practiced by Iranian revolutionary activists and iconoclastic lite-rati alike but yet to be grasped, let alone theorized, by Iranian intellectuals still lost in the wild-goose chase of "tradition versus modernity." The decentering of "the West" and the gradual ar-ticulation of an anticolonial modernity emancipated the prose and poetry of the Iranian presence in history.

Thus citing the site of world history, and the battlefields of ideas and aspirations, as the locus politicus of lived experiences, Iranian anticolonial modernity effectively surpassed the predica-ment of colonial modernity and defined the domain of its mate-rial origin and normative projects. "To achieve recognition," as Edward Said described the cultural formation of resistance against colonialism, "is to rechart and then occupy the place in imperial cultural forms reserved for subordination, to occupy it self-consciously, fighting for it on the very same territory once ruled by a consciousness that assumed the subordination of a designated inferior Other."[16] Neither territorially nor indeed in terms of the defiant inscription of its rebellious disposition against colonial domination was Iran ever the site of such impe-rial inscriptions, yet it was always the site of that rebellion—and thus our ever-defiant disposition to say no to all imperial inter-ventions in our collective destiny.

The reign of Mohammad Reza Shah, the second and last Pahlavi monarch, was coterminous with the rise of the United States as a global superpower, its worldwide competition with the Soviet Union, its imperial extensions as far as Vietnam, and its system-atic formation of satellite states such as Iran, Israel, Saudi Arabia, and Pakistan as major military bases and regional allies against the Soviets. Between 1941, when the young shah came to power, and 1979, when he was toppled, he systematically transformed Iran into a massive military base for the United States, facilitating its "containment" of the Soviet Union and supporting its drive for global domination.

Particularly during the Vietnam War (1956–75), Iran was instrumental in providing a logistical base and the necessary fuel for U.S. military machinery. Active U.S. involvement in Vietnam began in earnest three years after the CIA-sponsored coup of 1953 brought the shah back to power, and ended in disgrace a few years before a succession of events led to the collapse of the Pahlavi monarchy. The shah rightly thought himself indebted to the United States. "I owe my throne to God, my people, my army—and to you," the King of all Kings told Kermit Roosevelt, the American engineer of the coup, in a moment of theological hyperbole.[17]

The downfall of the first Pahlavi monarch and the ascendancy of the last were rooted in the wartime politics of the region and contingent on the global reconfiguration of powers in the course of World War II. The flirtation of Reza Shah with the Axis powers resulted in the Allied occupation of Iran soon after the war began, and he was forced to abdicate in favor of his son, Muhammad Reza Shah, who was installed and supported in power by the Allied forces. The pro-Nazi sentiments of Reza Shah would later be a source of embarrassment for the Pahlavis, particularly in the shah's close alliances with Israel. But apparently the Israelis did not mind this bit of history when they were helping the shah develop a nuclear program in the 1970s. Between 1941 and 1953, the young shah's reign was on very shaky foundations (in 1949 he was almost killed in an assassination attempt), but he had the full support of the Allies, the United States in particular.[18]

Soon after the Allied invasion and occupation of Iran in 1941, the infrastructure of the country was turned over to the occupying forces to help the Soviet Union in its war with Germany. Taking advantage of the chaotic conditions of military occupation, the Tudeh Party established the most far-reaching political organization in modern Iranian history. In 1943, Winston Churchill, Franklin Roosevelt, and Joseph Stalin ("The Big Three," as they were called at the time) came to Tehran for a crucial strategic meeting that, among other things, guaranteed Iranian national sovereignty. "We the President of the United States, the Prime Minister of Great Britain, and the Premier of the Soviet Union," solemnly declared the Tehran Declaration of December 1, 1943, "have met these four days past, in this, the Capital of our Ally, Iran, and have shaped and confirmed our common policy." Their common policy was to defeat Germany and Japan and divide the booty. By 1945, the Allied forces began to pull out of Iran—all except those of the Soviet Union, which embarked on a delaying tactic behind which Seyyed Ja'far Pishehvari, a socialist separatist leader, declared a free democratic republic in Azerbaijan and sought to secede from Iran and become part of the Soviet Union. Qavam al-Saltaneh, the Iranian prime minister, managed to prevent this. He gave certain economic concessions to the Soviets, including putting a number of Tudeh Party officials in his cabinet, and managed to persuade Stalin to pull out of northern Iran. By now the Tudeh Party had lost any semblance of autonomy and was effectively functioning as a fifth column for Stalin's megalomaniac designs for Soviet imperialism. After the Soviets left, Qavam al-Saltaneh took the economic concessions he had given to Stalin to the Iranian parliament to have them ratified and confirmed, knowing full well it would reject them, and once the parliament declined to ratify the proposal, Qavam al-Saltaneh resigned his post—giving Stalin nothing in return for having pulled out of Iran and allowing the disgraced Pishehvari separatist movement to self-destruct. Pishehvari's separatist initiative in 1945 caused a major split in the Tudeh Party, which forever lost much of its legitimacy as the vanguard of an autonomous socialist movement. The emergence of progressive and autonomous socialist leaders like Khalil Maleki in this period in Iran coincided with similar developments in Eastern Europe and Latin America.[19]

The first period of Muhammad Reza Shah's reign, from 1941 to 1951, ended with the nationalization of the Iranian oil industry—by now the most important point of global interest in Iran, particularly after World War II, with the commencement of economic reconstruction worldwide and the intensification of the cold war. Seeking finally to end British colonial control of the Iranian oil industry, newly elected prime minister Muhammad

Mossadeq (1882–1967) submitted to the parliament a bill seeking to liberate Iranian natural resources from this obscene colonial control. The bill was approved; the shah was scandalized, checkmated, and disgraced; the British were up in arms; and the Americans wondered what to do. The Anglo-Iranian Oil Company, which for decades had facilitated Britain's exploitation of Iran and outright thievery of its natural resources, was unable to continue operations after Mossadeq's nationalization, and as a result Britain boycotted Iranian oil and began an international campaign against Iran in both the UN and the International Court of Justice at The Hague. In a historic trip to New York and then to the Netherlands, Mosaddeq defended the cause of Iranian sovereign control over its natural resources. A power struggle between the shah (who did not mind Iranian natural resources being plundered by foreigners and was thus supported by the UK and the USA) and Mossadeq ensued.[20]

Iranian political history is a Trojan horse. Inside its belly is a hidden force never noted either for what it is or for its catalytic effect on that political history. The hidden force is the power of imagination, the force of a defiant intellect. Any attempt to reduce the cosmopolitan pluralism of Iranian political culture to an Islamist, nationalist, or socialist absolutism is at once analytically ludicrous and politically catastrophic. More than anything else, such lame and lazy reductionism distorts the inner grace and overriding power of a thriving culture that outsmarts its tyrant rulers and career opportunist observers alike. At this critical juncture, for example, when the shah and Mosaddeq were at the opposite ends of the political spectrum, something extraordinary happened that escaped almost everybody's attention, but that would have an enduring effect on the fate of the nation. During the tumultuous year of 1951, as the shah and his British and American supporters were wondering how to tackle the nuisance of Mosaddeq (representing a nation that had become fed up with outsiders plundering its wealth), very few people in Iran or anywhere else noted the publication of a slim little volume of poetry by an obscure young poet. Sohrab Sepehri (1928–79) would spend the following three decades after the appearance of his first collection of poetry in 1951 publishing his poems and painting his pictures, one after the other shaping and showing to his people visions of an invisible world, vistas of a world too close to see, too obvious to note, too precious to forget—and above all, infinitely more important than the political banality of an age feeding on its own insanity. In a glorious career that ultimately resulted in eight volumes of poetry and a small museum full of beautiful paintings, Sohrab Sepehri became the peace and serenity, grace and confidence, of a people otherwise too busy fighting in the streets for their inalienable dignity and their pride of place. Sohrab Sepehri neither rejected nor endorsed that battle. He was too busy laying the poetic foundations of a world in which those who could read him would never fear the loss of their dignity— for merely reading Sepehri was a gift of grace, his words the talismanic revelations of a world in the immediate gnostic vicinity of life. "I am from Kashan," Sepehri declared in one of his signature poems, "The Footsteps of Water," and he went on to map out the contours of a vision of our being we did not even know existed:

> *I paint for a living—*
> *Every once in a while I*
> *Make a cage*
> *With colors and sell it to you,*
> *So when you feel lonesome you can listen*
> *To the incarcerated songs of red poppies—*
> *What illusions, what illusions!*
> *I know well*
> *That my canvas has no life,*
> *I know quite well that there is no fish*
> *In the small pool of my paintings.*[21]

How did that happen? Where did this simplicity, vastness, and grace come from—in the midst of such systemic mendacity? Sepehri became the assured conscience of a nation otherwise too busy fighting to pause and ponder, too belittled and wronged to stand up and configure its measures of truth. Between the commencement of his career as a poet and a painter in 1951 and his untimely death in 1979, Sepehri was aware of every major and attentive to every minor incident of his homeland, took them gracefully in, and then gently transformed their banality into the visions and voices of an aesthetic confidence, a poetic poise, that to this day is the formative force behind a beleaguered people that no imperial hubris can intimidate and no colonial calamity may deter. *"Ta Shaghayegh hast Zendegi bayad Kard."* ("Until there are red poppies around, we must live.") I recently saw that line of Sepehri written in a celebratory calligraphy behind a truck traveling in the middle of an Iranian desert, from one unknown infinity to another. Imagine the power of a poet, the dignity of a simple line, decades after his death, giving solace and grace to the solitary passage of a tired truck driver pondering the boredom of his routine, going from one end of his life to the other. The problem with the historians and political scientists writing our story for the world to read is that they read too much into our political failures, and have no blasted clue wherefrom we get our moral rectitude, our dogged steadfastness—or by what means we defy the tyranny of our historical fate.[22]

The politics of despair, though, was all around Sepehri as he pondered the fate of his people. Between 1951 and 1953, Mosaddeq outmaneuvered both the shah and his colonial backers via a masterful succession of parliamentary moves. He nationalized Iranian oil, sustained a course of parliamentary democracy unprecedented in Iranian history, and forced the shah to accept constitutional limitations on his wanton disregard for that precious document. When things finally became too hot for the king, he took his newly wedded queen, Sorayya, and ran away to Rome, frolicking on the Via Veneto, waiting for the Americans and the British to do something about his predicament. As Iranians never get tired of repeating (for this is the defining trauma of their modern history), the CIA, aided by British intelligence, mounted, paid for, and executed a military coup, overthrew the democratically elected government of Mosaddeq, and brought the corrupt Mohammad Reza Shah back to power.[23] The CIA-sponsored coup of 1953 (a forerunner of what the United States did later throughout Latin America) became the most traumatic event in modern Iranian history, a trauma from which the people have yet to recover.

The nationalization of Iranian oil in 1951 by Muhammad Mosaddeq occurred in an era in which a major anticolonial movement was under way, not only in Iran but in the entire region—with Jawaharlal Nehru in India, Gamal Abd al-Nasser in Egypt, and the anticolonial movements spreading in North Africa and Latin America giving a new force to and widening the world revolutionary project. The Cuban Revolution of 1959, and the subsequent African mission of Che Guevara, opened a radical new chapter in a global revolution against capitalism and the Anglo-American custodial role, which required the commission of criminal atrocities to safeguard and propagate it. The increased involvement of the United States in Vietnam in this period, and Che Guevara's famous promise that he was going to ignite "a thousand Vietnams" when he returned from Africa to Latin America, unfolded against a background of the uprising of the poor and the disenfranchised against the already globalized imperialism of the United States and its Western European allies. Geopolitically, the world was now divided into two opposing camps, one led by the Soviet Union and its Warsaw Pact, the other by the United States and its NATO allies. In the Arab and Muslim world, Muhammad Reza Shah joined Israel, Pakistan, Saudi Arabia, and other retrograde Persian Gulf states as part of a major anti-Communist network in the region and, in alliance with the United States, crushed all secular, radical opposition to the status quo. This inevitably paved the way for Islamist movements, which gathered even more support after the June 1967 Arab-Israeli war, in which the Jewish state occupied even more Palestinian territory. The ideas and practices of a *Jewish* state, an *Islamic* Republic, a *Christian* empire, and a *Hindu* fundamentalist movement were now emerging as the absolute and absolutist terms of political engagement. The illustrious field of area studies in North American universities now emerged in earnest, effectively seeking to provide the United States with intelligence and strategies to control the spread of the Soviet Union, and prevent the formation of any progressive national liberation movement. Today U.S. think tanks like SAIS, the Washington Institute for Near East Policy, and the Hoover Institution have supplanted those area studies departments.

All these momentous global events had an immediate reflection inside Iran and in the wide spectrum of literary, intellectual, and artistic movements. The tragic suicide of Sadeq Hedayat in Paris in 1951 and the death of Nima Yushij in 1960 coincided with the birth of a new literary and poetic movement in Iranian cultural modernity. The progressive and enabling spirit of this cultural modernity was principally responsible for sustaining the hopes and articulating the aspirations of Iranians under the second Pahlavi monarch. As Muhammad Reza Shah sided with one imperial hubris against the other, sustaining his own illegitimate and repressive reign of terror and intimidation, it was left to our poets and filmmakers, novelists and short story writers, painters and photographers, dramatists and documentary filmmakers, to tell a different story, to help us dream and hope for better days. The rise of Forough Farrokhzad (1935–67) as a publicly celebrated (and also scandalous) poet in the early 1950s marked a crucial development not only in our literary modernity but also in the rise of a decidedly feminist (in the widest sense of the term) sensibility in the modern Persian creative imagination. Generation after generation of Iranian women had courageously fought for their freedom and articulated the terms of their emancipation. Forough Farrokhzad took those terms and carried them to unprecedented conclusions, in a beautiful, compelling, and pathbreaking poetic language that placed her right next to the most illustrious prophetic visionaries of her time. By the mid-1950s, Mehdi Akhavan Sales (1928–90) and Ahmad Shamlu (1925–2000) had joined Forough Farrokhzad and collectively emerged as the principal followers of Nima Yushij and his enduring poetic legacy—modern, modernist, committed, convincing, hopeful, joyous, uplifting. The pantheon of Persian poets in this period, by far the most significant public intellectuals of their country, gave Iranians a poetic modernism unparalleled in its elegant and visionary recitations of what was possible beyond our particulars and toward our potentials. By 1957, when Jalal Al-e Ahmad (1923–69) published one of his most significant works of fiction, *Modir-e Madreseh* (*The School Principal*), he in many respects defined a public intellectual. In his own character he combined and summarized the socialist, nationalist, and Islamist disposition of Iranian political culture. When in 1962 Al-e Ahmad published his most famous social essay, *Gharbzadegi* (*Westoxication*), modern Iranian political culture entered a whole new phase, in which socialist, nationalist, and Islamist components were urged to become part of a united ideological front against both U.S. and Soviet imperial influences in the region, and against the central role of the Pahlavi monarchy in facilitating the American drive for global domination. The publication of Ali Moham-mad Afghani's *Shohar-e Ahu Khanom* (*Ahu Khanom's Husband*) (1961) announced the entrance of modern Persian fiction into a new, socially far more significant, phase. Now the works of other literary modernists, from Sadeq Hedayat, Mohammad Ali Jamal-zadeh, Ebrahim Golestan, and Sadeq Chubak, to Gholamhossein Saedi, Houshang Golshiri, Mahmoud Dolatabadi, and Simin Daneshvar, came together and formed a mighty literary vision of our worldly whereabouts.[24]

The challenge that this cultural movement faced was stupen-dous. After the 1953 coup, the shah resumed his reign, though this time around with a vengeance and an iron fist that he would freely employ against "his own" people, and with full U.S. military support. The shah soon banned the Tudeh Party and established his infamous secret police to detect and prevent any political opposition against his authoritarian rule. The establishment of SAVAK in 1958 marked a particularly notorious chapter in the official repression of political dissent in Iran. Under pressure from the Kennedy administration (1961–63), the shah initiated his so-called White Revolution in 1963, a move to thwart more radical changes initiated by nationalist, socialist, and Islamist forces. The patently "secular" aspects of the move deeply angered the already radicalized elements within the clerical class. Mean-while, the death in 1961 of Ayatollah Seyyed Hossein Tabataba'i Boroujerdi, the supreme leader of the Shi'i community, marked the beginning of a new, radical phase in the political aspirations of the Shi'i authorities. Whereas Ayatollah Boroujerdi was a pac-ifist and conservative cleric, in less than two years after his death, in June 1963, Ayatollah Khomeini emerged as the unchallenged leader of the Iranian Shi'i community, which he led in his first, unsuccessful, challenge to the Pahlavi dynasty. The June 1963 up-rising, a dress rehearsal for the Islamic Revolution of 1979, was a widespread movement that was swiftly put down by the shah's army. Khomeini was arrested and exiled, things quieted down, and the shah resumed his authoritarian rule.[25]

In the domain of radical opposition, after the defeat and ban-ning of the Tudeh Party in the immediate aftermath of the 1953 coup, leftist (Marxist) activists began to join a whole new genera-tion of urban and rural guerrilla movements, culminating in the

legendary Siahkal uprising of 1971 in northern Iran. The nationalism of the Mosaddeq era went into hibernation after the coup of
1953, overshadowed by Islamist and Marxist ideologies. Taking
courage from anti-imperialist revolutions in Cuba, Algeria, and
Vietnam, as well as the Palestinian national liberation movement,
two major guerrilla movements wreaked havoc on the Pahlavi
monarchy between the June 1963 uprising and the Islamic Revolution of 1979. One was led by the Cherik-ha-ye Fada'i-e Khalq
organization (Marxist), and the other by the Mojahedin-e Khalq
organization (Islamist). These revolutionaries were the heroes of
their generation, striking fear into the heart of the ruling elite and
bringing hope to the rest of the nation in its darkest nights.
"*Kashefan-e forutan-e Shokaran,*" Ahmad Shamlu called them in
a beautiful revolutionary ode, "the humble discoverers of the
hemlock."

> *Joyandegan-e shadi dar mejri atashfeshanha.*
> *[Looking for happiness in the mouth of volcanoes.]*[26]

The names and faces of revolutionaries like Amir Parviz Pou-
yan, Hamid Ashraf, Bizhan Jazani, Mohammad Hanifnezhad,
Said Mohsen, and Ali Asghar Badi'zadegan became the cultural
icons of an entire generation of revolutionary activists. They
carried the revolutionaries' pictures in their pockets, put their
posters on their walls, read their defiant words, smuggled their
courageous pamphlets, and discussed their heroic deeds. Those
days did not last. Some of the leaders of these movements were
arrested, savagely tortured, and subsequently murdered, first by
the Pahlavi regime and then by the Islamic Republic. In the course
of the revolutionary events leading to the Islamic Revolution of
1979, Cherik-ha-ye Fada'i-e Khalq broke up into opposing and
warring factions, while Mojahedin-e Khalq gradually betrayed
the visions of their founding figures and systematically degenerated into a pathetic mercenary army, gathered around a medieval
cult of personality, and employed by Saddam Hussein to put
down various uprisings in Iraq.[27]

As the urban and rural guerrilla movements of the late 1960s
and early 1970s rose and peaked, so did the imaginative topography of a nation struggling to deal with its fears and hopes in an

age of autocracy. The tragic death of Forough Farrokhzad in an automobile accident in 1967, the accidental drowning of the leading Azerbaijani literary activist and folklorist Samad Behrangi in 1968, the death of Jalal Al-e Ahmad from a heart attack in 1969, and the concurrent establishment of the Association of Iranian Writers in 1968 might be considered the signposts of a major turning point in the later history of Iranian revolutionary literature and its increasing political consequences. The publication of Houshang Golshiri's *Shazdeh Ehtejab* (*Prince Ehtejab*) (1969) and Simin Daneshvar's *Savushun* (1969) ushered in a new generation of Iranian engagé writers. Soon after that Daryush Mehrju'i's adaptation of a short story by Gholamhossein Saedi (1935–85), *Gav* (*Cow*) (1969) brought international attention to the emerging Iranian cinema—and with that a major global catalyst in domestic Iranian cultural affairs was initiated. Modernist Persian poetry and fiction now blossomed and gave narrative space for ideals of freedom to come to fruition. When Ali Shari'ati, a leading Paris-educated Islamist revolutionary, died in London in 1977, and a brave band of Iranian poets gathered in the Goethe Institute for ten consecutive nights of revolutionary poetry recitation in the very same year, and subsequently Ayatollah Khomeini stepped up his public condemnation of the Pahlavi dynasty, signs of a massive social revolution were evident all around the country and for the whole world to see.

In the shah's palace, however, things looked otherwise. Encouraged by U.S. support, the shah had crushed a major rebellious movement in 1963, and checked and brutally repressed the urban and rural guerrilla movements that ensued soon after that; and by 1971 he felt so confident that he arranged for a massive, obscenely expensive celebration of the presumed 2,500-year anniversary of Persian monarchy. Heads of state, useless European and regional royal families, and European and American Orientalists and area studies professors came together in Persepolis to applaud the shah's pronouncement, addressed to Cyrus the Great: "Cyrus, sleep calmly, we are awake!" Cyrus could not hear. Cyrus was long dead. Whom was the shah talking to? The words echoed in his own head, reverberated throughout the country, and would soon ricochet and come back to haunt him. The autumn of the patriarch was fast upon us.[28]

After the celebration of 2,500 years of Persian monarchy, the last Persian monarch had barely a decade left before his own downfall, and with it the end of the long, languorous, and demented obscenity of monarchy as a political institution. The shah obviously did not participate in the Arab oil embargo of 1973 and as a result received millions of surplus dollars in oil revenue, which he spent lavishly—after first depositing his family's usual percentage in Swiss bank accounts—on even more U.S.- and European-made military gadgets. Iran was reduced to a client state and major U.S. military base in the last stages of U.S. involvement in Vietnam. (Iran was third in military importance to the United States, after Israel and Saudi Arabia.) When, in 1974, the shah ordered the execution of a leading dissident Marxist poet, Khosrow Golsorkhi, he thought he was invincible. When in 1976 he changed the Iranian calendar from its origin in the migration of Prophet Muhammad from Mecca to Medina to the presumed date of the coronation of Cyrus the Great, the shah clearly indicated his imperial agenda. We have a legendary king in our national epic, the *Shahnameh*. His name is Jamshid. He brought everything to humanity—life, liberty, and the pursuit of happiness, as it were. At the end he even eradicated mortality. Then he thought he was God. An Arab king named Zahhak soon emerged and killed Jamshid. Soon two monsters grew on Zahhak's shoulders. He had to feed these serpents the brain of young people lest they devour his own head. Finally a blacksmith named Kaveh, whose sons had been killed by Zahhak, raised his leather apron as a flag and led a revolutionary uprising against Zahhak and killed him. But (what was he thinking?) he went ahead and brought another king to power. We have had too many bad kings in our history; perhaps that is why we have so many good poets. Like Jamshid, the shah thought he was immortal; like Zahhak he feared for his head. He was wrong, for he was right.

There was a cosmopolitan worldliness in the air when I was growing up in the Pahlavi period, a deeply cultivated sense of our global whereabouts—a catholicity of learning that knew not where "the West" was or where "the East" began on the bipolar axis of a power that divided the world to rule it better, thus diminishing cultures, and neutralizing dissent. We recognized no such borders. We did not know or acknowledge where the "Third World" was. For us the world was squarely divided into two opposing parts: those who ruled it and those who resisted this tyranny and rose up against it, either in arms or else with a pen, a pencil, a brush, or a camera. We listened to an ongoing conversation made up of the voices of Muhammad Mosaddeq, Gamal Abd al-Nasser, Jawaharlal Nehru, Marshal Tito, Fidel Castro, Salvador Allende, Patrice Lumumba, Aime Césaire, and Ahmad Ben Bella, among many others. We were neither Islamist nor anti-Islamist. Our mothers may have prayed five times a day, but our fathers enjoyed Russian vodka, and never knew which way the Qibla was. Our uncles may have been Tudeh members, but our cousins were staunch Mosaddeq followers. Yes, we may wholeheartedly have attended Shi'i rituals in the month of Muharram, but we also dropped everything and ran for the nearest theater when there was a new Charlie Chaplin movie, an Indian musical, or an Egyptian melodrama. You would not be able to corner us or call us names—one thing or another. Nixon and Kissinger were evil people not because they were Americans, since Malcolm X, Martin Luther King Jr., Angela Davis, Muhammad Ali, W.E.B. Du Bois, Louis Armstrong, Langston Hughes, and Maya Angelou were also Americans, as were Herman Melville, Mark Twain, William Faulkner, Ernest Hemingway, John Steinbeck, and Jack Kerouac—and we loved them all. There was a momentous certainty about the location of our deeply committed culture of defiant knowledge—and that is where we had a strong sense of affinity with our friends, comrades, and heroes around the world, from Ho Chi Minh to Che Guevara, from Gandhi to Malcolm X, from Frantz Fanon to Jean-Paul Sartre. The terms of this emotive affinity extended from politics to poetry, from arms to arts. When we read Steinbeck or Hemingway, Dostoyevsky or Turgenev, Stendhal or Dickens, there was no sense that we were reading from "Western literature." We read everything in beautifully composed and exquisitely accessible Persian translations, and whatever we lost in translation we gained doubly by way of a global (worldly and material, liberating and imaginative) conception of literature that did not assign to any one group the privilege and to others the pejorative status of the West or the East, the First or the Last, the Second or the Third. There was a continuity of an emotive universe among Nikolay Gogol, Ignazio Silone, Émile Zola, George Orwell, John Steinbeck, Jack London, Bertolt Brecht, Arthur Miller, Harold Pinter, and Gabriel García Márquez—a way of reading Pirandello, watching Chekhov, and discussing Akira Kurosawa—that created a republic of emancipatory letters, a horizon of liberating visions. Revolutionary activists such as Said Soltanpour adapted and staged Henrik Ibsen's plays, and literary critics such as Amir Hossein Aryanpour wrote on them as if Ibsen were a native of Mazandaran. We were transported to the Europe of Ibsen, Fellini, Fassbinder, and Godard without having to go to any embassy, apply for any visa, stand in any long line for approval, or be humiliated at any border. There were no borders. We were already there—where Fellini's flamboyance met Visconti's sobriety, where Eisenstein's dark genius shed light on Truffaut's playfulness. John Ford was ours, as was Howard Hawks. We had no clue that Hitchcock or Bergman (the light and darkness of our heart) had anybody other than us in mind—the global citizens of a world they imagined when they made their movies. We read Faiz Ahmad Faiz, Nazim Hikmat, Pablo Neruda, Langston Hughes, Vladimir Mayakovsky, and Mahmoud Darwish as if they had all written their poems just for us; we read and memorized the works of Ahmad Shamlu, Nima Yushij, and Forough Farrokhzad as if they had written them for the whole world to read (for they had). Our most saintly poet, Sohrab Sepehri, had traveled around the world and written a poem that taught us the topography of our humanity at large, and prepared us for the swift magic of the Japanese haiku and the liberating joy of Latin American magic realism. Amir Naderi had the eye of the world in his lenses when he shot his films for us. Abbas Kiarostami had made Yasujiro Ozu look Iranian. Farhad Mechkat studied European classical music in the United States and in Europe and brought bundles of gifts for us at the Rudaki Hall, and he made sure when we went to see him conduct a Beethoven or a Brahms, a Mozart or a Schubert, we did not feel that we were standing outside some obnoxious aristocrat's drawing room and eavesdropping. We watched the World Cup on tiny and scarce television sets, in a few privileged homes and in coffeehouses, as citizens of a world that was not divided along the axis of any power other than the creative and defiant will of a solitary footballer, a ball, and the glory of a just and level playing field in sight (if only the political world were like that)—where German engineering genius, British industrial superiority, and French cultural arrogance all came together and in utter humility bowed down in reverence to the superior Brazilian poetry in motion. Pelé was our brother, as were George Best, Bobby Charlton, Franz Beckenbauer, and a generation or two later Diego Maradona, Ronaldo, Jürgen Klinsmann, Roberto Baggio, David Beckham, Lothar Matthäus, Roger Milla, Hidetishi Nakata, and Thierry Henry. There was a forgiving globality about the World Cup, where we were all on equal terms. We were an exceedingly lucky band of people, we the generation that was born and raised in the aftermath of a coup that the Mother of Parliaments and the children of Thomas Jefferson had plotted against our liberties, killing our hopes for democracy. We were taken aback by this treacherous act, and when the courageous and the imaginative among us picked up their guns and sharpened their pens and began to fight and read and write the world for us in an emancipatory and defiant way, we were all there—dreaming, fighting along with them, singing their praises, seeing the world in the glittering glory of their eyes, even as they were falling, even as we were defeated. The last years of the Pahlavi regime, between the Arab oil embargo of 1973 and the gathering of revolutionary momentum in 1977, were the longest years of our century—for the shah seemed stubbornly intractable, invincible, even (like Jamshid) immortal. He was not. We were all wrong—in more ways than one: we were not careful what we were wishing for, for it came true.

5

An Islamic Revolution

At the time of the Iranian Revolution of 1979, the total population of the country was almost 35 million people, of which some
5 million lived in Tehran. Other major Iranian cities such as
Mashhad, Isfahan, and Tabriz, had about one million inhabitants
each, while smaller cities such as Ahvaz, Kermanshah, Rasht, and
Qom had between one hundred thousand and five hundred
thousand inhabitants. Despite rapid urbanization, still about 50
percent of the total population lived in rural areas, with very limited and primitive means of transportation, communication, and
economic exchange. The reduction in the infant mortality rate,
which had not been accompanied by a corresponding rise in life
expectancy, had resulted in a noticeably young population, with
about 60 percent under the age of twenty-five. In 1970, when I
participated in the national entrance examination to attend college in Iran, some one hundred thousand high school graduates
did the same. The entire capacity of the Iranian university system
that year was only 10,000 seats, about 10 percent of all the ap-
plicants. (In 1997, the total number of high school graduates had
risen to 3 million students, but the percentage of college admit-
tance had remained almost the same, 240,000 seats, a bit less
than 10 percent). Only 10 percent of high school graduates were
admitted to college, and a corresponding 10 percent of the total
population lived in Tehran—but both these percentages, students at colleges throughout the country and the population living in the capital city, were disproportionately important in the
rise of the revolutionary momentum between 1977 and 1979.[1]

When one looks at the demographic makeup of Iran at the

time of the Islamic Revolution of 1979, one must note that despite the few concentrated centers of population in cities such as Tehran, Tabriz, and Isfahan, or the religiously charged pilgrimage destinations such as Mashhad and Qom, the country as a whole was integrated through a sustained and systematic network of physical and emotive connections. The connections were facilitated by both mass transportation and mass communications. During the reign of the Pahlavis, airplanes, trains, buses, cars, motorcycles, and bicycles had enormously expanded the transportation available in Iran. This all supplemented age-old vehicles such as horse-drawn carriages and beasts of burden: horses, camels, and donkeys. Travel throughout the country was far easier than it had been only a few decades earlier. In my own lifetime (I was born in 1951), I have covered the distance between traveling on donkeys and jumbo jets in the course of just one generation. I remember quite vividly that colorful droshkies were more available than taxis at the Tehran train station in the late 1950s when as a child I traveled from Ahvaz to Tehran to visit my extended family. We would travel by train from Ahvaz to Tehran (my father was a worker with the Iranian national railroad and as part of his benefits we got free third-class tickets once a year for our entire family), and then by droshky from the Tehran railroad station to my aunt's home in the Seyyed Khandan neighborhood. From there my younger brother and I would accompany my mother, taking a bus to Qom, where she performed her religious duties at the Hazrat-e Ma'sumeh shrine.

My mother was a devout Muslim of impeccable Shi'i convictions and unflinching piety; my father, however, oscillated between staunch Nasserite socialism when he listened to the legendary Egyptian singer Umm Kulthum on Radio Baghdad, devout Mosaddeq nationalism when the anniversary of the coup of 1953 came around, and Tudeh Party sympathies for the rest of the year; all of these sentiments depended on the time of the day, the weeks remaining till he got his meager monthly salary from the railroad, and above all the brand of Russian vodka he could afford and enjoy while cooking for us. This, incidentally, was not the only sharp difference between my parents. My mother's complexion was exceedingly fair, and she had light brown hair and hazelnut eyes, while my father was solidly black—we had quite an Othello and Desdemona situation there, minus of course the dramatic ending. They dearly loved each other, though, in a quiet and bashful kind of a way. The sharp contrast in my parents' skin colors alerted me to an astounding prevalence of Iranian racism very early in my life.[2] My father's nickname was "Dadi Siah," or "Dadi the Black"—his name being Khodadad, Dadi for short. When the television series *Shaft* (1973–74) came to Iran, my sixty-odd-year-old mother developed considerable affection for Richard Roundtree in the lead role. "He looks like your dad," she used to say, and then blush and bashfully add, "when he was young." (My father had passed away by then.)

From Qom, my mother, younger brother, and I would then take another bus to Mahallat, a small town close by, where my mother would hire three donkeys and a donkey driver to take us all to the nearby hot springs. (She very much enjoyed these obscure medicinal mud baths, and ritually dipped me and my young brother in and out of the boiling pools!)

The first and last time I boarded an airplane in Iran was when I left the country for the United States. There were Iranian jet-setters of course, flying between Iran, Europe, and the United States on a regular basis, but my family was hardly in that privileged class. From jumbo jets to donkeys, in the course of my own generation of Iranians, in our twenties at the time of the 1979 revolution, the four corners of the country were physically connected.

A sense of connectedness also came from the expanding realm of mass communications, including a national television network, a national radio network, a few leading daily newspapers (*Keyhan, Ettela'at*, and *Ayandegan* in particular), magazines (*Negin* and *Ferdowsi* were the leading progressive periodicals of the 1970s)— plus a network of movie houses, theaters, and teahouses, where public performances of classical Persian drama (*Ta'ziyeh* and *Shahnameh-khani*) were still very much a part of life. All the principal means of official mass communication were almost exclusively at the service of the Pahlavi propaganda machinery and entirely state controlled. But that does not mean that positive things did not happen there. When Reza Qotbi, a cousin of Queen Farah, was put in charge of Iranian television, he revolutionized the creative programming of that institution, and to this day generations of Iranian filmmakers and theater directors remember Qotbi fondly and consider him a major force in Iranian artistic revival—an art that definitive to its aesthetic disposition projected a powerful antiestablishment politics. Equally important was Kanun, a cultural institution, again directed by a relative of the queen, devoted to the education of young people. The most politically subversive stories, poems, and films of the leading Iranian writers and artists were produced and distributed by Kanun. But people such as Qotbi were exceptional. The rule was the systematic use of these institutions to propagate a monarchist view of our national identity and heritage. Before the screening of every movie we went to see we had to stand up in respect and watch the glorious achievements of the Pahlavi monarchy while our national anthem was played. (This was the best time to sneak out to the bathroom.)[3]

The globally projected image of Ayatollah Khomeini sitting under the shade of a tree in Neauphle-le-Chateau in France with a telephone right next to him, sending his revolutionary instructions to Tehran, requires a closer attention to the role of that mode of communication in Iran. Throughout the Pahlavi period, and even at the outset of the Iranian Revolution of 1979, private telephones were still rare and luxurious class privileges. In my entire childhood neighborhood in the 1960s, around the radius of almost a mile in the old part of Ahvaz, only one household had a phone. There were of course public phone centers (Telefon-Khaneh) that people would occasionally use to make a phone call to another city or country. It required a whole day to get to the Telefon-Khaneh, get a number, and wait for your turn, and you had to hope and pray that the party on the other end was at a phone too. Pay phones and phone booths were nonexistent in my hometown until the early 1970s, and were few and far between even in Tehran in the late 1970s.

Ayatollah Khomeini's telephone calls to Tehran were augmented by a massive and systematic body of cassette tapes that from 1963—when he first tried to topple the monarchy, failed, and was subsequently exiled to Iraq—he periodically recorded and sent to his followers in Iran. These cassettes were readily available in Tehran, Tabriz, Qom, and Mashhad bazaars. Understanding this communication technology requires an additional grasp of the network of mosques, Hosseiniyehs (establishments for ritual remembrance of the Third Shi'i Imam), religious seminaries, major Shi'i shrines, mausoleums, and Saqqa khaneh (water stations), and the widespread octopus of the clerical order. All that was needed from Najaf or later Neauphle-le-Chateau was one cassette tape smuggled into Tehran. The cassette could then be disseminated widely into centers of political activism and mass mobilization that extended from the major mosques in Tehran to private households in the remotest corners of the country. It is important to keep in mind that the network of the clerical establishment was not limited to major cities or even to public domains, but in fact extended into the inner sanctums of families around the country. Molla Javad, a blind mullah who came to our home once a month when I was a child and sang the praises and recited the glories of the Muslim saints and Shi'i imams to my mother and then answered her juridical inquires, was a staunchly radical cleric and a devout follower of Ayatollah Khomeini. Mullahs like Molla Javad, a very common feature of small towns and villages, were usually self-selected from among the blind mullahs so that their frequenting the private quarters of households would not be a problem for families. Molla Javad would sing beautifully in praise of our Shi'i imams, answer my mother's meticulous questions about ritual purity and her other pious duties and obligations, and then turn his attention to me, my younger brother Aziz, and my cousins Hossein and Abbas, and begin rhythmically (and chronologically) cursing from the rise to the (to him imminent) demise of the Pahlavis (while my mother took advantage of Molla Javad's political passion and quietly attended to her household chores). "These bastard British brought him back to power," he used to say, and I could swear his dark glasses shone with excitement. "They can take him to England, if they so much like kings and queens." Molla Javad refused to believe that the Americans had anything to do with the 1953 coup.[4]

In addition to telephones, the telegraph was also available, but it was rarely used by the public at large except for such rare occasions as weddings and funerals. But the telegraph did have official and commercial uses. The origin of the telegraph in Iran goes back to the nineteenth century and the British colonial interest in the region. Toward the end of the Pahlavi period telex communi-

cation had just become commercially viable for Iranian companies doing business with Europe and the United States. Though
during the Constitutional Revolution telegraphic communications between the revolutionary leaders was quite effective, that
function had been replaced by phone messages and cassettes
tapes by the 1979 revolution.[5]

The most popular mode of communication in the Iran of the
Pahlavi period was letter writing—raised to something of an art
form. (As a teenager I used to write love letters for my friends and
classmates, to be given to their potential girlfriends, for something like a dime a letter. For school-assignment compositions I
charged only a nickel.) The Iranian postal system was fairly reliable, though once in Isfahan in 1973 in the Hotel Shah Abbas I
saw the Iranian secret police checking a mailbox for bombs (in
anticipation of a visit by then crown prince Reza Pahlavi), and an
avalanche of postcards poured out of the yellow box, having accumulated there for months. Use of postal stamps for Pahlavi
propaganda was standard. Collecting rare stamps (or match
boxes) from Cuba, Vietnam, India, and China was a children's
mode of protest.

Between 1963 and 1979, Ayatollah Khomeini communicated
with his followers chiefly by writing letters to them. Letter writing as a medium connecting the distant parts of the nation (or
generating revolutionary momentum) raises the issue of literacy
in Iran. Despite a massive program of state-sponsored education,
the rate of illiteracy in rural areas and small towns was high.
What we would ordinarily see in front of the main post office of
every city were nameh nevises (letter writers), to whom would
flock migrant laborers from the surrounding villages and small
towns to have a letter written to their families, and then sealed,
signed, stamped, and mailed by these enterprising nameh nevises. These nameh nevises would also gather around the courthouse to write an *Arizeh*, or a petition for legal action. They were
something like American lawyers, though they charged a far more
humane fee for their services. Inside the courthouse itself, many
employees of the court also functioned as de facto lawyers, charg-
ing a small fee and helping the litigants write their petition in
proper legalese. If these litigations needed to have additional
documents attached to them, handwritten copies of those docu-

ments had to be prepared, for this was long before photocopy machines had been invented (or imported to my hometown). As a teenager, between the eighth and twelfth grades in high school, I spent most of my summers in Abadan, where my older brother Majid was a court clerk, and where I amassed quite a small fortune by copying (using carbon copies for multiple copies) various documents about land confiscations, family feuds, and inheritance disputations for despondent and illiterate litigants. Quite a number of tickets for James Bond movies, delicious sandwiches, and blessed Pepsi-Colas were paid for with my accrued tidy nest egg.

When we read Khomeini's revolutionary correspondence today, we may rightly wonder how many people in Iran could actually read and relate to it. The question of illiteracy in countries such as Iran is complicated. Both my parents, as well as most of my uncles and aunts, were illiterate. My two brothers and I, and our cousins, were the first generation in our extended family to attend school and learn to read and write—but that does not mean we were more literate, learned, or cultivated than our parents. My mother could not read or write a word. But she knew more lines of Persian poetry (of Omar Khayyam and Baba Taher Uryan in particular) by heart and recited them appropriately and on the right occasion, with impeccable prosody and elocution, than all my high school teachers put together. She would help me and my younger brother with school assignments, such as writing a composition, with appropriate Qur'anic references, prophetic traditions, and Persian literary and poetic allusions (all wasted on the inane topics we were asked to contemplate, such as "Is wealth better or knowledge?" or "Describe the benefits of a cow"). Because of her religious beliefs, my mother also had a thorough command of practical Shi'i jurisprudence, which she had learned from our Mulla Javad. Her command of our religious history, the lives of our saints, Sufis, imams, and prophets, as well as our folkloric heritage, storytelling traditions, popular plays, and above all herbal medicine, was typical of her gender and class and exquisitely effective. We had a Baha'i herbalist in our neighborhood, Baba Houshang we called him (the sweetest, wisest, and most gentle man of my entire childhood). Between Baba Houshang and my mother, we were raised on organic and herbal medicine and rarely needed modern medicine, which was not readily available to us anyway. Between our mothers and our neighborhood herbalist there was an available and effective medical knowledge infinitely more humane than what modern medicine had to offer poor and ordinary people.[6]

Illiteracy was no barrier to communication for people like my mother. She would sit me down and dictate to me, with perfect grammar and appropriate style, letters to the governor of Khuzestan about things that irked or concerned her. I would read the letter back to her, and she would make grammatical and compositional emendations, and then sign it with a metal seal that she had had carved with her name, Zahra Dabashi, in cursive Persian calligraphy. When we say "illiterate" in an Iranian context, this is the sort of "illiteracy" we have in mind. But my mother and her generation had neither a sense of official (secular) history nor indeed any conception of geography beyond the sacred sites of the Shi'i imams and Sufi saints that were important to her cosmic sense of piety and dignity. I still remember her sense of delight and amusement when upon my leaving Iran for the United States, I placed a small globe in front of her to show her where we were and where Philadelphia, Pennsylvania, was. She knew the world was round. But she could not quite get her mind around the idea.[7]

Our sense of nationhood at the time of the Islamic Revolution was thus formed around a network of physical and emotive interconnectedness, fashioned and fused together by a nationalist historiography, an iconic mode of fetishizing the catlike shape of our homeland on the map; by the canonization of Persian literature; and by a collective sense of statehood that our history had generated, sustained, and imprinted on the very fabric of our minds, the shape and shadows of our imagination.

The demographic and infrastructural foundations of the Pahlavi regime at the time of the 1979 revolution were matched by an equally volatile economic condition. The bifurcated class formation, between the merchant class and the poor (and pious) on one side and the ruling elite and the modern (mostly secular) middle class on the other, finally came to a head-on collision in

the course of the revolutionary period, when the political populism of Ayatollah Khomeini displaced the endemic elitism of the
secular left and liberal politics, by preaching a radical Islamism
predicated on the innate political propensities of Shi'i Islam.
About 40 percent of the Iranian labor force at the time of the
1979 revolution was agricultural, 20 percent was industrial, and
the remaining 40 percent belonged to the service sector. The Iranian economy at the time was more than 80 percent oil-based; oil
revenues between 1973 and the time of the revolution were at an
all-time high because of international political and economic factors (especially the Arab-Israeli war of 1973 and the ensuing Arab
oil embargo). The shah's economic expansions between 1953 and
1973, entirely due to a consistent rise in oil revenues, had created
(1) an expanded bourgeoisie that economically benefited from
the boost but was politically disenfranchised from any institutionally anchored democratic aspirations; (2) massive poverty and
an economic underclass, the direct result of a state capitalism
lucratively beneficial to the royal family; rapid and grotesque
urbanization; and endemic impoverishment of the rural areas;
(3) a disgruntled bazaar merchant class that was equally unhappy
with the incessant incorporation of the Iranian economy into a
corner of global capitalism that left them vulnerable; (4) an in-
censed clerical class poised to reignite its historical alliance with
the bazaar against the monarchy; and (5) a secular and Islamist
intellectual elite that had for decades cultivated a rebellious and
antigovernmental body of revolutionary ideas—in other words,
essentially a similar alignment of forces and factors predominant
during the Constitutional Revolution, but now cast in grander
and more global terms.[8]

Like these economic circumstances, the political condition of
Iran at the time of the Islamic Revolution cannot be viewed except ex post facto and in terms inevitably leading to that cataclysmic event. There are serious scholars of the Iranian Revolution of
1979 who believe that the revolution was entirely the result of a
spiraling synergy generated among three main actors: the shah,
Ayatollah Khomeini, and President Carter. They believe that if
any one of these actors had been replaced by a different person,
the revolution would not have taken place—and perhaps there is
a ring of truth to this claim. But it is ultimately a useless specula-

tion. The revolution did happen, the monarchy did collapse, and an Islamic republic did ultimately succeed it. The more pertinent question is, when do we start the political narrative that will give a coherent account of how it all came about? If we take the 1953 CIA-sponsored coup as our point of departure, the revolution will be read in essentially nationalist terms. If we start with the 1963 uprising led by Ayatollah Khomeini, the revolution will inevitably assume a Shi'i (Islamic) insurrectionary disposition. If we begin with the Siahkal uprising of 1971, then the revolution will have a markedly Marxist character. (In my account I will treat these three departure points together.) What is certain is that the systematic and brutal Islamization of the revolution after the hostage crisis (1979–80) cannot be read backward in order to give the course of the revolutionary momentum an entirely Islamic disposition. This was a national liberation movement that arose from a multiplicity of economic, social, and ideological sources and aspirations. One particularly powerful and merciless Islamist faction ultimately managed (shrewdly and brutally) to outmaneuver all other factions, hijack the revolution, and call it "Islamic." To be sure, many of the slogans and much of the visual iconography of the massive demonstrations leading to the shah's departure in January 1979 and Khomeini's return in February of the same year were indeed Islamic in character.[9] But (1) nationalist and socialist slogans and iconography were equally present during revolutionary mobilization, (2) the Islamist insignia of the revolutionary uprising borrowed freely from nationalist and socialist vocabularies, and (3) to put a united front against the monarchy, many nationalist, socialist, and even nonclerical Islamist forces (such as the Mojahedin) rallied behind the centralized leadership of Ayatollah Khomeini.[10]

What is historically evident, however, is that beginning in early 1978, when an article appeared in a Tehran daily insulting Ayatollah Khomeini, a succession of increasingly massive demonstrations was set in motion that in about a year forced the shah out of Iran. At this point, there was no operative political party in the country except the Rastakhiz Party, which the shah had established as the single political organization in the country. The two principal forms of political opposition to the monarchy at this point were (1) the urban guerrilla movements of Cherik-ha-ye Fada'i-e Khalq and Mojahedin-e Khalq and (2) the Shi'i clerical establishment, which was under the uncontested political leadership of Ayatollah Khomeini. He was both a leading grand ayatollah with impeccable scholastic credentials and, since 1963, a deeply respected radical revolutionary leader with widespread support both inside and outside Iran. When, on behalf of the National Front (the main political organ of Iranian nationalists), Karim Sanjabi went to Neauphle-le-Chateau early in November 1978 to ask Ayatollah Khomeini to drop the term "Islamic" from his proposal to establish an "Islamic republic" instead of the monarchy, the ayatollah told him to take a hike. When a courageous nationalist named Mostafa Rahimi wrote a defiant article, "Why I Am Against an Islamic Republic," there were many who agreed with him, but there was no major political apparatus to back up this position. Mosaddeq-era nationalism had been either in hibernation or else fused into a religious or secular leftist political apparatus. Neither Karim Sanjabi nor the National Front he led at the time of the revolution had substantial credibility or acceptable political credentials in the eyes of the mobilized masses.[11]

The ideological predisposition of the nation at large at the time of the Islamic Revolution was intertwined with its political configuration of power and opposition. The monarchy was systematically working to give a thoroughly royal definition to Iranian history. The coronation of Muhammad Reza Shah in 1968, his celebration of the 2,500-year anniversary of Persian monarchy in 1971, his changing of our calendar from its Islamic point of origin to the presumed date of the coronation of Cyrus the Great, and the royal patronage of the Shiraz Art Festival on the site of Persepolis all clearly and concisely indicated an ideological shift by the Pahlavi regime to a deliberately pre-Islamic, Persian, and monarchic claim to legitimacy. Opposing this monarchic ideological buildup (all orchestrated by an army of European and American Orientalists in collaboration with their Iranian counterparts) were alternative modes of anticolonial nationalism, pro-Soviet or independent socialism, and of course the endemic Shi'i millenarian Islamism. Of the three oppositional ideologies, the most readily available for public consumption was the Islamist, for very specific reasons. Anticolonial nationalism of the Mosaddeq era was severely censored and brutally repressed ever since the Shah of all Shahs had transformed Iran into a major U.S. military base, with the Iranian army effectively being an extension of the U.S. army (very much like Israel's then and now). Iran's status as a client of the United States also necessitated the suppression of Marxist and socialist ideas, in a country that was in the immediate vicinity of the Soviet Union and serving as a major U.S. bulwark to check and balance Soviet expansionism in the region and secure its own domination. This of course did not mean that radical and leftist ideas were totally absent in this period. Iranian Marxists used ingenious tactics to evade censorship and disseminate their rebellious ideas. From children's stories to fictitious "translations" (translations that were in fact books authored by Iranians and attributed to foreign—sometimes nonexistent—writers) to rampant oppositional symbolism in poetry and fiction to subversive films and suggestive plays, the post–1953 coup generation of Iranian artists, literati, and social scientists had produced a substantial body of leftist and progressive ideas that was readily available to those who sought them. (Remember the invisible library my friends and I had in circulation?)[12]

But the availability of both nationalist and socialist literatures was far less decisive than the public presence of revolutionary Islamist ideas. From 1963 forward, Khomeini's fiery speeches were readily available and widely disseminated on cassette tapes, both in and out of Iran, as were his letters, fatwas, and other pronouncements and proclamations. Even more widely available were similarly provocative Islamist ideas articulated by such leading revolutionaries as Ayatollah Mahmoud Taleqani and Ayatollah Morteza Motahhari. But the ideological prophet of radical Islamism in Iran in the late 1960s and the early 1970s was Ali Shari'ati (1933–77), a revolutionary thinker of unsurpassed charismatic charm and rhetorical power. Born and raised in Mashhad, educated in Iran and France, and profoundly influenced by the ideals and aspirations of Che Guevara, Frantz Fanon (with whom he actually corresponded), and Jean-Paul Sartre, Shari'ati returned to Iran to launch a career of radical activism unsurpassed in its tenacity, force, and consequences. A religious establishment in northern Tehran, called Hosseiniyeh Ershad, was the principal venue of his widely popular lectures between 1969 and 1972. They were taped, disseminated, transcribed, and published widely throughout the country. (I once attended one of his lectures, when I was an undergraduate student in Tehran, at the insistence of a roommate of mine at college who was his devotee. I found that Shari'ati had an uncanny ability to sugarcoat Marxist ideas with an Islamic vocabulary).[13]

The multifaceted condition of ideological preparedness at the time of the Iranian Revolution of 1979 roughly corresponds to the (political) culture of the time, which can very roughly be divided into two major, and diametrically opposed, components: (1) a rampant Eurocentric secularism almost exclusive to the ruling elite, the nouveaux riches, and the compradorial bourgeoisie, and (2) a grassroots Shi'ism that claimed the loyalty of the clerical clique, the bazaar merchant class, the working class and the urban underclass, and the peasantry. To this basic distinction must be added the social formation of a significant body of inorganic public intellectuals—poets, novelists, dramatists, filmmakers, social essayists. All of them (with rare exceptions) were left-radical in their political disposition but quite limited in their grassroots appeal (their influence was largely confined to Tehran) when compared to the clerical class, which could instantaneously stir and mobilize the populace for effective revolutionary purposes.

The Iranian political culture at the time of the 1979 revolution will have to be considered in a significant (though not exclusive) way in terms of its religious character. The overwhelming majority of Iranians, almost 90 percent, are Shi'is, some 9 percent are Sunnis, and the remaining 1 percent are Zoroastrians, Jews, Christians, and Baha'is. The definition of being a "Shi'i," however, radically differs from one class to another. By and large the most devout Shi'is are to be found among the rural and urban poor and the merchant (bazaar) middle class, exclusively beholden to the moral authority of the clerical establishment. The Shi'i disposition of other Iranians is more tenuous and evident mostly in their cultural character, emotive universe, normative behavior, ethical principles, moral imperatives, or cultural vocabulary—all minus the ritual practices and doctrinal beliefs definitive to their faith. The Shi'i Passion Play (Ta'ziyeh) and Muharram ceremonies, commemorating the death of the third Shi'i imam, must be exempted from this general characterization, for on those occasions the most lapsed Shi'i becomes curiously observant. Two Shi'i imams—Amir al-Mu'minin Ali ibn Abi Taleb and Hussein ibn Ali (the first and the third Shi'i imam, respectively)—are the objects of universal love and unconditional admiration in the Muslim world and transcend the religious-secular divide. Imam Hussein in particular is an almost universally admired figure of revolutionary defiance against tyranny and injustice. Other than these iconic figures, many other aspects of Shi'ism are interwoven with contemporary Iranian culture in even less perceptible ways. One of the most distinguished Iranian filmmakers and theater directors, Bahram Beiza'i (of a prominent and learned Baha'i family, though an avowedly secular intellectual), ingeniously adapted Ta'ziyeh dramatic techniques to our contemporary visual and performing arts. Other theater directors, such as Mohammad Ghaffari, made Ta'ziyeh performances an exceedingly successful component of the Shiraz Art Festival, the remainder of which was devoted to European and avant-garde theater. More recently, Abbas Kiarostami, the most widely celebrated Iranian filmmaker, had also turned his attention to creative adaptations of Ta'ziyeh performances. Therefore, Shi'i signs, symbols, and sentiments were present throughout Iranian culture, not just in the specific religious practices of believing Muslims. The almost universal acknowledgment of Ayatollah Khomeini as the leader of the 1979 revolution was (1) in part orchestrated by a highly organized revolutionary cadre among the clergy; (2) followed by a majority of the Shi'i believers out of their genuine belief in the sanctity of his leadership; (3) strategically adopted by secular Marxist and nationalist forces to form a unified front against the Pahlavi monarchy; and (4) the result of a charismatic instigation of latent Shi'i sentiments throughout the Iranian population (even the most staunchly secular and antireligious, almost despite themselves).[14]

Except for the sporadic persecution and systematic harassment of Iranian Baha'is, religious minorities were mostly tolerated. Of all the religious minorities, the Armenians have been the most politically integrated and active in Iranian revolutionary politics, since the dawn of the Constitutional Revolution early in the nineteenth century, and in fact from much earlier—as far back as the Safavid era. After 1948, segments of the Iranian Jewish community left their ancestral homeland for Israel, but by no means did all Jewish Iranians. Whether they immigrated to Israel or remained in Iran, Jewish Iranians are exceedingly proud of and deeply rooted in their Iranian heritage, which has found its way into their rituals—despite the fact that there is a horrid and persistent anti-Jewish racist trait endemic in Iranian popular culture and even in Persian literature. The critical position of the Islamic Republic vis-à-vis Israel (which is more a political ruse to cover its own atrocities at home than a genuine solidarity with the Palestinians) invariably translates into a troubling atmosphere for Jewish Iranians in and out of their homeland. Varied traces of Anti-Jewish, anti-Arab, anti-Turkish, and antiblack racism are unfortunate aspects of contemporary Iranian culture—all of which are predicated on a racist conception of a fictive Persian origin that European Orientalists taught Reza Shah's generation: that Iranians belonged to an imbecilic figment of their racist imagination called "the Aryan race." The generation of Reza Shah believed that nonsense, completely bought into it, and taught and thought itself into believing that we were really European in our origin but by some unfortunate geographical accident had ended up among Arabs and Semites. Traces of that astounding stupidity are still evident in Iran, particularly among the youth, whose legitimate anger against the Islamic Republic often assumes an illegitimate and racist anti-Arab disposition. And the bogus pro-Palestinian politics of the reigning regime degenerates into an anti-Jewish language.[15]

Iranian racism is particularly evident in Tehran, where similar racist negativity is directed at provincial Iranians—the Isfahanis, the Rashtis, the Azaris, the Kurds, the Lors, the Baluchis, the Arabs, or what the Tehranis in moments of unsurpassed white-washed racism call *dehatis*, a nasty derogatory term meaning "the peasants." The roots of this Tehrani-based racism is deeply buried in the whitewashed, Eurocentric Iranian bourgeoisie, who grotesquely identify with Europe, dye their hair blond, wear blue-and green-tinted contact lenses, and denigrate and ridicule provincial Iranians. Nikzad Nodjoumi, a distinguished Iranian artist and a close friend of mine, once told me that for years after he arrived in Tehran from Kermanshah he did not dare to talk publicly, because his Tehrani classmates at Tehran University made fun of his Kermanshahi accent. I have many other similar examples from my Azari friends from when I went to college in Tehran. To this day, much of the legitimate anticlerical anger of Tehrani residents invariably assumes a racist, antiprovincial, antipoor, and anti-Arab animus—a fact that became particularly acute during the presidential election of 2005, when an avalanche of racist and anti–poor people jokes about Ahmadinejad flooded the Internet. In many ways, the Iranian Revolution of 1979 was the revenge of the poor and the provincials against the Tehrani-based deep-rooted bourgeois racism, and the tyrannical (terrorizing and entirely wrong and abusive) imposition of mandatory veiling on Iranian women is the revenge of the poor and the provincial against the obscenity of rich Tehranis parading in the latest Christian Dior fashions as the most publicly ostensible sign of their class privileges. In a number of Iranian films, particularly by such prominent filmmakers as Jafar Panahi and Bahman Qobadi, who come from the provinces, a modicum of dignity is restored to non-Tehrani provincial accents and demeanors. But in the best of Iranian cinema—even in the works of such luminaries as Abbas Kiarostami and Mohsen Makhmalbaf (both born and raised in Tehran)—this arrogant, self-raising, other-lowering, anthropological view and treatment of provincial Iranians by Tehrani artists is all too evident.[16]

One of the most spectacular aspects of the massive demonstrations that led to the 1979 revolution was the overwhelming presence of women marching forward in the vanguard of the revolutionary force. Women were equally present in prominent positions of leadership in the various urban guerrilla movements, both Marxist and Islamist. This participation should be seen against a background of antiwomen, patriarchal misogyny definitive to Iranian culture at the time of the revolution. On one occasion the shah candidly expressed his view of the proper place of women in Iran. In an interview with the Italian journalist Oriana Fallaci he spat out the following: "You're equal in the eyes of the law but not, excuse my saying so, in ability." He added a clarification: "You've never even produced a great chef. You've produced nothing great, nothing! . . . You're schemers, you're evil. All of you."[17]

Iranian women have fought for their inalienable rights for centuries. A whitewashed international feminism (best repre-

sented by Azar Nafisi's *Reading Lolita in Tehran*) has now systematically sought to exploit the horrors of the status and
struggles of Iranian women (written into the very letter of Islamic
law), to facilitate and justify the (contemplated) U.S. invasion of
Iran and the presumed liberation of Iranian women that will follow it. Ill-informed members of the international feminist movement joined the celebratory rhetoric of the Bernard Lewis–Paul
Wolfowitz clique in hailing *Reading Lolita in Tehran*. But when a
courageous feminist activist like Golbarg Bashi dares to suggest
incorporating Iranian women who are active inside their own
homeland into a more grassroots and cross-cultural struggle, irrespective of their class or religious proclivities, she is viciously
attacked by a great many in the whitewashed international feminist camp—from the liberal-monarchist flank all the way to the
useless expatriate "radicals."[18] Iranian women have struggled for
their own freedom, in their own terms, in their own homeland,
for generations—both against the horrid patriarchal aspects of
their own ancestral culture and against the equally dehumaniz-
ing designs of outsiders on their homeland.[19]

Where were the opposing forces of the secular bourgeoisie
and the religious grass roots concentrated? A major music hall
(Talar Rudaki), a network of performing arts centers around the
country (chief among them the City Theater of Tehran), movie
theaters, playhouses, experimental theater groups (the most progressive of which was Kargah Namayesh in Tehran), libraries,
bookstores, record shops (the best of which, a store named
Beethoven, was in Tehran), sport complexes, cafés, restaurants,
organized tours to Paris, London, Rome, and New York, and Caspian Sea summer resorts were some of the principal sites of so-
cialization among the secular bourgeoisie. On the opposite side
of the battle lines, mosques, *Hosseiniyehs*, religious seminaries,
religious festivals, the shrines and mausoleums of imams and
saints, cemeteries, and pilgrimage tours to Mecca, Medina, and
the holy sites of Najaf, Karbala, and Kazemyan in Iraq were
prominent sites for convocations of religious activists and their
grassroots constituency.

Perhaps the single most important site of communal activity
in Iran during the 1979 revolution that crossed class lines was the
soccer stadium. As in the rest of the world (except the United

States, where it is a suburban phenomenon), in Iran soccer was the game of the urban poor and lower middle class. (Rich upper-middle-class Iranians preferred watching the silliest sport on planet Earth, Wimbledon tennis.) There were two chief soccer clubs—Taj and Persepolis—dividing soccer fans' loyalties. Soccer matches have historically had political dimensions beyond the control of the authorities.[20]

In the heat of revolutionary upheavals in 1978–79, the Tehran University soccer field was a major site of violent political confrontations. In July 1979, I was present for one such confrontation between the progressive nationalists and the militant Islamists. Soon after the violent Islamization of the 1979 revolution, the soccer field was permanently occupied by the Islamist forces and transformed into a makeshift mosque for Friday prayers and political sermons.

Cinema, too, crossed class lines in its universal appeal. There were of course hard-core religious believers who shunned cinema altogether (burning movie theaters was a major form of protest during the revolutionary uprising), but the appeal of its magic remained widespread. The actual movie theaters were of course divided according to class—first, second, and third, separating the poorer audience from the richer by ticket price. But when the lights were turned down and the film began there was a universal field of dreams all classes and factions could share. They could, at least for a couple of hours, escape from the nightmare of the history they momentarily repressed.

Spanning all economic, political, ideological, and cultural tendencies, the entire nation was alerted and mobilized during the massive revolutionary upheavals of 1977–79. To include the nationalist, Islamist, and socialist narrative points of departure leading to the revolution, we must begin with the CIA-sponsored coup of 1953 (and the profoundly *nationalist* sentiments it provoked); go on to the June 1963 uprising led by Ayatollah Khomeini (and the equally powerful *religious* sentiments it aggravated); and include the urban guerrilla movements led by Cherik-ha-ye Fada'i-e Khalq that began in 1971 after a by now legendary operation, the Siahkal uprising, heralded armed struggle against the Pahlavi regime (and the *social-*

ist revolutionary ideologies this struggle ignited). The Siahkal uprising inspired another urban guerrilla movement, Mojahedin-e
Khalq. Militant members of the Mojahedin had been preparing
ideologically since the early 1960s and training militarily with the
al-Fatah faction of the PLO in Jordan and Lebanon since the late
1960s to undertake, prematurely, a similarly spectacular operation
during the shah's celebration of 2,500 years of Persian monarchy.
But the operation was a fiasco, and almost half of their leaders were
arrested, tried, and executed. The organization went into a period
of regrouping and resurfaced in 1975, deeply split into Marxist and
Islamist factions, though both were more than prepared to take
part in the early stages of the 1979 revolution.[21]

Between August 1953, when the shah was put back on the Peacock Throne by the CIA, and the June 1963 uprising, the Iranian
monarch ruled with supreme power. Between the June 1963 uprising of Ayatollah Khomeini[22] and the crescendo of events beginning
in late 1977 that ultimately resulted in the downfall of the Pahlavi
monarchy, the battle was between the increasingly militarized monarchy, and the Cherik-ha-ye Fada'i-e Khalq and the Mojahedin-e
Khalq. These guerrilla movements were crushed brutally, and the
King of all Kings, as early as the mid-1970s, soon after his delusional
public address to Cyrus the Great ("Sleep calmly, we are awake!"),
had a sense of divine mission not unlike that of George W. Bush. "A
king," he told Oriana Fallaci, "when he doesn't have to account to
anyone for what he says and does, is inevitably very much alone. But
I am not entirely alone because I'm accompanied by a force that
others can't see. My mystical force. And then I get messages. Religious messages." When Fallaci expressed some skepticism about
this connection between His Majesty and God Almighty, the shah
told her that she could not understand such things. "Because you
don't believe. You don't believe in God, you don't believe me"—
whereby "God" and "me" suddenly fused and became interchangeable. Here are the words of the King of Kings:

> My reign has saved the country and it's saved it because
> God was beside me. I mean, it's not fair for me to take all the
> credit for myself for the great things that I've done for Iran.
> Mind you, I could. But I don't want to, because I know that
> there was someone else behind me. It was God.[23]

One might pause here (while His Majesty generously shares credit with the Almighty) and consider the idea that it was only *after* Ayatollah Khomeini took power that we ended up in a theocracy. But not once in all of his voluminous writing did Khomeini make such a claim to proximity with divinity. (This does not of course exonerate him from his own brand of lunacy and the responsibility for the terror that he would soon inflict on Iran and for sending thousands of its sons and daughters to death in a pointless war. Iran's history shows how we move from one monstrosity to another.) Dangerously delusional, the shah had an entire nation captive to his divine conception of himself—just like King Jamshid did in Ferdowsi's *Shahnameh*.[24]

The revolution began not in Tehran or any other Iranian city but in Washington, D.C., and the commencement of the presidency of Jimmy Carter (1977–81), who assigned human rights a place at the top of his policy agenda. That put his administration in the embarrassing position of accounting for the atrocious record of key U.S. allies. Among them in the Middle East were Iran, Israel, Saudi Arabia, and Pakistan. In November 1977, the shah traveled to Washington to discuss an array of issues with President Carter, including the thorny matter of the human rights violations in Iran. A massive antishah demonstration on November 16, 1977, forced the Washington police to use tear gas to disperse the demonstrators. The wind blew the tear gas to the White House lawn, where President and Mrs. Carter were officially welcoming the king and queen of Iran. The shah took out his white handkerchief to wipe his tears. As President Carter went to the podium to welcome him, he began by jokingly "apologizing to His Majesty for the temporary air pollution in the U.S. capital." The pictures of the shah and President Carter wiping their tears became a signal icon at the commencement of the revolutionary uprising in Iran.[25]

By the time President Carter, accompanied by Secretary of State Cyrus Vance and the National Security Advisor Zbigniew Brzezinski, went to Iran to return His Majesty's visit, the revolutionary uprising in Iran was taking on an ominous momentum. On December 30, 1977, a day before President Carter arrived in Iran, an explosion rocked a U.S.-Iran cultural exchange institute. At a New Year's Eve reception, President Carter toasted the shah at a state dinner and hailed Iran as "an island of stability" in an otherwise troubled Middle East. A week after that champagne toast, on January 7, 1978, an article that Ayatollah Khomeini's followers considered insulting to their leader appeared in an Iranian daily. The following day a massive demonstration was organized in Qom to protest this article. There were clashes with the police and casualties were reported. Commemorating the forty-day anniversary of this demonstration and those who were killed, on February 18, 1978, another large demonstration was organized in Tabriz. In what was later dubbed "the Bloody Tabriz Uprising," there were even more casualties. These two demonstrations set in motion an avalanche of events. No matter what the shah or President Carter did, Ayatollah Khomeini turned the events to his advantage. A tripartite chess game ensued among the shah, the ayatollah, and President Carter. Khomeini was now *leading* the course of events because he was responsive to and shaping the sentiments of the demonstrators. If the shah ordered his military to confront and disperse the demonstrators, more casualties would follow, angering the crowd even more, and even more massive demonstrations would ensue. If the shah did not order a crackdown on the uprising, the erosion of his authority and control would be dangerously apparent and his subjects would make more radical demands.[26] President Carter was also caught between a rock and a hard place. He had come to the White House demanding more consideration for human rights from U.S. allies, and Iran appeared to be the most blatant violator of these rights, pointing up the contradictions in that U.S. policy. Carter was the victim of his own campaign promises. Ayatollah Khomeini had both the shah and President Carter outmaneuvered and checkmated; it was now only a matter of time; a few more moves and the shah would be out.

By January 1978, Khomeini was in direct communication with his supporters, who were now fully in charge of organizing the demonstrations in all major cities. The demonstrations were relentless. Secular leftist and nationalist forces were now equally involved in (but not in charge of) organizing demonstrations. On the anniversary of the Iranian Constitutional Revolution, August 5, 1978, the shah made a speech in which he promised free elections. The speech was useless. The Carter administration was as baffled as the monarch, who now solicited the advice of foreign ambassadors. "The U.S. ambassador was telling us one thing," the King of all Kings told the British journalist David Frost in an interview later when he was in the Bahamas, "and Mrs. Carter was telling something else to our queen." His Majesty was confused. Where were Kermit Roosevelt and his Iranian counterpart, Sha'ban the Brainless, when he needed them?[27] The idea of arranging yet another U.S.-sponsored coup was obviously on the table. As early as April 1978, the shah had asked General Robert "Dutch" Huyser, the deputy commander of U.S. forces in Europe (serving under General Alexander Haig) to come to Tehran to consider the possibilities. General Huyser went to Iran again in August 1978 to assess what could be done and gave the shah the discouraging results of his assessment. Early in January 1979, just before the shah was forced to leave, General Huyser again spent almost a month in Tehran, where he was in regular contact with Iranian officers and the U.S. ambassador to Iran, William H. Sullivan. His mission failed because Carter's advisers gave him conflicting information and recommendations. In Huyser's own words, "there was not unity of effort in Washington. It was obvious the State Department had one view of the situation and the Department of Defense and Executive Branch another."[28]

On Friday, August 11, another violent demonstration broke out in Isfahan. On August 16 the Tehran bazaar, the lifeline of the merchant class (which was now fully committed to the clerical leadership) closed down in protest. On August 20 a movie theater, the Cinema Rex, in the southern city of Abadan, was set on fire. Close to four hundred people reportedly perished in the fire. Khomeini blamed the shah's secret police. The shah's police blamed Khomeini. It made no difference. The conflagration provoked even more anger against the Shah. Facts did not matter at this point. Revolutionary frenzy, mass hysteria, conspiratorial fantasies—this was a time of mythmaking and collective catharsis.[29]

The public impact of the fire in Cinema Rex was immense. On August 27, 1978, the shah dismissed Jamshid Amuzegar as his prime minister and appointed Ja'far Sharif Emami to the post, hoping that an old politician's modest credentials and good connections with the moderate clergy would keep him on his throne.

He was wrong. It made matters worse. The shah ordered Sharif Emami to give priority to religious matters, and he sent Queen Farah on a pilgrimage to the sacred Shi'i shrines. This backfired; it made Khomeini even more legitimate. He was seen now as the undisputed leader of the uprising and the cleric who could Islamize the revolution. Sharif Emami followed the shah's order and changed the Iranian calendar back to its original Islamic foundation date. Sharif Emami also attempted to address the financial corruption of the Pahlavi family and put an end to its depredations. This only served to confirm Iranians' belief that the royal family had been taking a cut of lucrative commercial contracts with European and American companies and feeding their private Swiss bank accounts. The demonstrations continued, not just in Tehran and Qom, but all over the country.

On September 4, 1978, which coincided with Aid Fitr on the Islamic calendar, the most massive demonstration against the shah in Iranian history took place. These were ecstatic days, unimaginable even weeks or months earlier. On September 7, more demonstrations followed: "Death to the shah" was the cry as the mass of demonstrators headed toward Shahyad Square—now renamed Azadi ("Freedom") Square. On the following day, "Black Friday," the army opened fire on demonstrators at Zhaleh Square. Many people were killed, the numbers were exaggerated, rumors swept the entire country, graffiti bloomed on walls everywhere, revolutionary banners waved, bloodied palms of hands marked street signs—the nation was up in arms. Demonstrations intensified—revolutionary events entered a whole new phase.

By September 1978, Khomeini was leading the revolutionary movement from Iraq. Hoping to stop Khomeini's agitation, Prime Minister Sharif Emami asked the Iraqi government to restrict the aging leader's activities. On September 24, 1978, Khomeini's house in Najaf was surrounded by Iraqi troops. Khomeini preferred to leave Iraq rather than remain silent. He first wanted to go to Kuwait, but he was denied entry on October 3. He then considered going to Algeria or Lebanon, but ultimately opted to fly to France, arriving first in Paris on October 12, and soon after that moving to a Paris suburb, Neauphle-le-Chateau, where he assumed active leadership of the revolution. The aging ayatollah was in close touch with his lieutenants in Iran. The shah was cornered. Carter was helpless. Khomeini now had access to international news organizations, to which he announced on October 19 that he would not hesitate to declare armed struggle against the Pahlavi monarchy. He was not just threatening the shah. He was dismissing almost a decade of armed struggle waged by Marxist revolutionaries. Marxist revolutionaries were in no position to protest. They acquiesced, remained silent. The monarchy was about to fall. That was the prime objective. On that day Khomeini also denied that there were Marxist elements in the Iranian opposition to the shah. The statement was blatantly false, but scarcely anyone took note of it. Dissident factions in the revolutionary front would not have been tolerated, and Khomeini was Islamizing the revolution day by day. No one objected.

On October 31, 1978, the revolution spread to the vital oil industry when oil workers announced a general strike in sympathy with the revolution and production came to a halt. The strikers demanded an end to martial law imposed by Sharif Emami's government, and the release of all political prisoners. Meanwhile student activists were out in the street demonstrating against the government, setting cars on fire, attacking banks and governmental offices, confronting the police, denouncing the monarchy. By early November, the riots were out of hand. Demonstrators were attacking banks, movie theaters, nightclubs, expensive hotels, liquor stores, foreign embassies—those of the United Kingdom and the United States in particular. On November 5, Prime Minister Sharif Emami resigned. The following day, the shah appeared on the national television to apologize ("I have heard the voice of your revolution," he said). He looked pale, pensive, remorseful, lost—and yet proceeded to declare that he had no choice but to appoint General Gholam Reza Azhari, chief of staff of the armed forces, as the next prime minister. Azhari declared a general curfew. From France, Khomeini responded quickly: *"Shah bayad beravad!"* "The king must leave!" This was no ordinary revolutionary. This was an ascetic mystic, fed for a lifetime on a simple diet of yogurt, dates, and vengeance. "You throw me out of my country," Khomeini was telling the shah— "I'll show you!" History was now in full epic proportions, daily events mythic.

General Azhari began yet another cycle of carrot and stick.

Khomeini had them both chewed up and spit out. On November 8, 1978, General Azhari ordered former prime minster Amir Abbas Hoveyda arrested and jailed on charges of corruption. Khomeini liked that. To him all Iranian prime ministers, the current one included, were corrupt. On November 9, Khomeini invited the major Shi'i clerics to join him in saving the country. No one dared to go against him; the charismatic cleric, Savonarola and Calvin combined in a Muslim guise, was now speaking for the nation. On the same day, General Azhari declared that he would have the financial dealings of the royal family investigated.

Fine, Khomeini had no objection to that—the shah's own prime minister further confirming the royal family's corruption. Everything that the shah did added more fuel to the bonfire of the revolution. Finally, on November 18, reports from Tabriz indicated that junior army officers and their soldiers were now refusing to follow their superiors' orders. The news from Washington was not any better. On December 7, President Carter told reporters that it was "up to the people of Iran to decide" what to do with the shah. During a particularly charged religious ceremony, held December 10–11, 1978 (coinciding with Muharram 9–10, 1399—the two holiest days on the Shi'i Islamic calendar, for it was on these days in 680 that the third Shi'i imam was killed in the famous battle of Karbala), massive demonstrations against the shah and for Khomeini virtually brought the country to a halt. By the end of December, General Azhari resigned.

Shapour Bakhtiar (1914–91), a moderately respectable figure of the National Front, was the only one who agreed to try to save the monarchy from final collapse. The shah appointed Bakhtiar as the next prime minister on December 28, 1978. The new prime minister spent January 1979 trying to establish a degree of respectability for himself. He failed. By now, the Persian monarch realized that he was no longer in charge. On January 1, 1979, the shah appointed a shura-ye saltanat ("royal council"), and on January 16 he left the country. He went first to Egypt and then, by way of Morocco, the Bahamas, and Mexico, finally arrived in New York for cancer treatment. He was accompanied by his family—crying. When an aide broke the news to Ayatollah Khomeini, "The brothers say that the shah has left the country and Radio

Tehran has broadcast the news," the ayatollah simply lifted his head, having just said his early-morning prayers, and, as if he had been told merely that his breakfast was ready, asked, "What other news?" As soon as word of the shah's departure spread, joyous pandemonium erupted in Iran—thousands of people took to the streets, some carrying trays full of sweets, singing and dancing and congratulating each other. *"Shah Raft,"* read a headline in the largest type size in the history of the Persian press. "The King Left." Others waxed poetic: "When the demon leaves," they began, quoting a poem of Hafez, "the angel will arrive." They wanted Khomeini to come back from France. On January 19, a euphoric crowd estimated at more than a million people demonstrated in Tehran, demanding the formation of an Islamic republic, pleading with Khomeini to return.[30]

On Thursday, February 1, 1979, Khomeini boarded an Air France jet in Paris and returned to Iran after fourteen years of exile, to a sea of rapturous supporters, a tsunami of affection. As the aging ayatollah was stepping down from the airplane, a reporter asked him what his emotions were. "Nothing," he said. "Nothing."

From the airport, Ayatollah Khomeini went straight to Behesht-e Zahra Cemetery, where thousands of young Iranians had been buried, victims of demonstrations that had led to Khomeini's triumphant return. The crowd circled around the aging revolutionary—fluttering moths around the proverbial Persian candle. "With the authority that this people have invested in me," the ayatollah declared in a voice at once triumphant, humble, arrogant, confident, prophetic, "I will slap this government in the face" ("Man silly to dahan-e in dowlat mizanam"). The phrase echoed through Iran and infused the mind and soul of every Iranian. It was a merciful, healing ointment applied to the bruised dignity of a mass of souls, their humanity hitherto denied. From the time that Mirza Reza Kermani killed Nasir al-Din Shah in the Shah abd al-Azim shrine in April 1898 to this very moment, defiant generations, fighting for a better life than history had allotted them, had been waiting for that phrase. *"Man silly to dahan-e in dowlat mizanam":* The phrase was liberating, emancipatory, cathartic, mythic, miraculous. It mattered not who said it. If the devil incarnate said it, it did not matter. Never mind what monstrosity later emerged from this revolution. At the moment of its utterance, the phrase was volcanic, revelatory, a sonnet, a soliloquy, sung to the worldly cause of a people's freedom.

Soon after that momentous utterance, Ayatollah Khomeini declared the Pahlavi monarchy null and void and appointed Mehdi Bazargan as the prime minister of a provisional government, and soon after that Shapour Bakhtiar fled the country. After a long and humiliating journey around the world, the shah finally went to Egypt, where he died on July 27, 1980. The monarchy was over. Khomeini was the sole, absolute law of the land. A sacred tyranny of unfathomable proportions was now fast upon the nation.

Between his return to Iran in February 1979 and his death in June 1989, Ayatollah Khomeini ruled over Iran with an iron fist, a fiery will, a steely determination, and a brutal matter-of-factness to his purpose rarely matched in history. Khomeini dispatched his Revolutionary Guards to eradicate rivals with the same implacable ferocity unleashed by Israel's Irgun and Stern Gang on Palestinian villages. Hitler's Gestapo, Mussolini's Black Shirt militia, Stalin's purges—they all had their counterparts in Khomeini's republic of terror. His was a purgatorial passage, a vindictive kingdom ruled with terrorizing vengeance and unsurpassed tyranny. The shah's tyranny seemed pathetic in comparison to the violence Khomeini inflicted on the nation. He ordered the swift and brutal execution of anyone who even seemed to challenge his vision of an Islamic republic. Old army officers and aging former politicians were arrested and summarily executed, as were young revolutionaries, juvenile activists, Kurdish rebels, women protesting the imposition of a medieval code of conduct on them, leaders of religious minorities, poets, journalists—anyone and everyone who dared to make the slightest public protest against the cruel theocracy that Khomeini had dreamed, ordered, legislated, and institutionalized with unsurpassed punishment, ascetic precision, and mystical conviction.

Initially some resisted Khomeini's assumption of absolute power: the Muslim Mojahedin, the Marxist Fada'ian, the resurrected Tudeh Party, the nationalist National Front, and the liberal Islamist Freedom Movement. He masterfully and cunningly used one against the other until he outmaneuvered, dismantled, discredited, and destroyed them all.[31]

The first thing Khomeini did in February 1979 was to appoint Mehdi Bazargan (1907–95) of the Freedom Movement as a transitional prime minister until the Islamic republic he wanted to establish was put to a referendum and an equally Islamic constitution was drafted. The appointment of Bazargan neutralized the Freedom Movement and its extremely popular spiritual leader, Ayatollah Taleqani, and it did little to antagonize other contending forces—Bazargan was liberal, good-hearted, and totally ineffective.[32] He had impeccable revolutionary credentials earned during the nationalization of oil by Mosaddeq but was no match for Khomeini. With Bazargan in ostensible control, Khomeini arranged for a national referendum, and asked people to vote yes or no on the idea of replacing the monarchy with an Islamic republic. Virtually all the factions approved of replacing the monarchy, but few Iranians other than Khomeini and his populist constituency wanted an Islamic republic—but to say no to an Islamic republic at this point meant saying yes to the monarchy. Khomeini's propaganda machinery and enforcers in the streets made sure that this was the sole, false choice available to Iranians. Virtually all the political alignments finally said yes to an Islamic republic. Only a few defiant rank-and-file members agonized over their choices; some did not follow their party's line and did not vote for an Islamic republic. *La Hobb-e Ali, bal Boghz al-Mu'awiyyah*, a very famous Arabic phrase sums up the choice—"Not out of the love of Ali, but out of the hatred of Mu'awiyyah." It was rather the same case in the U.S. presidential election of 2004; some people voted for John Kerry not because they approved of his politics but because they voted against President Bush. To be sure, there were millions of disenfranchised, pious, and mesmerized Iranians who did wholeheartedly vote for an Islamic republic. But organized political rivals—from nationalists to socialists to Islamists—were outmaneuvered; they had no alternative choices on the table.[33]

Khomeini declared victory on April 1, 1979, and triumphantly announced the establishment of the Islamic Republic. Then he proceeded to renege on his promise to oversee the creation of a constitutional assembly and appointed an Assembly of Experts (Majlis Khobregan), members of which were either his devoted followers or else those with no objection to an Islamic constitution. Between May and August 1979 was one of the most exciting periods of modern Iranian history (I went back to Iran in July and was present during many of these crucial events). As the official Assembly of Experts deliberated over the terms of the Islamic constitution, other factions held their own debates about the contents of the new constitution. I participated in one of them, which took place in a hall on the campus of Tehran University. Organized thugs, the emerging Hezbollah, systematically attacked these gatherings, prevented any debate other than what Khomeini had sanctioned, and brutalized people who dared to do otherwise. Newspapers were still struggling to remain free, *Ayandegan* in particular, and were full of heated discussions about the nature of the future state. But there was no organized resistance to this systematic Islamization of the revolution and its aftermath. There was both a genuine concern and a manufactured fear that the Americans would arrange for yet another coup and bring back either the shah or his son. The brutalities of Khomeini's rule in this period are unforgivable, but understandable given the domestic obstacles to laying out the theocratic foundations of an Islamic republic and the deep-seated fear of Iranians that the British and the Americans would try, yet once more, to impose a monarchy back on Iran.[34]

By the early fall, Khomeini faced three major problems: (1) armed factions were demanding a share of power, (2) the Kurds had revolted and were fighting for autonomy in western Iran, and (3) on October 22, 1979, the shah was admitted to a hospital in New York. On November 4, 1979, a group of militant students took American diplomats hostage in their own embassy. Thus began 444 days of crisis—public humiliation for the United States, accompanied by a possible forceful retaliation by the Americans if diplomacy could not resolve the stalemate. Two days after the U.S. embassy was taken over, Prime Minister Bazargan resigned. Khomeini probably did not know about the plan for or approve this takeover, but once it happened it was a godsend to him. The cunning revolutionary leader took full and immediate advantage of it. At a critical moment the students in the

U.S. embassy called themselves "Students Following the Line of the Imam," and Khomeini endorsed their actions. For days, weeks, and months, massive anti-American demonstrations were staged in front of the embassy. The blindfolded hostages were paraded before the assembled demonstrators, the U.S. flag was desecrated, and President Carter was humiliated, day after excruciating day. Operation Eagle Claw (or Operation Evening Light), launched to rescue the hostages, ended catastrophically on April 24, 1980, when the U.S. helicopters and airplanes collided in the middle of the Iranian desert with heavy casualties. The dead and burned bodies of the U.S. soldiers were displayed on Iranian television, and the fiasco was immediately used in propaganda—which, among other things, claimed that Americans were using the pretext of rescuing the hostages in order to conduct a coup and bring back the monarchy. Neither President Carter nor the Democratic Party could overcome the damage done by the crushing failure of the operation. President Carter would lose the presidential election to Ronald Reagan (who would in turn initiate the most dramatic right-wing swing in the history of the United States) largely because of this fiasco.[35]

Ayatollah Khomeini meanwhile put the hostage crisis of 1979–80 to four immediate and effective uses: (1) brutally and effectively destroying the armed challengers to his absolutist power, (2) harshly repressing the separatist movement of the Kurds, (3) safeguarding the revolution against a potential U.S.-sponsored coup on the 1953 model, and (4) rapidly ratifying an Islamic constitution, with draconian power given to himself and to his successor as the supreme leader of the nation, and once and for all Islamizing the 1979 revolution and the republic that followed it to its very constitutional core.[36] Thus while the world's attention was diverted by the fate of fifty-two Americans held hostage in their own embassy for 444 days, 35 million Iranians were being trapped inside a theocracy, and no one cared, or could do, much.

Once they served their purpose in helping Khomeini consolidate the Islamic Republic and outmaneuver all alternative revolutionary contenders for power, the American hostages were released on January 20, 1981, on the very day that Ronald Reagan was being inaugurated as the fortieth U.S. president, having defeated President Carter in no small measure because of the U.S. failure to prevent the Iranian Revolution or even safeguard its own diplomatic corps. "Who lost Iran?" was the burning question in that particular presidential election, as if an entire nation halfway around the globe were the collective property of the United States.

Meanwhile, the first-ever Iranian president, Abu al-Hassan Bani-Sadr, was inaugurated in Iran on January 25, 1980. When some six months later Mohammad Reza Shah died in Egypt on July 27, 1980, Khomeini had every reason to pause and reflect on his successes. He was the supreme leader of the republic, his authority written into the law of the land. What else could he want? That was "the end of history," if Francis Fukuyama were a Shi'i cleric and worked in a seminary in Qom instead of in a think tank in Washington, D.C.

Saddam Hussein's invasion of Iran on September 22, 1980, later aided and abetted by the United States, the Soviet Union, and Europe, opened up Iranian domestic politics to larger regional domains and provided Khomeini with additional momentum to consolidate the foundations of his newly established theocracy. Throughout his revolutionary career, Khomeini's intuitive strategy, or perhaps innate political disposition, was to pick a fight with a more powerful external enemy so his less powerful domestic opponents would be intimidated. His battles with the shah since the late 1950s had consolidated his undisputed leadership of the Shi'i community and given him an upper hand vis-à-vis other factions fighting the same war. The political postures he maintained against Israel and the United States in the course of the hostage crisis of 1979–80 were equally instrumental in discrediting his internal rivals. But this time around, he did not pick a fight with Saddam Hussein. Saddam Hussein launched a war against him—but he welcomed it, for this gave him an opportunity (1) to eradicate any remnant of domestic opposition to his theocracy, and (2) to up the ante in the region and have a larger regional domain for his revolutionary project—with the Palestinians' dispossession from their homeland both a genuine concern and a diversionary tactic high on his agenda. Saddam Hussein's invasion of Iran had given Khomeini a huge opportunity, since the country was now partially occupied by Iraqi forces. Khomeini could use the peril in which Iran found itself to silence, disarm, and suppress his political rivals—the Mojahedin, the Cherik-ha, the Tudeh, the National Front, and the Freedom Movement in particular. But Saddam Hussein was no match for Khomeini's expansive metaphysics of violence. Thus throughout the Iran-Iraq War (1980–88), Khomeini insisted that Iraq was only a passageway to fight Israel and to liberate Palestine, and ultimately to confront the United States—which he labeled "the Great Satan."[37]

One can argue that the Iran-Iraq War, and a series of ground-breaking events that happened around it, forever changed the geopolitics of the region and foreshadowed much that happened before and after 9/11. Just about a year after the success of the Iranian Revolution, the Soviets invaded Afghanistan in 1980 and deeply alarmed the United States during President Reagan's first year in office. Reagan immediately branded the Soviet Union "the Evil Empire." (Reagan and Khomeini shared almost identical theological dispositions in their perception of evil and Satan. Years later, President George W. Bush would place Iran on the "Axis of Evil" that included Syria and North Korea.)[38] Just before the Soviet invasion of Afghanistan, and as the Iranian Revolution was under way, General Zia al-Haq led a military coup in Pakistan in 1977, and in 1979 he had former president Zulfiqar Ali Bhutto hanged. He then quickly offered Pakistan as a major U.S. subcontractor, and a mercenary army, for American regional military operations. (The gross national product of Pakistan seems to consist primarily of mercenary military services to the United States—creating the Afghan Taliban today, dismantling it tomorrow.) Meanwhile in Saudi Arabia, in March 1975, King Faysal was assassinated by his nephew and was quickly succeeded by his brother, King Khalid Bin-Abd-al-Aziz al-Saud. In the wake of the Iranian Revolution, a group of militant Saudis seized the Grand Mosque of Mecca and precipitated a ten-day battle with the Saudi army that ultimately resulted in their capture and execution. Few remember now those bloody ten days. But the rise in prominence of Osama bin Laden and the militant uprising against the Saudi monarchy can be traced directly to that event—which, significantly, took place in the year 1400 on the Islamic calendar.

Further to the West, similarly groundbreaking events were in full swing. In March 1979, a peace treaty was signed between Egypt and Israel, and then, on October 6, 1981, President Anwar al-Sadat was assassinated by disaffected Egyptians. The Muslim Brotherhood was very much alive and active and obviously opposed to any peace treaty with Israel. Israel itself was not sitting quietly either. In March 1978, the Israeli army invaded and occupied southern Lebanon, with heavy casualties sustained by the Lebanese. Three years later, in June 1981, Israel launched an air strike on an Iraqi nuclear reactor (being built with the help of the French) and destroyed it. (Five years later, Israeli commandos lured Mordechai Vanunu from England to Rome and then kidnapped him, brought him to Israel, and charged him with exposing the secrets of the vast Israeli nuclear arsenal.) In June 1982, Israel disregarded all UN resolutions and the outcry of the international community and launched a full-fledged invasion and occupation of Lebanon. On September 16, 1982, and under the watchful eyes of their Israeli allies who had encircled the area (under the direct supervision of Ariel Sharon, later the Israeli prime minister), Lebanese Christian militiamen entered the Palestinian refugee camps of Sabra and Shatila and indiscriminately massacred men, women, and children. The Israeli invasion of Lebanon, already under effective Syrian occupation, in part facilitated the Iranian presence and influence in that country, and bolstered it with the active formation of the Lebanese Hezbollah. (There already existed Amal, the militia representing the disaffected Shi'i community historically disenfranchised from having a say in the affairs of their own homeland.) On October 23, 1983, some 241 U.S. marines and 56 French paratroopers were killed in two bomb explosions in Beirut. The winds of 9/11 had started blowing, almost a quarter of a century earlier and halfway around the globe.[39]

All these regional developments happened while Saddam Hussein's invasion of Iran gave Khomeini an opportunity to push the Islamic Republic into global prominence as a major force in the emerging power politics of the region. On June 22, 1981, Khomeini dismissed Bani-Sadr as the Iranian president. Bani-Sadr was no wartime president—a weak, entirely useless man who, soon after Khomeini rejected him, fled to France, allied himself with the already discredited Mojahedin, and led a parasitical political life.[40]

Eight years of senseless, horrid, murderous war ensued. Hundreds of thousands of Iranians and Iraqis perished on the battlefield, and the two nations exhausted each other's resources, to the full and vicious satisfaction of the United States and its regional allies, now guided by the doctrine of "Dual Containment"— or as Henry Kissinger put it with typically sadistic precision, "I hope they kill each other. Too bad they can't both lose." There were far more casualties on the Iranian side than on the Iraqi because the Iranians used the so-called human wave, which meant sending young and old soldiers to serve as minesweepers.

On December 20, 1983, Donald Rumsfeld, a special envoy of President Reagan, met with Saddam Hussein to endorse his side of the war and provide him with additional weapons. Some two years later, in 1985, and through the intermediation of the Israelis, U.S. defense secretary Caspar Weinberger approved the selling of arms to Iran as well. While the Soviet Union, the United States, and France were the main suppliers of weapons to Iraq, Iraq was also completely supported by most Arab countries (including Yasser Arafat and the PLO) and by the Iranian Mojahedin. Between 1983 and 1986 the Mojahedin moved their camps and headquarters to Iraq and fought on the side of Saddam Hussein against their own fellow Iranians, while helping the petty tyrant destroy his Kurdish and Shi'i opponents at home. Iran's suppliers were mainly North Korea and China.

Did the downing on July 3, 1988, of an Iran Air Airbus flying 290 civilian passengers and its crew, shot down by the USS *Vincennes* over the Persian Gulf, killing all aboard, have anything to do with Khomeini finally accepting the UN resolution for ending the war? Not likely. But he did. Less than a month after the passengers and crew of the Iran Air flight perished in the waters of the Persian Gulf, on July 20, 1988, Iran accepted a cease-fire agreement with Iraq and yielded to a UN-sponsored peace treaty. Khomeini would not live long after the end of Iran-Iraq War. "It is a hemlock I have to drink," he said on the occasion, and as the metaphoric poison was running through his veins he had one final bit of business he needed to address. He would not go with a whimper. He needed a bang.

Soon after the end of the Iran-Iraq War in July 1988, the Islamic Republic faced a constitutional crisis because the heir-designate to Ayatollah Khomeini, Ayatollah Hossein Ali Montazeri, had proved to be unreliable. Ayatollah Montazeri was initially totally devoted to Ayatollah Khomeini, and in anticipation of his own leadership after Khomeini he wrote extensively and enthusiastically on the merits of the absolute leadership of the Shi'i jurist (*velayat-e faqih*).[41] But he soon fell from grace because of his role in exposing a scandal that was later known as the Iran-Contra Affair. In 1985, the Reagan administration (through the lucrative mediation of the Israeli government and an international arms dealer named Manouchehr Ghorbanifar) began a series of secret negotiations with the Islamic Republic whereby U.S. hostages in Lebanon were being swapped for U.S. arms sold to Iran—all facilitated by Lieutenant Colonel Oliver North, a U.S. National Security Council staffer in the Reagan administration. The arrangement was rather bizarre: the Hezbollah in Lebanon would kidnap Americans in Lebanon, Oliver North would sell U.S. arms (from the Israeli stockpile, soon to be replenished by the United States) to Iran in exchange for the release of these hostages, and the proceeds would be channeled to the Contras fighting against the Sandinista government in Nicaragua.[42] So in effect illegal (and immoral) U.S. foreign policies in Latin America directly benefited from Americans being kidnapped in Lebanon.

Revolting against the military dictatorship of a corrupt tyrant named Luis Somoza, a band of Nicaraguan rebels known as the Sandinista National Liberation Front (FSLN) led a revolution and toppled the regime in July 1979. (I was in Iran, participating in a massive demonstration against the Islamist takeover of the revolution, held in the Tehran University soccer stadium, when we heard the news that the Sandinistas had triumphantly entered Managua.)[43] Concerned that the Sandinistas would create another Cuba, the Reagan administration immediately recruited an army of mercenaries including the disaffected former army officers of Somoza, dubbed this force the Contras, and began to arm them to fight the Sandinistas—against the specific articles of the Boland Amendment passed by the Congress. It was to circumvent the Boland Amendment, which made it illegal for the U.S. intelligence agencies to fund the Contras, that national security advisor Admiral John Poindexter and his subordinate Oliver North came up with the idea of diverting millions of dollars gained from selling arms to the Islamic Republic to the Contras. President Reagan was fully aware of the covert operation. (He would later claim that he knew little and remembered less.) The money that the ruling clerics gave to Oliver North for the arms they received—in exchange for having the Hezbollah in Lebanon free the kidnapped Americans—was given to the Contras to fight the Sandinistas.

Ayatollah Montazeri and some members of his family had a role in exposing this arrangement, which angered Ayatollah Khomeini, who dismissed Montazeri as his successor. Montazeri had committed an unpardonable offense by exposing the fact that, despite all Khomeini's anti-American and anti-Israeli ranting and raving, his Islamic Republic was secretly purchasing arms from them both.

The dismissal of Montazeri as successor to Khomeini created a constitutional crisis in the Islamic Republic. Who was now to succeed Ayatollah Khomeini? The obvious candidate was one of his young devotees, then the president of the Islamic Republic, Ayatollah Ali Khamenei. But Khamenei had no juridical credentials of any scholastic significance. He had devoted his life to revolutionary activities and was not much of a jurist, let alone a supreme jurist (a grand ayatollah, a *marja'-e taqlid*), and Shi'i scholasticism is particular about these sorts of things. So Khomeini had to have the constitution of the Islamic Republic changed to allow a lower-ranking cleric to become the supreme leader. But this would have opened a Pandora's box and might endanger the theocratic foundations of the Islamic Republic. Khomeini needed a diversion, yet another smoke screen.[44]

An obscure Pakistani novelist named Salman Rushdie provided that opportunity to Ayatollah Khomeini. Rushdie was a moderately successful novelist, having already established a reputation for himself with a succession of acclaimed works of fiction—*Grimus* (1975), *Midnight's Children* (1981), and *Shame* (1983), as well as a travel narrative, *The Jaguar Smile* (1987), which is an account of his visit to Nicaragua in 1986. Before the publication of his now infamous *Satanic Verses* (1988), his only connection to anything Iranian was limited to the title of his first book, *Grimus*, which is an anagram of the name "Simurg," a mythical bird at the center of the Persian medieval poet Farid al-Din Attar's *Conference of the Birds*.

The *Satanic Verses* would probably have been another moderately successful book for Rushdie had it not been for a succession of events that led Ayatollah Khomeini to a drastic step. Because of its perceived insults against the Prophet Muhammad, Rushdie's book was banned in India, burned in England, and caused a riot in Pakistan, in which a few people were killed. Capitalizing on events that did nothing more noteworthy than boost the international sale of *The Satanic Verses*, on February 14, 1989, Ayatollah Khomeini issued a death sentence against Rushdie in the form of a religious edict (fatwa) ordering Muslims to kill the Pakistani author wherever they found him.[45]

Khomeini's fatwa against Rushdie had two immediate results: (1) it turned Salman Rushdie into a cause célèbre for the bourgeois liberals of the Euro-American literati, who could not care less if scores of Iranian authors were killed or forced into exile by Khomeini but would now disguise their endemic racism and Islamophobia as a perfectly legitimate defense of freedom of expression; and while they were thus quite pleased with themselves, (2) Khomeini was given a golden opportunity to amend the Islamic constitution in a way that would perpetuate the reign of the theocracy. Thus Khomeini could use his fatwa in the Salman Rushdie affair in 1989 to do exactly what he had done in exploiting the hostage crisis in 1979—enable the clerical custodians of the Islamic Republic to strengthen the constitutional foundation of their theocracy. If in 1979 it was the fate of fifty-two American hostages that diverted the world's attention from the predicament of 35 million Iranians, now it was the life of one self-promoting and opportunistic novelist that hid the fate of almost 55 million Iranians.[46]

Khomeini's tactic worked. Salman Rushdie became a world-renowned author, with lucrative contracts for his future books, and the constitution of the Islamic Republic was revised in a manner that perpetuated the theocracy for the indefinite future. There was a momentary pause about the world—so Khomeini went ahead and died on June 3, 1989. On June 4, Ali Khamenei was appointed as the new supreme leader, marking the end of a decade of Khomeini's charismatic terror and the beginning of a nationwide project of reconstruction and reform (1990–97), all under the flailing, undemocratic, and beleaguered rule of a theocracy. An Islamic republic, a Jewish state, and a Hindu fundamentalism were now competing for attention in the region—and a Christian empire was now fast upon them all.

Conspicuously absent during the Iranian Revolution of 1979 was the cherished memory and the defiant alchemy of Persian literary and artistic modernity. To be sure, in what was later dubbed "Ten Nights," the crème de la crème of Iranian poets, artists, and literati gathered in the Tehran branch of the Goethe Institute during the preparatory stages of the revolution, between October 10 and 19, 1977, and received an enthusiastic reception from a large and excited segment of Iranians. It is important to keep in mind that this extraordinary event took place in October 1977, namely a month before the shah's visit to Washington, D.C., and the Iranian students' demonstrations against him; two months before Carter's visit to Iran; and three months before the appearance of that infamous article attacking Ayatollah Khomeini that triggered the protests in Qom and Tabriz, which brought things to a head in 1978 and, by January of the following year, forced the shah out of the country and brought Khomeini back to Iran.[47] In the course of these "Ten Nights," the leading Iranian public intellectuals spoke out valiantly and defiantly against censorship. Among those present during this extraordinary event were Simin Daneshvar, Mehdi Akhavan Sales, Tahereh Saffarzadeh, Manouchehr Hezarkhani, Bahram Beiza'i, Gholamhossein Saedi, Baqer Mo'meni, Said Soltanpour, Houshang Golshiri, Islam Kazemiyyeh, Daryush Ashuri, Mostafa Rahimi, Baqer Parham, and Isma'il Kho'i—the best and most courageous members of Iran's intelligentsia.

In addition to this groundbreaking event in 1977, in the course of the revolutionary upheaval in 1978, Ahmad Shamlu, the poet laureate of his nation at large, went to London (at the time of the "Ten Nights" in October 1977 he was visiting the United States) and founded *Iranshahr*, the leading political periodical published outside Iran during the revolution. In the crucial period of 1979–80, Shamlu returned to Iran and published thirty-six issues of yet another journal, *Ketab-e Jom'eh*, which became the most significant literary and political organ of the secular left. Meanwhile, Gholamhossein Saedi, another leading literary figure, established yet another literary and political journal, *Alefba*, to which the most prominent Iranian public intellectuals contributed. In addition to these organs, which were widely distributed in Tehran and other major cities, there were innumerable public meetings, political rallies, sizable demonstrations, and political debates on television and radio (even though they were under the control of the Islamists), in which the secular left and liberal voices were perfectly audible and enthusiastically received.

All these heroic deeds and defiant struggles against both the belligerent monarchy and the emerging clerical tyranny, however, pale in comparison with the passion and frenzy of the grassroots sentiments that Ayatollah Khomeini awakened and let loose. The poetic defiance and the literary uprising evident in the preceding century lost out to the deep and long-ignored needs and desires of the poor and the disenfranchised, who invested their hopes in those who spoke for the sacred Shi'i memory and the revelatory parlance of truth.

"Who is this Shamlu and what has he done for us?" I will never forget the face of the teenager on the campus of Tehran University in July 1979 who asked this question when I had gone back to Tehran some six months after Khomeini's return. "He is the greatest poet we ever produced over the last half a century," I said to a blank and indifferent face. "He wrote about and commemorated the struggles that have now been crowned with victory. He was the singer and songwriter of our hopes, the chronicler of our nightmares, the harbinger who kept us all awake, our dreamer defiant, who spoke of our aspirations, dignity, the claim that we were also a people, deserving a good name, a pride of place." The young man had walked away, screaming death to one thing or another, and I was talking to a vacant space.

Perhaps the secret of our poetic failure and the reason for the volcanic rise of a sacred violence hidden in the heart of our darkness are to be found in the figure and phenomenon of Khomeini himself. It is imperative that all Iranians own rather than conveniently disown him, both his disconcerting visionary discontent and the absolute and irreconcilable violence with which he executed it. Remember: when Khomeini returned to Iran after fourteen years of exile, a reporter asked him how he felt—and he said, "Nothing." What sort of a man was this? Who would say such a thing, without blinking an eye? From the very beginning, and for as long as Iranians could remember his austere, somber, and inscrutable face and figure, Khomeini seemed to have his gaze set, fixated, on an eternity beyond the pale of history, a celestial contemplation that made the mundane materiality of the world irrelevant, almost a nuisance. He was a mystic of punishing exactitude. Never had anything in the immediate vicinity of his world satisfied him. When Khomeini went from Iraq to France, he had the whole world focused on what he had to say. When he went back to Iran and led the revolution to success he in effect lost that global attention and became the local leader of a national liberation movement. When the U.S. hostages were taken, he recaptured global attention, and his edicts and pronouncements echoed all over the world. When the U.S. hostages were finally released, he again became an ordinary mullah managing the minutiae of a nascent theocracy. His opponents in Iran—the Mojahedin, the Cherik-ha, the Tudeh Party, the Freedom Movement—who were these people? Nothing, nobody to Khomeini.[48]

There was something of the absolutist metaphysics of certitude of Shi'i philosopher Mulla Sadra Shirazi (1571–1640) in Khomeini's thought and action—inherited from a philosopher he most admired and frequently taught. Mulla Sadra's most famous book is called *Asfar Arba'a* (*The Four Journeys*). These four journeys, Mulla Sadra explains, must be undertaken before one attains final and absolute Truth. First, there is the journey that the mortal man undertakes from the People (*Khalq*) toward God or Truth (*Haq*); then comes the second journey, a sojourn from the Truth thus reached toward the Truth internal to itself and in the company of that very Truth; third is the journey back from the Truth to the People in the company of the Truth thus attained; and finally the fourth journey is traveling from the People toward that very People and in the company of that Truth.[49] For Khomeini, these journeys seem not to have been mere philosophical metaphors. He had gone somewhere and come back to deliver what he had seen. The world was not real to him. To him the world was a mere metaphysical metaphor. He moved people, sent them to their deaths, or used them as disposable entities, as if they were concrete concepts, interchangeable ideas, logical premises, philosophical propositions, or mere mystical presuppositions. He was a metaphysician in motion—a philosopher of the minutest and most brutal precision.

It would be easy (and easily misleading) to conclude that Khomeini's efforts to attract the notice of worldwide media were the signs of a megalomaniac revolutionary demanding global attention. That would be too easy a reading. Khomeini was no megalomaniac. The shah was a megalomaniac. Khomeini was something else, something far more insidious. He was a mystic gone political, a revolutionary ascetic who forced the return of a mutated Islamic mysticism back to the point of its origin. One may read Islamic mysticism as the poetic transformation of the juridical fear of God into an ascetic love of God. Islamic law (Shari'ah) is predicated on a fundamental fear of a vindictive God who will punish you if you don't do as He says. Islamic mysticism (Irfan) grabs hold of that fear and gently transforms it into a love of God, the poetic articulation of an amorous reciprocity between humanity as the lover and God as the beloved, and thus the profoundly theo-erotic disposition of Islamic (Persian in particular) mysticism. The ease and mater-of-factness with which Khomeini sent tens of thousands of young people to their graves speaks of the convoluted mutation of that love of God into a material premise of death-in-God—or *fana*, as the mystics have called it.

> *Ro bemir ay Khwajah qabl az mordanat,*
> *Ta nabashad zahmat-e jan dadanat.*
> *An chenan margi keh dar nuri ravi,*
> *Ney chenan margi keh dar guri ravi.*

> *[Go and die, oh Sir, before you die,*
> *So you won't endure the pain of dying.*
> *A kind of death that leads you to light—*
> *Not a kind of death that buries you in a grave.]*

That poem is the quintessence of Islamic mysticism, and Khomeini seemed to have been absorbed by and in it—he "died before his death," a prophetic tradition that the mystics had turned into the cornerstone of their juridical laxity, universal humanism, peaceful disposition. Embedded in that peace, however, is a repressed violence, a millennial repression of the fear of death, camouflaged and sugarcoated in beautiful poetry. The entire poetic enterprise of Rumi, one may in fact argue, is the fear of death sublimated into the poetic fragility of an amorous moment.[50] Khomeini took that metaphoric moment literally—just like a floating bubble, which he then punctured with a political pin. He was resurrected from the depth of that poetic mutation of fear into love and from love into an absolutist certitude of death, a death before death, the convulsion of time and narration. Sometimes it seemed that this was Khomeini's second life—that he had already died, and gone away, and then come back to haunt the memory of a life he thought he had left unfinished on earth.

When Saddam gave Khomeini one final chance to have the world as his stage, he saw the war with Iraq as an excuse to march toward Israel, and ultimately toward Armageddon, to face the United States. *Emrika hich ghalati nemitavanad bekonad* (America cannot do a damned thing), he used to say. This might have been liberating at the moment, but it also had an apocalyptic tone to it no one dared to contemplate. Iran was too small for Khomeini, as was the Islamic world. He was a man of massive metaphysical abstractions, and "Islam" to him had a cosmogonic magnitude only the Muslim mystics have dared to ponder, narrate, navigate, fear, and love—all at one and the same time.

Before the Iran-Iraq War broke out, the local and nativist politics bored Khomeini, and his Iranian opponents were too puny to worry him. Wearied with Iranian politics, Khomeini welcomed the war with Iraq as an opportunity to go global. He dismissed Bani-Sadr like an irritating fly. He put a devoted follower, a pious and obedient underling called Mohammad Ali Raja'i (1933–81), in charge as president of the Islamic Republic, and entrusted the daily routines of the state to him and to two other followers, Ali Akbar Hashemi Rafsanjani (later the president for eight years) and Ali Khamenei (the future supreme leader), and then went after Saddam—and beyond.

The reason Khomeini went after Saddam and targeted the larger world beyond the Iranian imaginative borders was not just because he was a mystic revolutionary in search of ever vaster metaphysical abstractions to contemplate, combat, and conquer, but also because he knew intuitively that Shi'ism (and by extension for him Islam itself) is a religion of protest, that it can never be fully in power without fully discrediting itself. So he had to keep Shi'ism on its toes, as it were, always in a combative mode and a revolutionary posture, forever, for as long as he lived—for eternity. If he had been a Marxist he would have been a Trotskyist. But he was a Muslim, so he was a Shi'i, a permanent revolutionary. Statecraft did not just bore him. It in fact delegitimized him—not to the outside world, but to himself. As a religion of protest, Khomeini knew better than all his followers, Shi'ism has always survived by being in a combative mode. It was born in the seventh century as a religion of protest, when the first and after him the third Shi'i imam said no to power. From then on, protesting power and leading revolutionary outbursts against the status quo has been second nature to Shi'ism.[51]

As a Muslim, as a Shi'i, as a mystic, and as a permanent revolutionary, Khomeini knew the drama of his faith and religion from the inside out. As is evident in the Ta'ziyeh, the Shi'i dramatic Passion Play, on whose performative model Khomeini launched his revolution,[52] he knew that dramaturgically Shi'ism can never have a complete dramatic mimesis, a one-to-one Aristotelian correspondence between reality and representation—for the Shi'i mimetic mutation of fact and fantasy must forever remain incongruent, combative, inconclusive, at odds with itself, with representation never allowing reality to call and claim it completely, or vice versa.[53] Khomeini concluded his revolution, and with that revolution his account with the world, inconclusively—still having things to do. That is the way with all Shi'i mystics. They think there is, and thus they leave, something amiss about the world.

As Khomeini went around staging a massive revolutionary drama, the icons of Iranian cultural modernity were all alive and well— Ahmad Shamlu was alive, as were Mehdi Akhavan Sales and

Sohrab Sepehri. Gholamhossein Saedi was around, and so were Houshang Golshiri and Mahmoud Dolatabadi. But no one, even as they did their best and rose to the occasion, could do or offer or sustain anything even near the dramatic power of the spectacle Khomeini staged for the whole world to see.

Nothing breathed in the vicinity of that spectacle, nothing except, quietly and imperceptibly, the budding blossoms of a new turn in Iranian cinema. The single most important cultural achievement of this turbulent decade (1979–89) was the gradual rise of Iranian cinema to global prominence, updating and promoting Iranian cultural modernity, exposing the aesthetic rendition of the Iranian national fate on a wide screen, demanding and gradually securing the attention of the wider world.[54] Such prominent filmmakers as Amir Naderi, Abbas Kiarostami, and Mohsen Makhmalbaf became the visual chroniclers of the mind and soul of a people having hoped high, achieved very little, betrayed by its own hopes, abandoned by its own best wishes. It is as if everything—from poetry to fiction to drama—all gradually dissipated, entrusting the best they had ever hoped to achieve to Iranian cinema, and in a strange and convoluted way, Iranian cinema of the postrevolutionary and postwar period followed the same logic and lunacy of Ayatollah Khomeini—it too targeted a global audience and abandoned its local constituency. It too used the national trauma that had been the very source and inspiration of its visual energy to make a global spectacle beyond its own immediate borders. And above all, it too, particularly in its most glorious achievements—the works of Abbas Kiarostami and Mohsen Makhmalbaf—went for the inconclusive disposition of the Iranian (Shi'i) mimesis, borrowing from what the Ta'ziyeh had to offer and making it global. Iranian cinema thus emerged as the mirror image, the celluloid negative, of the nightmare Khomeini had violently interpreted in the darkest noon of Iranian political modernity. Iranian cinema was bright and early, where Khomeini was dark and delayed.

Between the success of Khomeini's revolution inside Iran and the rise of Iranian cinema to global recognition, Iranian cultural modernity oscillated between a provincial convulsion internally and a cosmopolitan effervescence externally. The success of the Islamic Revolution in Iran was the Manichaean victory of one side of the Iranian political paradox over the other: the triumph of Qomi clericalism over Tehrani cosmopolitanism, the victory of Bernard Lewis's Orientalist reading of our history over Edward Said's emancipatory humanism. Tehran was the capital of our future hopes (where Edward Said's literary humanism would have felt at home), Qom the clerical corner of our fearful past (where Bernard Lewis would find plenty of clerical kindred souls). To Tehran we had imported and invested, from the four corners of our country, the best that we had to offer our future. The clerical clique that ultimately hijacked and stole our revolution did so through a more organic link with our fears, leaving our hopes dangling in the air, right in front of our eyes and at the mercy of phantom liberties our poets and filmmakers had envisioned for us. As the urban poor and the disenfranchised peasantry—the two major revolutionary forces that were left to their own devices, and which the clerical tribalism seized upon and catapulted into a revolutionary frenzy—were incorporated into the body politic of the Islamic Republic, the middle class either fled the country, went into domestic hibernation, or put on the garb of a mercantile provincialism and catered to the clergy. By the time Khomeini died in 1989, something else in Iran had already died; something exceedingly precious: the cosmopolitan urbanism of our hopes, a syncretic humanism that was the flowering achievement of two hundred years of anticolonial modernity. Mourning the death of Ayatollah Khomeini were not just the proverbial inky cloak of Hamlet, nor customary suits of solemn black, that his devoted followers donned, mourning a father, bidding him farewell unrevenged. Together with all the forms, modes, and shows of grief customary to such rituals, Iranians had in them that which passes show—they were mourning the death of their cosmopolitan dreams, for they had become the walking embodiment of their own tribal nightmares.

6

To Reconstruct and Reform

It is now hard to imagine, but it is imperative to remember, that the initial success of the Iranian Revolution of 1979 in toppling a corrupt monarchy (and as usual a major U.S. ally) sent shock waves throughout the region, from Pakistan to Morocco. Fear and hope of a domino effect, of people rising up and repeating what Iranians had done with their bare hands, were rampant in the region. Ever since the end of World War I and the rise of the United States as a major global power, the single most consistent American foreign policy around the world (from Latin America to Asia and Africa) has been to generate, sustain, and endorse corrupt and subservient governments, which obsequiously serve U.S. material and strategic interests. It did not matter how much any of these tyrannical regimes abused their people—the United States needed and supported them. Between 1941 and 1978, the shah of Iran was an outstanding example of a tyrant at home and a lackey abroad, subordinating the interests and welfare of his country to the imperatives of American foreign policy. But the man the Americans had put in power was finally deposed in what, to disenfranchised people around the globe, appeared to be a legitimate, grassroots revolution. The United States and its regional and European allies were alarmed by this widespread perception; it spelled trouble for them. The jinni of revolutionary uprising had come out of its proverbial bottle. The menacing apparition had to be put back in.

The Iran-Iraq War provided a golden opportunity for the United States and its allies to create a buffer zone between Iran and the rest of the Arab and Muslim world. Supporting and arming Saddam Hussein, while making sure that Iran also had enough arms to fight back, was essential to the doctrine of "Dual Containment." While Iran was thus preoccupied on its western borders for eight years, a similar opportunity arose soon after the Soviet invasion of Afghanistan. From 1979 to 1989 the United States banked on Saudi money to support Afghan resistance to the Soviets and asked the Pakistanis for operational intelligence to assist them in furthering the creation of what became the Taliban, initially known as the Mojahedin, or as President Reagan liked to call them, "Freedom Fighters." The staunch Sunni (Wahabi) disposition of the Afghan Taliban also made them a useful instrument for limiting the spread of the Shi'i-based Iranian Revolution of 1979 eastward into Muslim nations in central Asia.[1]

Thus trapped on both its eastern and western borders, Iran saw the healthy and robust energy of its revolution turned inward and diverted to the furtherance of a repressive and corrupt theocracy. It is imperative to keep in mind that when the Iranian Revolution began its momentous course it was *not* an Islamic revolution; it mutated into a radical Islamic movement through a long, repressive, brutal, and viciously calculated process, with the followers of Khomeini systematically destroying all their political rivals—both Islamist and secular.[2] Though the United States and its allies did succeed in curtailing the spread of the Islamic Revolution and protecting their regional interests, they soon had ample reason to regret that success. At the time, however, the systematic mutation of a robust, cosmopolitan, effervescent, syncretic, and pluralistic revolutionary energy into the pathological Islamic Republic very much mirrored what was taking place in the Jewish state to its west, the ever-brewing Hindu fundamentalism to its east, and the emerging Christian empire that did everything in its power to support Arab potentates from Jordan to Morocco in their repression of any emerging revolution and their resistance to democratic changes.

But history, as the great Abu al-Fazl Beyhaqi knew a very long time ago, cannot be cheated—or, to put it bluntly, what goes around comes around. The two monsters that the United States had created to stop the spread of the Iranian Revolution into the rest of the region—Saddam Hussein and Osama bin Laden—soon came back to haunt their creators. The ink on the UN resolution ending the hostilities between Iran and Iraq had not yet dried when Saddam Hussein began planning to use the armaments generously given him by the United States to invade Kuwait, which he did on August 2, 1990.³ This triggered what is now referred to as the First Gulf War (1990–91), or Operation Desert Storm, when the United States and its allies mobilized a massive army and forced Saddam Hussein out of Kuwait, but wisely kept him in power for fear of destabilizing the region even more. The United States also cynically encouraged the Shi'is in the south and the Kurds in the north to revolt against Saddam—but not to demand more than the United States was ready to allow. There were times that the commander of the U.S. Army, General Norman Schwarzkopf, seemed not to agree with his president and wanted to march on Baghdad. But he was ordered not to do so. Another Bush in another administration would later take care of that bit of unfinished business.⁴

Soon after Saddam Hussein's forces were expelled from Kuwait, the other U.S. chicken came home to roost. Osama bin Laden was on the move—transferring his headquarters from Afghanistan (where the United States and its Pakistani subcontractors had helped him operate against the Soviets) to Sudan (where they had no control), where he began his global assault on the United States. On February 26, 1993, a band of militant Muslims launched a major attack on the World Trade Center in New York, but failed to do extensive damage to it. In October of the same year, eighteen U.S. servicemen were brutally killed in Mogadishu by a group of Somali militia. Three years later, in 1996, Osama bin Laden returned to Afghanistan to launch a devastating assault on U.S. interests and facilities in the region. On June 25, 1996, a U.S. military housing complex was destroyed in Dhahran, Saudi Arabia. Two years after that, on August 7, 1998, the U.S. embassies in Nairobi, Kenya, and Dar es Salaam, Tanzania, were destroyed, with massive casualties. On October 12, 2000, the USS *Cole* was the target of an attack in the principal port of Yemen—seventeen American sailors were killed. Finally, the most spectacular operation of this cycle of violence was executed on September 11, 2001, when nineteen people hijacked four U.S. airplanes and crashed them into World Trade Center in New York, the Pentagon in Washington, D.C., and a field in Pennsylvania. All of these operations were attributed to Osama bin Laden and a shadowy organization called al Qaeda that he presumably controlled. A decade after the conclusion of the Iran-Iraq War and the expulsion of the Soviets from Afghanistan, the "weapons of mass destruction" that America had created in Iraq and Afghanistan to prevent the spread of a revolutionary movement in the region were exploding in its own face.[5]

The geopolitical circumstances of the Iranian Revolution of 1979, the fall of a major U.S. ally in the region, the spectacular success of an Islamic revolution, the global embarrassment of the U.S. inability to rescue its diplomatic corps held hostage in Iran, the subsequent U.S. manufacturing of two regional monsters (Saddam Hussein and Osama bin Laden), in the larger regional context, in particular the continued Israeli occupation of Palestine—all came together to condition a major epistemic shift in the geopolitics of the region. One might trace much of what has happened ever since to this shift, which has eclipsed the cosmopolitan disposition of the political cultures of the region (a cosmopolitanism irreducible to "religious" or "secular" binaries), collapsing them into a tribal fixation with characterstics specifically Jewish (Israel), Islamic (Iran), Hindu (India), and Christian (United States). It is within this larger religious frame of reference, and the systematic destruction of alternative cosmopolitan cultures, that much of Iranian history of the post-Khomeini era must be understood—a condition categorically collapsed into the most brutal and irreducibly violent bare bones of what the German political philosopher Karl Schmidt stripped of all its metaphysical innuendos and simply called "the political."

At the threshold of the twenty-first century, and in the immediate aftermath of the coded cacophony of 9/11, the German political philosopher Karl Schmidt's "concept of the political," and its corollary anchorage on the notion of "the enemy," have assumed a renewed and added significance. Of the centrality of the concept of "the enemy" in the formation of the political, Schmidt had a categorical, definitive, and almost insular conception. "The distinction of friend and enemy," Schmidt stated categorically, "denotes the utmost degree of intensity of a union or separation, of an association or dissociation. It can exist theoretically and practically, without having simultaneously to draw all those moral, aesthetic, economic, or other distinctions." Schmidt's intention here is to produce a categorical distinction that locates "the enemy" as the locus classicus of "the political," and by virtue of "the political" "the state." "The political enemy," Schmidt stipulated, "need not be morally evil or aesthetically ugly; he need not appear as an economic competitor, and it may even be advantageous to engage with him in business transactions. But he is, nevertheless, the other, the stranger; and it is sufficient for his nature that he is, in a specially intense way, existentially something different and alien, so that in the extreme case conflicts with him are possible."[6]

In the aftermath of 9/11 and the systematic demonization of "the Arab" and "the Muslim" as "the enemy" in not just pure political terms but in extended moral and aesthetic terms (for as the Christian element of the American empire insists on the evil disposition of Muslims, "the Axis of Evil," etc., the CNN–*New York Times*–*Time* magazine nexus makes sure that its visual apparition appear as nothing but ugly), the geopolitics of the region in which Iran is squarely located is brought to bear on the very moral and political fabric of the imperial globalization of U.S. interests. The dichotomous manufacturing of "Islam" and the "West" by the ideologues of the U.S. imperialism (Bernard Lewis in particular) entered a new phase in the course of the pestiferous construction of an enemy (by Samuel Huntington and Francis Fukuyama in particular) that can be physically located, politically identified, morally despised, visually vilified, and militarily conquered. The clerical codification of Iranian political culture in the course and aftermath of the Islamic Revolution, at the heavy price of eclipsing and institutionally destroying its cosmopolitan ecumenicalism, coincided with the rise of American neocons and the manufacturing of a binary opposition at once moral and political in its disposition. Much of the rest of Iranian history—indeed, the history of the region at large, and in fact the history of the U.S. empire—must be read in terms definitive to this dangerous mutation of cosmopolitan cultures the world over into extremist banalities of religious tribalism—Jewish, Christian, Islamic, and Hindu in particular.

*   *   *

By the time the Iran-Iraq War ended and Ayatollah Khomeini died on June 3, 1989, Iran was in utter ruins and the Islamic Republic in a shambles—but its state apparatus and territorial integrity had remained intact.[7] For the next decade or so, the Islamic Republic, having failed to foment Islamic revolutions in neighboring countries, turned much of its attention inward, by and large (but not entirely) determining only the fate and future of Iranians, collectively trapped inside their own homeland and subjected to a totalitarian theocracy. President Ali Khamenei was promoted and anointed as the next supreme leader on June 4, 1989, and by August 17, Ali Akbar Hashemi Rafsanjani was sworn in as the new president. The U.S. release of more than $500 million in frozen Iranian assets early in November of that year may have indicated a slight improvement in U.S.-Iran relations. When on June 21, 1990, a major earthquake killed more than forty thousand people in Iran, the natural disaster diverted the attention of people from politics and mobilized their energy and resources to help the survivors, which had the effect of ratifying the status of the clerical custodians of the Islamic Republic as the legitimate leaders of the nation and the protectors of the collective well-being of the Iranian people. For all intents and purposes, the Islamic Republic seemed to be there to stay. It had outmaneuvered and eliminated all its rivals, defended the territorial integrity of the country, and emerged as a major contender in the geopolitics of the region.

Domestically, much of the 1990s was devoted to postwar reconstruction, with Ali Akbar Hashemi Rafsanjani, twice elected president (1989–93 and 1993–97), turning the attention of the nation to repairing the heavily damaged infrastructure of the country. Dubbed "Sardar-e Sazandegi" ("the Leader of Reconstruction"), Rafsanjani presided over a massive project of rebuilding Iran, essentially funded by oil revenues that by now constituted more than 80 percent of the Iranian national economy. A bureaucratic state capitalism, now integrated into the world market and globalized capitalism, managed the lion's share of the economy, while Rafsanjani did his best to promote the private sector, with modest success. A large percentage of the Iranian bourgeoi-

sie had either fled the country after the revolution or else with-
drawn from active economic participation for fear of the volatile
and unpredictable conditions in the society at large. Be that as it
may, billions of dollars in foreign exchange reserves derived from
oil revenues, and a substantial decrease in outlays for purchasing
arms, helped boost the economy even in its unproductive and
parasitical disposition.[8]

Ali Akbar Hashemi Rafsanjani has been a figure definitive to
the establishment of the Islamic Republic from its very inception.
Few remember today that in his youth he actually wrote a book
on Amir Kabir (1807–52), the great reformist prime minister
under Nasir al-Din Shah. The book, which he called *Amir Kabir
or the Hero of Fighting Against Colonialism*, was published in
Qom in March 1968. The then thirty-four-year-old Rafsanjani
(he was born in 1934, studied with Khomeini in Qom, and was
imprisoned under the shah several times) wrote this book some
five years after the brutally repressed June 1963 uprising and long
before there was any hope of anything on the scale of the 1979
revolution. Rafsanjani's book on Amir Kabir, however, has a quite
obvious celebratory tone when its author mirrors the aspirations
of his own youthful idealism in those of Amir Kabir—he clearly
and strongly identifies with his subject. As Rafsanjani says in his
preface, "My main purpose in writing this book is mainly to describe Amir Kabir's anticolonial struggles. . . . In this book, I do
not wish to engage in historical research. As a result, the readers
should not expect any historical detail or thorough research. Instead, my main objective is to investigate the position of Amir
Kabir vis-à-vis colonialism and colonialists."[9] This was a coded
and common language at a time when political activists resusci-
tated historical figures for contemporary purposes. While in a
Pahlavi prison, for example, Mehdi Bazargan also wrote a book
on Mahatma Gandhi, for largely similar reasons.[10]

Rafsanjani has quite properly been described as a "pragmatic
conservative"—someone politically invested in and totally committed to the Islamic Republic, part of the clerical establishment,
and yet far from holding any idea, principle, or political position
to be inviolable. He is perhaps the shrewdest politician the Islamic Republic has produced. If any Iranian were ever to match
Henry Kissinger's politically criminal mind and Thatcher's in-

sidious statesmanship, it would be Rafsanjani. One can argue that many of the inner tensions within the Islamic Republic that surfaced after President Mohammad Khatami's election in 1997 were in fact already present during Rafsanjani's presidency, but by a combination of uncanny statesmanship and subtly applied brutality he managed to co-opt all the Islamic (and even some of the secular) dissenters by appearing to be their only hope, thereby saving the Islamic Republic (and with it his own prominence in it) from internal dissent. He is among the rare Iranian politicians who know how to speak an exceedingly populist and anti-American language at home, and yet sound conciliatory and pragmatic to their foreign interlocutors. He has a blasé and quite disarming smile carved on his otherwise blank face. Before becoming the president of the Islamic Republic, for nine years (1980–89) he occupied the powerful position of the speaker of the parliament. For a short time he was also the commander of the Iranian armed forces, and reportedly the man who persuaded Khomeini to accept the UN resolution ending the grueling Iran-Iraq War.

Rafsanjani's presidency was marked by a consistent attempt to invigorate the private sector without creating social unrest or economic instability—and to some degree he succeeded in doing so, largely thanks to massive oil revenue. Substantiating Rafsanjani's economic project was his contribution to the political consolidation of power in six major organs within the administrative apparatus of the Islamic Republic: (1) first and foremost, the revolutionary leadership of the supreme leader, predicated on the idea of the absolutist authority of the jurisconsult (*velayat-e faqih*), which was now squarely in the hands of Ali Khamenei; (2) the office of the president, which was occupied for eight years by Rafsanjani; (3) the Guardian Council, which sought to institutionalize the power of the clergy within the constitutional framework of the Islamic Republic, for without its approval no law could be legislated by the legislative body of the government; (4) the Expediency Council (an afterthought of the Islamic constitution), which would make sure juridical hairsplitting by Shi'i jurists in the Guardian Council would not jeopardize the Islamic Republic; (5) the parliament, which always remained a wild card depending on the political disposition of the nation; and (6) the judiciary, which remained securely in the hands of the clerical establishment. In other words, the system worked because the clerics, trained in and speaking a common seminarian and juridical language (largely incomprehensible to the rest of Iranians), were incorporated into the official organs of the Islamic Republic. The clerics shared power while allowing only two democratic components of the constitution, the presidency and the parliament, to remain relatively democratic and unpredictable but always constrained to bow to the will of other, extremely powerful and clerically controlled offices.

Despite its ironfisted control of the political apparatus of the state, mostly maneuvered by the politically savvy Rafsanjani, the Islamic Republic was ideologically in deep trouble almost immediately after the death of Ayatollah Khomeini, if not earlier. This was largely due to the doctrinal disposition of Shi'ism itself, which as a historically combative and intransigent religion of protest must always be in a position of defiance and rebellion and thus can never come to power without immediately discrediting itself.[11] The specific form that this discrediting assumed, however, was initially the anti–Islamic Republic forces, secular or Islamist, that fundamentally and militarily challenged the very constitution of the state. But once they were eliminated, a form of robust ideological opposition emerged from within the bosom of the Islamic Republic itself, led by a group of activist intellectuals who eventually called themselves *Roshanfekran-e Dini* ("Religious Intellectuals"). The most salient ideological challenge to the very epistemic foundation of the Islamic Republic came from the work of one such religious intellectual, Abdolkarim Soroush.[12]

In a succession of highly erudite books, essays, interviews, and public lectures, Abdolkarim Soroush gradually emerged in the postwar period as the leading Muslim theorist constitutionally critical of the clerical reign in Iran. Soroush was born in 1945 in Tehran, educated in Iran and England in pharmacology, and became increasingly attracted to philosophy. Early in the course of the revolution, Soroush was among the leading cadre of revolutionaries revamping and Islamizing Iranian universities, which meant a systematic purging of the faculty and curriculum of what this censorial body (the Cultural Revolution Council, the members of which were appointed by Ayatollah Khomeini directly) considered anti-Islamic and/or antirevolutionary. That ignoble role of policing thoughts and curtailing freedom of inquiry early in his involvements with the Islamic Republic had enabled him, after he resigned from that shameful post in 1983, to have a vast and increasing audience inside and outside his homeland, both among the religious intellectuals and even among the religiously not so conscious activists—to the point that in the 1990s he became persona non grata among the Iranian political elite, while vastly popular with the emerging body of opposition from within the Islamic Republic.[13]

Abdolkarim Soroush's most significant idea was articulated in a book he published in 1990, *Qabz-o-Bast-e Teoric-e Shari'at* (*The Theoretical Expansion and Contraction of Religious Law*). The principal argument of this book is that before any discussion of a conservative or progressive interpretation of Islamic jurisprudence, or any other aspect of any other religion, the primary task is to address the implicit question of religious hermeneutic, or how a religion is read, received, and interpreted in a given time and place. What Soroush proposed here was a rather innocuous idea, simple (if not simpleminded) and modest in a comparative context; the historicity of any form of understanding. But in the suffocating context of an Islamic republic, permeated by a hermetically essentialist and violently politicized conception of "Islam," the suggestion quickly became iconoclastic. Soon after Ayatollah Khomeini died (Soroush did not publicize these thoughts while Khomeini was still alive), the organs of the Islamic Republic sought to consolidate their grip on power by predicating their authority on the implicit assumption of divine will and providential intervention. In the context of the Islamic Republic, Soroush's suggestion rightly emerged as the most subversive idea challenging the essentialist claim to Islam and Islamicity that was the very raison d'être of the ruling elite.

Whatever the innate merits of Soroush's ideas, in the immediate domain of the Islamic Republic they were seen as an eruption of theoretical resistance to and ideological defiance of the Islamic Republic. A band of disaffected revolutionary idealists, who had devoted their lives to the cause of the revolution, watched as their side took power and soon mutated into a horrid theocracy. They began to flock around Soroush. The phenomenon of Soroush and what he had made possible led to a major social movement that quickly gained momentum and deeply angered and concerned the religious establishment, for it rightly considered Soroush one of its own who had now turned against it. Perhaps the most disconcerting aspect of Soroush for the clerical elite was that he was not a seminarian but a lay (though deeply devout and religious) intellectual, yet he had outsmarted, outjurisprudenced, outmaneuvered, and altogether beaten them at their own game. Conservative religious authorities such as Ayatollah Mesbah Yazdi detested Soroush; the young revolutionary Shi'i had in effect deturbaned them all out of their clerical position and disrobed their claim to canonical authority. This, perhaps, was infinitely more damaging to seminarian fraternity brothers who had historically held the Shi'i establishment together and privileged their position in society at large.

The downside of Soroush's major intellectual intervention and ideological subversion of the Islamic Republic was that he actually intensified the further Islamization of Iranian political culture by presenting the principal theoretical challenge to the Islamic Republic in a deeply cultivated Islamic language. Over the preceding two hundred years, contemporary Islamic ideas were all articulated in dialectical debates and creative conversation with non-Islamic ideas that came from all over the world. Of particular importance were liberation movements and emancipatory ideas coming from the battle zones of Latin America, Africa, and Asia. One can in fact extend this observation to the entirety of Islamic intellectual history, where the introduction of Chinese, Indian, Persian, and Greek (the real Greeks, not the Greeks that the Germans invented for Europe) ideas has been instrumental in facilitating the dialectical disposition of Islamic philosophies and sciences. In the context of the Islamic Republic, Soroush's ideas were brilliant, creative, critical, and deeply cultivated; but they were conveyed in a vacuous, flat, and tepid language. His argument courageously targeted the reigning theocracy, but its conceptual muscles were atrophied from a lack of contrapuntal exercises that could only have come from Soroush's being challenged on an open and democratic playing field. There is thus something antiquarian at best and provincial at worst about So-roush's ideas, a tepid tempest in a rather modest teacup.

The best that less religiously inclined intellectuals in Iran such as Daryush Shayegan, Ramin Jahanbegloo, and Morad Saqafi could do under these circumstances was to get caught up in the pointless wild-goose chase of the "tradition" versus "modernity" debate, which bought deeply into the Islamic primacy in political discourse; consequently, they were left wondering if there was any way out of this dilemma. Those secular intellectuals such as Daryush Ashuri and Mashallah Ajoudani who lived outside Iran were equally trapped in this binary opposition and thought Iran had only two options: become either "Westernized" or even more "Islamized." The poverty of ideas in this period of Iranian intel-lectual history is almost unprecedented. The Islamists were both in power *and* in opposition, and those intellectuals, whether for or against the Islamic Republic, who could function in a wider field of ideas were stuck in the less than enviable position of being the fifth wheel of an already operative ideological machine. In this respect, intellectuals such as Morad Saqafi, the courageous and imaginative editor of a wonderful journal called *Goft-o-Gu* (*Dialogue*), deserve particular recognition for their sustained (but ultimately futile) record of creating an alternative site of reflec-tion in the heyday of these limitations.[14]

The entrapment in an Islamist narrative became increasingly evident yet remained highly influential with the oppositional re-ligious intellectuals. The phenomenon assumed vast societal pro-portions when it included other major public figures such as Mohsen Kadivar and Hasan Yousefi Eshkevari—members of the younger generation in the clerical establishment, deeply steeped in its scholastic learning and thoroughly enmeshed in the juridi-cal language of their profession. The position of the Islamic Re-public vis-à-vis these religious intellectuals oscillated between regarding them as a loyal opposition, which gave a democratic coloration to their reign of theocratic terror, or else condemning them as deeply troubling and subversive. These young and criti-cal clerics were exceedingly courageous and indeed endured great hardship and prison terms for their criticism of the ruling clerical elite, their own fellow jurists. But the arguments of these courageous clerics were even more problematic than Soroush's—for as they did their best to articulate a more liberal, tolerant, and expansive conception of Shi'i jurisprudence, they in fact buried the Iranian political culture even deeper in an exclusively juridical and thoroughly Islamist language. By virtue of all the positive features of their diction and disposition, the liberal language they spoke and the more tolerant vision of an Islamic republic they offered, they in fact pushed the Iranian political culture even deeper into the grave of a thoroughly Islamic consciousness—as if more than two hundred years of a creative cultivation of a globally conversant, comparative, cosmopolitan, expansive, and emancipatory set of critical discourses had never existed or, even before that, the vast effervescence of Persian literary humanism was not equally definitive to the Iranian cultural disposition.[15]

The critical language that Soroush and other religious intellectuals like him best represented gradually expanded and included a wider circle of ideas expressed by other extraordinary religious theorists, political activists, and creative strategists, such as Sa'id Hajjarian, who gradually (toward the end of Rafsanjani's presidency and early in the course of Khatami's term) emerged as the principal theorist and an insightful tactician for what was now dubbed a "reformist movement"—a movement that originated within the Islamist camp itself. Helping Hajjarian, who was the target of an assassination attempt in March 2000, were such courageous and defiant journalists as Abdollah Nouri, Mashallah Shams al-Va'ezin, and Akbar Ganji. All of these public intellectuals opposed and actively discredited the Islamic Republic (and endured short or long prison terms) even though they had initially been its staunchest supporters and had played major roles in its success. Before he became a leading dissident intellectual late in the 1990s, Abdollah Nouri had attained a high position in the ruling clique as a personal representative of Ayatollah Khomeini with the Revolutionary Guards, and then a vice president and minister of the interior. Nouri came to prominence as an oppositional thinker after he established a daily paper, *Khordad*, in which he advocated freedom of expression and civil rights. He used his impeccable revolutionary credentials to call for constitutional limitations on the authority of the supreme leader, Ali Khamenei. In 1999, he was sentenced to five years' imprisonment for insulting the supreme leader and instigating resistance to the Islamic Republic. Akbar Ganji was equally outspoken in his criticism of the regime. In a succession of relentless investigative reports he implicated the highest-ranking members of the clerical clique in numerous criminal activities.

One of the most remarkable figures of this period of internal defiance against the tyrannies of the Islamic Republic is Mohsen Makhmalbaf, a globally celebrated filmmaker, novelist, and social activist, who like the other members of this group was initially totally committed to the cause of the Islamic Revolution and involved with the propaganda machinery of the Islamic Republic. But he soon broke ranks with its leadership and maintained an independent and highly public position of opposition to the horrors of the regime. No other filmmaker's career in Iran so clearly parallels and illustrates the rise and subsequent plunge of the Islamic Republic from a utopian ideal to a nightmarish reality. Makhmalbaf's early films (which he started making soon after serving more than four years in Pahlavi dungeons), such as *Nasuh's Repentance* (1983) and *Two Sightless Eyes* (1984), were completely at the service of creating the ideological and metaphysical underpinnings of the nascent Islamic Republic. By the time he made *The Marriage of the Blessed* (1989) and *The Nights of Zayandeh Rud* (1991), however, he was completely disillusioned with the regime and publicly scandalized its ruling elite. While with *Peddler* (1987) and *The Cyclist* (1989) he remained committed to enduring social causes, with *Once Upon a Time Cinema* (1992) and *A Moment of Innocence* (1996), he not only distanced himself from the militant Islamism to which he had once been integral but also took a stand against its violent metaphysics.[16]

From Abdolkarim Soroush to Mohsen Makhmalbaf—on two ends of a spectrum that both ground and liberate a political culture—the major public intellectuals of the immediate postwar period emerged from the bosom of the Islamic Republic itself and began to influence profoundly the course of its troubled and tumultuous history.

The evident parallel between Abdolkarim Soroush and Mohsen Makhmalbaf, one grounding the Iranian political culture deeper in an exclusively Islamist commitment as he seeks to liberate it, the other liberating it from even a verbal bondage to history and thus letting it flower in a fresh, surreal, and thus more promising visual universe, became definitive to the post-Khomeini circumstances of the nation at large. The binary was not false but sculptural to a full-bodied perception of the culture at large. The same correspondence could be seen between Soroush and other religious intellectuals (liberating the juridical Islamism of the reigning regime from an exclusively positivist jurisprudence toward a more hermeneutic liberalism) on one side, and their clerical nemesis in Qom (insisting on their custodial prerogative to guide the Muslim flock) on the other. A similarly disjoined dualism might be seen and suggested between the religious and secular intellectuals, or between the invariably pragmatic Rafsanjani and the rampant idealism of Mohammad Khatami—soon to emerge as a champion of a reformist movement.

Here, Karl Schmidt's definition of "the political" as the realm of the distinction "between friend and enemy" becomes increasingly significant in reading the modus operandi of the Islamic Republic—the positing of an *internal* enemy, on either side of the ideological divide, that makes the political possible. "The friend and enemy concepts are to be understood in their concrete and existential sense, not as metaphors or symbols," Schmidt insisted; "the concern here is neither with abstractions nor with normative ideals, but with inherent reality and the real possibility of such distinction."[17] Thus stripped of all its metaphysical sugarcoating, the political becomes impossible without the positing of an enemy, an emotive dissonance that makes the communal resonance possible.

By the time we reach that lower depth and common denominator of the political, the formative society (gesellschaft) has already mutated down to its tribal affiliations and communal gatherings (gemeinschaft). In the aftermath of 9/11, it is safe to suggest that positing "the Arab" or "the Muslim" as the enemy has collapsed the universal gesellschaft of humanity at large to the tribal gemeinschaft of "the West" seeing itself against "the Rest." The fences that now mark the U.S. border with Mexico are the visible signs of a similar tribalism that seeks to insulate the tribal formation of "American" from its darker and poorer neighbor, "the Immigrant." The enemy without has a reflection in the enemy within. What we are witnessing at this point in Iranian normative and moral history, soon after the exhaustion of Khomeini's charismatic terror holding it violently together, is the rapid mutation of the society at large, of the cosmopolis of anticolonial social modernity into tribal affiliations, in effect the Qomification of the entire nation. The dialectic of rapid mutation from society to communities, from gesellschaft to gemeinschaft, from Iran to Persia and all its racialized subsidiaries, mirrors, reflects, and exacerbates the more global mutation of the universal gesellschaft into communal gatherings of tribal affiliations—and thus the self-fulfilling banality of Samuel Huntington's thesis of "the clash of civilizations" (which amounts to clash of tribalisms), in effect corroborating a global mutation of humanity to the basest, lowest common denominator of their tribal fears: Huntington would be most at home in Qom.[18]

The phenomenon known in Iran as the Second of Khordad (which in the year 1376 on the Iranian calendar corresponds to Friday, May 23, 1997, when Mohammad Khatami was elected president) and outside Iran as the "reformist movement" did not begin with Khatami but in fact anticipated him all through the two terms of Rafsanjani's presidency. It came to a climax with the spectacular and unanticipated election of Mohammad Khatami as the fifth president of the Islamic Republic (in its seventh presidential election, with the two preceding presidents, Rafsanjani and Khamenei, each having served twice). Given the later defeat of the reformist movement, it is now difficult to imagine, but necessary to remember, the extraordinary joy of Iranians from all walks of life who embraced Khatami with an enthusiasm ordinarily reserved for rock and movie stars in Europe and the United States. It is hard to figure out what exactly was the extraordinary charismatic appeal of Khatami in the late 1990s. Perhaps it can be understood if one first looks at the symbolic and iconic aspects of the phenomenon.

Reza Shah was dubbed "the Father of the Nation" or "the Crowned Father" (*Pedar-e Tajdar*), the epical patriarch who made the nation possible. Dwarfed by that towering presump-

tion, his son, Muhammad Reza Shah, overcompensated by building the tallest dam over the Karun River, claiming the longest
history in the world for Iran, or trying to make it the most potent
political power in the region—the Japan of the Middle East, as he
used to say. In the Iranian Revolution of 1979, Iranians chose to
turn to their grandfather figure—Khomeini—and reject their
royal father figure. Once victorious, the grandfather, fearing his
own imminent demise, dispatched tens of thousands of his
grandchildren to premature death in the course of revolutionary
uprising, the war with Iraq, and the purging of oppositional
forces. The deaths of the shah and then Khomeini amounted to
the demise of both the father and the grandfather. The downfall
of the Iranian father figure was followed by the rise of two split
characters in its stead: Ali Khamenei and Hashemi Rafsanjani,
one the leader and the other the president. The visible problem
with these two would-be father figures was that one (Khamenei)
had no right hand, and the other (Rafsanjani) no proper "manly"
beard. (The right hand of Khamenei was paralyzed after an assassination attempt, and Rafsanjani is *kuseh*, as we say in Persian, or
bi-rish, meaning he lacks facial hair.) The right hand and the substantial beard being the iconic insignia of patriarchy from time
immemorial, the split characters of Khamenei and Rafsanjani cut
the patriarchal image into two useless halves (we should remember here that in the Iranian national epic *Shahnameh* the legendary King Jameshid was cut into half by a saw). The sawed-through,
split character of the father figure in Khamenei-Rafsanjani facilitated the next antipatriarchal move, when in the course of the
presidential election of 1997, the two candidates—Ali Akbar
Nateq Nuri and Mohammad Khatami—presented two very
different images. While Nateq Nuri had an uncanny similarity
to Khomeini—he looked almost identical to the grandfather—
Khatami had a soft, gentle, kind, almost feminine face. In the
presidential election of 1997, with 70 percent of the votes going
to Khatami, Iranians voted for an image closest to that of their
mothers. It is a marvelous piece of added confirmation of this
symbolic reading of contemporary Iranian history that the public's nickname for Khatami after the failure of the reformist
movement became "Fariba," which is a Persian feminine name

that also means "she who seduces and deceives" or "seductively promises and does not deliver"!

Even outside such fictive and epical insignia of how a culture might operate, the shaky legitimacy of the Islamic Republic faced its most serious domestic survival test with the advent of the Khatami phenomenon. With the so-called reform movement, the Islamic Republic entered a stage that would either kill or cure it. Khatami's landslide victory gave him a national mandate to deliver on his campaign promises: political liberalization, economic transparency, rule of law, limitation of abusive clerical rule, increasing civil liberties, greater participation for women, and allowing people to present alternative political visions of the republic in an open and democratic space. The conservative ruling elite, led by the unelected occupant of the office of the supreme leader, Ayatollah Khamenei, was now in complete disarray. The reformists also prevailed in the February 2000 parliamentary elections, when liberal legislators and political supporters of President Khatami won an overwhelming majority of the 290 seats in the sixth parliamentary elections, gaining control of the Majlis, which for almost two decades had been dominated by the clerical and lay architects of the Islamic Republic. Now two of the most powerful ruling organs of the Islamic Republic, both elected—the presidency and the parliament—were controlled by the more open-minded, progressive, and liberal wing of the Islamic Republic.[19]

The euphoria of Khatami's election notwithstanding, the repressive measures of the state were still very much in place. No opposition (other than the increasingly faint dissent of those doctrinally loyal to the Islamic Republic) was tolerated. In November 1998, just a year after President Khatami was elected, the revelation of the systematic murder of a number of leading secular opposition intellectuals, the so-called serial murders (*qatl-ha-ye zanjireh'i*), exposed the brutal savagery with which the custodians of the Islamic Republic dealt with the slightest opposition to their rule. A year later, in July 1999, prodemocracy students at Tehran University sparked a nationwide series of demonstrations after the reformist newspaper *Salam* was closed down by the government. These demonstrations were the first indication of a deep dissatisfaction with the Islamic Republic, which threatened the leadership far more than the so-called reformist movement did. Clashes with the security forces led to six days of rioting and the arrest of thousands of students. The thuggish brutality with which armed hooligans attacked the students and repressed their movement was reminiscent of the Islamist hijacking of the revolution in its early days.

The following year, on April 5–7, 2000, the Heinrich Böll Institute in Berlin invited a number of leading Iranian public intellectuals to participate in a conference discussing the future of democracy in their homeland. The Berlin Conference, as it was later dubbed, revealed the widespread malignancy in the politics of the Islamic Republic. As soon as the participants in the conference returned to Tehran, they were charged with antirevolutionary ideas and un-Islamic behavior, subjected to atrocious kangaroo courts, and imprisoned. In the same month, the judiciary branch of the Islamic Republic, following the adoption of a new press law, banned the publication of scores of reformist newspapers. It seemed that the beleaguered President Khatami could do nothing to oppose this. In June 2003, yet another violent and widespread student uprising, assailing the undemocratic practices of the clerical establishment, rocked the Iranian capital. It was brutally suppressed. In December of that year, another earthquake killed forty thousand people in southeast Iran; the ancient city of Bam was devastated. Once again, disaster gave the Islamic Republic's leaders an opportunity to play the role of a responsible government, enhance their legitimacy, and consolidate their power.

By the end of his first term, Khatami had managed to put a benevolent face on a government that ostensibly cared about the hopes and aspirations of the nation, but his administration had failed to deliver anything substantial. The unelected officials of the Islamic Republic still had the decisive role in determining the fate of the nation. The serial murders of secular intellectuals in 1998, the student uprising of 1999, and the Berlin Conference debacle in 2000—all happened on Khatami's watch, and he could do, or did, nothing about any of them. Nonetheless, in June 2001 Khatami was reelected for a second term, winning just under 77 percent of the vote. The clerical clique was now angry. The supreme leader (*Rahbar-e Ali Qadr*, literally, "His Noble Highness the Leader," as they call him officially) did not allow the inauguration of the newly elected president to proceed in August 2001 until the Majlis approved the new members of the Guardian Council, all handpicked to assure the clerical reign for perpetuity. The second term of President Khatami did not make much of a difference either. In June 2003, student activists again led tens of thousands of people in protests against the clerical establishment.

After the humiliating defeat of Hashemi Rafsanjani in the parliamentary election of February 2000, when he failed even to be elected a member of the parliament, he managed to get his political career back on track when he was appointed head of the powerful Expediency Council in 2002. By the second presidential term of Mohammad Khatami, it was evident that the clerical custodians of the Islamic Republic were thinking about its future after the death of Ali Khamenei. The ideological ferocity with which the very doctrine of *velayat-e faqih* ("the custodial power of the supreme jurist") had been argued and institutionalized had made it clear that if the rule of the ayatollahs was to survive, the office of *velayet-e faqih* had to be dismantled or substantially modified. They moved to strengthen the Expediency Council as the primary means for carrying out the political will of the clergy, safeguarding the Islamic Republic against Shi'i juridical hairsplitting, on a pattern that might facilitate a role for politically contentious clerics such as Ayatollah Montazeri or the younger Mohsen Kadivar; against the unpredictable institutions of the presidency and the parliament; and above all, against ideological, political, or institutional alternatives to the Islamic Republic—a real possibility: calls for putting the nature of the state to a national plebiscite under UN supervision was on the opposition's agenda just before President Bush invaded Iraq and (paradoxically) strengthened the hand of the clerical clique.

The internal dynamics of the Islamic Republic were of course strongly influenced by the geopolitics of the region. The hostility of the United States toward the Islamic Republic was evident throughout the periods of reconstruction and reform. By 1995,

two years before Khatami became the president, and as courageous journalists, students, oppositional young clerics, public intellectuals, artists, and even expatriate activists were struggling
for anything ranging from moderate reforms to radical changes
in the Islamic Republic, the United States imposed oil and trade
sanctions on Iran, accusing the Islamic Republic of sponsoring
terrorism and seeking nuclear arms. The hostility of the Islamic
Republic to the U.S.-initiated Israeli-Palestinian peace process
was an equally compelling factor in placing Iran and the United
States on a collision course. Moreover, as late as 1998, the Islamic
Republic remained wary of a possible plot against its territorial
integrity by the U.S.-Saudi-Pakistani-manufactured Taliban in
Afghanistan. In 1998, Iran amassed a major force on its border
with Afghanistan after the Taliban killed eight Iranian diplomats
and a journalist in Mazar-e Sharif.[20]

Successive U.S. administrations paid little attention to the internal dynamics of Iranian politics when formulating policy in
the region. In preparation for the March 2003 invasion of Iraq, in
his State of the Union address in January 2002, President Bush
designated Iran, Syria, and North Korea the "Axis of Evil." In the
tense post-9/11 environment, and while the United States was
still in the middle of its military invasion of Afghanistan (on one
side of Iran) and about to attack Iraq (on its other side), the designation of the Islamic Republic as a member of the "Axis of Evil"
amounted to an open declaration of war against Iran—and whatever success, or hope and aspiration for change, the reform
movement had managed to secure or institutionalize went up in
smoke. Once again the regime and the country were braced for a
fight for survival, and all reformist bets were off. The terror that
President Bush's "Axis of Evil" address created in Iran put courageous Iranians, who had actively opposed the criminal atrocities
of the Islamic Republic for decades, in a false light: they could be
accused of being allied with the imperial hubris of an empire now
plotting to invade their country. Because there had not been such
an open expression of U.S. hostility and such an explicit threat
for about two decades, dissident Iranians had been able actively
to oppose the medieval theocracy ruling over their destiny. With
one speech, President Bush managed to turn all of them into trai-
tors to their own country. One can argue that after the coup of

1953, the "Axis of Evil" speech was the second most damaging thing the United States has done against the cause of democracy in Iran.[21]

The failure of the reform movement in Iran went hand in hand with the increased involvement of the Islamic Republic in the national liberation movements in its region. Once it was trapped inside Iran and degenerated into an Islamic republic, the revolutionary energy that had been the cause of great hope and widespread aspirations for freedom in the region was now channeled into the business of exporting the regime's failures and its plots to clone itself into additional Islamic republics. This was being done through the clandestine activities of the Supreme Council for Islamic Revolution in Iraq (SCIRI), Hezbollah in Lebanon, and Hamas in Palestine, and by provoking unrest in other countries from the Persian Gulf states to Yemen, then in the throes of an antigovernmental rebellion. The geopolitics of the region facilitated this involvement. Soon after the Israeli invasion of Lebanon in June 1982, the Islamic Republic was instrumental in the creation of the Lebanese Hezbollah. Meanwhile, the emergence of the First Palestinian Intifada in 1987, and then the Second (al-Aqsa) Intifada in 2000, resulted in Hamas assuming a leading role in the Palestinian national liberation movement, a movement in which the Islamic Republic became invested. The Islamic Republic played an equally significant role in supporting SCIRI and its leader, Ayatollah Muhammad Baqer Hakim (1939–2003), who spent more than two decades (preparing his Badr Battalion) in exile in Iran and was subsequently assassinated on August 29, 2003, upon his return from exile to Iraq. Such involvements of the Islamic Republic came into obvious and direct conflict with U.S. imperial interests, while the ruling clergy sought externally to legitimize its internally delegitimized reign of fear and intimidation by appearing to side with legitimate national liberation movements.

Paradoxically, with the defeat of the reform movement inside Iran, the only hope of salvation for the future of Iran as a free nation-state seems to come from the very national liberation movements the clerical rulers have consistently sought to Islamize. The fundamental problem of an exclusionary Islamism in Iran is predicated on the fact that the overwhelming majority of Iranians (up to 90 percent) are Shi'is (with their usual minority complex), while in Iraq and Lebanon the Shi'is comprise smaller majorities (not more than 60 percent in Iraq or 50 percent in Lebanon). The same is true about Hamas as an Islamist component of the Palestinian national liberation movement. Therefore, in Iraq, Lebanon, and Palestine, Muslims in general and Shi'is in particular will have to be part of a larger, pluralistic and cosmopolitan, political movement if they are to have a fair share of power and realize their political aspirations. Should that historic experiment with pluralism take place in Iraq, Lebanon, and Palestine (possibilities that the U.S. invasion and occupation of Iraq, the continued Israeli occupation of Palestine, and the receding Syrian occupation of Lebanon have hitherto thwarted), these movements can indeed have a catalytic effect on the Islamic Republic, and side with oppositional forces inside Iran. Then, instead of the Islamic Republic exporting its medieval theocracy to these countries and cloning itself, these movements could export their pluralist political disposition to Iran and save it from its current stalemate. In this respect, the future success of Shi'i political organizations in Iraq (when and if the U.S. occupation ends), of Hezbollah in Lebanon (now that the Syrians have left), and of Hamas in Palestine under Mahmoud Abbas's leadership (should the Israelis finally comply with countless UN resolutions, withdraw from their illegal occupation of Palestine, and pull back to their 1967 borders), could indeed transform Iran, strengthen the hands of those offering alternative visions of the republic, and, in a pluralist experiment with democracy, re-create and sustain the anticolonial cosmopolitanism definitive to the political culture of the region.[22]

Precisely when Khatami's reform movement and his notion of a "dialogue among civilizations" promised a more cosmopolitan reading of Iranian political culture (between 1997 and 2005), the most reactionary tribalism of global proportions—in the shape of Samuel Huntington's thesis of "the clash of civilizations," and Francis Fukuyama's idea of "the end of history" and a singular victory of "Western liberal democracies"—became the reigning ideology of the neocons in the United States. The reformist movement identified with Mohammad Khatami was much more open-minded and tolerant than the imperial tribalism that Samuel Huntington and Francis Fukuyama narrated for the U.S. neocons. While Khatami's reform movement was ultimately defeated by the clerical counterparts of the U.S. neocons in Qom, American neoconservative tribalism went global and began to redraw the moral map of the region in pathetically tribal terms— necessitating an Islamic republic in the neighborhood of a Jewish state and a Hindu fundamentalism, all of them welcoming the advent of a Christian empire.

The problem with Fukuyama's notion of history, now definitive to the millenarian triumphalism of the Bush administration, is obvious: the singularity of a history that remains definitive to a teleological narrative that posits humanity at large as a Hegelian preface to what Western Europe and North America look like today—a choo-choo-train theory of a world history that begins somewhere in the Oriental haze of the past, with India, China, Egypt, and Persia as its archaeological way stations; gains momentum in Greece; hurtles thunderously foward in Rome; and then comes to full *geistlich* glory in Germany for Hegel, as it does in the bureaucratic banality of Washington, D.C., for Fukuyama.

While Fukuyama tried to dance his argument around "Islam,"[23] for Huntington, "Islam" remained "the enemy," the exception that proved the rule. Meanwhile, far beyond the intellectual horizons of these two imperial functionaries, the centrality of the notion of "the enemy"—on the continuum of "friend-and-enemy"—in making the very conceptual category of "the political" possible, the way that it was first theorized by Karl Schmidt, loses its potent presence in the distinguished Italian political philosopher Giorgio Agamben's theorization of the "state of exception" and becomes subsumed under the dialectic that Agamben posits between life and law—in terms dialectically entirely domestic to "Western" legal and political theories. "The juridical system of the West," Agamben proposes, "appears as a double structure, formed by two heterogeneous yet coordinated elements; one that is normative and juridical in the strict sense (which we can for convenience inscribe under the rubric *potestas*) and one that is anomic and metajuridical (which we can call by the name *auctoritas*)."[24]

What Agamben describes in his frightfully insightful argument in *State of Exception* (2005), written in the immediate aftermath of the events of 9/11, is the blind spot of "Western" political thought in which a state of siege casts a definitive shadow on the state of normalcy, an exception that in fact becomes the rule, and thus exposes the hidden barbarity at the heart of "Western" liberal democracies. This phenomenon was detected and clearly identified long before Agamben by Theodor Adorno and Max Horkheimer in their *Dialectic of Enlightenment*, in which they trace the horrors of the German concentrations camps and the Jewish Holocaust to the very doorsteps of European Enlightenment modernity.[25] What Agamben further unearths is the way the state of exception reveals the thin layer of civility (a mere fiction) that holds liberal democracies together:

> As long as the two elements [the normative *potestas* and the anomic *auctoritas*] remain correlated yet conceptually, temporally, and subjectively distinct ... their dialectic— though founded on a fiction—can nevertheless function in some way. But when they tend to coincide in a single person [such as President George W. Bush], when the state of exception, in which they are bound and blurred together, becomes the rule, then the juridical-political system transforms itself into a killing machine.[26]

Verifying Agamben's frightful insights, it is imperative to note that Alan Dershowitz's and Michael Ignatieff's ideas and theories of how to torture people (Arabs and Muslims to be precise) emerged not despite but in fact through "Western" legal theories.[27] In the most terrifying moments of American imperial expansionism, precisely when the revelation of U.S. torture chambers in Abu Ghraib (Iraq), Bagram Air Base (Afghanistan), Guantánamo Bay (Cuba), and a labyrinth of subterranean torture halls in Europe had created a horror around the world, criminal minds like Dershowitz and Ignatieff theorized the specific legality and mechanics of torturing people straight from the very heart of "Western liberal democracies"—a point made clearly and with ingenious precision by Agamben.

* * *

Throughout the same post-Khomeini period, the incorporation of the Islamic Republic into the global geopolitics of Islamism was (by serendipity) matched and mixed with the extraordinary rise and worldwide reception of Iranian cinema. When in May 1997 Abbas Kiarostami joined Shohei Imamura in receiving the prestigious Palme d'Or at the Cannes Film Festival, the effervescent creativity of Iranian cinema was a matter for global celebration. While the custodians of the Islamic Republic sought to sustain their own illegitimate reign at home by allying themselves with legitimate national liberation movements abroad, Iranian filmmakers were the harbingers of a radically different vision of their homeland, their region, and the wider world that embraced both. One particular example shows the significance of this phenomenon. During the 1996 Jerusalem Film Festival, a few of Mohsen Makhmalbaf's films were selected for a special screening. A number of leading Arab and Muslim filmmakers had boycotted the Jerusalem Film Festival in response to an incident in which pictures of pigs were placed on Muslim Palestinian houses in Palestine. Mir Salim, at the time the Iranian minister of culture and Islamic guidance, put official pressure on Mohsen Makhmalbaf to withdraw his films from the Jerusalem Film Festival. In an article that he published in a Tehran daily, Makhmalbaf said he would do no such thing—first because this was legally not his decision but the decision of his French distributor, and second, because "if the Israeli people want to watch my films, I am very pleased and have absolutely no objection, and if the Israeli government wants to abuse my cinema, they are not any different from the Islamic Republic."

For over a quarter of a century since the tumultuous rise of the Islamic Revolution, Iranian cinema has spread around the world, serving as evidence of a rich and diversified culture, neither daunted by the calamities of a medieval theocracy masquerading as a revolutionary regime and an Islamic republic nor enamored of the Christian empire and its arrogance. When, during the New York Film Festival in 1999, Abbas Kiarostami was denied a visa to enter the United States (on the grounds that he might be a terrorist), and when three other prominent Iranian filmmakers—Jafar Panahi, Mohsen Makhmalbaf, and his wife, Marziyeh Meshkini—were subjected to the systematic indignities one encounters in attempting to enter the United States on an Iranian passport, the official harassment of Iranian filmmakers by the U.S. authorities was not very different from what they experienced at the hands of an Islamic republic. Despite such limitations and harassment both at home and abroad, Iranian filmmakers managed to keep the best aspirations of their nation (and with it the world) alive. As two opposing but ultimately identical forms of militant mendacity, the Islamic Republic and the Christian empire were in fact the least exposed to Iranian cinema—in one, Iranian filmmakers were subjected to systematic harassment and blinding censorship; and in the other, they were denied entry and exposure.[28]

For the rest of the world, Iranian cinema became a harbinger of hope—an antidote, a medicinal cure made of the same poison that had not killed but invigorated it. With its own roots going all the way back to the origin of cinema late in the nineteenth century, Iranian cinema became, in the immediate aftermath of the Islamic Revolution, the solitary beneficiary of all other art forms that had, since early in the nineteenth century, profoundly influenced and shaped Iranian cultural modernity. The result was then tested by a gut-wrenching revolution and a devastating war, in which hundreds of thousands of innocent youths perished, while the nation was turned upside down and seared in the flames of its own revolution. National cinemas, like all other national art forms, often emerge from the heart of national traumas. At the commencement of the Iranian Revolution of 1979, New Persian poetry declined, for it lost the collectivity of its creative effervescence. The legendary Ten Nights of poetry reading at the Goethe Institute in October 1977 that signaled the revolutionary uprising in Iran was not the beginning but the end of the public relevance of Persian poetry. Thus also ended Persian fiction, despite the fact that most of the great poets and novelists of Iran in the latter part of the twentieth century were still around when the revolution took place. A decade into the 1979 revolution, all forms of cultural expression but cinema had lost their collective demeanor, social significance, and public domain. It was as if these poets and writers, caught up in a cultural relay race, had passed the baton to a younger, more creatively potent and poised running mate, and then rested at the sidelines. As the Iranian Revolution was systematically corrupted and gradually degenerated into a malignant theocracy, in the shadow of its cruel banality grew the green pastures of its exact opposite: the bitter anger and boiling banality of one were channeled and churned over into the flowering of colorful blossoms in a vast, beautiful, and worldly cinema. Iranian cinema became worldly both by virtue of apologizing to the world for having given it a tyrannous theocracy, and by way of making up for that horror with hope.[29]

An equally positive and hopeful sign became evident for both Iran and the region when in October 2003 Shirin Ebadi became the first Iranian recipient of the Nobel Peace Prize. Ebadi represented generations of Iranians fighting for their inalienable rights against daunting odds. As a civil rights and human rights activist, she represented the aspirations of people in a much wider domain of denial and denigration. As a lawyer, she highlighted the absence of due process of law in the countries that were now particularly proud to celebrate her prize. As a woman, she was a symbol of resistance to generations of systematic abuse and gender apartheid in her own homeland and in the region at large. And finally, as a Muslim, she could now bear witness to the far wider spectrum of terror and tyranny perpetrated by a homegrown patriarchy as well as by imported cultural imperialism. Against the background of a religious tradition in which endemic gender apartheid is definitive to the very letter of its medieval laws, Muslim women have for generations fought against a jurisprudence of misogyny and patriarchy. Ebadi represented not just other heroic Iranian women who had stood up to both domestic and foreign tyranny but also those who continued to identify and resist forces that were responsible for such continuing calamities the world over.[30]

As the presidency of Mohammad Khatami came to an end (and a decisive and ominous turning point became evident in the fate of the reform movement in Iran), aspects of Iranian cultural and social modernity had now opened the perils and promises of Iranian society to a much wider spectrum of regional and global concerns. As best represented in Iranian cinema and Shirin Ebadi's social activism, more than two centuries of anticolonial

modernity, in both social and cultural terms, had made it impossible for the political elite of the Islamic Republic, or its imperial
nemesis, to silence the voices and blind the visions of alternative
dreams of the nation. The social activism of an Iranian woman
and the artistic effervescence of a national art form spoke loudly
of the textured cosmopolitanism at the creative roots of a society
that no Islamic republic could incarcerate in its feudal jurisprudence, and no imperial hubris could denigrate and deny with its
wanton disregard for people and their pride of place.

The regional and global implications of Iranian domestic politics
were of course not limited to attempts to clone the Islamic Republic in Iraq, Lebanon, and Palestine; nor were the global celebration of Iranian cinema and the universal attention to the plight
of civil and human rights in Iran the only indices of a thematic
and territorial expansion of the Iranian national sphere of presence and influence. But U.S. imperial maneuvers in the region
were equally palpable. By August 1990, when Saddam Hussein
(reinvented, encouraged, and heavily armed by the Reagan administration) invaded Kuwait, Iranian domestic politics had already become integral to Iran's position in regional and global
contexts. The Islamic Republic condemned the Iraqi invasion of
Kuwait but refused to cooperate with or even endorse the U.S.-
led invasion of Iraq. Events on the western borders of Iran were
matched by equally troubling developments on its eastern borders. Throughout the 1980s, as the Iran-Iraq War was raging, the
Soviet occupation of Afghanistan and the U.S.-Saudi-Pakistani
creation of the Taliban kept the flames of war ablaze in that central Asian domain. Soon after the Taliban succeeded in forcing
the Soviets out and establishing a theocracy even worse than the
one in Iran, the border between Iran and Afghanistan became the
site of increasing tension. Soon, with the massive U.S. military
presence on three of its four sides (in Iraq, Afghanistan, and the
Persian Gulf), plus the paramount U.S. presence in Saudi Arabia,
Pakistan, and Israel, Iran and the United States were set on a collision course.

The second term of Mohammad Khatami's presidency
(2001–4) coincided with the most cataclysmic events in the history

of the region, with the United States and its regional allies assuming an increasingly militant posture. Soon after Khatami began his second term and George W. Bush began his first, 9/11 assumed an entirely iconic significance in the U.S. imperial calendar. For precisely that reason it is imperative to turn the clock back and get some distance from the overtly fetishized 9/11, and to understand the history of U.S. involvement in the region over the past two decades. This most recent phase of history originated in the Reagan administration (1981–89), and before that in the 444 relentless days and nights during the Carter administration (1977–81) when ABC News anchorman Ted Koppel reminded the bruised American militarists how impotent and incompetent they were. Indeed, one has to go back to the catastrophic rescue mission of President Carter that ended (on April 24, 1980) in tragic humiliation in the middle of a remote Iranian desert, where U.S. helicopters and aircraft collided during the operation. From 1977 to 1981, President Carter put a stamp of official approval—with his human rights policies and military incompetence alike—on the enduring phenomenon known as the "Vietnam Syndrome."

President Carter left office stigmatized as the man "who lost Iran," and who could only stand by impotently as U.S. diplomats and their nation were publicly humiliated. The rising tide of U.S. imperial arrogance began on the very first day of Ronald Reagan's presidency, on the very day of his inauguration, as the U.S. hostages in Iran, having served as a means for radically Islamizing a multifaceted national liberation movement, were finally released. During the two Reagan administrations the United States finally emerged from its Vietnam Syndrome and began flexing its military muscles around the globe.[31] The two monsters that President Reagan created, Saddam Hussein and Osama bin Laden, soon came back to haunt the interim presidency of George H. W. Bush (1989–93) and the Democratic presidency of President Bill Clinton (1993–2001), paving the way for the full-fledged globalization of the U.S. empire during George W. Bush's presidency (2001–present). Toward the end of Khatami's presidency and the commencement of George W. Bush's second term, the politics of the region were largely determined by an Islamic republic, a Jewish state, and a Christian empire—with a persistently brewing Hindu fundamentalism always on the horizon. One form of patrimonial tribalism was thus cast against another. At the very same time, the domestic politics of all these religiously attenuated nation-states was almost entirely at the mercy of an even more ghostly apparition called "al Qaeda" and its shadowy reflection called "the War on Terror."

As Iranian cinema was universalizing expansive Iranian cosmo-politanism, the U.S. empire was globalizing American provincial-ism, rampant and evident in the ideas and pronouncements of its leading ideologues—Francis Fukuyama and Samuel Huntington, one telling the world that history had ended and "the West" had won (and "the Rest" had lost) the game, the other warning that still one more victory over "Islam" was necessary.

As in the aftermath of 9/11 the superior wisdom of the pre-eminent Italian philosopher Giorgio Agamben saw through the combined banality of Huntington and Fukuyama and detected precisely the opposite of their cumulative mendacity and nar-rowed in on "the state of exception" that effectively holds and destroys the "Western liberal democracies" at one and the same time, the world at large was at the mercy of his darkest insight: "What the 'ark' of power contains at its center is the state of ex-ception—but this is essentially an empty space, in which a human action with no relation to law stands before a norm with no rela-tion to life."[32] What Agamben has revealed is less a blind spot of European Enlightenment political philosophy, much less a warn-ing against the imperceptible mutation of liberal democracies into totalitarian states, and far more a paradox at the heart of the jurisprudence of liberal democracies—not just its Achilles' heel, but in fact its traumatic repression. How could that state of ex-ception be the rule for a liberal democracy, let alone the rhetoric of an overtly Christian empire?

What even the great Agamben has left untheorized, having already predicated his theory of the state of exception on Karl Schmidt's notion of "the enemy," is the prospect of "the enemy" itself, or the threat of the enemy, to be more exact, the ghostly ap-parition that prompts and summons the "state of exception"—the bugbear of Osama bin Laden having always been hidden at the heart of "Western liberal democracies." The state of exception is predicated not just on the notion of "the enemy" but far more insidiously on "the threat of the enemy," a political fact as pertinent to the neoconservative reign of "the state of exception" in the United States as to the reign of the clerical cliques in Iran. Feeding on each other's real and fabricated fears, the United States and Iran, ruled by two identical sets of banalities, have cast their respective fears of their enemy without on the face of their opponents within, or conversely, the exorcism of the demon slumbering within on the lurking specter without—for here the state of exception proves to be the rule.

7
The End of Islamic Ideology

Let me begin this last chapter with what is reported to be an actual radio conversation released by the U.S. chief of naval operations:

> —Please divert your course fifteen degrees to the north to avoid a collision.
> —Recommend you divert *your* course fifteen degrees to south to avoid a collision.
> —This is the captain of a U.S. Navy ship. I say again, divert *your* course.
> —No. I say again, you divert *your* course.
> —THIS IS THE AIRCRAFT CARRIER *ENTERPRISE.* THIS IS A LARGE WARSHIP OF THE U.S. NAVY. DIVERT YOUR COURSE NOW!
> —This is a lighthouse. Your call.

There are certain things that power, no matter how super, cannot move. Immobile lighthouses, solid and serene, suggest a modest lesson in humility that commanders of aircraft carriers, and commanders in chief of empires, capable of projecting monumental destructive force, may or may not wish to learn—always at their own peril. This old navy joke resurfaced on the Internet just around December 2005, more than two years into the carnage that the United States had unleashed in Iraq, and its rosy plans to end states, change regimes, promote democracies, and secure lucrative oil deals all went awry. It is said that the United States is the most powerful country on the face of the earth. Despite its power to blow our planet to kingdom come, one must in all modesty question the factual validity of any phrase like that. The entire U.S. military, estimates suggest, comprises only one million people (there are two million prison inmates in the United States, of whom 50 percent are African Americans, whereas they are only 12.3 percent of the population). Of this force, more than 250,000 soldiers were reportedly deployed in the course of the second Gulf War, which pretty much tied up the entire global capability of the U.S. military. Despite the presence of substantial U.S. forces in South Korea, North Korea flaunted its alleged capability to manufacture (or continue to manufacture) nuclear warheads, and there was little that President Bush could do, since a credible military response would have required disengaging from Iraq and Afghanistan first.

All evidence suggests that this notion of "al Qaeda" that the United States is projecting has scarcely anything to do with the actual organization operative somewhere in a proverbial Afghan cave. In reality, al Qaeda seems to be more like a blueprint of a global guerrilla operation that gives the Pentagon a pretext to reconfigure its military forces to engage in a U.S. version of a "counterterrorist" guerrilla operation. Al Qaeda is presented by the United States as a shadowy organization that is omnipotent, omniscient, and omnipresent, one that can strike anywhere, anytime, and with deadly and unpredictable consequences. This also describes how the United States wishes to project its own military power around the globe. The United States may indeed have the military power and political wherewithal to do so, but the world that that deadly power ultimately faces is really a lighthouse that cannot be moved or shoved around at will. Yet the United States persists in believing that it can not only advance its military and political objectives against other nations and their collective will to resist imperial tyranny but also ignore the environmental catastrophe that now threatens the planet. The United States may foolishly refuse to sign the Kyoto agreement, for to do so might derail its plans for global economic domination. But when the ozone thins even more, and the greenhouse effect accelerates, and the polar ice caps begin to melt even faster, there isn't any bunker in Camp David that can hold 265 million Americans and their SUVs. There may be enough room in it to offer safe haven to the entire regiment of neocons, but alas they will have no world left to rule. The Project for the New American Century will be rendered pointless if we come to the *real* "end of history."[1]

Resisting the onslaught of the misbegotten U.S. empire, its military might and faltering hegemony alike, are tall and graceful lighthouses of the collective will of people around the globe insisting on their pride of place, the dignity of their communal gathering to oppose and end tyranny in terms conducive to a future that is rooted in their own unending and unfolding history. In Iran as indeed in much of the rest of the world, that history speaks a cosmopolitan language cultivated over millennia and conjugated in an anticolonial modernity at once progressive and liberating, syncretic and urbane. If the success of the Islamic Revolution in Iran amounted to the exhaustion and end of the Islamic ideology and as such occasioned the momentary triumph of a parochial clericalism over an urbane cosmopolitanism—an emancipatory urbanity earned by lifetimes of struggle the world over against domestic tyranny and foreign domination alike and thus made possible by visions and vistas informed from the four corners of the country and every continent of the globe—neither the means nor the measures of that cosmogonic dream of emancipation have lost their grip on the nation (or the world). The key task is to sift through the rubble of defeat and look for the cornerstones of liberation.

What at the threshold of the twenty-first century both Hashemi Rafsanjani and Mohammad Khatami (along with the reform movement he represented) left behind and completely ignored, namely a massive impoverished urban and rural underclass, came back to haunt them both (and with them the established leadership of the Islamic Republic itself) during the parliamentary election of February 2004 and even more drastically in the course of the presidential election of June 2005. Mahmoud Ahmadinejad, a radical conservative who appealed directly to the poor and the disenfranchised, won a landslide victory that sent a tsunami shock, as the expression then went in Iran, through the spine of the reform movement. He received 63 percent of the vote and was elected president. The crisis of Iranian political culture had now come full circle: the urban poor turned to a populist Islamism to dislodge the middle class and derail its program to make Iran a player in the globalized neoliberal economy. Colonial modernity, the enduring paradox of Iranian political culture, had now entered a planetary phase, where a global (war on) terrorism has radically changed the terms of engagement in domestic and regional political conflicts. That Mahmoud Ahmadinejad, the newly elected populist president, would soon plunge Iran even deeper into the throes of that very neoliberal economy amounts to precisely the very same paradox that has at once moved and paralyzed Iranian political economy.

The ironic result of the failure of reform is that those who once hoped to see it prevail now must look up to the potentially emancipatory aspects of the national liberation movements that the clerical leaders of the Islamic Republic have sought to Islamize. The clerical leaders of the Islamic Republic, however, seem to have forgotten (if they ever really understood) that the central paradox of Shi'ism as a state ideology—that it is legitimate only to the extent that it is in opposition, and that it loses its legitimacy the instant it assumes power—is finally catching up with the Islamic Republic.

The *Islamic Republic* is a categorical contradiction in terms— it is neither a *republic* nor *Islamic*. It is not a republic because it is a theocracy; it is not Islamic because Islam (Shi'ism in particular) cannot be in power without instantly discrediting itself. From its very earliest manifestation, Islam emerged as a religion of protest, and in its long and tumultuous history, both political and doctrinal, it has never lost that initial defining moment of its political potency.[2] The dialectical paradox that has remained textual to the Qur'anic revelation—its Meccan chapters charismatic and revolutionary, its Medinan verses somber and institution building—has never abandoned the long and arduous Islamic history. In these terms, Shi'ism is the quintessence of Islam as a religion of protest and can only remain valid and legitimate as long as it posits itself as a revolutionary project. The instant that Islam (Shi'ism) becomes a dominant (state) ideology it contradicts itself. This paradox is definitive to Islamic political and doctrinal history. The Islamic Republic, as a result, and ipso facto, has placed Islam in a position of tyranny, which in turn discredits and dismantles Islam itself—in the most basic tenets of its doctrinal principles. From the Umayyads (661–750) to the Abbasids (750–1258) down to all other major and minor Islamic empires and dynasties, there has never been an Islamic form of government that has not been radically challenged and opposed in precisely Islamic terms. As soon as a dynasty has come to power in Islamic terms of legitimacy, a revolutionary movement has arisen to challenge it in precisely Islamic terms. This paradox is now the central dilemma of the Islamic Republic, in which it is trapped and from which it has no escape, except dismantling itself. A *regional* integration of the most progressive forces in both the reformist and the conservative camps in Iranian politics is the only way it can at once sustain its domestic legitimacy and pose a highly effective politics of resistance to the predatory demands of globalized capitalism and the empire it has engendered. But it cannot do so without radically revising its very doctrinal basis—and thus the self-defeating paradox that at once animates and contradicts it.

A radical reformulation of "Islam," now incarcerated within the clerically anchored "Islamic Republic," effectively amounts to (1) recognizing its own discursive polyvocality—its jurisprudence historically checked and balanced by its philosophy and mysticism; and (2) allowing the cosmopolitan context of its contemporary anticolonial modernity to work the dialectic of its polyvocality out—its Islamism placing itself next to the nationalism and socialism that have historically checked and balanced it.[3] Among the myriad consequences of such an emancipatory reimagining of Islam in its modern and medieval history is the effective abandoning of the faulty Eurocentricity of a singular modernity, by which the rest of humanity must abide. In its contemporary context, this full-bodied version of Islam will posits the terms of an anticolonial modernity that is worldly in its roots and cosmopolitan in its consequences.

The nationwide loss of the reformists during the parliamentary election of February 2004 may be considered the ultimate sign of the collapse of the movement and the resurgence of radical Islamists.[4] During this parliamentary election, conservative Islamists gained almost complete control of the parliament, while thousands of reformist candidates were disqualified by the staunchly conservative Guardian Council. The antireformist, conservative, and combative factions of the Islamic Republic were now in complete control of all the major organs of the state—all belligerent in their defiant theocracy, which is only strengthened by the overwhelming U.S. military presence in the region.

A similar tendency was all but evident in the presidential election of June 2005, when again the Guardian Council disqualified hundreds of reformist candidates from running for office, and recognized only eight candidates—four conservatives (Mohsen Reza'i, Ali Ardeshir Larijani, Mohammad Baqer Qalibaf, and Mahmoud Ahmadinejad), three reformists (Mostafa Mo'in, Mehdi Karrubi, and Mohsen Mehr Alizadeh), and a key figure in the ruling clerical elite, the pragmatic Ali Akbar Hashemi Rafsanjani. Days before the election, Mohsen Reza'i, a former commander of the Pasdaran (the Islamic Militia) stepped aside and left the competition to his rivals. On election day, on Khordad 27, 1384 (June 17, 2005), many reformist candidates, particularly Mehdi Karrubi, the former speaker of the parliament, cried foul. He accused military personnel, the Guardian Council, Iranian television, and even Supreme Leader Ayatollah Khamenei's son of interfering in the election process.

Karrubi wrote a scathing public letter to Khamenei, objecting to the abuse of the democratic process, resigning from his official posts, and promising that he would soon establish and run an independent political party. Khamenei rebuked Karrubi in an equally public letter but promised to make sure that the electoral process would be fair and votes would be counted accurately. Karrubi expressed his anger and frustration because he and his supporters believed that he had in fact come in second (with about 19 percent of the vote) after Rafsanjani (with about 20 percent). The surprise of this round of the election was the unanticipated success of the staunchly conservative mayor of Tehran, a politically obscure former Islamic Militia leader named Mahmoud Ahmadinejad. He topped Mehdi Karrubi and was officially announced as second to Rafsanjani.

Of 47 million eligible voters, close to 29 million people voted in the first round, in which Rafsanjani received upwards of six million votes (6,179,653), while Ahmadinejad (5,710,354) and Kar-rubi (5,066,316) received more than five million votes each. The other candidates received the following number of votes: Mo-hammad Baqer Qalibaf, four million; Mostafa Mo'in, three mil-lion; Ali Ardeshir Larijani and Mohsen Mehr Alizadeh, one million each. Rafsanjani and Ahmadinejad went into a second round in the election.[5]

Above the internecine bickering of the presidential candi-dates, and beyond the red-herring question of whether or not the electoral participation was a testament to the legitimacy of the Islamic Republic, a far more crucial fact was evident in this round of the presidential election. Participation in this election meant nothing for the legitimacy or illegitimacy of the Islamic Republic. Some 65 million people are trapped inside their own country and in the claws of a clerically controlled medieval theocracy. Al-though it is easy for expatriates to issue revolutionary communi-qués from Los Angeles, Washington, D.C., and Paris, telling the people to rise up against their rulers and establish a democratic republic—with open neoliberal arms extended toward the IMF and the World Bank for the expatriate bourgeoisie to be able to spend their summer holidays at the Caspian Sea—it is far more difficult to secure a modicum of decency in the material and moral life of a nation.

The result of the first round of the presidential election in June 2005 meant something far simpler, far more elementary. Most of the calls to boycott the election came from opposition forces outside the country.[6] The problem with most such calls was that they represented appeals from those with a variety of ideological positions—the Mujahedin, the monarchists, the re-formists, remnants of the secular left outside Iran. But each of these factions was, as the saying goes, barking up the wrong tree. Of the 47 million eligible voters, close to 29 million voted in the first round, and the least successful candidates were the most ideologically committed: Mostafa Mo'in, the leading reformist candidate endorsed by President Khatami himself, on one side, and Ali Larijani, the detested former head of Iranian national television, on the other. These two candidates stood for the two opposite poles of the ideological spectrum—the reformists and the conservatives. The voters rejected them both. For this was the season of migration to the southern side of all absolutist convictions, toward the end of (Islamic, and all other) ideologies.

The two candidates who received the most votes represented no absolutist ideologies, for they stood for the most basic and crudest cases of class division in the country: the middle-class, upwardly mobile, Yuppie International, and Eurocentric voters opted for Ali Akbar Hashemi Rafsanjani, while the poor, the disenfranchised, those heavily dependent on state social subsidies, and the religiously more pious voted for Mahmoud Ahmadinejad. The question of cheating on behalf of Ahmadinejad was quite beside the point. He was the handpicked candidate of the Pasdaran, the Basijis, the Hezbollah (the three heavily militarized layers of Islamic *Sturmtruppen*), and their families—the poorest Iranians, the people most adversely affected by the postwar economic boom that had been engineered by Rafsanjani. If an abusively powerful clerical class and its militant vigilantes were rooting for and blatantly bribing or intimidating people to vote for Ahmadinejad, it does not mean that in his populist demeanor and socialist rhetorics he did not appeal to the most disenfranchised and impoverished classes of people.

Also on the side of Ali Akbar Hashemi Rafsanjani was an array of prominent Iranian filmmakers, artists, novelists, public intellectuals, and prominent reformists—among them the globally celebrated filmmaker Abbas Kiarostami. Just a few days before the second round of the election, Kiarostami wrote a short open letter to Ahmadinejad in which he endorsed Rafsanjani. Now that their favored candidate, Mostafa Mo'in, had failed to gain enough votes to compete with Rafsanjani, the reformists (and with them the secular intelligentsia) had opted to endorse the old and wily pragmatist, for fear of what the staunchly conservative Ahmadinejad would be up to if he was elected.[7]

Breaking his usual habit of staying away from overtly political postures, Kiarostami told Ahmadinejad that although he loved him most because he reminded him of the idealism of the 1979 revolution, he was going to vote for Rafsanjani, though he did not like him half as much as he liked Ahmadinejad. Then, and here was the rub, in a delicate combination of endearment and condescension, Kiarostami told Ahmadinejad that the presidential hopeful was a *"vasleh-ye najur"* ("an awkward patch"—an obvious and demeaning reference to the blacksmith's son's modest manner of dressing) upon the garment of contemporary politics, which in Kiarostami's judgment was devoid of ideals and corrupted by political games that Ahmadinejad did not know how to play. He is too simpleminded and too fundamentalist (*usulgara*) to understand such things.

The theme of the open letter was that Kiarostami believed the time of idealism of the early revolutionary period was over and that people needed a seasoned politician such as Rafsanjani—a pragmatist who would know how to deal with the dirty world of politics. Was it fair and accurate for Kiarostami to say that Iranians lived in a world in which ideals had been replaced by pragmatism? Was this the way to read the depressing saga of the Iranian Revolution and how it degenerated into its predicament in the early twenty-first century? No doubt Rafsanjani was a wily pragmatist. That people attracted to Mahmoud Ahmadinejad were by and large poor and disenfranchised was equally evident. But was Kiarostami's article a valid assessment of where we are in history?[8] Certainly the age of (Islamic) ideology is over; but is this also the end of idealism, of hope, aspirations, struggle?

One should not look for the origin of Kiarostami's pessimism in the Khayyamesque traits of his cinema. There is something far more mundane and far less sublime at work here. Abbas Kiarostami's statement about Mahmoud Ahmadinejad more than anything else reveals the depth of a moral malady at the heart of a class division that separates those Iranians who voted for Ahmadinejad from those who did not. This class division is now definitive to Iranian political culture. From his physical demeanor to his manner of clothing, from the rhetoric of his vacuous political speeches to the absolutism of his archaic convictions, from the simplicity of his fanaticism to the grandiosity of the zealot impatience lurking under his gaze, Ahmadinejad screams a bit too loudly the poverty of the underclass he represents, the religious resonance of his intolerant politics—a rough, coarse, jagged, and toothed disposition that reveals too much of the impoverished underbelly of the Iranian whitewashed bourgeoisie. He is, to that class, an international embarrassment—he is short, stocky, and unpresidential, and looks far too militant. He looks brutish and fanatical in an age of neoliberal aesthetics and soft-spoken banalities. He is Tom Doniphan (John Wayne) of John Ford's *The Man Who Shot Liberty Valence*. He may have been wild and attractive in the revolutionary heyday of conquering Monument Valley; but this was the reason that Kiarostami wished for a Ransom Stoddard (James Stewart) but would settle for Ali Akbar Hashemi Rafsanjani. Ahmadinejad was Ethan Edwards (John Wayne) of Ford's *The Searchers*. He may have looked fine and dandy fighting Indians in the Iranian Wild West of the revolutionary uprising. But Debbie Edwards (Natalie Wood)—the success of the revolution—delivered, he had no seat at Mrs. Jorgensen's table and must turn around from her doorstep and walk away from Kiarostami's (Ford's) camera—he and all his outdated vices and virtues.

Kiarostami's open letter to Ahmadinejad—the condescending tone and his open endorsement of the wiliest and most pestiferous political hack in the manufacturing and salvaging of the Islamic Republic (and all its criminal and repressive measures)—also spoke of a far more unfortunate calamity: the chronic degeneration of Iran's cosmopolitan political culture into ideological and class-based tribalism. The tribalism of the Shi'i clerical class had metastasized itself and spread into the rest of society. The more the cosmopolitan integrity of Iranian political culture degenerates into tribal affiliations (on the model of the Shi'i clerical cliques), the more "the West," the hallucinatory figment of a perturbed imagination, becomes central to defining national and world histories. While his superlative cinema reveals precisely the emancipatory visions of a cosmopolitan culture born out of a material encounter with the world, Kiarostami's open letter to Ahmadinejad speaks of the predicament of that culture trapped in its frightened subconscious. Kiarostami is a far superior gift to Iran when he is wielding his camera, and throwing away his pen.

Beginning at 9 A.M. Tehran time on Friday, Tir 3, 1384 (June 24, 2005), Iranians went to poll stations across the country in their millions. No matter who won the election, the real winner, so the clerical custodians claimed, would be the Islamic Republic—namely its ideological foundations of a medieval theocracy.

Any Iranian citizen born on or before Tir 3, 1369 (June 24, 1990) was invited to vote in this presidential election. Some 47 million Iranians, not just in Iran but all over the globe, were reportedly eligible to vote. (The first votes were in fact cast in Japan.) As the day dawned on major Iranian cities, people poured into voting stations. Reports of chaos and confusion, cheating and irregularities, almost immediately filled the air. Officially in charge of the election was the Ministry of the Interior. But the clerically controlled Guardian Council did not trust the ministry's reformist leadership under President Khatami, and accused it of favoring Rafsanjani and the reformist coalition against Ahmadinejad. Representatives of the Ministry of the Interior and the Guardian Council were soon at each other's throats, making accusations of interference and arguing about which body was in charge. At one point the special inspector of the Ministry of the Interior in charge of the election process, Ali Mir Baqeri, was arrested by military personnel under the command of the Guardian Council, for interrupting the election at a number of polls where it was reported that the Pasdaran, the Basijis, and the Hezbollah were bribing or intimidating voters. The Guardian Council members, conversely, were accusing the Ministry of the Interior of trying to disrupt the elections because Rafsanjani was falling behind.

Be that as it may, turnout was overwhelming, and the time allotted for voting was extended until almost midnight to facilitate the latecomers. At the closing of the polls, supporters of both candidates immediately declared victory, before the counting of the votes had even started. The daily newspaper *Keyhan*, openly rooting for Ahmadinejad, was reported to have prepared its lead headline, celebrating his victory: *"Mellat Kar ra Tamam Kard"* ("The Nation Finished the Job"), and then in a smaller screamer adding, *"Khabar-ha az Piruzi-ye Chashmgir-e Ahmadinejad Hekayat Mikonad"* ("Reports Indicate Spectacular Victory for Ahmadinejad"). The principal rival of Keyhan, *Sharq*, openly siding with Rafsanjani, started giving statistical proof from some of the polling stations that showed him winning. As the open war of the dailies was raging, reports of irregularities were still in the air. Later in the evening, reports from a polling station, Madreseh-ye

Pirovan-e Zeynab (the School of the Followers of Zeynab— Zeynab was a sister of the third Shi'i imam) indicated that electricity had been cut off and someone had walked away with a box full of votes! At another point, a few representatives of the Ministry of the Interior were thrown out of the polling centers by military personnel acting on behalf of the Guardian Council.

Toward the end of the day, as the polling stations were closing, Ayatollah Khamenei, the supreme leader, sent an urgent message, urging both parties not to declare victory prematurely and stir up civil disorder. He called for calm and serenity so that the votes could be counted by the officials in charge. But the officials in charge—the Ministry of the Interior and the Guardian Council—were openly fighting against each other and favoring one or the other candidate.

At 1:18:13 A.M. on Saturday, June, 25, 2005, the Iranian Students News Agency (ISNA) announced Mahmoud Ahmadinejad as the winner of the ninth presidential election of the Islamic Republic. All indications were that Ahmadinejad had won a resounding victory with 60 percent of the vote. According to BBC News, "On a count of 80% of the 22m ballots cast, he [Ahmadinejad] had won 61 percent with his more moderate opponent, Akbar Hashemi Rafsanjani, trailing on 35%. Turnout was 47%, down from 63% in the first round."[9]

Altogether three ideological movements were active in the Iranian presidential election of 2005: (1) the conservatives, or the fundamentalists, as they call themselves—*usulgara*, supporters of the regime and its status quo; (2) the reformists, those who are not in fundamental disagreement with the regime and wish to reform it from within; and (3) those who boycotted the elections altogether and wanted radical changes in the Islamic Republic, perhaps through a UN-sponsored referendum, perhaps through a revolutionary uprising, perhaps even a "regime change," through a U.S. invasion, following "the Wolfowitz Doctrine."

To understand the nature of this presidential election and what it means in the current context of the Islamic Republic we need to understand a paradox. In Iran, we have a deeply flawed democracy. But it is a democracy. The ruling clerical elite is an entirely parasitical band of illegitimate and unelected theocrats— but they are integral to a political process that has generated a grassroots democracy. That democracy is riddled with flaws and constitutionally compromised by a number of undemocratic institutions definitive to the Islamic Republic; yet neither a king nor a dictator, neither an American emperor nor a Persian monarch, decides Iranians' fate. People do. They go to polling stations and vote. They are the fiercest, most unpredictable voters the world has ever seen. I am an Iranian. I oppose the Islamic Republic. I root for a free and democratic state, cosmopolitan in its political culture, embracing all of its religious and secular proclivities, religious and ideological pluralities. I was among those who boycotted the election. Having lost my hope that the reform movement could accomplish anything significant, I had no candidate in the first round of the election, and in the second round not even my dead body could be dragged to vote for Rafsanjani. Given the obscenity of the Tehrani bourgeoisie rooting for him, if I had been in Tehran I might have even sneaked out and voted for Ahmadinejad—just to spite them. But voting for Ahmadinejad was out of the question for me, and thus not voting, I was a very proud Iranian during that presidential election, anxiously searching for news about the election while sitting in my small apartment on the Columbia University campus in New York City. Considering Iraq and Afghanistan, I would choose Ahmadinejad over Bush and Bin Laden without a second's hesitation—while opposing every single idea that he stands for. This is the paradox at the heart of the Islamic Republic, at the root of Iranian political culture.

The paradox is not debilitating but empowering. The victory of Ahmadinejad was the will of the Iranian people, the majority of them, caught and compromised as they are within the democratically flawed constitution of a theocracy. That Iranians deserve better and that their struggle is still unfolding does not compromise their current victory. In the vicinity of such undemocratic states as Saudi Arabia, Kuwait, Egypt, and Jordan (all major U.S. allies in the region), Iran is light-years ahead in democratic terms. Compared to the U.S.-ravaged Iraq and Afghanistan, Iran is the beacon of hope for the region. Next to the Israeli apartheid state, a Jewish state built on the broken backs of Palestinians, Iran is the proverbial Switzerland of fairness and justice. That Iran is governed by a medieval, clerically dominated, brutally oppressive, tribally fragmented, politically factitious, savagely intolerant of opposing ideas, horridly misogynist Islamic Republic, yet is still the best in its neighborhood, is the saddest commentary on where the world is today.

The election of Ahmadinejad, and before him Khatami, is the clearest indication that as a people Iranians in and out of their homeland have a collective will, a shared determination, and that they demand and exact a pride of place and a significant say in their destiny—a collective will that was not given to them by "the West" and cannot be denied them by any empire. That collective will is the crowning achievement of more than two hundred years of consistent struggle for liberty, equality, and national sovereignty. That collective will speaks the vernacular prose and poetry of an anticolonial modernity that Iranians did not borrow or steal, copy or plagiarize, from European Enlightenment modernity—they earned it on the battlefields of their collective struggle for emancipation from domestic tyranny and foreign domination alike. If we abandon the flawed Eurocentricity of a singular notion of modernity, we enter the battlefield of history, where anticolonial struggles the world over have generated and sustained a particular kind of modernity—a historical agency, a revolutionary reason for trusting the world and fighting to make it better. That anticolonial modernity has historically dismantled and decentered the self-proclaimed centrality of "the West," summoning the prose and poetry of world history to articulate the terms of its own emancipation. Citing the site of world history as the *locus politicus* of anticolonial modernity, the domain of its material origin would no longer be the vacuous and exclusionary philosophical speculations in Europe, but the battlefield of anticolonial struggles the world over, from Latin America to Africa, from Asia to all the disenfranchised communities within the metropolitan "West"—the poor, the racialized minorities, women. An organic link thus holds the emancipatory forces of any culture of resistance to colonialism and the anticolonial modernity that bestows agency by virtue of facing up to injustice. Anticolonial modernity thus sidesteps and exposes the shallow validity of such false binaries as "tradition" and "modernity," which has now for generations wasted the precious time of so many gifted Iranian intellectuals.[10] "Islam and the West" is a dangerous delusion, a nightmare of

Bernard Lewis and all his Orientalist brethren, and as such at odds with the cosmopolitan disposition of a worldly culture that has over the last two hundred years defined the ideals and aspiration of Iranian people. Anytime any Iranian public intellectual begins a singsong oscillation between "Islam" and the "West" or "tradition" and "modernity," he (and all those who engage in such debates are male) is playing into the hands of Bernard Lewis and disregarding the very cosmopolitan culture that has made Iranian intellectuals (and the glory of their cantankerous disagreements) possible.

Right in the middle of that cosmopolitan claim on Iranian political culture, the question remains, and the question is revealing: Who is this Ahmadinejad and what might he be up to?

Ahmadinejad is a poor people's president, and the vindictive glory that sets him apart from Iranian Gucci revolutionaries who opposed him is precisely the recipe for a populist fascism that has always been lurking under the clerical robes of the Islamic Republic. The poor and the disenfranchised who voted for Ahmadinejad lack any coherent ideology except the beliefs that stem from their memories of the founder of the Islamic Republic, the time of the "Imam," as they now call it reverently. The Iranian chapter of the whitewashed Bourgeois International daydreams a neoliberal economy, its open market of goods and ideas, and an active integration into a faceless globalization in both economic and cultural terms. There is a direct correspondence between the reform movement of the Khatami era and the Gucci revolutionaries—one wants freedom of expression, democratic institutions, the challenge of new ideas, and a neoliberal and transparent economy; the others want the Gucci bags and designer jeans and sexy scarves and oversize sunglasses that go with it.

There is nothing wrong with these Gucci revolutionaries. They are in fact quite essential to a healthy and robust society, a thriving economy, and the institutions of civil society and full-fledged democracy. But opposing them is the combined will of some seventeen million poor Iranians, who voted the son of a blacksmith into the highest elected office of their country. The aspirations of poor Iranians who voted for Ahmadinejad and the anonymity of the president they have elected are integral components of a future that is yet to be assayed. Unless and until these poor Iranians—laborers, peasants, and the unemployed—are actively incorporated into the Iranian political economy and allowed to form independent and autonomous unions and cooperatives, their legitimate concerns will continue to be systematically abused by a band of illegitimate clerical power-mongers. Only from a sustained clash between the organized labor and the Bourgeois International can one hope for enduring institutions of democracy to emerge.

Soon after the election of Mahmoud Ahmadinejad, everyone in the press spoke of his anonymity, that he came from nowhere. Not just foreign correspondents and analysts but also Iranians themselves. This is very strange indeed. Mahmoud Ahmadinejad is a very well-known person. His first name is Mahmoud, but Ahmadinejad is also Haji, and he is also Hussein.

Haji is the protagonist of one of the most popular films of Mohsen Makhmalbaf, *The Marriage of the Blessed* (1989). A fanatical idealist who put his life on the line, Haji fought in the Iran-Iraq War to save the Islamic Revolution. He returns to Iran traumatized by his experiences and is shocked by the crass materialism of his prospective father-in-law. Haji now fully realizes the futility of the entire revolution. He is about to get married when he realizes the depth of corruption and dishonesty, moral decay and economic decadence, that have engulfed his nation, a sacred land to him and a sanctified polity that he and his comrades sacrificed their lives to preserve. There is a haunting scene in *The Marriage of the Blessed* where Haji interrupts his own wedding ceremony and bursts into a hallucinatory recitation of revolutionary slogans and militant battle hymns—much to the horror of the guests at the wedding. Makhmalbaf made *The Marriage of the Blessed* just about a year after the end of Iran-Iraq War, when the unsurpassed sacrifices of a generation of poor Iranians in defending their country ended, and a rapid reconstruction period that left most of the nation disenfranchised began. Presiding over that reconstruction between 1989 and 1997 was none other than Ali Akbar Hashemi Rafsanjani. The seventeen million Iranians who voted for Mahmoud Ahmadinejad voted for Haji in *The Marriage of the Blessed.* Mahmoud Ahmadinejad is Haji coming back from the dead to reclaim the revolution, a bit too late and completely out of season.[11]

Mahmoud Ahmadinejad is also Hussein, the lead character of one of the most important films of Jafar Panahi, *Crimson Gold* (2003). Hussein (Hussein Emadeddin) is a pizza deliveryman mesmerized and bewildered by the injustice he sees all around him. He has a stillness, a grounded quality, that is concealed behind a poker face that gives no indication of the depth of the anger that has built up in him during and soon after the futility of the Iran-Iraq War. Through his friend and prospective brother-in-law, Ali (Kamyar Sheissi), who has just snatched a woman's handbag and found in it the receipt for an expensive piece of jewelry, Hussein becomes obsessed with a posh jewelry shop. The condescending attitude, the veiled contempt, of the owner gradually begins to stoke Hussein's anger. *Crimson Gold* is the story of Hussein navigating somberly through his disillusion with the promises of the Islamic Revolution, the futility of heroic sacrifices poor people made to fight for its survival, the obscenity of those who got rich after the war ended, and above all a paralyzing awareness of profound class differences decades after the Islamic Revolution. As he says to his friend Ali, he was about seventeen when the revolution happened, and he fought for its victory and then its survival—and now he sees Tehran divided almost exactly as it used to be, deeply bifurcated along class lines.

Hussein, Ali, and Ali's sister (Azita Rayeji) finally decide one day to visit the posh jewelry shop. When they go there the owner treats them like what Abbas Kiarostami would call *vasleh-ye najur,* "a mismatched patch upon a garment." Hussein and his fiancée cannot afford that kind of jewelry, and the owner condescendingly sends them off to downtown jewelry shops, where things are much cheaper. Hussein leaves the premises and almost faints from an anxiety attack triggered by the humiliation he has suffered. He takes his fiancée home, comes back to the jewelry shop the following day, and, when his plan to rob the store is foiled, kills the owner. Then, trapped inside the jewelry shop, he pulls the trigger and kills himself. Mahmoud Ahmadinejad is Hussein coming back from the dead to haunt the early promises of a catastrophically failed revolution.[12]

Between 1989, when Makhmalbaf made *The Marriage of the Blessed*, and 2003, when Jafar Panahi made *Crimson Gold*, just the year before the reformists lost the parliament and then the presidency, Makhmalbaf and Panahi were acute observers of an entire generation of postwar poverty—of a rising population entirely disenfranchised by the postwar economic boom spearheaded by Rafsanjani between 1989 and 1997. During the eight years that followed and that they were in power, from 1997 to 2005, the reformists, too busy looking radical and liberal and open to Gucci revolutionaries, did nothing but cater to the social liberties of the middle class that had come into existence during Rafsanjani's presidency, and thus failed to address the massive poverty it had left behind. Apparently at odds with each other, Rafsanjani and Khatami were in fact complementary. One championed a postwar reconstruction economy and its contingent middle class on the artificial wealth of an oil-based economy (1989–97), and the other sought to secure the very same class's social liberties (1997–2005)—but both neglected the overwhelming majority of their constituents. Some seventeen million Iranians who were left behind during Rafsanjani's reconstruction and could not care less about Khatami's "dialogue of civilizations" thought of teaching them both a lesson.

The danger that Ahmadinejad poses for Iran and by extension the region at large, should he not be effectively sidestepped by the clerical intrigues plotting the post-Khamenei Islamic Republic above his head, is the dangerous liaison between a massive underclass and the fanaticism of a true believer. What might save Iran from that frightful possibility is hidden in a scene in *Crimson Gold*, the script of which was written by none other than Abbas Kiarostami. In this scene Hussein has brought a large pizza to deliver to a party at a posh house in a wealthy neighborhood, but he is stopped by the morality police guarding that house and arresting anyone who comes out of it. As the arrested young couples coming out of the party, the disheveled members of the morality police, the concerned parents of the youngsters partying in that house, and other neighbors gather in the street, Hussein suddenly realizes that the pizza he was about to deliver is getting cold and useless. He opens the box and goes around the street, offering a slice to everyone in sight—rich and poor, pious and unbelieving, Muslim and secular, men and women, young and old, prorevolutionary and antirevolutionary. In the dimly lit haze of the street, in the ritual mannerism of that Shi'i version of the Eucharist, Kiarostami and Panahi bring their whole nation together in an emancipatory act of forgiveness that collects and stages the collectivity of their cosmopolitan tolerance of each other—all implicit in the accidental gathering of their enduring differences, definitive to the cosmopolitan character of their historical survival as a nation.[13] To that cosmopolitanism, Islam is always integral but should never be definitive.

Constitutionally threatening—yet paradoxically invigorating—the cosmopolitan disposition of Iranian political culture is the charismatic appeal of Shi'ism, always evident on the horizon and shimmering seductively at the edges of its cosmic claims on history. The cultural condition of the victory of Mahmoud Ahmadinejad extends from its anticipation in Iranian cinema deep into Shi'i political culture, and from there to the central paradox of its cycles of conferring legitimacy on, and withdrawing it from, power. Ahmadinejad emerged from the most disappointed, the most disenfranchised, and the most impoverished segments of the country—those who had invested every hope in the course and cause of the Islamic Revolution, were at the forefront of its sacrifices, and yet received none of its promised benefits. The poor and the disenfranchised were those who were in the front lines of the revolution, sacrificed their lives in the course of the war, yet were systematically left behind in the course of Rafsanjani's presidency. The corruption and astronomical wealth imputed to Rafsanjani during and after his presidency may have been exaggerated. But the imputation reflects the resentment of those he abandoned to poverty and desperation while he implemented his economic policies. How could the poor and the disaffected vote for Rafsanjani when they could vote for a man coming from just as humble a background as theirs? The sheer stupidity of the reformists—and the public intellectuals and artists who supported them—between the first and the second rounds of the presidential election in 2005, their desperate stand against Ahmadinejad and on behalf of Rafsanjani, is simply staggering.

Rarely has reformist liberalism been so totally implicated in paving the way for a potential rise of populist fascism.[14]

The normative pattern of poor and desperate people turning to Ahmadinejad is prototypically identical with the rise of Shi'ism at its very inception, when the early promises of the Prophet Muhammad had been rendered hollow during the reign of the Umayyads (661–750) and the Abbasids (750–1258). The charismatic disposition of the attraction to such populist figures is at once historically grounded and potentially dangerous. Ahmadinejad—representing a group of so-called Abadgaran ("the Builders")—rises from the same zealous revolutionaries who took the U.S. diplomatic corps hostage in November 1979, fearing that the United States would engineer yet another coup to bring back the shah.[15] They are staunch followers of Khomeini (in a rather cultic and mystical way) and believe things have gone seriously wrong since he died. They love and admire the current supreme leader, Ayatollah Khamenei, because he occupies the office of *velayat-e faqih* that the ascetic revolutionary created, and then left vacant after his death. They are holding the Islamic Revolution responsible for its early promises.

Throughout Islamic history, proto-Shi'i movements have mobilized the poor and the disenfranchised, referred to the inaugural moment of their faith, invoked the moral authority of their prophet, and launched revolutions. The reference of Ahmadinejad to Khomeini (through Khamenei) is the reference of all Shi'i revolutionary leaders to the moral authority of the Prophet Muhammad. The reference is always paradoxical. It invokes authority as it launches a revolutionary movement, and it fails as soon as it succeeds. The prevailing paradox of Shi'ism—gaining legitimacy while saying no to power, losing it when in power—suggests that the presidency of Ahmadinejad will fail in one of two equally catastrophic ways. At best, he will fail miserably to deliver on his promises to his poor constituency and will thus degenerate into a weak president, manipulated by wily politicians such as Rafsanjani, whom he defeated, or by Ali Khamenei, whom he treats like a mystical mentor—this scenario will drastically compromise the office of the presidency, one of the few quasi-democratic institutions of the Islamic Republic. At worst, he will abuse the hopes and aspirations invested in him and resume an Islamic reign of terror over those young yuppie voters with their stylish hairdos, chic scarves, and sexy sunglasses—in which case he will turn them and their innocent semiotics of resistance into the real inheritors of the moral authority of Shi'ism. Either result reveals both the curse and the source of the curious resiliency of Shi'ism: it is always on the side of the tyrannized and discredits those who are in power, a charismatic disposition at once mythic in its revolutionary endurance and curiously effervescent in its social-democratic implications.

At an innately emotive level, Ahmadinejad invokes the collective (now definitive) sentiments of the earliest nucleus of revolutionary Shi'ism, the early supporters of the first Shi'i imam, Ali ibn Abi Taleb (d. 661) and his descendants, who thought the promises of their prophet to the poor and the wretched were not fulfilled by the increasingly opulent, powerful, and worldly rulers of the Umayyads and the Abbasids. As it was in the beginning, so shall it be today. Trapped in the charismatic appeal of that abiding memory, Ahmadinejad may indeed go to war—with the United States, with Israel, with any one of the Persian Gulf states (or perhaps the United States and Israel may hand him that opportunity by invading Iran)—for the fire of war cleanses and purifies the evil that this zealotry sees dominant in the world.

The presence of enemies without always reflects on the mutation of enemies within. The effective transmutation of a popular vote into populism, its alliance with the militarism that helped bring it to power, and the belligerent presence of U.S. imperial hubris at the borders of the Islamic Republic are the classical recipe for fascism at home and war abroad. A combustible mixture of populism and militarism will put Ahmadinejad's presidency on a catastrophic course leading to a frightful fascism. He has come to office with a huge popular mandate. That popular support can very easily mutate into a vacant and vacuous populism, very high on rhetoric and low on delivery. The systematic support of the Pasdaran, the Basijis, and the Hezbollah in bringing Ahmadinejad to power does not bode well for the future of democracy in Iran. This, perhaps, is the fear that drove the reformists to stake their very last remnant of credibility on their support for Rafsanjani, the most discredited force in the very core of the Islamic Republic, and yet the man who could save the

Islamic Republic—not just from the democratic aspirations of Iranians, but from a theocratic fascism even worse than the Islamic Republic.[16]

The republic of fear that will result will impose draconian limitations on the latitude that has, in the past, been allowed to the social behavior of middle-class Iranians, the flamboyant youth, and the Gucci revolutionaries. This will scare and dishearten middle-class Iranians, and force them even more into belligerent secularism, vulgar consumerism, and ultimately escape from the claws of the Islamic Republic—most immediately to Dubai and other United Arab Emirates locations, but ultimately (if they can afford it) to Turkey, Europe, and the mecca of their mendacity, Los Angeles. The impoverished classes will most certainly not be the beneficiaries of this exodus of capital. The Islamic Revolution never had the economic courage of its political imagination, never dared to opt for a socialist economy, even from its very ideological basis in the ideas and principles of ideologues such as Ayatollah Mahmoud Taleqani and Abu al-Hassan Bani Sadr.[17] So-called Islamic economics are fundamentally based on a secured niche in global capitalism. But this economics wants to have its cake and eat it too. It needs foreign investments and a robust capitalist economy, but it does not want the Bourgeois International and its preference for tight jeans, loose scarves, and the democratic institutions that go with global capitalism. The Iranian economy under Ahmadinejad will thus remain heavily dependent on oil revenue. Jobs will remain scarce unless Ahmadinejad can transmute the oil revenue into a productive, labor-intensive economy—a critical task that all his predecessors have failed to meet. Chances are that he will not succeed, for he is very much at the mercy of the global economy, which allots Iran only a role as an oil producer. The Iranian economy under his administration will be even further incorporated into globalized neoliberal economics and the logic of its planetary need for cheap labor, raw materials, and expansive markets.

This all assumes, however, that Ahmadinejad plays ball with the ruling clerical elite. It is also possible that he will remain honest, innocent, and true to the persona with which his constituency identifies. In that case he will become isolated, insular, and entirely irrelevant to the conniving course of the clerical politics.

At the end of *The Marriage of the Blessed*, Haji goes back to war; at the end of *Crimson Gold*, Hussein kills himself. These two fictional options may offer themselves to Ahmadinejad. The two options might in fact be only one—if the United States opts for a military confrontation with Iran.

The chronically charismatic disposition of Shi'ism characteristically compromises the Iranian cosmopolitan political culture and yet paradoxically invigorates its underlying predisposition to social democracy. The problem is that left to its own sacred devices, further complicated by its anticolonial mutation into a combative ideology, Shi'ism (and by extension Islamism) has no room for any sort of cosmopolitan culture, Iranian or otherwise, while the cosmopolitanism of Iranian anticolonial modernity has had plenty of room for Shi'ism (and Islamism in general).

The hope for the restitution of that cosmopolitan culture, now compromised by a militant Islamism that has no patience or tolerance for anything it deems un-Islamic, can come from an entirely unexpected corner if we consider the flowering relationship between President Hugo Chávez of Venezuela and his Iranian counterpart.[18] Chávez has been an unflinching supporter of the Islamic Republic ever since he came to power in 1998, and following repeated trips to Iran, reciprocated by visits to Caracas by then president Khatami. So far Chávez has not uttered a word about the systematic human rights abuses in Iran, or the horrid status of women in medieval Shi'i jurisprudence, or the undemocratic institutions within the constitution of the Islamic Republic. Out of his legitimate anger with the Bush administration, which has repeatedly tried to topple his democratically attained presidency, Chávez has a categorical admiration for the Islamic Republic, and sees in it a potential ally across the globe. This admiration can extend beyond a mere transcontinental but vacuous camaraderie, with occasional economic benefits for both, only if Chávez uses his leverage with the Islamic Republic to have it open up its medieval gates to political dissent and institutional changes in its theocracy. The relationship is of course reciprocal—namely, if Chávez fails to raise principled questions with the Islamic Republic and thus help restore the Iranian cosmopolitan political culture, then the theocratic disregard for human rights and the mutation of Iranian cosmopolitan political culture into a clerical tribalism of the worst kind, now definitive to the Islamic Republic, will turn around and corrupt the social democratic aspirations of Chávez. There is no third way: either along with lucrative business deals the Islamic Republic will export its tribal clericalism and destroy the social democratic aspirations of Venezuela, or else Chávez will speak forthrightly to the medieval clericalism of the Islamic Republic and help restore the Iranian cosmopolitan political culture.

One must look at the nuclear standoff between Iran and the United States, which came to a full rhetorical crescendo early in 2006,[19] as yet another occasion in which the United States has in fact helped strengthen the position of the beleaguered clerical clique, in effect reflecting its own categorical collapse into tribal fanaticism of the worst sort, code-named neoconservatism. There is a belligerent tribalism, almost identical in its pestiferous essentialism, linking the most recalcitrant clerics in Iran to the most obstinate neocons in the United States—making Ayatollah Mesbah Yazdi and his associates in Qom indistinguishable from Bernard Lewis and his cohorts in Washington, D.C. The frightful proliferation of nuclear arms is thus contingent on two forms of fanaticism, one worse than the other; one is homegrown in the United States and is code-named neoconservatism, and the other is domestic to Iranian clericalism and dubbed fundamentalism (*usulgara'i*). The first step toward any way out of the impasse is the simultaneous discrediting of these two identical forms of ideological fanaticism that feed on each other.

The origin of the international crisis over the Islamic Republic and its development of a nuclear program must be traced back to the political environment soon after 9/11, although the roots of this ambition go back to the shah's time, when the United States and Israel were actively involved in providing their principal ally in the region with the necessary technology to attain nuclear capabilities. When, in January 2002, President George W. Bush included Iran in the "Axis of Evil," accusing it of supporting international terrorism, the political elite of the Islamic Republic was of course highly alarmed that after the assault on the Taliban in Afghanistan, it might be next. Its fear was not entirely misplaced if we consider that soon after the "Axis of Evil" speech, the chief neocon strategist, the author of the "Wolfowitz-Bush Doctrine," the man who had promised that the United States would "end states" that in its judgment endorsed terrorism, Deputy Secretary of Defense Paul Wolfowitz, in collaboration with his chief Orientalist ideologue Bernard Lewis, helped Azar Nafisi publish and widely disseminate her *Reading Lolita in Tehran* in 2003, and thus set propaganda psyops against Iran into full gear.[20] So at least since October 2001, when the United States invaded Afghanistan, and certainly after January 2002, when President Bush placed Iran on the "Axis of Evil," the officials of the Islamic Republic must have felt that they had been put on notice; and thus they intensified their nuclear programs—for they took a quick look at North Korea and concluded that the only reason it stood firm against the United States was that it wielded its nuclear capabilities. By September 2003, Russian technicians had begun construction of a nuclear reactor in Bushehr, despite U.S. objections.

The U.S. invasion of Iraq in March 2003 put a stamp of finality on all the real and fictive fears of the Islamic Republic that it would be next on the neocon list—and thus encouraged its clerical leadership to speed up its nuclear program. That in June 2003 a nationwide student-led protest challenged the clerical establishment clearly indicates how internal assaults on the legitimacy of the Islamic Republic always have a reciprocal relationship with U.S. pressure on Iran. The student uprising was violently crushed in part under the ludicrous pretext that its leaders were financed and encouraged by the United States. Throughout that year the United States, through the UN nuclear watchdog, the International Atomic Energy Agency (IAEA), pressured Tehran to prove that it was not pursuing an atomic weapons program. Under these circumstances, when in October 2003, Shirin Ebadi received the Nobel Peace Prize, the global recognition she received failed to elevate the critical issue of human and women's rights in Iran and the Muslim world at large to any significant level, principally because by then the United States and its European and regional allies had consistently abused the absence of those rights in Iran and similar countries for their own imperial and colonial purposes.[21] The eventual revelations about U.S. torture chambers in Bagram Air Base in Afghanistan, in Abu Ghraib in Iraq, in Guantánamo Bay in Cuba, and throughout an entire network of interrogation dungeons in Europe, as well as revelations of U.S. Marines raping, murdering, and massacring civilian Iraqis in Fallujah, Haditha, and Mahmoudiya had totally discredited the United States as an arbiter of human rights abuses—a fact further corroborated by the endorsement of such prominent advocates of human rights as Michael Ignatieff who openly, barefacedly, and with sadistic precision theorized the legal and "moral" necessity of torturing people.[22] As I have tried to show throughout this book, the nuclear standoff between Iran and the United States functions as the worst possible catalyst—it strengthens a tyrannical regime, blocks democratic developments, and effectively helps the ruling clerical clique assume a warring posture. This gives the clerics a perfect excuse to suppress any form of opposition to their theocratic reign. Responding to international pressure, in November 2003 the leadership of the Islamic Republic suspended Iran's uranium-enrichment program and allowed tougher UN inspections of its nuclear facilities. In response, the IAEA concluded that there was no evidence that the belligerent ayatollahs were in fact developing a nuclear weapons program.

By February 2004, the conservatives had regained complete control of the Islamic parliament, and in June of that year, the IAEA condemned Iran for having failed to cooperate with its inquiries into nuclear activities. By November, Iran again agreed to suspend most of its uranium enrichment as part of a deal with the European Union. The conservatives, now in full control of the parliament, felt more confident about negotiating on nuclear issues. When in June 2005 Mahmoud Ahmadinejad became president, the crisis over the nuclear issue entered a new and ominous phase. In August, Iranian authorities declared that they had resumed the conversion of uranium while insisting that their program was for peaceful purposes. The year 2005 came to a close with President Ahmadinejad provocatively stating that the state of Israel must be "wiped off of the map," and appearing to deny the reality of the Jewish Holocaust, slyly suggesting that if Europeans felt particularly responsible, then they ought to relocate Israel to Europe, which caused an international uproar. This had the felicitous effect of encouraging neighboring states to assume belligerent postures. History is indeed first tragedy and then farce—having an Islamic republic point the finger at a Jewish state, or vice versa. Unfortunately, Armageddon is no joke. The most direct way to resolve this situation was for all these fanatical religious states, Jewish or Islamic, and above all the Christian empire that had done so much to encourage them, be dismantled, and a set of democratic republics, cosmopolitan and tolerant of people's religious and ideological differences, to emerge—giving free and independent citizenship to people, a freedom not predicated on their presumed religious identity but based on their citizenship in free and democratic states. But that sort of language was now so indigestible to the propaganda machinery of the Christian empire that it would dismiss it as utopian and impractical—while what was practical was disastrous.[23]

Thus in the shadow of a deadly game now played between the globalized U.S. empire and its nemesis, the equally globalized al Qaeda, Mahmoud Ahmadinejad presided over a discredited Islamic republic, held together against the collective will of its own citizens. The catastrophic prospect of a nuclear Islamic republic would seal the fate of some seventy million people held hostage within their own homeland. Furthermore, Iran is surrounded by four nuclear powers—Israel to its west, Pakistan to its east, Russia to its north, and the United States to its south in the Persian Gulf. None of these four states is in a moral or even a military position to point the finger at a sovereign nation-state and object to its pursuing of a nuclear program. Least of all can a Jewish state (itself sitting on a massive stockpile of nuclear arms) find fault with an Islamic republic, or vice versa. The Jewish state and the Islamic Republic are in fact mirror images of each other. The horrors of the Jewish Holocaust, in which European Jewry was almost eradicated by criminal European atrocities, justify the existence of a Jewish state as much as the obscenities of a Persian monarchic history justify the existence of an Islamic republic. The current cycle of violence pits an Islamic republic against a Jewish state, both of them at the whimsical mercy of a Christian empire, all in the neighborhood of an equally horrid Hindu fundamentalism. This cycle is undermining any hope for a civil society (in Iran or in Israel/Palestine) that entitles all its citizens to equal and identifiable rights and responsibilities.

The so-called U.S. war on terrorism is being used to cover up a far more dangerous reality: a systematic mystification of world politics in violent theological terms—corroborated as much by the reciprocal atrocities of Osama bin Laden's "Islam" and George W. Bush's "Crusade" as by the reactionary and infallible fatwas of Pope Benedict XVI, whose unwavering hostility to liberation theology (the Christianity of the poor people) is the most disturbing sign of where institutionalized Christianity is headed—not too far from where Osama bin Laden's followers and Meir Kahane's sect are taking Islam and Judaism.[24]

In the crossfire of these variations on the common theme of fanaticism, more than anything else it was the nativist hold and the captured imagination of leading Iranian public intellectuals that most delimited the horizon of their collective concern for national liberation. Left to its own devices, the Islamic Republic cannot but generate more of its kind, and the terms of its so-called dissent are measures of even more entrapment within an exclusively Islamist imagination. Two almost concurrent events in the summer of 2006 came together to punctuate and demonstrate this entrapment. Ramin Jahanbegloo, a leading Iranian public intellectual, was arrested in Iran on May 2, 2006, and was later charged with being involved in what the overanxious clerical authorities term "a velvet revolution" against the Islamic regime—a ludicrous, bogus, and Kafkaesque charge brought against a sincere social activist deeply concerned about the fate of his nation. A few months later, Akbar Ganji, another leading Iranian dissident who had just endured years of imprisonment in Iran, found his way to the United States and announced that he planned to engage in a hunger strike in front of the UN—very much following the model of what he had done while in prison in Iran— to protest the atrocious record of human rights abuses inside his country and, more specifically, demand the release of Ramin Jahanbegloo and other political prisoners.

Under ordinary and isolated circumstances this was a noble and perhaps even heroic gesture. But the global condition that surrounds the geopolitics of the Islamic Republic is anything but normal and far from isolated. The reaction of Iranian expatriate intellectuals to Ganji's idea was twofold and diametrically opposed. A powerful array of exiled leftists inundated the Internet with details of Akbar Ganji's own involvement with the earliest stages of the Islamic regime, his active participation in consolidating the nascent institutions of the theocracy, and his silence, indifference, and complacency in the savage execution of secular leftists in the 1980s. The more liberal wing of expatriate intellectuals, meanwhile, opted to support Ganji's call for a hunger strike in front of the UN as a way of alerting the world to egregious human rights abuses in Iran.

The problem with Ganji's call for a hunger strike against these abuses in Iran, and with much of the debate that emerged around it, is symptomatic of a larger issue that will engage the Iranian political predicament for decades to come. Those who were pointing out Ganji's own past and implicating him in the criminal atrocities of the Islamic Republic were of course correct. Ganji and practically all of his stated heroes—Ayatollah Montazeri and Abdolkarim Soroush in particular—have been and in fact continue to be instrumental in a radical Islamization of Iranian political culture. After Ayatollah Khomeini, Ayatollah Montazeri was the principal theorist of the doctrine of *velayat-e faqih*—a medieval Shi'i dogma that labels 70 million Iranians, simply because they are Muslims, inferior in their collective reasoning, and thus flawed in their autonomous judgment, to just one of them who considers himself to be a Supreme Jurist—namely Ayatollah Khamenei. Abdolkarim Soroush was chiefly responsible for the ideological cleansing of the Iranian university system of faculty and administration with views contrary to his. The fact that Montazeri, Soroush, and Ganji all now repent what they have done and seek to cultivate a different reading of Islam (and a different vision for the future of their homeland) neither completely exonerates them of their past deeds nor validates their current stands concerning the political disposition of their country. The ideas and aspirations of people like Montazeri or Soroush have developed in an undemocratic and imbalanced atmosphere, and they have never been subject to an open and democratic challenge by people who will be directly affected by their political implications.

The Islamic Republic's record of human rights abuses is not limited to Zahra Kazemi, the Iranian Canadian journalist savagely raped and murdered in its dungeons, or before her to Ali

Akbar Sa'idi Sirjani, the distinguished scholar and courageous essayist, or after him to scores of other literary and political figures, all at odds with the medieval banalities of the Islamic Republic, and who all lost their lives defending the integrity of their ideals and aspirations. Thousands of Iranians, mostly leftist political activists, have been tortured and murdered by the custodians of the sacred rage in the Islamic Republic, the very Islamic Republic that Akbar Ganji had helped to succeed in eradicating all its secular and Islamist opponents—political movements as legitimate and integral to Iranian political culture as any other. The leading clergy now reaping the political benefits of those criminal atrocities will have to be held accountable for their crimes against humanity.

Be that as it may, history cannot be held hostage to vindictiveness. People are entitled to growth and emancipation, and they do indeed change their positions—that is all good. The reformist movement inside Iran was a temporary sign of hope, and it could have resulted in drastic and enduring changes—all for the better, for a more democratic and tolerant state apparatus. That it did not, and that the Khatami phenomenon is in effect the record of a catastrophic failure, cannot be blamed solely on the reformists. So the problem is not with people changing their minds and altering their politics. The problem is with the direction into which they change and mutate, and the degree that the terms of their dissent against the Islamic Republic are informed and invalidated by larger and more global parameters.

The most fundamental problem that people like Ganji face, as they come out of their nativist cocoon and wish to address a more global audience, is rooted in their legitimate anger against a feudal theocracy that they in fact helped to bring to power. They are now completely enamored with the grand delusion of what they still care to call "the Western civilization" and the promises of a neoliberal economics, which in turn (and there is the rub) makes them very natural bedfellows of the U.S. neocons—as indeed has already been evident in the case of one such leading ex-Islamist, the born-again reformer and former comrade of Akbar Ganji Mohsen Sazegara, who has now joined forces with the band of U.S. neocons gathered together at the Washington Institute for Near East Policy. If Mohsen Sazegara's current cozy status with the U.S. neocons is the model to be followed by the rest of the Islamist reformists who come to the United States, then their initial betrayal of the Iranian Revolution by brutally helping it degenerate into a militant theocracy will be repeated by swinging to the opposite extreme, a neoliberal/ neocon nightmare.

While the Iranian expatriate left was busy documenting a rather useless history for Ganji, and while the liberals were equally busy projecting their oppositional postures toward the Islamic Republic from the safe distance of Europe and the United States, all of them were trapped in a myopic and astoundingly nativist position—none of them placing the Iranian situation within the larger geopolitics of the region (this of course is a symptom of a much deeper malady among Iranian intellectuals who have always seen themselves as interlocutors of "the West," considering the Arab, the Muslim, the South Asian, or the Central Asian context of their immediate surroundings just beneath their decorum and as such too small a feat for their grand delusions).

As historical fate would have it, Ganji had come to New York at a particularly acute and tumultuous point in history. His call for a hunger strike protesting human rights abuses in Iran happened to have occurred in mid-July 2006, and nothing, not a word, in the statement that his supporters and admirers circulated for signature, or in his own interviews, pointed to monumental global events surrounding the issuing of that call, as if there were a safe, insular, subterranean, secure, and entirely airtight tunnel between Tehran and New York. Ganji's call occurred at a time when the daily carnage the United States had initiated and caused in Iraq had reached unprecedented dimensions, with tens of thousands of Iraqi civilian casualties the innocent victims of an illegal, immoral, and deceitful war. And yet the U.S. invasions of Iraq and Afghanistan, occurring as they did on both sides of the Islamic Republic, were notably absent from Ganji's call for the protection of human rights, as was the barbaric invasion of Lebanon by Israel, committing war crimes that ranged from the massacre of civilians (mostly children) to creating close to a million refuges in southern Lebanon. Ganji and his handlers could not have been entirely unaware that the U.S. government may indeed heap folly upon deceit and invade yet another country in the region; Seymour

Hersh's article in the April 2006 *New Yorker* alerting the American public to such an eventuality was just too well known and too widely discussed.

Somewhere in the vicinity of Akbar Ganji's hidden promises, of the hope that still cries for freedom in him (the Nelson Mandela that is waiting to be born in him), and in the crossfire of fear and fanaticism that defines the age, a political commitment of an entirely different sort is needed than the one he managed to bring to New York during that sad and solicitous summer. The only way that human rights abuses in the Islamic Republic or any other degenerate theocracy or tyranny in the world can be brought to global attention is for them to be connected to a larger frame of reference.

In the midst of this mad game of power and politics, if national liberation movements do not degenerate into corrupt totalitarian regimes, there is a chance for the resurgence of cosmopolitan political cultures endemic to the region. Regional geopolitics, liberation movements feeding on each other's promises and curtailing each other's terror, can both mount a legitimate and viable resistance to globalization and all its imperial designs (by the United States or the European Union), while resisting xenophobic nativism and tribal absolutism of homegrown ideologies—allowing the pluralistic reality of these nations to save instead of sink them. The salvation of Iran depends entirely on tapping the resources of its syncretic and pluralistic political culture. Instead of *exporting* its disastrous tribal fears, it will have to allow for the *importing* of the cosmopolitan hope it once generated in its neighborhood—and that is only possible through cross-national, regional alliances among progressive forces against both retrograde domestic tyrannies and the predatory U.S. imperialism that sustains and feeds on them. The alternatives do not bode well for humanity.

At the end of Islamic ideology, where the revolutionary charge of the Islamic Revolution has lost all its momentum and retained scarcely anything of its variegated ideological origins, the clerical tribalism of the Shi'i elite is matched and balanced by the globalized tribalism of a different sort put forward by the American neocons. What is lost between them, perhaps forever, perhaps not, is the cosmopolitan dream of people—Americans, Iranians, and others—a dream that is neither Islamist nor Western, nei-

ther nativist nor Westoxicated, neither religious nor secular, neither ideologically dwarfed nor politically lame, yet embraces all
such claims and credulities, brought together in a dream too
beautiful to betray.

How exactly can a lapsed Muslim and an erstwhile Iranian,
the most recent immigrant and a forever grateful guest of this
blessed land of Native Americans, far from all nostalgic claims on
any faith let alone the faded rings of a homeland, and quite content by the boisterous banks of a magnanimous river that links
together all the memories of his past and present, fears fading
and hopes rising, just to switch places and mark despair, ever
dream in a language he still cannot but call home—the language
of kings and clerics before history placed them outside the fold of
humanity, the language of soothing lullabies, of cries and whispers public and private, the language of poets, mystics, and philosophers long since forgotten, the language of the prose and
poetry of his youthful convictions and aging wisdom?

But wisdom wanes as it wonders at the calamities the world
now harbors. The world was not at peace as I brought this book
to an end and sought to rest my case. About a week before the
Israelis began bombing the living daylights out of Lebanon in
mid-July 2006, Golbarg and I spent about ten days in Beirut visiting our friends and colleagues. Beirut was beautiful when we left
it—and all in one piece. Once in New York and two days into
watching Beirut burn on CNN, my fears for people dear to me
who were now trapped and in danger inside Beirut made it impossible to take one more minute of the criminal complacency of
the U.S. media—all slight variations on an obscenity called Fox
News. It was far easier to look straight at the banality of evil
itself—as the Israelis were bombing Beirut and the Beirutis into
rubble and ashes, broken bones and pieces of flesh, slaughtering
an entire nation with total impunity—than to listen to or read
the American media whitewashing this criminal thuggery. Might
now the Israelis or Americans or both (are they two different
things?) go ahead and hit Syria, invade Iran, bomb North Korea,
and set the whole globe on fire? Things were just too hot and ugly
in New York in that July of our despair, and this barefaced savagery had opened a vision of inferno too vile to fathom. "I love
Melville's *Moby Dick*," my filmmaker friend Amir Naderi once

told me, "but I cannot have that kind of ending. I need a smidgen of hope." So did I. But how? I finally gave up and picked up my aging copy of Rumi's *Mathnavi* and headed for a bench I know by the Hudson River, near where I live and where the sun sets on a horizon that seems entirely oblivious to what shade of orange, yellow, gold, or indifference it casts on the tall and luscious trees, the hurried and speeding cars, the playful and boisterous children, and the shimmering and unhurried waters of the Hudson. I turned my back to New York, faced the ponderous river (it was unusually calm and gray), and opened the *Mathnavi* randomly and began to read out loud to myself:

Jang-ha-ye khalq bahr-e khubi ast,
Barg-e bi-Bargi neshan-e Tubi ast.
Khashm-ha-ye khalq bahr-e ashti ast,
Dam-e rahat dayeman bi-rahatist.
Har zadan bahr-e navazesh ra bovad,
Har geleh az shokr agah mikonad.
Buy bar az jozv ta koll ay karim,
Buy bar az zed ta zed ay hakim.
Jang-ha mi ashti arad dorost, [. . .]

[The wars of nations are all in search of kindness,
The impoverished leaves are reminiscent of the luscious tree of
  paradise.
The angers of people are all in want of peace,
The way to gain comfort is to be always in turmoil.
All slapping in the face are caressing kindness,
All complaints inform of gratitude.
Take the trace of the particular and go toward the universal,
Smell from every opposite exactly its opposite.
Wars will bring about peace for sure]

I sat there watching the sun set for a while. Then I collected my *Mathnavi* and went home to my Golbarg.

Postscript

I have taken you through a long journey of more than two hundred years of Iranian history with the single abiding purpose of showing you the cosmopolitan disposition of a worldly political culture at once conversant with factors and forces, moral and material, that are domestic to its collective heritage, and yet shared by its regional predicament, and thus definitive to its global whereabouts. In telling the story of the Iranian encounter with colonial modernity, I have sought to retrieve that cosmopolitan history not by way of an idle bystander reporting to an indifferent audience (for we are both invested in what I have written and you have read), but as a way of sharing my perception of what that cosmopolitanism means, where its origin is, what its disposition is, and how it can be restored and safeguarded—for I see it as the solitary source of hope for our future.

"It behooves both the Jews and the Arabs," says the governor (Charles Durning) in Colin Higgins's *The Best Little Whorehouse in Texas* (1982), "to settle their differences in a Christian manner!" If the world at large were only to do as the good governor suggests! It would indeed have been good of "the Jews and the Arabs" to do as they were told—but alas, the wisdom of Christian morality is a bit blurred, especially to "the Jews and the Arabs," considering the Crusades and all the pogroms and the mayhem that that particular Christian manner has entailed. Over the last two hundred years in particular, "the Jews and the Arabs," and indeed much of the rest of the world, have been plagued not just by failing to see the wisdom of the good governor's recommendation, but also by the method and madness of the universal condition of a simple economic fact: that the accumulated capital in major industrial economies has necessitated the ever increasing expansion of a global capitalism in which a few get incessantly richer, while the overwhelming majority get inevitably poorer by the day.

The mechanism that has globalized that accumulated capital and generated this global condition of calamity and destitution is called *colonialism*—whereby European merchants and Christian missionaries have got together with a good number of mercenary Orientalists and their counterparts among the soldiers of fortune and gone around the world ruling people, plundering their wealth, forcing them into slavery, writing a subservient history for them, and then telling them, in a good "Christian manner," to turn the other cheek. Colonialism is not accidental to the operation of accumulated capital but in fact definitive to it. The ideological disposition that has given universal validity, in moral and normative terms, to the global operation of capital is called *modernity*, and the way that much of the rest of the world has received this modernity must perforce be called *colonial modernity*. Within that simple, if not altogether simplistic, reading of the modern world, much of our contemporary history has been assayed and narrated—as must all national histories, and as I have done in this book about Iranian history, a reading that I thus wished to share.[1]

My reading of modernity, thus the code name of a global peril and promise yet to be mapped out and ascertained, is entirely against the categorical distinction habitually made between "tradition" and "modernity"—a wild-goose chase that has preoccupied generations of debates by well-meaning but bewildered public intellectuals. The history of Iran over the last two hundred years has invariably been cast in the bogus binary opposition between "tradition" and "modernity." To this day, the leading Iranian intellectuals, both in and out of their homeland, continue to run after their own tails and ask whether they should be "modern" or "traditional," or posit the problem "between tradition and modernity" as the defining moment of their national destiny. Throughout this book, I have sought to demonstrate that this binary opposition is entirely false and epistemically fabricated on the quintessential principality of a figment of imagination colonially manufactured and code-named "the West." At its European origin, Enlightenment modernity was a self-raising/other-lowering project that, to benefit a small fraction of the world's population code-named "Europe," disenfranchised the overwhelming majority of humanity, which it called "the Orient." For the father of European Enlightenment modernity, Immanuel Kant himself, the Orient extended from the east of the Danube River all the way around the globe to within a millimeter to the west of the English Channel.[2] It is my contention that all the "traditions" that mercenary Orientalists have manufactured for non-Europeans were contrived to authenticate and corroborate the principality of a European modernity that at its core was racist and essentialist, and as such excluded (not by omission but by a deliberate, Kantian and Hegelian, commission) the vast majority of the world. Whether because of a limited critical imagination (e.g., Daryush Shayegan, Daryush Ashuri, and Ramin Jahanbegloo) or because they were paid lucratively to reduce their own nation to "security issues" for the U.S. empire, Iranian intellectuals continue to send an entire nation on the wild-goose chase of whether they ought to be "modern" or "traditional"—in terms identical to those in which the ruling clerical establishment, their presumed enemies but evident counterparts, see the world. Both the traditionalists, as they call themselves, and the modernists, as they congratulate themselves for being, are caught in a vicious circle that necessitates and authenticates the circularity of their futile pursuit.

Against this prevailing trend and predicating my assessment of the cosmopolitan political culture I have sought to retrieve and demonstrate in this book, my reading of modernity runs as follows: There is no center to capitalist modernity and thus no periphery to it either—thus all the so-called traditions manufactured at the periphery of capitalist modernity are the classical cases of Saussurean (and later Derridean) binaries made up just to make *modernity* mean something it inherently does not. Capitalism from its very inception was contingent on the global circulation of accumulated capital, cheap labor, raw materials, and expansive markets. The economic mechanism of that global operation of capitalism was ipso facto colonialism, which is in fact nothing but the abuse of labor by capital writ global. What we have in Iran, as indeed in much of the rest of the world, is thus not *modernity* but *colonial modernity*—and the difference here is between day and night.[3] European modernity is not universal, and as we have received it, it is categorically European in its texture and disposition, and as such it has privileged a few, by giving them agency and endowing them with the primacy of reason and progress, at the horrendous cost of denying such prerogatives to the overwhelming majority of the world's population.[4] *Colonial modernity*, as I understand and propose it here, namely a kind of modernity that brings European reason and progress to the world but delivers them through the gun barrel of European colonial officers, has in the course of colonial history generated its dialectical opposite, namely the epistemic and practical domains of an *anticolonial modernity*—the terms of which are not borrowed from Europe but in fact are articulated on the battlefield of opposing the effective consequence of European modernity, namely colonialism. My proposal here is that fighting back (picking up a gun and shooting back like José Martí and Che Guevara, or picking up a pen and writing back like Frantz Fanon and Edward Said) against European (and later American) colonialists was conducive to the effective articulation of a particular mode of modernity, an *anticolonial modernity*, which has always been contingent on the historical attendance of the colonized upon the modernity of history.

Anticolonial modernity, the way I perceive and articulate it here, is not *reactive* against the philosophical articulation of modernity in the course of European Enlightenment—which Hegel and Kant saw as limited to Europeans and by commission (and not by omission) excluded the (Orientalized) others[5]—but entirely *proactive* and rooted in the anticolonial struggles of peoples around the globe. On that battlefield, the terms of anticolonial modernity were articulated not in merely pragmatic and combative terms, but in terms of a praxis that was ipso facto theoretical: in terms of the paramount parameters of modernity (public reason and universal progress), it posited *a revolutionary reason* that ascribed agency to the subaltern and the way he or she talks, and *an unfolding conception of history* that is open-ended in its quest for freedom. There is thus a prose and a poetry that matches the gun and the machete that the colonized pick up against their colonial tormentors—and the dialectic of this particular enlightenment is what I understand from Frantz Fanon's cultured theorization of violence, or more immediately by Malcolm X's liberating phrase, "by any means necessary."

The idea of *anticolonial modernity* is predicated on a fundamental contradiction at the heart of colonial modernity, namely a modernity that needed an extended colonial domain to have its moral and material disposition assayed and mapped out. The overwhelming majority of the inhabitants of this earth were promised Enlightenment emancipation at precisely the moment that they were denied political agency. What Habermas now calls *societal* and *cultural* modernities have as a result had an entirely different disposition in our neck of the woods.[6] Our *societal modernity* was entirely aborted, while our *cultural modernity* was achieved neither through (what Habermas calls) an instrumental nor indeed through a communicative reason (so for us, even if we were to follow Habermas's path, the problem of the subject is *not* resolved). What has defined our *cultural modernity* (the imaginative symbolics of our worldly self-awareness) has been a creative dialectics charged against both the material condition of our colonially ravaged lands and also the inner dynamics of the culture itself, all leading to a dialectics of cultural inauthenticity, a kind of guerrilla warfare against both its material conditions and its generic ossification—and thus the underlying logic of our movement from one genre of creative cultural resistance to tyranny to another, from prose to poetry to fiction and then to film in the Iranian case. Because our *societal modernity* (the institutional foundations of a participatory presence in globalized capitalism) has been utterly vicarious and not predicated on a robust bourgeoisie with a vested interest in the economic production of reality in their homeland, our *cultural modernity* is precarious and predicated on a body of disembodied intellectuals and their multifarious discourses, in effect producing one set of phantom liberties after another. The reason operative at the heart of our cultural modernity as a result is neither *instrumental* nor *communicative*, but in fact *dialectical* and self-negating, stipulated intermittently against a colonial economy and the logic of its own inauthenticity. This *cultural modernity* has been invariably predicated on a poetics of resistance, an imaginative dialectics of inauthenticity, of crafting and dismantling its own narrative mode of resistance and thus our periodic movements from one dominant cultural medium to another—from prose to poetry, from poetry to performing arts, and from there to cinema and other visual arts.

Habermas's notion of *communicative reason*, as a result, may indeed posit a moment of pause against the postmodernity that has internally dismantled the Enlightenment project, but in fact for much of the rest of the world it means nothing more than perhaps a visual delight in seeing the European Enlightenment self-destruct. But that self-destruction is not constructive for the rest of humanity, where the terms of modernity have been articulated and attested to on the battlefields of their anticolonial history. What has triggered the European soul-searching of the terror of Enlightenment modernity,[7] namely the horrors of the Jewish Holocaust, has been definitive to the structural violence at the heart of European colonialism around the globe. Joseph Conrad's Kurtz in *Heart of Darkness* is the key iconic figure to that structural violence, linking the internal blind spot of Europe to its colonial savageries around the world. The *anticolonial modernity* I detect in Iranian (and I daresay other) encounters with colonial modernity and have tried to articulate in this book takes the disenfranchised position of the colonial person, fighting his or her battles against the colonial robbery of the moral and material foundations of his or her historical agency with creative effervescence, transforms it into the functional equivalent of what Habermas calls *societal modernity*, and from there weds it to the vibrant power of its incessant variations on the theme of *cultural modernity*. The result is a modernity at once anticolonial in the dialectic of its own enlightenment (to give an entirely different and extended twist to Adorno and Horkheimer's critique of the European Enlightenment), and equally empowering at all the colonial ends of European modernity. Thus what I propose as an *anticolonial modernity* at the postcolonial sites is the functional equivalent of *postmodernity* at the capitalist presumption of its epicenters. But whereas at the edge of a normative nihilism postmodernity has dismantled moral and political agency, from the edges of a normalized alterity anticolonial modernity in fact engenders, justifies, and theorizes it.

The normative condition of this anticolonial modernity is what I have suggested as the cosmopolitan disposition of Iranian political culture. What in the aftermath of an Islamic revolution in Iran in 1977–79, and particularly since the cataclysmic changes in world geopolitics since the horrid events of September 11, 2001—and subsequently after the U.S.-led invasion of Afghanistan on October 7, 2001, and the U.S.-led invasion of Iraq on March 20, 2003, is hard to imagine but absolutely necessary to envision is the factual evidence of a cosmopolitan political culture in much of the so-called Third World, a cosmopolitanism now categorically covered under the thick cloud of rapid ramifications of a seismic change dialectically manufactured and sustained among a Jewish state, a Christian empire, an Islamic republic, and a Hindu fundamentalism. In Iran in particular, what we have witnessed ever since the successful Islamization of the Iranian Revolution is a systematic clerical Qomification of Iranian political culture, a militant Islamism taking over and dismantling the nationalist and socialist elements within Iranian political culture at large—all in the name of a bogus and vacuous essentialism called going back to "ourselves," a dangerously delusional and romanticized identity politics that has never been definitive to Iranian (or any other) political culture. Islamism is as definitive to contemporary Iranian political culture as nationalism and socialism; and if the origin of modern ideologies were to be traced back to European colonialism, then the origin of Islam might also be traced back to early Arab conquests—all of which is a futile and ludicrous quest for essentialist authenticity about a culture that in its organic totality flies in the factual face of history: always syncretic, always cosmopolitan, always multicultural, always irreducible to one fictional authenticity or another.

An obvious and perfectly legitimate question to ask at this point is why the Islamists won the game, outmaneuvered all other possible and potential normative claims on Iranian cosmopolitan political culture and established an Islamic republic (and one might add here precisely at the moment that Fukuyama thought "the West" had won the game). The most immediate answer is the sociological fact that the Shi'i clerics in particular have historically been closest to the poorest and the most disenfranchised, and because the secular left and liberal center could not break through the class barriers of their ideological formations. The success of the clerical class, because of its organicity with the urban poor and the impoverished peasantry, is tantamount to its destructive force in breaking down the organicity of the Iranian cosmopolitan culture into a retrograde clerical tribalism that then successfully subsumes and radically changes the face, the form, and even the substance of Iranian culture.[8] As such the clerical class has subsumed the Iranian cosmopolitan culture and has no room for it, while the Iranian cosmopolitan culture has plenty of room for the clerical class. Here is the issue: the triumphant clerical culture has no room for the secular, and the alienated secular no patience for the clerical, but if one were to take a step away from them both and look at the wider spectrum of Iranian culture, there is an evident cosmopolitanism that transcends and embraces them both, accounts for their fictive bipolarity, and can still include much more. It is that cosmopolitan generosity of epistemic space that has escaped the so-called Iranists and has never been properly theorized, or viewed and understood in liberating terms out of this crocked vision of Iranian political culture that keeps going back to a cleric here or an equally dwarfed vision of a secular intellectual there, for salvation and solution. That cosmopolitanism is the modus operandi of the anticolonial modernity that has been the result of more than two hundred years of fighting against colonialism, wherein a new historical person has been born who is neither European in modernity nor Islamic (Oriental) in the presumptions of any tradition—but a historical person with at once local and global agency, and in this particular case with a proverbial Persian accent to her or his prose and poetry of dissent and defiance.

The cosmopolitan culture that underlies much of Iranian history over the last two hundred years is neither entirely Islamic nor anti-Islamic, neither exclusively nationalist nor antinationalist, neither solely socialist nor antisocialist—and yet it is the dialectical culmination of all such political and ideological forces that have come together to form its thick description of our moral and material history. The single most definitive fact of our lives over the last two hundred years has been our consistent battle against the colonial and imperial domination of our destiny—a domination facilitated too eagerly by its local beneficiaries—

which has made the racialized minorities, the disenfranchised communities, the urban poor, and the impoverished peasantries of Europe and the United States our most natural allies in the post/colonial world. The result is that ours in the colonial corner of the capital is not an exclusively Islamic (nativist) or nationalist or socialist position—this is the historical fact of our contemporary history, the semiotic solidarity of all the mosaic signs of our collective identity as a people at the receiving end of a predatory machinery. Our modernity, as a result, is not attained via a borrowed piece, or a stolen page, of a promissory note from European Enlightenment; for ours is a modernity that we have earned on the battlefields of our anticolonial struggles, a struggle we have shared with our neighbors and comrades from Asia to Africa to Latin America, with comrades in the equally brutalized sites internal to the so-called cosmopolitan West.

Anticolonial modernity, as I read and understand it here, is the dialectical logic of an open-ended hermeneutics, an *il pensiero debole* ("weak thought"), as the preeminent Italian philosopher Gianni Vattimo would say, and thus lacks all the teleological narratives of any metaphysics of absolutist certainties.[9] A definitive counter-metaphysics of spontaneity, a morality without an ethic, as John Caputo would say,[10] defines and sustains this cosmopolitanism—the abiding spirit by which Guido Orefice (Roberto Benigni) acts in Benigni's *Life Is Beautiful* (1998), always doing the right thing, without ever uplifting (or more accurately in this case drifting) the right thing into a superlative metaphysics, an abiding ethic, a frightful and violent metaphysics. Thus I imagine anticolonial modernity, and the emancipatory cosmopolitanism that it engenders and entails, as a battlefield between the Nietzschean will to power and Shamlu's will to resist power—from which encounter arises both the politics of our despair and the poetics of our liberties. That there is an erotics of bodily resurrection against spiritual decadence in this, an erotics that links that politics and poetics together, is perhaps best left unsaid, so it remains physically evident, aesthetically sublime, politically rebellious, and thus mysteriously prolific.[11]

Anticolonial modernity has a strong antiracist element in it that understands the prevalent Persian racism directed against all racialized minorities and the Azaris and Mazandaranis in particular as an insidious manifestation of a whitewashed conception of modernity that sees the origin of European Enlightenment as its principal point of reference and thus its primary interlocutor—and so is entirely blinded to the fact that the prevalence of anti-colonial ideas in central Asia and Azerbaijan and Mazandaran has been definitive to Iranian modernity, a fact that renders the exclusive Eurocentricity of the very notion of "modernity" dubious, a phenomenon that needs to be underscored by way of shifting the epistemic site of modernity away from philosophical speculation in Western Europe and toward the anticolonial struggles around the world. To see the presumption of a Eurocentric interlocutor operative in any discussion of modernity in Iran, it is exceedingly important to note that most contemporary Iranian public intellectuals, lost inside the "tradition versus modernity" vicious circle, were either born and bred in Tehran or else are deeply Tehrani-identified, and so cannot see that the origin of Iranian anticolonial modernity is not in Europe but in fact (and as best represented in the monumental significance of such figures as Mirza Fath Ali Akhondzadeh) in central Asia—a major crossroad of anticolonial struggles against British, French, Russian, and even Ottoman imperialisms.

The anticolonial modernity that is evident throughout Iranian social and cultural modernity, its current clouding by an Islamic republic notwithstanding, has been equally conscious of the extraordinary contribution of Iranian women as a doubly abused subcategory of the national agency. Working-class, tribal, and rural Iranian women in particular have been the subaltern of the subaltern—abused and repressed not only by the colonial domination of their homeland and the endemic patriarchy of their own culture but also by a rampant form of bourgeois international feminism that has nothing for them but a class-based contempt.[12] Throughout this book I have sought to highlight the grassroots significance of social movements in which women have had a major presence. In any nativist adaptation of a Eurocentric modernity, a rampant form of masculinist nationalism has in the very definition of the nation negated and dismissed half of the national population by a built-in semiotics of misogyny and patriarchy. It is not accidental that without a single exception all the major Iranian public intellectuals wondering and meandering between "tradition" and "modernity" (from Jalal Al-Ahmad to Daryush Ashuri, from Daryush Shayegan to Ramin Jahanbegloo) are not just men, but men with a built-in blind spot toward Iranian women and their collective predicament in their own homeland. Neither the socialist nor the Islamist component of Iranian political culture has had any better record of having a pride of place for half of humanity. But in the general fabric of Iranian cosmopolitan political culture, and in the conception of anticolonial modernity that excavates the site of struggle against domestic patriarchy and foreign domination alike, a grassroots feminist presence has always been definitive to Iranians' collective struggle for the modernity of their historical agency—an agency most evident in Iranian literary, visual, and performing arts.

The locus classicus of both anticolonial modernity and the cosmopolitan culture that has been historically cultivated through the instrumentality of that historical evidence is the nation-state—flawed, compromising, colonially manufactured, and fastidiously artificial as it is. The domain and disposition of the nation-state is the lemon of colonial history turned into the lemonade of anticolonial modernity.[13] To this day the nation-state remains the optimum domain of cosmopolitanism, for it is in the context of anticolonial nationalism that the emancipatory terms of our modernities have been articulated. Subnational categories (such as Kurdish-, Azari-, or Arab-Iranians), obviously the indices of a nationalism of a different sort, break down the effervescence of that cosmopolitan nationalism in terms of racialized and ethnic and tribal affiliations that more than anything else reduce the cosmopolitan nation into tribal formations, with the most divisive and defeating consequences. If Kurds were to collect themselves from Iran, Turkey, Iraq, and Syria and form a purely Kurdish country, the nightmare of an ethnically cleansed nation-state would only exacerbate the model of clerical tribalism now ruling over Iran. If Kurds were to remain in Iran and as Kurds have a normative, material, and moral presence in the restoration of the Iranian cosmopolitan culture (and the same holds true for Kurds in Iraq, Turkey, and Syria), then a Kurdish component would become instrumental in the making of similar cosmopolitanisms. The same holds true for the Azaris and the Arabs. Suppose the local inhabitants of Khuzestan seceded—what is the point of yet another sheikhdom in the Persian Gulf? But a legitimate Arab, Azari, Kurdish, etc., presence within the cosmopolitan context of Iran as a nation-sate, once the horrid Persian racism is checked and balanced, will result in a mosaic of cosmopolitan disposition true and definitive to Iranian historical experiences.[14] The same holds true for supra-national affiliations such as Islamic, Jewish, and Arab. The nightmare of a transnational Islamic *ummah* is as frightful a proposition as that of an exclusively Jewish state, or a metanational Arab superstate from Morocco to Syria to Yemen. Supratribal categories are even more phantasmagoric and delusional than subnational categories—all of which compromise the anticolonial cosmopolitanism that has historically occasioned and invigorated them.

As a nation-state, Iran remains the site of that cosmopolitan political culture even a quarter of a century after the successful Islamization of its political institutions. One can in fact begin with the current clerical regime in Iran and epistemically and historically peel away at its exclusionary claim to legitimacy by placing and positing it within the larger frame of reference that challenges its absolutist and essentialist claims on the entirety of Iranian cosmopolitan political culture. To begin with the Shi'i juridical clericalism that now rules ruthlessly over Iran (even if we were to extend it to Sunnism and thus the entirety of juridical Islam), that medieval jurisprudence has absolutely no historical ground for claiming Islam in its entirety. Islam has always been a multifaceted and cosmopolitan culture—polyfocal in its discursive dispositions, polyvocal in its linguistic domains in the Arabic, Persian, Turkish, or Urdu languages, and above all polylocal in the geographical expanse of its historical unfolding. Islamic philosophy or Islamic mysticism (Sufism) has as much moral authority to claim the entirety of Islam as does Islamic jurisprudence, the exclusive and very limited domain of the clerical class that now rules over Iran in the name of Islam in its entirety. A bizarre coalition between juridical clericalism, pestiferous ideological Islamism, and the merchant-class bazaar petit bourgeoisie has taken over the entire intellectual and social history of a vastly multifaceted civilization, claiming it all to itself. That claim is both factually fraudulent and historically flawed.[15]

Islamic culture is not exclusively Islamic—not everything said and done in the domain of Islam can be traced to the Qur'anic revelation and the Prophetic traditions. Definitive to what we call Islamic culture are not only multiplicities of technically Islamic discourses ranging from theology and jurisprudence to Islamic philosophy and mysticism but also an abiding literary humanism (Adab) that in its multilingual manifestations—Arabic, Persian, Turkish, and Urdu in particular—has expanded the normative cosmogony and moral imaginary of Muslims far beyond their doctrinal beliefs and dogmatic principles. With the roots of this literary humanism deeply embedded in the most cosmopolitan period of the Abbasid era (750–1258), Adab is as integral and definitive to Islamic (Arabic, Iranian, Turkish, Indian, etc.) culture as the most sacrosanct principles of Islam.[16] The later rise and creative effervescence of literary humanism in Arabic, Persian, Turkish, and Urdu literatures in particular would directly link its institutional authority to this glorious period of Adab.[17] The reigning clergy in Iran not only have no institutional or discursive claim over the nonjuridical dimensions of the religion, but are entirely ignorant of the literary domain of a cultural claim to legitimacy, ipso facto entirely outside their domain of knowledge and authority. Their sole and solitary claim to authority is through their knowledge of Islamic (Shi'i in particular) law, historically at odds with and hostile to Islamic philosophy, Islamic mysticism, and above all literary humanism of all sorts.

The cosmopolitan context and content of Islam at large (and not just in its Shi'i aspects) have in the course of their historical encounters with colonialism been even more vastly complicated by anticolonial cosmopolitanism deeply rooted in a prolonged history of resisting imperial designs on Islamic countries. Here it is crucial to keep in mind that throughout Islamic social history, a major external intellectual force has always acted as the principal interlocutor of its epistemic formations and subsequent ruptures. Islamic philosophy emerged in a dialogue with Greek philosophy; Islamic mysticism was conversant with Christian asceticism and Buddhist spirituality; Islamic theology cultivated its doctrinal disposition in normative juridical exchanges with Jewish theology. The same is true of the rise of the post/colonial Islamic cosmopolitanism that has emerged on the battlefield of

Muslims fighting against the barbarity of colonial intrusions into their homelands. The anticolonial cosmopolitanism that has perforce emerged in Muslim lands has wedded the medieval intellectual history of Islam to its modern affinities with anticolonial movements across continents and cultures—all the way from Latin America to Africa to Asia. Consider Che Guevara going from Latin America to Africa; imagine Malcolm X crossing the boundaries of his African American experience to become a worldly Muslim; notice Frantz Fanon moving from the Caribbean context of European colonialism to its adjacent African domains; imagine Edward Said trespassing his Palestinian predicament and transforming it into a liberation humanism of global dimensions. Those are a few good examples of how trespassing from one limiting domain, without abandoning its normative significance, expands and universalizes a cross-current mobilization of sentiments and reasons, agencies and authorities, moral and material forces, against tyranny and injustice. The same is true about much of the history of the last two hundred years in the so-called Islamic countries, where anticolonial modernities have enriched premodern cosmopolitanism.

Between the premodern cosmopolitanism of worldly cultures and the anticolonial modernities that have emerged in the course of Third World encounters with European colonialism, the modernity of history has found a global theater of operation. It is nonsensical gibberish to trace the origins of contemporary debates about "modernity" to anything prior to the rise of European colonial modernity in the late seventeenth and early eighteenth centuries.[18] It is far more accurate to speak of multiple modernities.[19] But the notion of anticolonial modernity that I have sought to outline in this book, while giving you a panoramic view of Iranian history, neither collapses into the delusional hallucinations of a modernity that goes back a million years, nor falls into the binary trap of "tradition versus modernity," nor does it have to posit the perfectly legitimate proposition of multiple modernities. It accepts the historical fact of the colonially militated European Enlightenment modernity, refuses to succumb to its presumptuous universality, and instead seeks to navigate the site of the rise of an alternative mode of modernity in the anticolonial battlefield of real people fighting against real colonizers.

Rooted in the open-ended liberality of its premodern imagination, predicated on its anticolonial struggles over the last two hundred years, and more than a quarter of a century into the successful formation of an Islamic theocracy notwithstanding, the Iranian cosmopolitan culture, conducive to a liberating reason and a vastly empowering historical agency, is more evident than ever. At the writing of these final words to this book, the prominent Iranian filmmaker Mohsen Makhmalbaf is roaming somewhere in the deep thickets of Afghanistan making yet another film on the predicament of Afghans to show it to the world and promote the cause of justice and democracy there, having already made films in Afghanistan, Tajikistan, Iran, Pakistan, and India, thus transgressing all the received and presumed boundaries of his homeland. Inside Iran, yet another globally celebrated filmmaker, Abbas Kiarostami, has already wedded the horrors of AIDS in Africa to the most miasmatic mysteries of his aesthetic syncopation of poetry on polity and produced a body of cinematic masterpieces beyond the wildest dreams of any neocon artist in Washington, D.C., or his or her clerical counterpart in Qom—a cinema at once ennobling and emancipatory, expansive in its moral imagination and liberating in its aesthetic celebration of the ordinary. Here in New York, the kindred soul of Makhmalbaf and Kiarostami, Amir Naderi, has pushed the boundaries of Iranian cinema, and with it the cosmopolitan culture that has over decades sustained and enriched its miraculous achievements, into ever more effervescent domains. Naderi's two successive cinematic careers, first in Iran in the 1970s and 1980s and now in the United States in the 1990s and 2000s, is the palimpsestic synergy of two convergent measures of worldly aesthetics, at once universal and yet Iranian, planetary and yet particular, a characteristic that makes it almost impossible to tell where Iran ended in Naderi's cinema and where the world began, where the particularities of the sublime rose to meet the universalities of the human condition. Also in New York, Shirin Neshat has already far transgressed into aesthetic domains that have uplifted her Iranian aesthetics well into the global trajectory of her moral and political ecumenicalism. Where did Nikzad Nodjoumi, yet another legendary Iranian artist living in New York, and Ardeshir Mohasses, yet another iconic figure in Iranian graphic art, find the globality of their vision, the planetary parameters of their worldly aesthetics? None of these particular parameters of a national nourishment of a global presence upon the fact and phenomenon of history have been wasted on the limited nativity of the culture. Consider the mind-boggling flourishing of the younger generation of Iranians' presence on the Web. "With an estimated 700,000 blogs," writes one observer, "Farsi [Persian] is now the fourth most popular language for keeping online journals."[20] In the sinuous meanderings of the Web thus thrives the globality of a cosmopolitan culture that will forever speak its cyberspace language with an Iranian accent.

The abiding fact that determines the cosmopolitanism I propose here and shapes the anticolonial modernity that becomes the breeding ground of historical agency is history itself. For much of the rest of the world, those with the patience of a solemn river running quietly through the elongated valleys of any notion of home and habitat, history has not ended. For them history has just begun—for they have just entered it, for they never exited it. Them is also us—for the anticolonial modernity I propose here embraces as much the disenfranchised and racialized minorities within the so-called Metropolitan West as much as it does the rest of the world—and thus the only way that Americans can help promote democracy in Iran or anywhere else in the world is by first and foremost restoring and safeguarding it in their own country.

Notes

Introduction

1. See Francis Fukuyama's *The End of History and the Last Man* (New York: HarperPerennial, 1993) and Samuel P. Huntington's *The Clash of Civilizations and the Remaking of World Order* (New York: Simon & Schuster, 1998).

2. See Azar Nafisi's *Reading Lolita in Tehran: A Memoir in Books* (New York: Random House, 2003) and Kenneth Pollack's *The Persian Puzzle: The Conflict Between Iran and America* (New York: Random House, 2004).

3. See Kenneth Pollack's *The Threatening Storm: The Case for Invading Iraq* (New York: Random House, 2002).

4. The publication of Azar Nafisi's *Reading Lolita in Tehran* achieved three objectives, (1) systematically and unfailingly denigrating an entire culture's revolutionary resistance to a history of savage colonialism; (2) blatantly advancing the cultural foregrounding of a predatory empire; and (3) catering to retrograde and reactionary forces within the United States, forces waging all-out war against various immigrant communities seeking curricular recognition on university campuses. For more detailed critiques of Nafisi's *Reading Lolita in Tehran* see Negar Mottahedeh's "Off the Grid: Reading Iranian Memoirs in Our Time of Total War," *MERIP*, September 2004, and my "Native Informers and the Making of the American Empire," *al-Ahram* no. 797, June 1–7, 2006.

5. See Thomas Cushman, ed., *A Matter of Principle: Humanitarian Arguments for War in Iraq* (Berkeley: University of California Press, 2005).

6. Identifying the United States as an empire is not a radical or left-wing conspiracy by a handful of renegade historians and observers. Mainline observers such as Chalmers Johnson in his extraordinary *The Sorrows of Empire: Militarism, Secrecy, and the End of the Republic* (New York: Henry Holt, 2004) have persuasively argued the case, as have right-wing apologists like Niall Ferguson, who in *Colossus: The Price of America's Empire* (New York: Penguin Press, 2004) encourages the United States to do a better job in being an empire, and come out of the closet and flaunt its imperial hubris more freely. For a classical statement on U.S. imperialism see V.G. Kiernan's

America: The New Imperialism—from White Settlement to World Hegemony (London and New York: Verso, 2005).

1. On Nations Without Borders

1. See Robert O'Meally's *The Jazz Cadence of American Culture* (New York: Columbia University Press, 1998).

2. This remarkable first appearance of Persian literature in the United States is covered in the wonderful scholarship of John D. Yohannan in his *Persian Poetry in England and America: A 200-Year History* (Delmar, NY: Caravan Books, 1977), ix–xviii and 107–58—from which I take this story.

3. As quoted in ibid., 137–38.

4. For an exquisite discussion of the predicament of nationalism in its colonial context, with consequential insights in narrating post/colonial histories, see Partha Chatterjee's *Nationalist Thought and the Colonial World: A Derivative Discourse* (Minneapolis: University of Minnesota Press, 1993).

5. One can only hope to suggest the original Persian in which Farrokhzad wrote her satirical dismantling of Iranian jingoism. For the original of the poem in its entirety see Forough Farrokhzad, "Ay Marz-e Por Gohar," in *Tavallodi Digar (Another Birth)* (Tehran, 1964). The translation of this passage is mine.

6. Shahla Haeri is the author of a pioneering book on temporary marriage in Shi'ism. See her *Law of Desire: Temporary Marriage in Shi'i Iran* (Syracuse, NY: Syracuse University Press, 1989).

7. Critical reconsideration of nations and their narrations have been the subject of groundbreaking work, including Benedict Anderson's *Imagined Communities: Reflections on the Origin and Spread of Nationalism* (London and New York: Verso, 1991), Partha Chatterjee's *The Nation and Its Fragments* (Princeton, NJ: Princeton University Press, 1993), and Homi K. Bhabha's *Nation and Narration* (London: Routledge, 1990). By and large the field of modern Iranian historiography has remained innocent of these developments. An excellent exception is Firoozeh Kashani-Sabet's *Frontier Fictions* (Princeton, NJ: Princeton University Press, 2000). Kashani-Sabet is part of a generation of young historians and social scientists who are radically rethinking the question of modernity in Iran. See also Mohamad Tavakoli-Targhi's *Refashioning Iran: Orientalism, Occidentalism, and Historiography* (London: Palgrave, 2001), Afsaneh Najmabadi's *Women with Mustaches and Men Without Beards: Gender and Sexual Anxieties of Iranian Modernity* (Berkeley: University of California Press, 2005), Janet Afary's *The Iranian Constitutional Revolution, 1906–1911* (New York: Columbia University Press, 1996), Houchang E. Chehabi's *Iranian Politics and Religious Modernism* (Ithaca, NY: Cornell University Press, 1990), and Mansoor Moaddel's *Islamic Modernism, Nationalism, and Fundamentalism: Episode and Discourse* (Chicago: University of Chicago Press, 2005). These scholars are building on a previous body of solid scholarship, best represented by Said Amir Arjomand's *The Turban for the Crown: The Islamic Revolution in Iran*

(London: Oxford University Press, 1989) and Ervand Abrahamian's *Iran Between Two Revolutions* (Princeton, NJ: Princeton University Press, 1982).

8. See Edward Said, *Orientalism* (New York: Vintage, 1978).

9. I have argued this point in some detail in "For the Last Time: Civilization," *Journal of International Sociology* 16, no. 3 (September 2001): 361–68.

10. For the most recent scholarship in the ancient history of Iran see Josef Wiesehofer's *Ancient Persia* (London: I.B. Tauris, 2001), and J. Curtis and N. Tallis's *Forgotten Empire: The World of Ancient Persia* (Berkeley: University of California Press, 2005).

11. I have given a detailed account of these epistemic changes, from Orientalism to area studies to the rise of right-wing think tanks, in my introduction to a new edition of Ignaz Goldziher's *Muslim Studies* (New Brunswick, NJ: Transaction, 2006).

12. The current (early-twenty-first-century) attack of such propagandist hoodlums as Martin Kramer, Daniel Pipes, Stanley Kurtz, and David Horowitz on U.S. academics has a much longer history. The quintessential anti-intellectual disposition of the United States has a long pedigree that was known and diagnosed as early as the mid-nineteenth century, when Alexis de Tocqueville wrote his *Democracy in America.* "I think that in no country in the civilized world is less attention paid to philosophy than in the United States," Tocqueville began the first book of the second volume of his *Democracy in America* (New York: Vintage Books, 1945), 3. This anti-intellectual tradition was picked up and intensified soon after the antiwar and civil rights movement of the 1960s and came to a crucial pinnacle during the Reagan administration (1981–89), with the publication of such deranged documents as Roger Kimball's *Tenured Radicals: How Politics Has Corrupted Our Higher Education* (New York: Ivan R. Dee, 1990). More recently, and particularly after the global outcry against Israeli criminal atrocities in occupied Palestine, and the concerted efforts of the Zionists to silence it, and then following the events of September 11, 2001, in the United States, which occasioned the U.S.-led invasions of Afghanistan and then Iraq, departments of "Middle Eastern" studies became the principal targets of such neocon charlatanism. The publication of the nauseating pamphlet by Martin Kramer, *Ivory Towers on Sand: The Failure of Middle East Studies in America* (Washington, DC: Washington Institute for Near East Policy, 2001); the establishment of the McCarthyite Web site of Campus Watch by a miserably failed academic named Daniel Pipes; the launching of the so-called David Project to defame and character-assassinate the leading scholars of the field; and the publication of *The Professors: The 101 Most Dangerous Academics in America* (New York: Regnery, 2006) by a militant thug named David Horowitz are the major landmarks of this otherwise unfathomable intellectual travesty, marked by a unique and clinically pathological constellation of illiteracy, charlatanism, banality, mendacity, and above all vulgarity. Nowhere other than in the United States, with the possible exception of Israel, would such a constellation of vulgarity and illiteracy be imaginable—and with such access to money, power, and a willing audience to sustain it.

13. For a revealing essay on the power of these neocon think tanks, con-

servative foundations, and their collective effort to manufacture consent to the neocon project, see Lewis H. Lapham's "Tentacles of Rage: The Republican Propaganda Mill, a Brief History," *Harper's*, September 2004. For an excellent account of Leo Strauss, the intellectual guru of this cabal of neocon artists, and his extraordinary influence on American imperial hubris, see Anne Norton, *Leo Strauss and the Politics of American Empire* (New Haven, CT: Yale University Press, 2004).

14. For narrative adaptations of other Che tactics see Ernesto Che Guevara, *Guerrilla Warfare* (Lincoln: University of Nebraska Press, 1998), 7.

15. See Immanuel Kant, *Observations on the Feeling of the Beautiful and Sublime*, trans. John T. Goldthwait (Berkeley: University of California Press, 1960), 109–10. Kant was willing to perform certain moral surgeries on Arabs, Iranians, or Japanese to endow them with the hope of becoming like Europeans. No such luck for other Orientals in Kant's book. "The Negroes of Africa," believed the author of "What Is the Enlightenment" (1784), "have by nature no feeling that rises above the trifling. Mr. [David] Hume challenges anyone to cite a single example in which a Negro has shown talents, and asserts that among the hundreds of thousands of blacks who are transported elsewhere from their countries, although many of them have even been set free, still not a single one was ever found who presented anything great in art or science or any other praiseworthy quality, even though among the whites some continually rise aloft from the lowest rabble and through superior gifts earn respect in the world. So fundamental is the difference between these two races of man, and it appears to be as great in regard to mental capacities as in color" (ibid., 111). On another occasion, Kant quotes a statement about women that is attributed to an African and reported by a certain Father Labat, to which the author of *Critique of Pure Reason* adds, "And it might be that there were something in this which perhaps deserved to be considered; but in short, this fellow was quite black from head to foot, a clear proof that what he said was stupid" (ibid., 113).

16. "Westoxication" (Gharbzadegi) was a term coined by Jalal Al-Ahmad (1923–69) in an essay bearing that title. See his *Gharbzadegi: Weststruckness* (Costa Mesa, CA: Mazda Publications, 1997). For a detailed discussion of his ideas, and a critique of Islamism as in fact the worst kind of ideological affliction with "the West," see my *Theology of Discontent: The Ideological Foundation of the Islamic Revolution in Iran* (New Brunswick, NJ: Transaction, 2006). For an excellent critique of Islamism as afflicted with the delusion of authenticity see Aziz al-Azmeh, *Islams and Modernities* (London and New York: Verso, 1993).

17. For a detailed discussion of the interplay among these three ideologies in modern Iranian history see the new introduction to my *Theology of Discontent*.

18. No other Orientalist in history, and no pestiferous ideologue of any empire, has done more to manufacture this false binary between "Islam" and the "West" than Bernard Lewis. See, among a myriad of other similar works, his *Islam and the West* (Oxford, UK: Oxford University Press, 1994). Where Bernard Lewis left off, his kindred soul, the French neo-Orientalist Gilles Kepel, has picked up. See *The War for Muslim Minds: Islam and the West*

(Cambridge, MA: Harvard University Press, 2006). For a critique of Kepel and his Orientalist pedigree see the new introduction to my *Theology of Discontent*.

19. For more on Iranian cinema and the centrality of its role in the Iranian encounter with colonial modernity see my *Close Up: Iranian Cinema—Past, Present, Future* (London and New York: Verso, 2001).

2. The Dawn of Colonial Modernity

1. Iradj Amini has studied this period of French colonial interest in Iran in his *Napoleon and Persia: Franco-Persian Relations Under the First Empire* (Washington, DC: Mage Publishers, 1999).

2. Sir Denis Wright has two important books on this period: *The English Amongst the Persians* (London: Heinemann, 1977) and *The Persians Amongst the English: Episodes in Anglo-Persian History* (London: St. Martin's Press, 1990). These are two competent and well-researched books, written from the perspective of an English diplomat entirely sympathetic to and in fact a participant in the colonial interventions of his country in Iran. Sir Denis was the first British ambassador to Iran after his government helped the CIA topple the democratically elected government of Muhammad Mosaddeq. His services to British colonialism in the mid-twentieth century were not unlike Major D'Arcy's early in the nineteenth century.

3. The distinguished Iranian scholar Mojtaba Minovi has a wonderful essay on these first groups of students to Europe. See his "Avvalin Karevan-e Ma'refat" ("The First Caravan of Knowledge") in his collected essays, *Tarikh va Farhang* (Tehran: Khwarazmi Publishers, 1973), 380–437. The essay was first published in 1953. Another equally brilliant essay on these early groups of students, written before Minovi's, is by Abbas Iqbal Ashtiyani, another prominent Iranian literary scholar. See "Ketab-e Hajji Baba va Dastan-e Nakhostin Mohasselin-e Irani dar Farang" ("James Morier's *The Adventures of Hajji Baba [of Ispahan]* and the Story of the First Iranian Students in Europe"), *Yadegar* 1, no. 5 (Dey 1323/December 1944–January 1945): 28–50.

4. There are two critical editions of Mirza Saleh's travelogue, covering his trip to England between 1815 and 1819, one by Isma'il Rai'n and the other by Homayun Shahidi. The latter is more accurate and comprehensive. See Mirza Saleh Shirazi, *Gozaresh-e Safar*, edited with an introduction and notes by Homayun Shahidi (Tehran: Rah-e No Publishers, 1983). I gather my account from the early pages of Mirza Saleh's own travelogue.

5. For a classical study of the Qajar period see Ann K.S. Lambton, *Qajar Persia* (London: I.B. Tauris, 1987). For the most recent scholarship in the field see Edmond Bosworth and Carole Hillenbrand, eds., *Qajar Iran: Political, Social, and Cultural Change, 1800–1925* (Costa Mesa, CA: Mazda Publishers, 1992). For an equally important account of the Qajar period, from the perspective of its religious institutions, see Hamid Algar, *Religion and State in Iran: 1785–1906* (Berkeley: University of California Press, 1969). The best theoretical examination of the retardation of capitalist economy in the Qajar period is Ahmad Ashraf's *Mavane'-e Roshd-e Sarmayeh dari dar Iran:*

Doreh-ye Qajar (*The Historical Obstacles for the Growth of Capitalism in Iran: The Qajar Period*) (Tehran: Zamineh Publications, 1980). Ann S.K. Lambton's *Landlord and Peasant in Persia: A Study of Land Tenure and Land Revenue Administration* (London: I.B. Tauris, 1991) is a classic and comprehensive study of the economic condition of Iran in this period. For the most recent scholarship on the subject see Willem Floor's *Agriculture in Qajar Iran* (Washington, DC: Mage Publications, 2003).

6. The most reliable source of information about the literary history of the Qajar period is Yahya Aryanpour's two-volume *Az Saba ta Nima* (*From Saba to Nima*) (Tehran: Amir Kabir, 1976). Mashallah Ajoudani's *Ya Marg Ya Tajaddod: Daftari dar She'r va Adab-e Mashruteh* (*Either Death or Modernity: A Study of the Prose and Poetry of the Constitutional Period*) (London: Fasl-E Ketab, 2002) is a groundbreaking study of Persian literary modernity in the nineteenth century.

7. As quoted in Aryanpour, *Az Saba ta Nima*, vol. 1, 48. This is my translation of the original Persian.

8. As quoted in Amini, *Napoleon and Persia*, 101.

9. For an excellent essay on the relationship between Qaem Maqam Farahani's prose and politics see Mirza Yahya Dolatabadi's introduction to Seyyed Badr al-Din Ahsa'i's collection of Farahani's letters in *Munsha'at Qaem Maqam Farahani* (*Letters of Qaem Maqam Farahani*) (Tehran: Sharq Publications, 1987): xvi–xlvi.

10. As quoted in Denis Wright, *The English Amongst the Persians*, 53.

11. See Immanuel Kant, "What Is Enlightenment?" in Carl J. Friedrich, ed., *The Philosophy of Kant: Immanuel Kant's Moral and Political Writings* (New York: Modern Library, 1993), 145.

12. For extended reflections on the red-herring question of "tradition" and "modernity," all of them trapped inside the binding binary, see the works of Abdolkarim Soroush, Hasan Yusefi Eshkevari, Alireza Alavi Tabar, Ramin Jahanbegloo, Mohsen Kadivar, Hossein Bashiriyeh, Houshang Mahruyan, Daryush Ashuri, Mashallah Ajoudani, and Jamshid Behnam—all in Persian. All these thinkers, without a single exception, take the binary opposition between "tradition" and "modernity" at face value. For them Europe is the center of modernity, while Iran (alas) is caught in the periphery of that modernity and afflicted with tradition. Completely off the mark and hallucinating in the U.S. neoconservative think tanks, wasting our tax money, is Abbas Milani, who in his *Lost Wisdom: Rethinking Modernity in Iran* (Washington, DC: Mage Publishers, 2004), believes Iranians had modernity from about a thousand years ago! Such old and tired clichés, fortunately, are now being discarded and surpassed by a vital set of studies by a new generation of scholars. For the most recent critical examination of the Iranian encounter with modernity see Farzin Vahdat's pathbreaking book, *God and Juggernaut: Iran's Intellectual Encounter with Modernity* (Syracuse, NY: Syracuse University Press, 2002). For an insightful reflection on this book and the issues that it raises see Afshin Matin-Asghari's review in *Critique: Critical Middle Eastern Studies* 14, no. 3 (Fall 2005). The conversation that is now emerging between Farzin Vahdat and Afshin Matin-Asghari on the question of modernity is

infinitely more informed and insightful than anything offered before them. Equally brilliant and insightful is the exquisite work of Darius M. Rejali, *Torture and Modernity: Self, Society, and State in Modern Iran* (Boulder, CO: Westview Press, 1994). Rarely have Foucault's theories of body as the site of political engraving of violence been so perceptively extended and examined in any national context as in Rejali's wonderful work. Perhaps the most baffling problem with such Iranian intellectuals as Daryush Ashuri and Ramin Jahanbegloo, representing a much larger group of captured imaginations and colonized minds blindly defending what they call "modernity," is an arcane ignorance of groundbreaking critiques of modernity launched over the last half-century. Entirely innocent of constitutional critiques of modernity that from Adorno through Heidegger, Foucault, and Derrida, and down to Lyotard and Baudrillard, have shredded the iconic notions of *reason* and *progress* into metaphysical pieces and catapulted the history of continental philosophy to a categorical implosion, these nativist Iranian intellectuals still consider "modernity"—within an archaic cocoon of insularity—the panacea that will cure all the ills and backward "traditions" that have hitherto hindered the entry of Iran into the modern age. Between the paralyzing neutralization of postmodern theories in the United States and the nineteenth-century positivism of Iranian intellectuals still chasing after the mantra of "modernity," what is missing is a post/colonial critique of modernity from within the post/colonial site and with a solid and uncompromising commitment to political action.

13. See Hegel's *Philosophy of History* (New York: Dover Publications, 1956) to see how he casts world history into a programmatic progression from "the Oriental World" toward the "the German World," via two stopovers at the Greek and the Roman worlds. For Hegel, the Orientals are prehistorical and thus prepolitical. The same is true for Kant in his *Observations on the Feeling of the Beautiful and the Sublime* (Berkeley: University of California Press, 1960), in which the Orientals are categorically identified as incapable of the beautiful and the sublime and systematically characterized as "grotesque." The unabashed racism of Kant, particularly against Africans—typical of Europeans at the time—should not distract us from the more fundamental project he outlines. "The Orient" for Kant extends from the Danube River all the way around the world and back to the English Channel. His exclusion of Orientals (which means humanity at large minus Western Europeans) from the beautiful and the sublime is tantamount to and coterminous with his more insidious philosophical denial of historical agency to them—a project he exclusively outlines for the European subject in his three critiques. The endemic problem with Third World reflection on the predicament of modernity, particularly in the postcolonial theories emerging from the South Asian context, is a systematic neglect of this inaugural moment of European Enlightenment modernity in which non–Western Europeans have no place. A similar blind spot is evident in Dipesh Chakrabarty's recent pronouncement, in his *Provincializing Europe* (Princeton, NJ: Princeton University Press, 2000), that in his estimation the European Enlightenment is really a global project and we better come to terms with it. It is not, and we should

never come to terms with it. This insistence on the universality of the European Enlightenment modernity is what Frantz Fanon and generations of anticolonial theorists and activists meant by a "colonized mind."

14. Mohamad Tavakoli-Targhi, a distinguished historian of the Qajar period, has studied these travelogues extensively in his *Refashioning Iran: Orientalism, Occidentalism, and Historiography* (London: Palgrave Macmillan, 2001). This book provides exceptionally well-researched coverage of eighteenth- and nineteenth-century Indo-Persian sources contemporaneous with the rise of European Orientalism. Tavakoli-Targhi has unearthed a particularly significant body of archival material that few scholars before him had examined so thoroughly—though simultaneously with him another gifted young Iranian historian, Firoozeh Kashani Sabet, has far surpassed her generation in an astounding body of scholarship on this very period (see her *Frontier Fictions* in particular). Despite his groundbreaking archival work, the central thesis of Tavakoli-Targhi's book, that there was such a thing as "Occidentalism" on the part of Orientals, paralleling and balancing Orientalism, is of course fundamentally flawed. There was no systematic discipline of "Occidental studies" anywhere in the Muslim or "Oriental" world, and the term "Occidentalism" is Tavakoli-Targhi's own invention, a vacuous copycat imitation of "Orientalism" (something that Tavakoli-Targhi and others like him have fabricated) that corresponds to and means absolutely nothing. A few years after Tavakoli-Targhi's book came out, Ian Buruma and Avishai Margalit published a book with that very title, *Occidentalism: The West in the Eyes of Its Enemies* (New York: Penguin Press, 2004), which, as its subtitle, a variation on the theme of "Why do they hate us?" suggests, carries Tavakoli-Targhi's "Occidentalism" to its neocon conclusions. Tavakoli-Targhi has alternatively used the term "Europology," which is an equally chimerical concoction of his own and has no correspondence to any institutional and formative discipline anywhere in the Arab, Iranian, Indian, or Muslim world. That Iranians and other Muslims traveled to Europe and on occasion wrote about their experiences (particularly, as Tavakoli-Targhi repeatedly points out, imagined European women the same way that the Orientalist did the Oriental women) does not amount to a system of knowledge production called "Occidentalism." Orientalism was not just an accidental aggregate of a multifaceted body of interrelated scholarly works, paintings, musical scores, operas, plays, films, photographs, and travelogues. It was a massive and systematic body of knowledge and fantasy all predicated on a particular epistemic mode of knowledge and illusion production constitutional to European colonialism. Indians, Iranians, and Arabs were not the only "Orientals" that mercenary European Orientalists invented. "The Orient" for Kant and Hegel (and by extension for European Orientalists) extended from the west bank of the Danube River, all the way around the globe, and back to the east of the English Channel. The Indians, the Chinese, the Japanese, the Latin Americans, the Native Americans, the Africans—none of the inhabitants of any part of the world had any delusional construction called "Occidentalism" or "Europology." Iranians and Arabs, like the rest of humanity, were not colonizing Europe, nor were they producing knowledge and illusion to sustain and support any such colonial domination. The occasional travelogues

by those very few who happened to go to Europe, and any other writing they did on Europe, are in fact indices of their bewilderment, awe, admiration, envy, and what Nietzsche called—and, after him, Max Scheler characterized as—*ressentiment*. These are not the epistemic indices of an arrogant, abusive, and manipulative mode of a massive body of knowledge and delusion production about the entirety of the colonized world all around the globe—the way Orientalism was—all designed and executed in order to dominate conquered people and rule them more effectively. Tavakoli-Targhi has either categorically failed to understand the nature of Edward Said's argument in *Orientalism*, or else he is making a positively ludicrous attempt for epistemic ecumenicalism. People around the world did of course resist Orientalist manufacturing of their culture and history, but not through what Tavakoli-Targhi calls "Occidentalism." They did so by both narrative and revolutionary uprisings—something that Edward Said extensively considered and examined (contrary to Tavakoli-Targhi's assertion) in his magnum opus, *Culture and Imperialism*, almost a decade before Tavakoli-Targhi published his *Refashioning Iran*.

15. The most reliable source on Amir Kabir's life and career is Abbas Iqbal Ashtiyani, *Mirza Taqi Khan Amir Kabir*, ed. by Iraj Afshar (Tehran: Tus Publications, 1961).

16. For more details on these translations see Fereydun Adamiyyat, *Andisheh-ye Taraqqi va Hukumat-e Qanun: Asr-e Sepahsalar* (*The Idea of Progress and the Rule of Law: The Era of Sepahsalar*) (Tehran: Khwarazmi Publishers, 1972), 13–28.

17. For more details see Hamid Algar, *Religion and State in Iran: 1785–1906* (Berkeley: University of California Press, 1969), 170.

18. For more on Sepahsalar's reforms see Adamiyyat, *Andisheh-ye Taraqqi*. Adamiyyat's sanguine reading of Sepahsalar's reforms, attraction to European ideals, and visceral anticlericalism ought to be tempered with a more nuanced grasp of all these factors. Adamiyyat is a historian of acute critical intelligence, and his secular reformist reading of the Qajar history is a healthy counterbalance to both the Orientalist and the Islamist readings of the period. But at times his admiration for court-affiliated reformists like Sepahsalar is thematically tinted and critically animated by a visceral hatred of the clerical class, a rather common trait of his generation of secular intellectuals. He scarcely makes a distinction between the positive revolutionary role that certain components of the clerical class played in the course of the Constitutional Revolution and the corrupt leadership of the clerical class that was squarely vested in the Qajar dynasty. Hamid Algar, meanwhile, is exactly the opposite of Adamiyyat and has an entirely positive and uncritical stance vis-à-vis the clerical class and has nothing but praise for them. For a far more balanced assessment of the period see Said Amir Arjomand, ed., *Authority and Political Culture in Shi'ism* (Stony Brook: State University of New York Press, 1988). For more on my own take on the Shi'i clerical role in these and other periods see my "The End of Islamic Ideology," *Social Research* 67, no. 2 (Summer 2000): 475–518.

19. For more on Amin al-Dowleh see his political memoir, *Khaterat-e Siyasi*, ed. Hafez Farman Farmaian (Tehran: Ketab Iran, 1962).

20. Fereydoun Adamiyyat's *Andisheh-ha-ye Mirza Fath Ali Akhondza-deh* (*The Ideas of Mirza Fath Ali Akhondzadeh*) (Tehran: Khwarazmi, 1970) is the most comprehensive study of the life and thoughts of Akhondzadeh.

21. Again, the most reliable source on the ideas and aspirations of Mirza Aqa Khan Kermani is by the indefatigable social and intellectual historian of nineteenth-century Iran, Fereydoun Adamiyyat. See his *Andisheh-ha-ye Mirza Aqa Khan Kermani* (*The Ideas of Mirza Aqa Khan Kermani*)(Tehran: Payam Publications, 1978). For a comprehensive study of these reformist and revolutionary thinkers see also Mohammad Reza Fashahi's *Az Gatha-ha ta Mashrutiyyat: Gozareshi Kutah az Tahavvolat-e Fekri va Ijtima'i dar Jame'eh Feodali Iran* (*From the Gathas to the Constitutional Revolution: A Brief Report on Social and Intellectual Developments in the Iranian Feudal Society*) (Tehran: Gutenberg Publications, 1975), 283–504.

22. The most authoritative study of the Babi movement is Mohammad Reza Fashahi's *Vapasin Jonbesh-e Qorun-e Vosta'i-ye dar Doran-e Feudal* (*The Last Medieval Movement in the Feudal Period*) (Tehran: Javidan Publications, 1977). Also important is Abbas Amanat's *Resurrection and Renewal: The Making of the Babi Movement in Iran, 1844–1850* (Ithaca, NY: Cornell University Press, 1989).

23. I have examined the theoretical foundations of this position of Shi'ism in comparison with other branches of Islam in my *Authority in Islam: From the Rise of Muhammad to the Establishment of the Umayyads* (New Brunswick, NJ: Transaction, 1989). For a discussion of the fundamental paradox at the heart of the Shi'i notion of authority see my "The End of Islamic Ideology."

24. For a comprehensive study of the Tobacco Revolt see Ebrahim Teymouri's *Tahrim Tobacco: Avvalin Moqavemat-e Manfi dar Iran* (The First Negative Resistance in Iran) (Tehran: Jibi Publications, 1982). See also Ann K.S. Lambton's "The Tobacco Régie: A Prelude to the Revolution" in her *Qajar Persia* (London: I.B. Tauris, 1987), 223–76. While in the Islamic Republic the role of the clerical establishment in the making of the Tobacco Revolt is highly exaggerated, revisionist historians like Rudi Matthee (*The Pursuit of Pleasure: Drugs and Stimulants in Iranian History, 1500–1900* [Washington, DC: Mage Publishers, 2005], 230–35) completely downplay it. They are both wrong. The rich and corrupt members of the clerical class had indeed a vested interest in opposing the tobacco concession. Other members of the clergy sided with the native merchant class and opposed it. But the younger, poorer, and more radical elements within the clerical class saw in it a more fundamental cause to oppose the Qajars, and once the popular forces, ranging from the lower to the middle classes, joined the movement, then the event assumed revolutionary proportions, which came to full fruition in the course of the Constitutional Revolution. The fundamental problem endemic in Qajar historiography, both in assessing the clerical class and otherwise, and ranging from Anne Lambton to Rudi Matthee, from Islamists to Iranists, is the conspicuous absence of even a rudimentary appreciation of class formations within the clerical class.

25. From Gayatri Chakravorty Spivak, "Deconstructing Historiography,"

in Donna Landry and Gerald MacLean, eds., *The Spivak Reader* (London and New York: Routledge, 1996), 205.

26. For more detail on Mirza Habib Isfahani see the excellent introduction of Ja'far Modarres Sadeqi to his critical edition of Mirza Habib Isfahani's Persian translation of James Morier's *The Adventures of Hajji Baba of Ispahan*, as *Sargozasht-e Hajji Baba-ye Isfahani* (Tehran: Nashr-e Markaz, 2000), 16–18. Sadeqi's edition of this crucial text is by far the best and most accurate. My gratitude to Mahmoud Omidsalar and Iraj Afshar for procuring this text for me.

27. Ja'far Modarres Sadeqi discusses all these issues in his learned introduction. See also Seyyed Mohammad Ali Jamalzadeh's introduction to his edition of Mirza Habib's translation of Morier's *Adventures of Hajji Baba of Ispahan* (Tehran: Amir Kabir, 1969); Iraj Afshar, "Mirza Habib Isfahani," *Yaghma* 13, no. 10 (Dey 1339/December 1960–January 1961); Mojtaba Minovi, "Hajji Baba and Morier," in *Panzdah Goftar* (Tehran: Tus, 1988); Abbas Iqbal Ashtiyani, "The Book of Hajji Baba and the First Group of Iranian Students in Europe"; Homa Nateq, "Hajji Morier va Qesseh-ye Iste'mar" ("Hajji Morier and the Story of Colonialism"), *Alefba*, 4 (1974); and Abbas Amanat's article on James Morier's *Adventures of Hajji Baba of Ispahan* in *Encyclopedia Iranica*. In a recent PhD dissertation at Columbia University (2004), Kamran Rastegar has also extensively discussed this controversy.

28. See Abbas Amanat, "Hajji Baba of Ispahan," in *Encyclopedia Iranica*.

29. In his assumptions about "masochistic Persian modernists," Abbas Amanat in effect adds yet another racist trait to the abuses that Morier had already heaped on Iranians—but this time by neglecting the political culture of literary receptions. It is now common sense in postcolonial critical literary theory that "the itinerary from colonial through national to post-colonial and/or migrant subjects is complex, diverse, many-leveled . . . [while] the method of reading [of the sort that Abbas Amanat here best represents] has kept to the representation of agency" (Gayatri Chakravorty Spivak, "How to Teach a 'Culturally Different' Book," in *The Spivak Reader*, 261). In contradistinction from Amanat, Ja'far Modarres Sadeqi falls into the opposite trap by being enamored of James Morier's original (see Modarres Sadeqi's introduction to his edition of Mirza Habib's translation, 27), in which it is not quite clear what premise he believes to be a masterpiece of English literature. He takes the continued printings and availability of James Morier's *The Adventures of Hajji Baba of Ispahan* as a sign of its literary significance. The instrumental function of these sorts of colonial texts in the continued racial profiling of nations to this day seems to have completely escaped Ja'far Modarres Sadeqi. Instead, complementing Abbas Amanat's comments, he too accuses those Iranians, like Homa Nateq, who have taken issue with the racist premises of Morier, of being "ignorant and stupid" for having failed to understand the literary significance of Morier's book (ibid., 26). These serious flaws in Sadeqi's introduction, mostly stemming from the fact that he has written it without any critical awareness of English literature, should not detract from his extraordinary scholarship in critically editing Mirza Habib's translation.

30. Fereydoun Adamiyyat has extensively examined these texts and their implications in his *Andisheh-ha-ye Mirza Aqa Khan Kermani*, 213–40.

31. For more on Akhondzadeh's literary achievements see Fereydoun Adamiyyat's *Andisheh-ha-ye Mirza Fath Ali Akhondzadeh*, 32–68 and 238–64, as well as Yahya Aryanpour, *Az Saba ta Nima*, vol. 1, 342–57. The history of Persian theater is now the subject of two brilliant studies: Hamid Amjad, *Teatr-e Qarn-e Sizdahom* (*The Theater of the Nineteenth Century*) (Tehran: Nila Publications, 2002) and Willem Floor, *History of Theater in Iran* (Washington, DC: Mage Publishers, 2005).

32. Mohammad Ali Sepanlu has critically edited and published Zeyn al-Abedin Maraghe'i's *Seyahat-namah Ebrahim Beik* (Tehran: Asfar Publications, 1985).

33. Edward Said, *Culture and Imperialism* (New York: Vintage Books, 1993), 51.

3. A Constitutional Revolution

1. All the questions and answers I quote here, as well as the details and logistics of the scene, are from the official interrogation of Mirza Reza Kermani after he assassinated Nasir al-Din Shah Qajar, as it is reported in Nazim al-Islam Kermani, *Tarikh-e Bidari-Ye Iranian* (*The History of Iranian Awakening*), ed. Ali Akbar Sa'idi Sirjani (Tehran: Agah Publishers, 1983), vol. 1, 97–124.

2. The best biography of Nasir al-Din Shah available in English is by the distinguished Qajar historian Abbas Amanat. See his *Pivot of the Universe: Nasir Al-Din Shah Qajar and the Iranian Monarchy, 1831–1896* (Berkeley: University of California Press, 1997).

3. Edward Said, *Culture and Imperialism*, 196.

4. It is crucial to mark the commencement of these three ideologies during the Constitutional Revolution, because since the successful Islamization of the Iranian Revolution of 1979, the Islamist component of Iranian political culture has taken over and systematically denied—politically suppressed and narratively repressed—the non-Islamist (nationalist and socialist) dimensions of the same political culture. Academic intellectuals, even (or particularly) those who do not live in Iran, have been instrumental in this systematic Islamization of Iranian political culture. The pathology is representative of a larger trend that has now successfully bought into the dominant Islamist language and institutions of the Islamic Republic, engages it with its U.S. neocon counterparts, and thus adds an academic legitimacy to a politically manufactured repression of the cosmopolitan disposition of Iranian political culture. For a more comprehensive critique of this pathology in its larger Asian and African context—which includes people like Gilles Kepel, Olivier Roy, and Bernard Lewis—see the new introduction to my *Theology of Discontent*.

5. See Frantz Fanon, *The Wretched of the Earth* (New York: Grove, 1968), 96 and 102, and Said, *Culture and Imperialism*, 197.

6. The best book on the role of the Shi'i clergy in this period is Hamid

Algar's *Religion and State in Iran: 1785–1906.* The problem with Algar's otherwise impeccable scholarship is that he is too much beholden to the clerical class, has a categorical conception of its functions as quintessentially antigovernmental, and as a result systematically whitewashes the clerics' at times criminal support of the Qajar dynasty. Algar repeatedly talks about the "traditional role of ulama," and characterizes it as being on the side of the people and against the ruling class. There is no such tradition. The clerical class was not uniform in its political functions in this or any other period. At the outset of the Constitutional Revolution it was divided along the class divisions of the society at large. Some of the Shi'i clerics supported the Qajar monarchy; others opted to oppose it because of their anticolonial stance, rooted in their historic connection to the Iranian merchant class. The fragmentation of the Shi'i clerical class in Iran reflected the contemporary class formation of the society at large: the entrenched and beleaguered feudal aristocracy, the emerging and faltering bourgeoisie, and the rural and urban poor. All these classes had their respective representatives among the Shi'i clergy. The endemic retardation of political parties in Iran may in fact be attributed to the fact that these factions within the clerical establishment in effect functioned as political parties. Either romanticizing the clergy, the way Algar does (the current official historians of the Islamic Republic do the same), or demonizing them, the way secular historians such as Fereydoun Adamiyyat do, simply distorts the fact of their at times diametrically opposed, and entirely class-based, loyalties, convictions, and political positions and practices.

7. By far the best account of these preparatory stages of the Constitutional Revolution and their aftermath is Janet Afary's *The Iranian Constitutional Revolution, 1906–1911: Grassroots Democracy, Social Democracy, and the Origins of Feminism* (New York: Columbia University Press, 1996). The classic study of the Constitutional Revolution in Persian is by Ahmad Kasravi, *Tarikh-e Mashruteh-ye Iran* (*The History of Iranian Constitution*) (Tehran: Amir Kabir, 1951). Equally important is E.G. Browne's *The Persian Revolution of 1905–1909* (Cambridge, UK: Cambridge University Press, 1910). These latter books, however, have by now assumed the status of primary sources. Afary's book surpasses all these and other studies of the Constitutional Revolution in the range, depth, and complexity of her scholarship and insights.

8. Said Amir Arjomand has extensively studied the historical vicissitudes of the political function of the Shi'i clerics in his groundbreaking book *The Shadow of God and the Hidden Imam: Religion, Political Order, and Societal Change in Shi'ite Iran from the Beginning to 1890* (Chicago: University of Chicago Press, 1984). See also my "The End of Islamic Ideology."

9. Janet Afary, *The Iranian Constitutional Revolution, 1906–1911*, 18–19.

10. Ibid., 19.

11. For more details on the economic conditions of Iran in this period see Ahmad Ashraf's "The Historical Obstacles for the Growth of Capitalism in Iran," Ann Lambton's *Landlord and Peasant in Persia*, Willem Floor's *Agriculture in Qajar Iran*, and Charles Issawi's *The Economic History of Iran: 1800–1914* (Chicago: University of Chicago Press, 1971). Chapters 1, 6, and 12

in Janet Afary's *The Iranian Constitutional Revolution, 1906–1911*, dealing with the economic foregrounding of the Constitutional Revolution, are equally insightful.

12. Here I distinguish between the historically variable class interests of the clerical establishment and the doctrinally revolutionary disposition of Shi'ism, for which argument see my "The End of Islamic Ideology."

13. For more on the contradictory role of the Shi'i *ulama* in the course of the Constitutional Revolution see chapter 4 of Afary's *The Iranian Constitutional Revolution, 1906–1911*. For additional insights into the role of the *ulama* in this period see chapter 4 of Vanessa Martin's excellent *Islam and Modernism: The Iranian Revolution of 1906* (London: I.B. Tauris, 1989). Equally insightful in this regard is Abdul-Hadi Hairi's *Shi'ism and Constitutionalism in Iran* (Leiden: E.J. Brill, 1977).

14. Fanon, *The Wretched of the Earth*, 148.

15. In *Culture and Imperialism*, Edward Said takes pains to prove that anticolonial movements in much of the world were not limited in their ideological formations to emancipatory ideas coming from imperial nations themselves. "A standard imperialist misrepresentation," Said points out, "has it that exclusively western ideas of freedom led the fight against colonial rule, which mischievously overlooks the reserves in Indian and Arab culture that always resisted imperialism, and claims the fight against imperialism as one of imperialism's major triumphs" (199). This is an entirely misplaced anxiety. The very site of anticolonial movements generates and sustains its own revolutionary ideas, irrespective of their point of origin, irreducible to native or foreign influences, and thus dismantling any claim to cultural authenticity, one way or another. From Che Guevara to Frantz Fanon to Malcolm X, all revolutionary activists have fully realized that it is in the very disposition of the necessary violence at the core of anticolonial movements that emancipatory ideas emerge—ideas that ultimately make a mockery of any colonially constituted East–West divide. For Fanon's reflection on revolutionary violence see *The Wretched of the Earth*, 35–106.

16. For more on Baskerville see Janet Afary's *The Iranian Constitutional Revolution, 1906–1911*, 225, 337. See also Ahmad Kasravi, *Tarikh-e Hijdah Saleh Azerbaijan* (*The Eighteen-Year History of Azerbaijan*) (Tehran: Amir Kabir, 1978), 881, and Ibrahim Safa'i, *Rahbaran Mashruteh* (*The Leaders of the Constitutional Revolution*) (Tehran: Javidan, 1984), 401–2. For more on the letter that Annie Rhea Wilson wrote to Baskerville's parents see Robert D. Burgener, "Iran's American Martyr," *The Iranian*, August 31, 1998, at http://www.iranian.com/History/Aug98/Baskerville (accessed November 2, 2005).

17. See Morgan Shuster, *The Strangling of Persia* (Washington, DC: Mage Publishers, 1987), xiii. See also Robert A. McDaniel, *The Shuster Mission and the Persian Constitutional Revolution* (Minneapolis, MN: Bibliotheca Islamica, 1974). For the text of Aref Qazvini's song for Morgan Shuster see Yahya Aryanpour, *Az Saba ta Nima*, vol. 2, 167–68.

18. Amy Kaplan, *The Anarchy of Empire in the Making of U.S. Culture* (Cambridge, MA: Harvard University Press, 2002), 212.

19. See Willem Floor, *Agriculture in Qajar Iran*, 11.

20. For a pioneering study of the role of women in the course of the Constitutional Revolution see chapter 7 of Janet Afary's *The Iranian Constitutional Revolution, 1906–1911,* Chapter 9 of this book, "International and Multiethnic Solidarity," is equally informative. Groundbreaking new work on the history of Iranian women in the nineteenth and early twentieth centuries is now done by Firoozeh Kashani-Sabet. See her "Patriotic Womanhood: The Culture of Feminism in Modern Iran, 1900–1941," *British Journal of Middle East Studies* 32 (May 2005); see also her "The Politics of Representation: Materialism and Women's Hygiene in Iran, 1896–1941," *International Journal of Middle East Studies* 38, no. 1 February 2006). See also Afsaneh Najmabadi's *Women with Mustaches and Men Without Beards: Gender and Sexual Anxieties of Iranian Modernity* (Berkeley: University of California Press, 2005), and Minoo Moallem, *Between Warrior Brother and Veiled Sister: Islamic Fundamentalism and the Politics of Patriarchy in Iran* (Berkeley: University of California Press, 2005).

21. For a discussion of the social foundation of a parliamentary democracy after the Constitutional Revolution in Iran see chapter 2 of Said Amir Arjomand's *The Turban for the Crown: The Islamic Revolution in Iran* (New York: Oxford University Press, 1988).

22. Edward Said, *Culture and Imperialism,* 195.

23. See in particular the section "Jane Austen and Empire" in Edward Said's *Culture and Imperialism,* 80–97, in which Said repeatedly emphasizes that "it is, as I have been saying throughout, too simple and reductive to argue that everything in European or American culture therefore prepares for or consolidates the grand idea of empire" (80). For a misreading of Said on Jane Austen that maliciously distorts his ideas in order to appease Bernard Lewis, see Nafisi's *Reading Lolita in Tehran,* 289–90.

24. See Gauri Viswanathan, *Masks of Conquest: Literary Study and British Rule in India* (Oxford, UK: Oxford University Press, 1988).

25. See my discussion of this translation in chapter 2 of this book.

26. See chapter 5 of Janet Afary's *The Iranian Constitutional Revolution, 1906–1911* for a discussion of the press in the course of the Constitutional Revolution. The classic study of the press during this period is by E.G. Browne, *The Press and Poetry of Modern Persia* (Cambridge, UK: Cambridge University Press, 1914). There is of course a massive body of recent scholarship on the subject in Persian as well.

27. For an English translation of this poem of Dehkhoda see Ahmad Karimi-Hakkak, *Recasting Persian Poetry: Scenarios of Poetic Modernity in Iran* (Salt Lake City: University of Utah Press, 1995), 68–89.

28. For pioneering research and a thorough discussion of Persian periodicals in this period see Yahya Aryanpour, *Az Saba ta Nima,* vol. 2, 21–117.

29. Ibid., 62.

30. Ibid., 42.

31. Edward Said, *Culture and Imperialism,* 212.

32. See Antonio Gramsci, *Selections from the Prison Notebooks* (New York: International Publishers, 1971), 520. Gramsci's reference is to Georges Sorel (1847–1922), a pioneering theorist of revolutionary violence; see *Reflections on Violence* (New York: Collier Books, 1950).

33. For more on these later developments in Edward Said's thought see his first posthumous book, *Humanism and Democratic Criticism* (New York: Columbia University Press, 2004).

34. See Yahya Aryanpour, *Az Saba ta Nima*, vol. 2, 49.

35. See Janet Afary's *The Iranian Constitutional Revolution, 1906-1911*, 1-13.

36. As noted by Yahya Aryanpour, *Az Saba ta Nima*, vol. 2, 50.

37. Ibid., 86.

38. Ibid., 50. Aryanpour is among the rare literary historians who have paid systematic attention to the significance of the Caucasus, Azerbaijan in particular, in the making of the Iranian Constitutional Revolution. Focusing on this significance, which has scarcely been documented let alone theorized, challenges the Eurocentricity of the very question of "modernity."

39. In the malady of that "Persianist" historiography, Iranian historians, just like their Orientalist counterparts, see the modernity of Iranian history only in categorical juxtaposition for or against "the West." Rarely do these historians (with the notable exception of Yahya Aryanpour, who is light-years ahead of American and American-trained historians in the globality of his regional awareness of modern Iranian history) place Iran in the immediate context of its regional affiliations in central Asia, western Asia, or south Asia.

40. For a discussion see Yahya Aryanpour, *Az Saba ta Nima*, vol. 2, 65.

41. Ibid., 68-69.

42. For a collection of Dehkhoda's *Charand-o-Parand* articles and other writings see Seyyed Muhammad Dabir Siyaqi, ed., *Maqalat-e Dehkhoda* (Tehran: Tirazheh, 1983). For a collection of Dehkhoda's political correspondences see Iraj Afshar, ed., *Nameh-ha-ye Siyasi Dehkhoda* (Tehran: Ruzbahan Publications, 1979). For more on Persian satire see Paul Sprachman, "Persian Satire, Parody and Burlesque," in Ehsan Yarshater, ed., *Persian Literature* (New York: Bibliotheca Persica, 1988), 226-49.

43. See Nazim al-Islam Kermani, *Tarikh-e Bidari-Ye Iranian (The History of Iranian Awakening)*.

44. For further details of these debates see Yahya Aryanpour, *Az Saba ta Nima*, vol. 2, 433-65.

45. For further details see ibid., 456.

46. For a comprehensive study of the lives and poetry of Muhammad Farrokhi Yazdi, Aref Qazvini, Mohammad-Reza Mirzadeh Eshqi, and Malek al-Sho'ara Bahar, see Muhammad Ali Sepanlu, *Chahar Sha'er-e Azadi (Four Poets of Freedom)* (Spanga, Sweden: 1994).

47. For more on Aref's life and poetry see Yahya Aryanpour, *Az Saba ta Nima*, vol. 2, 349-60; see also Muhammad Ali Sepanlu, *Chahar Sha'er-e Azadi*, 27-142.

48. Yahya Aryanpour, *Az Saba ta Nima*, vol. 2, 161.

49. Ibid.

50. For a discussion of the origin of modern Persian fiction and drama in this period see ibid., 236-316. Equally informative is Muhammad Ali Sepanlu's *Nevisandegan-e Pishro-e Iran (Progressive Writers of Iran)* (Irvine, CA: Iran Zamin Publications, 1986). See also Muhammad Este'lami, *Adabiyat-e Doreh-ye Bidari va Mo'asser (The Literature of the Period of Awakening and*

Contemporary Literature) (Tehran: Sepahian-e Enqelab University Press, 1976). On the origin of Iranian cinema in this period see the first chapter of my *Close Up: Iranian Cinema, Past, Present, Future.*

4. The Pahlavis

1. See Fredric Jameson, "Third-World Literature in the Era of Multinational Capitalism," *Social Text* 15 (1986): 65–88. For a critical conversation with this essay see Aijaz Ahmad, *In Theory: Classes, Nations, Literatures* (London and New York: Verso, 1992).

2. Edward Said, *Culture and Imperialism*, 209. In the last part of the passage, Said is quoting from Basil Davidson's *Africa in Modern History: The Search for a New Society* (London: Allen Lane, 1978).

3. Hans-Georg Gadamer, *Truth and Method* (New York: Crossroad, 1989), 301.

4. Ibid., 302. The Gadamerian notion of "horizon," through which understanding is not only not limited but in fact made possible, is the premise of Gadamer's revelatory restitution of "prejudice" not as a hindrance but in fact as the condition of understanding. See his discussion in "Prejudices as Conditions of Understanding," ibid., 277–85.

5. For the vicissitudes of Ayatollah Khomeini's thoughts before and after his exile in Iraq, including his doubts that he would live to see the Pahlavi regime toppled, see the Khomeini chapter in my *Theology of Discontent: The Ideological Foundations of the Islamic Republic in Iran* (New Brunswick, NJ: Transaction, 2006).

6. For an excellent account of the collapse of the Qajars and the rise of the Pahlavis see Cyrus Ghani, *Iran and the Rise of Reza Shah: From Qajar Collapse to Pahlavi Power* (London: I.B. Tauris, 1998). Equally useful is Cyrus Ghani's edited volume of his father's memoirs, *A Man of Many Worlds: The Diaries and Memoirs of Dr. Qasem Ghani*, trans. Cyrus Ghani and Paul Sprachman (Washington, DC: Mage Publishers, 2006). See also Nikki R. Keddie, *Roots of Revolution: An Interpretative History of Modern Iran* (New Haven, CT: Yale University Press, 1981), chapter 5, and Ervand Abrahamian, *Iran Between Two Revolutions* (Princeton, NJ: Princeton University Press, 1982), chapter 3.

7. For more details on this meeting between Aref Qazvini and Rabindranath Tagore see Jamal Omid, *Tarikh-e Cinema-ye Iran* (Tehran: Rozaneh Publications, 1995), 64. For the early history of Iranian cinema see the first chapter of my *Close Up: Iranian Cinema, Past, Present, Future.* For more detail see also Hamid Naficy's forthcoming book, *Cinema and National Identity: A Social History of the Iranian Cinema* (Durham, NC: Duke University Press).

8. The jaundiced history of political parties in Iran, with the obvious exception of the Tudeh Party, is both a cause and a consequence of this endemic populism in Iranian politics. For a study of the history of Iranian political parties see Malek al-Sho'ara Bahar, *Tarikh-e Mokhtasar-e Ahzab-e Siyasi Iran* (Tehran: Jibi Publications, 1942).

9. Leading Iranian public intellectuals on both sides of the argument—from Alireza Alavitabar to Sadeq Ziba Kalam, from Daryush Shayegan to Daryush Ashuri, from Ali Shari'ati to Abdolkarim Soroush, from Seyyed Hossein Nasr to Ramin Jahanbegloo—are the principal examples of captured minds and limited imaginations, epistemically trapped in this myopic distortion of the Iranian encounter with colonial modernity, systematically positing it as a malignant case of an ahistorical binary opposition between "tradition" and "modernity," and thus mistaking the ideological formation of two opposing classes—the Bourgeois International on one side and the urban and rural poor on the other—for essentialist attributes separating a fictitious "tradition" from a metaphysical "modernity." The two most representative examples of this malady are Daryush Ashuri, who has a metaphysical (almost fanatical) conception of and a blind trust in what he calls "modernity," and Seyyed Hossein Nasr, who has an equally mystical and entirely ahistorical conception of "tradition." They are mirror images of each other and as such reflect the epistemic entrapment of an entire generation of intellectuals in a blind alley of history. For a cogent reflection on these figures and their ideas see Mehrzad Boroujerdi, *Iranian Intellectuals and the West: The Tormented Triumph of Nativism* (Syracuse, NY: Syracuse University Press, 1996). Equally insightful is Ali Gheissari's wonderful book *Iranian Intellectuals in the Twentieth Century* (Austin: University of Texas Press, 1997), and Ali Mirsepassi, *Intellectual Discourse and the Politics of Modernization: Negotiating Modernity in Iran* (Cambridge, UK: Cambridge University Press, 2000). The central, and entirely unexamined, problem with all these pathbreaking works is that they all take the epistemic centrality of "the West" for granted and never subject it to historical or epistemic scrutiny.

10. For a classic study of reforms under Reza Shah, albeit one too sanguine about their intents and consequences, see Amin Banani, *The Modernization of Iran, 1921–1941* (Stanford: Stanford University Press, 1961). For a more critical perspective see Keddie, *Roots of Revolution*, chapter 5; and Abrahamian, *Iran Between Two Revolutions*, chapter 3.

11. For an English translation of Hedayat's masterpiece see *The Blind Owl* (New York: Grove Press, 1989). See also Michael Beard's *Hedayat's Blind Owl as a Western Novel* (Princeton, NJ: Princeton University Press, 1990), as well as Ehsan Yarshater's "Sadeq Hedayat: An Appraisal," in Ehsan Yarshater, ed., *Persian Literature*, 318–23. The theme of "annihilation" is now the subject of a superb doctoral dissertation by Jason Bahbak Mohaghegh, defended in 2004 at Columbia University.

12. For a study of the history of Communist movements in Iran see Sepehr Zabih, *The Communist Movement in Iran* (Berkeley: University of California Press, 1966).

13. For an essay on the significance of Nima see my "Nima Yushij and the Constitution of a National Subject," *Oriente Moderno* 22 no. 83 (2003). Good translations of Nima's poems are scarce. Preliminary and moderately successful attempts have been made by Ahmad Karimi-Hakkak to translate Nima into English in his *Anthology of Modern Persian Poetry* (Boulder, CO: Westview Press, 1978), 29–38. For more on Nima Yushij see also Ahmad

Karimi-Hakkak and Kamran Talattof, eds., *Essays on Nima Yushij: Animating Modernism in Persian Poetry* (Leiden: E.J. Brill, 2004).

14. The unveiling of Iranian women in the late nineteenth and early twentieth centuries was a widespread and pervasive phenomenon essentially rooted in the course of the Constitutional Revolution. The attribution of this development to Reza Shah is both false and misleading. For an excellent account of women's participation in the course of the Constitutional Revolution, including the issue of veiling, see Janet Afary's *The Iranian Constitutional Revolution, 1906–1911*, chapter 7.

15. Such unsavory records of the Shi'i clerical establishment are now systematically suppressed, not just by the entrenched propaganda machinery of the Islamic Republic but also by ideologically compatible scholars such as Hamid Algar and Ziba Mir Hosseini, who systematically distort the cosmopolitan disposition of Iranian political culture. For latest intervention in this narrative pacification of Iranian political culture in an Islamist direction, see Ziba Mir-Hosseini and Richard Tapper, *Islam and Democracy in Iran: Eshkevari and the Quest for Reform* (London: I.B. Tauris, 2006).

16. Edward Said, *Culture and Imperialism*, 210.

17. See Kermit Roosevelt, *Countercoup: The Struggle for the Control of Iran* (New York: McGraw-Hill, 1979), ix. For a comprehensive study of the CIA coup in Iran in 1953 see Stephen Kinzer, *All the Shah's Men: An American Coup and the Roots of Middle East Terror* (New York: John Wiley & Sons, 2004).

18. For a comprehensive study of U.S.-Iranian relations, including this crucial period, see James A. Bill, *The Eagle and the Lion: The Tragedy of American-Iranian Relations* (New Haven, CT: Yale University Press, 1988).

19. For more on the Tudeh Party in this period see Ervand Abrahamian, *Iran Between Two Revolutions*, chapters 6–8.

20. For an excellent collection of essays on Mosaddeq's nationalization of the Iranian oil industry see James A. Bill and William Roger Louis, *Musaddiq, Iranian Nationalism, and Oil* (Austin: University of Texas Press, 1988).

21. The translation of this stanza of Sepehri's "The Footsteps of Water" is mine; see Sohrab Sepehri, *Hasht Ketab* (Tehran: Tahuri, 1984), 271–72.

22. There are no good translations of Sepehri available in English. David L. Martin's translation, *The Expanse of Green: Poems of Sohrab Sepehry* (n.p.: Kalimat Press, 1988) must be avoided like a plague. Far superior, but still wanting, is Ahmad Karimi-Hakkak's translation in his *Anthology of Modern Persian Poetry*, 95–104. There is also a good translation of a poem of Sohrab Sepehri by Massud Farzan in Naomi Shihab Nye, *The Space Between Our Footsteps: Poems and Paintings from the Middle East* (New York: Simon & Schuster, 1998), 74. The calamity that the English-speaking world (the United States in particular) faces today, so far as a direct understanding of cultures such as Iran is concerned, is the scarcity of reliable and graceful translations of such primary sources as Sepehri's poetry, while rootless expatriate charlatans write and widely publish nauseating accounts of a fictive Iran that facilitates its cultural denigration.

23. The engineer of the coup, Kermit Roosevelt, has given his own ac-

count of this treachery in his *Countercoup: The Struggle for the Control of Iran*. But far superior in its analytic detail of the CIA coup and based on a more comprehensive body of evidence is Stephen Kinzer's *All the Shah's Men: An American Coup and the Roots of Middle East Terror*.

24. There are two excellent studies of these writers and their significance: M.R. Ghanoonparvar, *Prophets of Doom* (New York: University Press of America, 1984), and Kamran Talattof, *The Politics of Writing in Iran: A History of Modern Persian Literature* (Syracuse, NY: Syracuse University Press, 2000).

25. For more on the June 1963 uprising see Keddie, *Roots of Revolution: An Interpretative History of Modern Iran*, chapter 7. See also Shahrough Akhavi, *Religion and Politics in Contemporary Iran: Clergy-State Relations in the Pahlavi Period* (Albany: State University of New York Press, 1980), particularly chapter 4.

26. For more on Ahmad Shamlu and his revolutionary significance see my essay, "Ahmad Shamlu and the Contingency of our Future" in Negin Nabavi, ed., *Intellectual Trends in Twentieth-Century Iran: A Critical Survey* (Tallahassee: University Press of Florida, 2003), 53–90.

27. The best study of the Mojahedin is by Ervand Abrahamian, *Radical Islam: The Iranian Mojahedin* (London: I.B. Tauris, 1989).

28. There are two good studies of the shah's last few years: Marvin Zonis, *Majestic Failure: The Fall of the Shah* (Chicago: University of Chicago Press, 1991); and William Shawcross, *The Shah's Last Ride* (New York: Touchstone, 1989).

5. An Islamic Revolution

1. For more detail on the demographic and economic condition of Iran at the outset of the 1979 revolution, see A.H. Pesaran, "Economic Development and Revolutionary Upheaval in Iran," in Haleh Afshar, ed., *Iran: A Revolution in Turmoil* (London: Macmillan, 1985), 15–50. For more on the economic condition of Iran during the Pahlavi period, see Jamshid Amuzegar and M.A. Fekrat, *Iran: Economic Development Under Dualistic Conditions* (Chicago: University of Chicago Press, 1971). For an excellent account of urbanization in Iran see Masoud Kheirabadi, *Iranian Cities: Formation and Development* (Austin: University of Texas Press, 1991).

2. The rampant antiblack, anti-Arab, anti-Azeri racism of the manufactured "Persian" Iranians has been a historical cause of many separatist movements in Iran—in Khuzestan, Kurdistan, and Azerbaijan in particular. In late May 2006, the appearance of a racist cartoon in an Iranian daily angered the Iranian Azeris deeply, and major riots erupted in many cities. According to Matthew Collins of BBC: "There have been demonstrations in several parts of north-west Iran, with thousands of ethnic Azeris protesting at a newspaper cartoon. Azeris said the cartoon, which was published earlier this month, compared them to cockroaches. Reports from the cities of Ardebil, Naqadeh and Meshkin Shahr say Iranian security forces fired on demonstrators, killing at least five people. Dozens of others were injured and hundreds arrested"

("Iran Azeris Protest over Cartoon," BBC News, *World Edition*, May 28, 2006). Similar unrest was reported throughout 2005 in Khuzestan province. While the Islamic Republic blamed the British for causing the unrest, to divert attention from the terror they were causing in neighboring Iraq, and while British colonialism has been chiefly responsible for many calamities in Iran, the underlying cause of much such unrest remains the prevalent "Persian" racism.

3. For more on the culture of moviegoing in Iran see my *Close Up: Iranian Cinema, Past, Present, Future*.

4. In his classical exposition on the education of a mullah, Roy Mottahedeh has written extensively and beautifully on the subject. However, the subject that has provided the model of his study comes from an elitist family and is far removed from grassroots figures like Molla Javad that I introduce here. See Roy Mottahedeh's *The Mantle of the Prophet: Religion and Politics in Iran* (New York: Pantheon Books, 1985).

5. For an excellent study of the mass media in the making of the Iranian Revolution of 1979 see Annabelle Sreberny-Mohammadi and Ali Mohammadi, *Small Media, Big Revolution: Communication, Culture, and the Iranian Revolution* (Minneapolis: University of Minnesota Press, 1994).

6. Erika Friedl's exquisite *Women of Dehkoh: Lives in an Iranian Village* (Washington, DC: Smithsonian Institution Press, 1989) captures the stories of ordinary and illiterate Iranian women with unusual care and sensitivity. Friedl's introductory remarks, however, are filled with pestiferous assumptions about "middle-class, educated, Westernized Iranian women," whom she believes consider peasant and small-town women "dirty, dumb, downtrodden, filled with superstitions, and in dire need of enlightenment" (4). There is of course an element of truth in what Erika Friedl argues here. But Friedl's own vindictive prose here seems to have been affected by her interlocutors. The substance of her book, however, is outstanding in revealing the lives of ordinary Iranian women.

7. The pride of place and abiding dignity of ordinary Iranian women of the lower and middle classes are particularly lost, dismissed, and denigrated in the memoir industry of Lipstick Jihadists. In *Reading Lolita in Tehran* we learn that Azar Nafisi has a home servant (more a home slave, really) whom she calls Tahereh Khanoom (not even the dignity of a last name), the person who cleans her house, attends to her children, and does all sorts of other chores while Azar Nafisi and her "girls," as she calls her so-called students, are busy reading *Lolita* and other masterpieces of "Western literature." Restored to her full name and dignity, Tahereh Khanoom is the subaltern figure, the repressed subconscious of the text, whose voice is categorically muttered and silenced—a voice that is in dire need of recognition and global utterance—all against the mendacious, useless chorus of career opportunists who come from exceedingly privileged backgrounds and now barefacedly sit with militant warmongers, plotting against the fate and dignity of an entire nation.

8. For more on the economic condition of Iran during the Pahlavi period see Homa Katouzian, *The Political Economy of Modern Iran: Despotism and Pseudo Modernism, 1926–1979* (London: Macmillan, 1981). On economic

planning during the Pahlavis see George B. Baldwin, *Planning and Development in Iran* (Baltimore, MD: Johns Hopkins University Press, 1967). On the transitional period between the Pahlavis and the Islamic Republic see Hossein Razavi and Firuz Vakil, *The Political Environment of Economic Planning in Iran, 1971–1983: From Monarchy to Islamic Republic* (Boulder, CO: Westview Press, 1984). For a Marxist critique of the Iranian economy of the Pahlavi period see Bizhan Jazani, *Capitalism and Revolution in Iran* (London: Zed, 1980), as well as chapters 13 and 14 of Petter Nore and Terisa Turner, eds., *Oil and Class Struggle* (London: Zed, 1980).

9. In collaboration with Peter Chelkowski, I have studied the iconography of the revolution in *Staging a Revolution: The Art of Persuasion in the Islamic Republic of Iran* (New York: New York University Press, 1999).

10. In this respect an excellent account of the revolutionary mobilization is to be read in Sepehr Zabih, *Iran's Revolutionary Upheaval: An Interpretative Essay* (San Francisco: Alchemy Books, 1979).

11. The political force of the mobilized masses at the time of the revolution was not an empty rhetorical device but had substantial revolutionary character. For a brilliant study of the mobilized poor in this period see the extraordinary work of Asef Bayat, *Street Politics: Poor People's Movements in Iran* (New York: Columbia University Press, 1997). Equally magnificent is Asef Bayat's other pathbreaking book, *Workers and Revolution in Iran* (London: Zed, 1987).

12. I have studied the political dimensions of Persian literature in this period in "The Poetics of the Politics: Commitment in Modern Persian Literature," *Iranian Studies* 18, nos. 2–4 (Spring–Autumn 1985) special issue, *The Sociology of the Iranian Writer*, ed. Michael C. Hillmann. See also the excellent work of M.R. Ghanoonparvar, *Prophets of Doom*.

13. I have studied in some detail the ideas and aspirations of all these ideologues in my *Theology of Discontent*. See also the excellent work of Mansoor Moaddel, *Class, Politics, and Ideology in the Iranian Revolution* (New York: Columbia University Press, 1994).

14. I have examined this charismatic disposition of Shi'ism as a prototype in my *Authority in Islam*. See also Said Amir Arjomand's classic study of the subject in his *The Shadow of God and the Hidden Imam*. Arjomand and I are both deeply influenced by Max Weber's sociological theory of charisma. See Max Weber, "The Sociology of Charismatic Authority," in Hans Gerth and C. Wright Mills, eds., *From Max Weber: Essays in Sociology*, 245–52.

15. For an exquisite collection of essays on Iranian Jews see Houman Sarshar, ed., *Esther's Children: A Portrait of Iranian Jews* (New York: Jewish Publication Society of America, 2002).

16. This prevalent mode of Iranian racism against all provincial cultures is usually predicated on the fabricated notion of a racial construct called "Persian." The construct is utterly meaningless, except as a linguistic designation; it is not a racial, ethnic, national, or cultural designator. The majority of Iranians are not "Persian," meaning the Persian language is not their mother tongue. But even a cursory look at the history of Persian literature shows that all the masterpieces of classical Persian literature were in fact cre-

ated by poets and literati from "the provinces." Rudaki and Ferdowsi were from Khurasan; Nezami was from Azerbaijan; Sa'di and Hafez were from Shiraz; Rumi and Jami were from modern-day Afghanistan. None of them were from Tehran (for Tehran is a very recent urban calamity perpetrated on the Iranian landscape), and if these poets were around today Tehranis would make fun of their accents, were they to recite their own poetry. Rumi's ghazals will not even rhyme properly sometimes unless we read them with what today the Tehranis would condescendingly call an "Afghani accent." The decision of the *Encyclopedia Iranica* to replace "Iran" with "Persia" was an entirely misguided choice—and not just because of such absurd expressions as referring to the Iran-Iraq War as the "Persia-Iraq war." The decision was wrong because it alienates and disenfranchises non-Persian-speaking Iranians from their own culture, and because it is predicated on a fictive construct called "Persia" and ethnically racializes a culture in the historical making of which non-Persians have had an overwhelming role. Today, Iran is a better name for the country than Persia because (1) that is the legitimate and internationally recognized name of the country, (2) it includes all Persian and non-Persian components of Iran, as it includes millions of people who are certainly Iranian but not Persian, and (3) the term "Iran" refers to the contemporaneity of our historical pride of place (dignities and indignities combined), whereas "Persia" refers to an antiquated, antiquarian, and exotic fascination with Persian cats, caviars, and carpets (and now even an empire) that categorically dehumanizes an entire nation to items and icons of European and North American Oriental fantasies. It is of course a horrid legacy of colonialism that a people with a long and proud culture behind them still have to haggle and argue over such rudimentary issues as what to call themselves or even the language they speak—as in this recent Los Angeles affectedness of calling the Persian language "Farsi." You only refer to Persian as "Farsi" when and if you speak Persian. We don't say, "Do you speak Deutsch?" or "I speak français." This particular banality started in the United States during the hostage crisis of 1979–80, when suddenly Iran became "Persia" and "Persian" became "Farsi." Iranian expatriate bourgeoisie trying to distance themselves from the clerical rule of their country stopped calling themselves Iranians and started referring to themselves as "Persians" because Americans, with their legendary and spectacular knowledge of geography, had no blasted clue where this Persia was. "It's somewhere near Transylvania," an acquaintance of mine at Penn used to say upon further inquiry.

17. See Oriana Fallaci, *Interview with History* (New York: Houghton Mifflin, 1977), 272. Fallaci (1929–2006) conducted this interview at a time when she still had some legitimacy to her name. After the events of 9/11, she mutated into a racist Islamophobe of demented proportions. The traces of her phobia of the "Third World" and the danger it poses to "We Europeans" are of course evident even at this stage. For Fallaci's rage against Muslims see her *The Rage and the Pride* (Rome: Rizzoli, 2002). The terror of Fallaci's views is not in the rampant racism evident in her post-9/11 writing; it is in the fact the she is a bestseller both in Europe and in the United States.

18. For a courageous and revealing conversation between Golbarg Bashi

and Ayatollah Montazeri see Golbarg Bashi's "Eyewitness History: Interview with Ayatollah Montazeri," *Payvand News,* 2006 at http://www.payvand.com/news/06/mar/1067.html (accessed May 21, 2006).

19. For an excellent account of women's social and literary movements in Iran see Farzaneh Milani's *Veils and Words: The Emerging Voices of Iranian Women Writers* (Syracuse, NY: Syracuse University Press, 1992). For post-revolutionary developments see Mohammad Mehdi Khorrami and Shouleh Vatanabadi, eds., *A Feast in the Mirror: Stories by Contemporary Iranian Women* (New York: Lynne Rienner Publishers, 2000). For a study of Iranian women outside their homeland see Halleh Ghorashi, *Ways to Survive, Battles to Win: Iranian Women Exiles in the Netherlands and United States* (Huntington, NY: Nova Science, 2002). Equally insightful is Mahnaz Kousha's *Voices from Iran: The Changing Lives of Iranian Women* (Syracuse, NY: Syracuse University Press, 2002).

20. A bureaucratic functionary and neocon artist named Patrick Clawson wrote an article in the heat of the Iranian nuclear crisis (2004–6) in which he suggested that one way of forcing the Islamic Republic to abandon its nuclear project was to ban Iran "from participation in the World Cup" (*Middle East Forum: Promoting American Interest,* September 16, 2005). The problem with intellectual Tweety Birds like Patrick Clawson, chirping around Washington, D.C., wasting our tax money, is that every time they turn around they think they see a pussycat. The soccer match between Iran and the United States in the course of World Cup 1998, which Iran won 2–1 (the goals were scored by three magnificent footballers, Estili at 40', Mahdavikia at 84', and McBride at 87'—and the game was refereed by Meier from Switzerland), was a noble occasion when the two nations came together in a moment of rare friendship and shared humanity. May God save Americans if pathological warmongers such as Clawson are "promoting their interests." Soccer is the only global game in which there is a glimmer of hope that the world might in fact be saved from the terror of subterranean creatures such as Patrick Clawson.

21. The best study of the Mojahedin remains Ervand Abrahamian's *Radical Islam: The Iranian Mojahedin.* There is no comparable study of the Cherik-ha-e Fada'i-e Khalq organization. But in his *Iran Between Two Revolutions,* Abrahamian does discuss them in chapter 10. See also Abrahamian's essay, "The Guerrilla Movement in Iran, 1963–1977," in Haleh Afshar, ed., *Iran: A Revolution in Turmoil,* 149–74. For a pioneering study of the Iranian student groups see Afshin Matin-Asgari's *Iranian Student Opposition to the Shah* (Costa Mesa, CA: Mazda Publishers, 2001).

22. An excellent study of the role of the *ulama* in this and other political uprisings is Hamid Algar's "The Oppositional Role of the Ulama in Twentieth Century Iran," in Nikki R. Keddie, ed., *Scholars, Saints and Sufis* (Berkeley: University of California Press, 1972). For an economic explanation of the causes and failure of the June 1963 uprising see M.H. Pesaran, "Economic Development and Revolutionary Upheaval in Iran," 20–31.

23. Oriana Fallaci, *Interview with History,* 268.

24. When an early Persian translation of Fallaci's *Interview with History* appeared in Iran, the table of contents indicated that the interview with the

shah started on a certain page. But when one turned to that page one discovered that the shah's censors had removed the entire interview, torn it out of the printed sheets before they were bound!

25. For a somber reflection on this early phase of the revolution from the perspective of a British ambassador to Iran at the time see Anthony Parsons, *The Pride and the Fall: Iran 1974–1979* (London: Jonathan Cape, 1984), chapters 5 and 6. For an account of the American position at the same time see the U.S. ambassador's account in William H. Sullivan's *Mission to Iran* (New York: W.W. Norton, 1981). See also Marvin Zonis, *Majestic Failure: The Fall of the Shah*, chapter 9.

26. For a pioneering study of the function of crowd mobilization in Iranian politics see Ervand Abrahamian, "The Crowd in Iranian Politics, 1905–1953," *Past and Present* 41 (December 1968): 184–210.

27. Sha'ban Ja'fari, aka Sha'ban the Brainless, was a legendary thug instrumental in mobilizing a crowd on behalf of the runaway monarch in preparation for the CIA coup. Homa Sarshar has interviewed this Sha'ban in Los Angeles and written a wonderful book on him. See her *Shaban Jafari* (Los Angeles, CA: Naab Publishers, 2002). For more details on this character see also Stephen Kinzer, *All the Shah's Men: An American Coup and the Roots of Middle East Terror*, 180–94. A note on the nomenclature of Sha'ban the Brainless seems necessary. It is a common practice among a particular group of the lumpen underclass in Iran, the so-called Jahels or Lutis, to add adjectives to each other's names. The name of this person is actually Sha'ban Ja'fari. The addition of "the Brainless" (*bi-mokh*) is usually gained in the course of an adventurous and parasitic life. The Jahels gain their adjectival surname by virtue of something specific they have done or are fond of doing. One might be called, for example, Hassan Chap Dast (Hassan the Left-Handed), Abbas Tighi (Abbas the Knife), Reza Tofu (Reza Who Spits Too Much). Sha'ban the Brainless does not mean that he was stupid, but that he did daring and foolhardy things. He had that name before he mobilized a crowd for the shah. But after that event, the epithet assumed an added meaning.

28. See General Robert E. Huyser, *Mission to Tehran* (New York: Harper & Row, 1986), 23. For more detail see Marvin Zonis, *Majestic Failure: The Fall of the Shah*, 246–48. As Zonis clearly documents, the American authorities—from National Security Advisor Zbigniew Brzezinski to the majority leader of the U.S. Senate, Robert C. Byrd of West Virginia (whose son-in-law was apparently Iranian)—were encouraging the shah to use force and were in fact in favor of a military solution. General Huyser's mission to Iran was precisely to see through such a possibility. That a military coup on the model of 1953 did not happen in 1978 was the result of three factors: (1) confusion and disagreement in the Carter administration, which had come to the White House on the premise of safeguarding human rights; (2) the shah's reluctance to use force, hoping to leave the possibility of a graceful exit for himself and to secure his throne for his son; and (3) the massive revolutionary momentum that the killing of a few thousand more people would not have stopped, and in fact would have aggravated. Nevertheless, a coup was a strong possibility.

29. The distinguished Iranian theater and film director Parviz Sayyad later collected a massive body of evidence that pointed the finger at Khomeini's supporters for this fire. He wrote and staged a play on the basis of these documents. For a translation of that play see my edited volume *Parviz Sayyad's Theater of Diaspora* (Costa Mesa, CA: Mazda, 1993).

30. There is an excellent eyewitness account of these tumultuous days in Asef Bayat's *Street Politics*, chapter 3.

31. For a cogent analysis of this period in postrevolutionary development see Said Amir Arjomand, *The Turban for the Crown*, chapters 5–8.

32. The best study of the Freedom Movement that Mehdi Bazargan and Ayatollah Taleqani led is Houchang Chehabi's magnificent *Iranian Politics and Religious Modernism: The Liberation Movement of Iran Under the Shah and Khomeini* (Ithaca, NY: Cornell University Press, 1990). Chehabi's study remains exemplary for both its detail and its theoretical sweep. For the details of Bazargan and Taleqani's ideas see chapters 4 and 6 in my *Theology of Discontent*.

33. For more details of this period see Said Amir Arjomand, *Turban for the Crown*, chapter 8.

34. That systematic pattern of imperial intervention in other people's destinies of course intensified under the neocons during George W. Bush's presidency. Under the delusional rubric of the "war on terrorism" (in effect generating and sustaining terror), the U.S.-led invasions of Afghanistan (2001) and then Iraq (2003) carried the logic of the 1953 coup in Iran to its obscene conclusions. Consider also the fact that the only moderately free and autonomous media in the Arab world, the television and Web site network of Aljazeera, was the subject of a systematic campaign of slander and defamation not just by the Bush administration but by the U.S. media; in fact, Bush contemplated bombing Aljazeera in the course of the U.S. invasion of Iraq. For the details of this report, after the *London Daily Mirror* exposed it, see the BBC News *World Edition* coverage in late November 2005, particularly "Arab TV Staff Blast Bush 'Threat,'" November 24, 2005. The U.S. media remained categorically silent about this atrocious report.

35. For a firsthand account of the American hostages' ordeal see Bruce Laingen's *Yellow Ribbon: The Secret Journal of Bruce Laingen* (New York: Brassey Publications, 1992). Bruce Laingen was the U.S. chargé d'affaires in Iran at the time of the hostage crisis. For more recent studies of the incident see Mark Bowden, *Guests of the Ayatollah: The First Battle in America's War with Militant Islam* (New York: Atlantic Monthly Press, 2006), and David Patrick Houghton, *US Foreign Policy and the Iran Hostage Crisis* (Cambridge, UK: Cambridge University Press, 2001). Colonel James H. Kyle, USAF (Ret.), an expert in special operations and the officer in charge of the air force component of the U.S. rescue mission, has written his account of this operation in *The Guts to Try: The Untold Story of the Iran Hostage Rescue Mission by the On-Scene Desert Commander* (New York: Ballantine Books, 2002). See also Hamilton Jordan's *Crisis: The Last Year of the Carter Presidency* (New York: Berkley Publications, 1983) for an account of the hostage crisis from the perspective of the Carter administration.

36. Ayatollah Khomeini had articulated the specific Shi'i terms of his the-

ocracy decades earlier in his writings. For the details of Khomeini's political ideas see chapter 8 in my *Theology of Discontent*. Hamid Algar has also translated and edited Khomeini's own writings in *Islam and Revolution: Writings and Declaration of Imam Khomeini* (Berkeley, CA: Mizan Press, 1981).

37. Dilip Hiro has provided a fairly reliable account of the Iran-Iraq War in *The Longest War: The Iran-Iraq Military Conflict* (London: Routledge, 1991).

38. Very strange that precisely when under Ronald Reagan (and soon after him under George W. Bush) the notions of evil and Satan were definitive to U.S. political culture, Andrew Delbanco, a distinguished American literary critic, wrote a book, *The Death of Satan: How Americans Have Lost the Sense of Evil* (New York: Noonday Press, 1996), in which he decried the liberal eradication of the central role of evil in American society, and asked for it to come back. All around Delbanco was the systematic demonization of anything and everything non-American, yet Delbanco blamed American liberalism for having wiped out the notion of evil. Coterminous with Ronald Reagan, Ayatollah Khomeini too systematically invoked the notion of the "Great Satan" about the United States. Ronald Reagan's "Evil Empire" (the Soviet Union), Ayatollah Khomeini's "Great Satan" (the United States), and later George W. Bush's "Axis of Evil" (Iran, Syria, and North Korea) are endemic and definitive to a global conception of the world that Delbanco wished for, and yet it was already there—though he wrote a very learned book arguing that alas Satan was dead! Under George W. Bush's administration, and particularly after 9/11, a massive, systematic, and officially sanctioned demonization of Arabs and Muslims, and Islam in general, was rampant in U.S. culture. But presumably Muslims and Islam did not quite figure in the antiliberal, strangely Christian conception of evil that Delbanco harbored and hoped to revive.

39. For the modern history of the civil war in Lebanon, because of all these developments, see Robert Fisk, *Pity the Nation: The Abduction of Lebanon* (New York: Nation Books, 2002). For more historical depth see Kamal S. Salibi, *A House of Many Mansions: The History of Lebanon Reconsidered* (Berkeley: University of California Press, 1990).

40. Abu al-Hassan Bani-Sadr did have a modest role in articulating the economic dimensions of Islamic ideology in the decades leading to the revolution. For more details see my discussion of his ideas in *Theology of Discontent*, chapter 7.

41. I have extensively documented Ayatollah Montazeri's enthusiastic endorsement of the idea of *velayat-e Faqih* before his fall from grace in the new introduction to my *Theology of Discontent*, xxi–xxii.

42. There is a plethora of books on the Iran-Contra Affair. Perhaps the most detailed and reliable is Lawrence E. Walsh's *Firewall: The Iran-Contra Conspiracy and Cover-Up* (New York: W.W. Norton, 1998). Walsh was the independent counsel for the Iran-Contra investigation (1986–93). See also Theodore Draper, *A Very Thin Line: The Iran-Contra Affairs* (New York: Hill & Wang, 1991). Both President Reagan and then vice president George H.W. Bush are implicated in the cover-up and abuse of executive power in these studies. An excellent chronology of the events that clearly outlines the illegal

activities of Oliver North and his superiors was researched and edited by Scott Armstrong, Malcolm Byrne, and Tom Blanton from the National Security Archive. See their *The Chronology: The Documented Day-by-Day Account of the Secret Military Assistance to Iran and the Contras* (New York: Warner Books, 1987).

43. For more on the Sandinista revolution in Nicaragua see Matilde Zimmermann, *Sandinista: Carlos Fonseca and the Nicaraguan Revolution* (Durham, NC: Duke University Press, 2001), and Dennis Gilbert, *Sandinistas: The Party and the Revolution* (London: Blackwell Publishers, 1988).

44. Anoushiravan Ehteshami has covered the crisis of succession to Khomeini in some detail in the first chapter of his excellent *After Khomeini: The Iranian Second Republic* (London: Routledge, 1995).

45. For a collection of cogent essays on the Salman Rushdie affair see Jeremy Jennings and Anthony Kemp-Welch, ed., *Intellectuals in Politics: From the Dreyfus Affair to the Salman Rushdie Affair* (London: Routledge, 1997). See also Gayatri Chakravorty Spivak's "Reading Satanic Verses" in her *Outside in the Teaching Machine* (London: Routledge, 1993), 217-42. Ever since the Salman Rushdie affair, the Arabic word *fatwa* has been used in the U.S. and European press as if it means "a death sentence." *Fatwa* means no such thing. All it means is a "religious edict," not a "death sentence."

46. In the aftermath of Khomeini's fatwa, and even more rabidly after the events of 9/11, Salman Rushdie mutated into a pestiferous anti-Muslim crusader, indistinguishable from his U.S. neocon artist cohorts. It is as if the pre-fatwa Rushdie, with a modicum of progressive politics about him, *was* in fact assassinated, and a neocon imposter took up his name. For my take on the later Salman Rushdie see my "Islam and Globanalization," *al-Ahram*, March 23-29, 2006.

47. I insist on the exact dates of these ten nights not only to note that they occurred *before* the Islamists took over the cause of the revolutionary developments but also in part because these dates have been incorrectly represented on a number of occasions, most notably by Roya Hakakian in her article "In 1979, It Was Blood. In 2005, Is It Pragmatism?" (*Washington Post*, June 19, 2005). These ten nights of public speeches and poetry recitation took place between Monday, Mehr 18, and Wednesday, Mehr 27, 1356, on the Iranian calendar, which corresponds to October 10-19, 1977 (and *not* October 1978, as Hakakian reports to her *Washington Post* readers). Details of these nights are very well known in Iran and are duly recorded in a meticulously collected book edited by Nasser Moazzen, *Dah Shab* (Tehran: Amir Kabir, 1978), which was published in Persian soon after the event. The Ten Nights have been lovingly remembered by Iranians of subsequent generations such as in a beautiful essay by Soheil Assefi in *Sharq*, reprinted in *Asr-e No* of Sunday, Ordibehesht 20, 1383 (May 9, 2004), "Negahi beh Dah Shab-e She'r dar Institute Goethe: Baradar Kakolesh Atashfeshuneh." For additional sources verifying the same dates see the same Soheil Assefi's conversation with Javad Mojabi in *Sharq*, May 6, 2006, as well as a chronology of Houshang Golshiri's life at http://www.golshirifoundation.org/1346-1356.htm. (accessed May 17, 2006) These nights, moreover, were not just "poetry, poetry, poetry," as

Hakakian erroneously reports to her American audience, but in fact contained many brave and straightforward speeches in defense of freedom and against tyranny and censorship, by such noble writers, activists, scholars, and filmmakers as Rahmat Allah Moqaddam Maraghe'i and Simin Daneshvar (first night), Manouchehr Hezarkhani (second night), Shams Al-e Ahmad and Bahram Beiza'i (third night), Gholamhossein Saedi (fourth night), Baqer Mo'meni (fifth night), Houshang Golshiri (sixth night), Islam Kazemiyyeh (seventh night), Mostafa Rahimi (eighth night), Baqer Parham (ninth night), and Mahmoud Etemad Zadeh (tenth night). None of these people read a poem, but they all gave speeches on a range of social and political topics. Yes there were poets too—poets such as Mehdi Akhavan Sales, Ismail Kho'i, Tahereh Saffarzadeh, and Said Soltanpour (just released from the Pahlavi dungeons and soon to be murdered by the Islamic Republic). The events of these ten nights, in which some sixty top-notch Iranian literary and artistic intellectuals and activists participated (fifty-seven men and three women), were so significant that all major foreign embassies in Tehran in fact noted and reported them back to their respective countries. "The educated youth of Tehran," writes Anthony Parsons, who was the British ambassador to Tehran at the time, "were also finding different outlets to express their views in the new atmosphere of relative freedom, or at least of immunity from the mass arrest of the past. In October an important series of poetry readings was held at the (West) German Cultural Centre at which Iranian poets read extracts from their works. One of these poets [Said Soltanpour] had been released from political detention only days earlier. He and others took the opportunity to voice powerful criticisms of the regime in the poems which they read." Sir Anthony then adds, "The audiences were huge, estimated at 62,000 over a period of a week [actually ten days], and demonstrably appreciative. There was no retaliation from the regime" (Anthony Parsons, *The Pride and the Fall*, 56).

48. There is no satisfying biography of Khomeini. What exists is either hagiographical canonization or else dismissive anticlericalism. Baqer Moin's *Khomeini: Life of the Ayatollah* (London: I.B. Tauris, 1999) is a fairly reliable narrative but quite thin in gaining access to the man's character.

49. For a good introduction to Mulla Sadra's philosophy see J.W. Morris's excellent English translation of his *The Wisdom of the Throne: An Introduction to the Philosophy of Mulla Sadra* (Princeton, NJ: Princeton University Press, 1982). For more on the philosophical spirit of the age from which Mulla Sadra emerged see my "Mir Damad and the School of Isfahan," in Oliver Leaman, ed., *A History of Islamic Philosophy* (London: Routledge, 1994).

50. I have explored this theme extensively in my book on the medieval mystic Ayn al-Qudat al-Hamadhani. See my *Truth and Narrative: The Untimely Thoughts of Ayn al-Qudat al-Hamadhani* (London: Curzon Press, 1999).

51. I have discussed this central paradox of Shi'ism in detail in "The End of Islamic Ideology."

52. For more on the iconography and the dramaturgical dimensions of the Islamic Revolution see my (with Peter Chelkowski) *Staging a Revolution:*

The Art of Persuasion in the Islamic Republic of Iran (London: Edward Booth-Clibborn Editions, 1999).

53. I have explored this mimetic aspect of the Shi'i passion play in my "Ta'ziyeh: Theater of Protest," *Drama Review*, 2005.

54. For more on Iranian cinema see Shahla Mirbakhtyar, *Iranian Cinema and the Islamic Revolution* (New York: McFarland & Company, 2005); Richard Tapper, ed., *The New Iranian Cinema: Politics, Representation and Identity* (London: I.B. Tauris, 2002); Hamid Naficy, *Cinema and National Identity: A Social History of the Iranian Cinema* (Durham, NC: Duke University Press, forthcoming); and my *Close Up: Iranian Cinema, Past, Present, Future*. In addition to my essay "Ta'ziyeh: Theater of Protest," I have explored this notion of Shi'i mimesis and its relation to Iranian cinema in my forthcoming volume, *Masters and Masterpieces of Iranian Cinema* (Washington, DC: Mage Publications, 2007).

6. To Reconstruct and Reform

1. For an excellent example of how post-9/11 politics succeeds in eradicating the pre-9/11 memory of the U.S. support for Saddam Hussein and the creation of the monster that later came to haunt the United States, see George Packer's *The Assassins' Gate: America in Iraq* (New York: Farrar, Straus and Giroux, 2005). For Packer and the generation of amnesiac historiography he represents, history begins on 9/11. Infinitely superior in its grasp of history and geopolitics of the region is Ahmed Rashid's excellent study of the Taliban in Afghanistan, *Taliban: Militant Islam, Oil, and Fundamentalism in Central Asia* (New Haven, CT: Yale University Press, 2001).

2. In the post-9/11 historical amnesia, it is imperative to keep in mind the systematic mutation of the cosmopolitan, syncretic, and multifaceted dimensions of the Iranian Revolution of 1979 into an Islamic theocracy. The official historians of the Islamic Republic are not the only ones adamant in categorically Islamizing the revolution. Two prominent foreigners have made significant contributions in that regard. V.S. Naipaul and Michel Foucault visited revolutionary Iran and wrote two entirely different accounts of what they saw—and they both spectacularly missed the point. One made a prominent literary career by consistently missing the point all the way up to a Nobel Prize in literature; the other's theoretical insights into the nature and function of the abnormal and peripheral blinded him to what was right in front of him when he visited Tehran. One of the earliest signs of a pathological Islamophobia, V.S. Naipaul's *Among the Believers: An Islamic Journey* (New York: Vintage, 1981) is an astounding piece of racist hubris by a self-loathing Oriental lashing out against a nation about whom he knew absolutely nothing. Meanwhile, Michel Foucault's dispatches from Tehran for the Italian newspaper *Corriere della Sera* missed the point in an entirely different way. Foucault's ten-day visit to Tehran in September 1978 was predicated on three falsifying facts: (1) he went to revolutionary Iran in search of political oddity and radical antinomies; (2) most if not all his handlers and interpreters in Iran were Islamists or else fascinated by Islamism; and

(3) about a month before Khomeini left Iraq and came to France in October of that year, Foucault was already convinced that what was happening in Iran was an "Islamic" revolution. As a result, Foucault categorically failed to see the underlying multifaceted dimensions of the revolutionary uprising, completely missed its syncretic ideological disposition, and set for himself the task of reading an "Islamic" revolution into what he saw. Janet Afary and Kevin Anderson have collected and translated Foucault's writings on the Islamic Revolution in a recent (and quite unfortunate) study, *Foucault and the Iranian Revolution: Gender and Seduction of Islamism* (Chicago: University of Chicago Press, 2005). The problem with this volume first and foremost is that it shares the outlandish accusation that Foucault was seduced by the Islamic Revolution in Iran, a ludicrous notion that in fact predates Afary and Anderson's study back to 1994, when the French versions of Foucault's Tehran dispatches were first published. Of all people, Janet Afary, a distinguished historian of the Constitutional Revolution, should have been the first to note Foucault's misreading of the ideological complexity of the Iranian Revolution of 1979. Having failed to note this, she and Kevin Anderson go on a bizarre rampage against Foucault, accusing him of being so hasty to criticize "Western" narratives of reason and progress that he collapsed into celebrating premodern forms of solidarity—an accusation at once fallacious in theory and misapplied to Foucault's reading of the Iranian Revolution. The problem with Foucault's reading of the Iranian Revolution was not that he was seduced by a premodern revolution, which he of course was not, but that he took the ideological disposition of it far too Islamically than it actually was at the time. It took a brutal campaign of eliminating all their non-Islamic rivals and a barbaric eight-year war with Iraq, both long after Foucault packed and left Iran and lost interest in its revolution, for the Islamists to appropriate the revolution for themselves. Instead of noting this crucial fallacy, Afary and Anderson have joined the fashionable neocon anti-Foucault tirade of defending the cause of an inanity called "Western reason." For an excellent critical review of Afary and Anderson's book see Jonathan Rée's "The Treason of the Clerics," *The Nation*, August 15–22, 2005. The fundamental problem with Foucault's reading of the Iranian Revolution remains definitive to his groundbreaking critique of Enlightenment modernity, which in his theoretical limitations he grounded only in such peripheral domains as the European asylum houses, leaving the far more exotic Oriental dungeon of the "Western reason" untapped—and thus my insistence throughout this book to articulate a mode of anticolonial modernity that once and for all discards the false perception of "tradition" and "modernity" into which, alas, Foucault fell when he put pen to paper to write about the Iranian Revolution.

    3. The U.S. involvement in arming Saddam Hussein and empowering his megalomaniac designs for the region, including his mass murder of Kurds in Halabja, as well as the U.S. media's complicity in all of these atrocities, is now the subject of an extraordinary study by Sheldon Rampton and John Stauber in their *Weapons of Mass Deception: The Uses of Propaganda in Bush's War on Iraq* (New York: Penguin Books, 2003).

    4. For a good narrative of the First Gulf War, see Alastair Finlan, *The Gulf War 1991* (London: Osprey Publishing, 2003).

5. Bruce Lawrence has collected, edited, and introduced a series of speeches by Osama bin Laden: *Messages to the World: The Statements of Osama bin Laden* (London and New York: Verso, 2005). These speeches are the most solid evidence of the thinking and political behavior of Osama bin Laden. Any attempt, however, to link these utterances to a larger frame of political ideology is fallacious and premature. The phenomenon of Osama bin Laden is the commencement of a whole new phase in radical Islamism that requires a serious consideration, now made almost impossible under the propaganda machinery shifting gears between the United States and its Islamist nemesis. For a preliminary argument against assimilating the phenomenon of Osama bin Laden backward to two hundred years of legitimate Islamic ideological and political resistances to European colonialism (the way such observers as Olivier Roy and Gilles Keppel are doing) see my new introduction to *Theology of Discontent*. There is a vast and growing body of literature by theoretically and historically illiterate writers, suffering even more dangerously from serious scholarly flaws, who seek to satisfy the sensational market for things "Islamic" by providing outlandish formulas as to how and why things have happened in the Islamic world, as if libraries of scholarship do not already exist on the subject. For two recent, and particularly misguided, examples see, Ladan Boroumand and Roya Boroumand's "Terror, Islam, and Democracy," *Journal of Democracy* 13, no. 2 (April 2002), and Reza Aslan's *No god but God: The Origins, Evolution, and Future of Islam* (New York: Random House, 2006). The problem with these sorts of quick-buck takes on Islamic political and intellectual history is that they begin by trying to account for the sensational interest that now exists for matters Islamic and then fabricate a genealogy for their fantasies back to the earliest phases of Islamic history, without the slightest even nominal respect for the vast body of scholarship that exists on these issues. The problem with the Boroumands' take on Islamism (which is the worst of the two examples I cite) is the usual analytic fallacy of beginning with a traumatic event, in this case 9/11, and then fabricating a genealogy for it irrespective of the historical context of the event they thus narrate into a teleology. The same holds true for Aslan's book, which has an even more transcontinental claim on explaining what is happening today in Islam. Aslan's assumption that Islamic juridical legalism has obscured the variegated possibilities of alternative Islams is categorically flawed and suffers from serious lack of exposure to a vast body of scholarship in the field. It is exceedingly instructive to note that in his infamous *The End of History and the Last Man*, Francis Fukuyama continues to rely on such dubious, flawed, and misguided studies of contemporary Islam as the Boroumands' "Terror, Islam, and Democracy." (See Fukuyama's new afterword to the 2006 edition of *The End of History and the Last Man*.) Because of this limitation, Fukuyama comes up with such outlandish conclusions as the assumption that what he calls "radical Islamism" is a sign of identity politics caused by the process of modernization. This singular sign of illiteracy about the rise and fall of Islamic ideologies over the last two hundred years is straight out of mid-twentieth-century modernization theories that wasted so many department of political science faculties for genera-

tions. Muslim ideologues and their followers are not alienated from anything. They are most convinced and connected to their ideas and aspirations, societies and communities—and above all, their ideologies have emerged out of a vast and multifaceted encounter with colonialism: a term, a fact, and a phenomenon for which Fukuyama's analytics simply has no room. To him "the West" (aka the white man) has had a civilizing mission called modernization; this has caused alienation and anomie among "traditional societies" such as those of Muslims (or "Arabs" as he believe is more the case); and these Muslims or Arabs have become violent reactionaries because this modernization process has alienated them from their "traditional" cultures. This is the nonsense that the Boroumands et al. are feeding people like Fukuyama—bad data provided by ill-informed natives to outdated First World theorists. For an infinitely superior study of contemporary Islamism's see Mansoor Moaddel's *Islamic Modernism, Nationalism, and Fundamentalism: Episode and Discourse* and Aziz al-Azmeh's *Islams and Modernities* (London and New York: Verso, 1996). For my extended theoretical reflection on multiple medieval Islamic discourses of legitimacy, which frames Islamic legalism in its proper social and intellectual context, see my *Truth and Narrative*.

6. Karl Schmidt, *The Concept of the Political* (Chicago: University of Chicago Press, 1996), 26–27.

7. For details of the politics of post-Khomeini developments see Anoushiravan Ehteshami, *After Khomeini: The Iranian Second Republic.*

8. Chapters 11 and 12 of Nikki Keddie's *Modern Iran: Roots and Results of Revolution* (New Haven, CT: Yale University Press, 2003) are solid points of reference for developments in the post-Khomeini reconstruction period.

9. See Ali Akbar Hashemi Rafsanjani, *Amir Kabir ya Qahreman e Mobarezeh ba Este'mar* (Tehran: Farahani Publications, 1967), 10.

10. See the chapter on Mehdi Bazargan in my *Theology of Discontent,* 354–55.

11. For a full account of my argument on this proposition see my "The End of Islamic Ideology."

12. For more on Abdolkarim Soroush see the excellent volume prepared by Ahmad Sadri and Mahmoud Sadri, eds., *Reason, Freedom, and Democracy in Islam: Essential Writings of Abdolkarim Soroush* (Oxford, UK: Oxford University Press, 2000).

13. For a critical essay on Soroush's thoughts see my "Blindness and Insight: The Predicament of a Muslim Intellectual," in Ramin Jahanbegloo, ed., *Iran: Between Tradition and Modernity* (New York: Lexington Books, 2004).

14. For more on the intellectual context of these philosophical thoughts see the excellent work of Farzin Vahdat, *God and Juggernaut: Iran's Intellectual Encounter with Modernity.*

15. Abdolkarim Soroush's prolific writings, reflecting much of this paradox, are best represented on his official Web site: http://www.drsoroush.com. See the most recent interview with him, "Democracy, Justice, Fundamentalism and Religious Intellectualism: An Interview with Abdolkarim Soroush" by Ali Asghar Seyyedabadi, cited on this Web site and dated November 2005.

16. For more on Makhmalbaf's early cinema see my "Dead Certainties: Makhmalbaf's Early Cinema," in Richard Tapper, ed., *Studies in Iranian Cinema* (London: I.B. Tauris, 2002). For a comprehensive study of Makhmalbaf's cinema see Eric Egan, *Films of Makhmalbaf: Cinema, Politics and Culture in Iran* (Washington, DC: Mage Publishers, 2005). See also my forthcoming book on Makhmalbaf, *Makhmalbaf at Large* (London: I.B. Tauris, forthcoming).

17. Karl Schmidt, *The Concept of the Political*, 27–28.

18. For my critique of Samuel Huntington's thesis of the "clash of civilizations" see "For the Last Time: Civilizations," *International Sociology* 16, no. 3 (September 2001): 361–68.

19. For a sample of Khatami's ideas see Mohammad Khatami, *Islam, Liberty and Development* (New York: Global Academic Publishing, 1998). An entirely useless and banal set of observations about the Khatami phenomenon is collected in Patrick Clawson et al., *Iran Under Khatami: A Political, Economic, and Military Assessment* (Washington, DC: Washington Institute for Near East Policy, 1998).

20. Scarcely anyone other than historians of the region remembers now, but there is a history of Afghan invasions of Iran that goes all the way back to the early 1700s, when the declining Safavid dynasty was subjected to repeated Afghan incursions into Iranian territories, including the invasion and occupation of Iran all the way down to Isfahan and Qazvin during the reign of Sultan Hossein (reign, 1694–1713). To this day the names of the invading warlords, Mahmoud Afghan and Ashraf Afghan, are mentioned in a tone of anxiety and disgust in Persian chronicles of the period.

21. For a critical set of reflections on the notion of the "Axis of Evil" see Bruce Cumings et al., *Inventing the Axis of Evil* (New York: The New Press, 2004). It was precisely at this point and soon after President Bush placed Iran on the "Axis of Evil" that Fouad Ajami's protégée, Azar Nafisi, published her ignominious *Reading Lolita in Tehran*, telling Americans how horribly women were treated in Iran and how they needed to be liberated. The assumption of a U.S. invasion of Iran—before, during, and after the invasion of Iraq—was very much in the air. In both *Reading Lolita in Tehran* and an array of op-ed pieces that her PR firm (Benador Associates) had arranged for her, Nafisi spoke of the deep pro-American sentiments among Iranians, who hoped for the United States to liberate them from the reign of the ayatollahs. Fouad Ajami and Kanaan Makiya were feeding Americans the same sort of gibberish just before the U.S. invasion of Iraq—that the Iraqis would welcome U.S. soldiers with rose petals and baklava—but when the body bags started coming home, no one held these commentators accountable for their share in these crimes against humanity. No doubt the legitimate anger of some segments of the Iranian population against the atrocities of the ruling elite may indeed degenerate into an illegitimate wish for the U.S. Army to liberate them. But the problem that the United States faces is that people uttering such sentiments to Nafisi and Christopher Hitchens will flee and hide in a hole the minute a shot is fired their way, while the people who will remain and fight to the death are those who have a material and moral investment in the Islamic Republic, those who have not read *Lolita* in Tehran, and

do not converse in English with Christopher Hitchens when he is touring Tehran hotel lobbies—the poor, the disenfranchised, the angry, the same people who stood and fought against Saddam Hussein during the earlier U.S. invasion of Iran camouflaged in the form of the Iraqi army. In a succession of brilliant critical essays, Joseph Massad has exposed the bankruptcy of the ideas of such self-loathing Orientals as Fouad Ajami, Kanan Makiya, and Bassam Tibi. See Joseph Massad's review of Bassam Tibi, *Political Islam and the New World Disorder* (Berkeley: University of California Press, 1998), in *Middle East Journal* 53, no. 3 (Summer 1999); Fouad Ajami, *The Dream Palace of the Arabs: A Generation's Odyssey* (New York: Pantheon Books, 1998), in *Al-Ahram Weekly*, April 30–May 6, 1998; and Samir al-Khalil (aka Kanan Makiya), *Republic of Fear: The Politics of Modern Iraq* (Berkeley: University of California Press, 1990), in *Against the Current*, January 1991; more generally, see Joseph Massad's "Dham al-'Arab bi-Lisan 'Arabi," in *al-Hayat*, December 30, 2002. See Brian Whitaker's "US Thinktanks Give Lessons in Foreign Policy," *Guardian*, August 19, 2002, to read the extent of the stupefying calamity that the PR firm Benador Associates has perpetrated on American, and by extension world, public opinion.

22. This definitive cosmopolitanism of the region, constitutional to its anticolonial social modernity, is entirely lost to such neo-Orientalists as Gilles Keppel and Olivier Roy, who have vastly popularized a singularly Islamist reading of the region. Their reading of the modern history of the region, reflecting and updating Bernard Lewis's, is identical to that of the most reactionary clerical circles in Qom. See Gilles Keppel's *The War for Muslim Minds: Islam and the West* (Cambridge, MA: Belknap, 2004); and Olivier Roy, *Globalized Islam: The Search for a New Ummah* (New York: Columbia University Press, 2004). For a critical reflection on such dangerous misreadings of the region see my new introduction to *Theology of Discontent*. The Israeli invasion of Lebanon in July and August 2006 may very well have expedited the mutation of the Lebanese Hezbollah into a national liberation movement and the rise of a subsequent cosmopolitan political multiculturalism that will include not just Lebanon and Palestine but also both Iraq and Iran, and may indeed have a larger catalytic effect on the regime at large.

23. Fukuyama sought to dance around Islam by relying on such illiterate commentators on contemporary Islam as Ladan Boroumand and Roya Boroumand, or on the neo-Orientalist Islamism of Olivier Roy (see Fukuyama's new afterword to his *The End of History and the Last Man*). There are libraries of work on contemporary Islam of the last two hundred years (even in English—the only language that most of these Washington-based neocons read) that would radically compromise Fukuyama's understanding of what Islam (or any other religious tradition for that matter) has done over the last two hundred years, and of which Fukuyama remains blissfully ignorant.

24. Giorgio Agamben, *State of Exception* (Chicago: University of Chicago Press, 2005), 85–86.

25. See Max Horkheimer and Theodor Adorno's *Dialectic of Enlightenment* (Palo Alto, CA: Stanford University Press, 2002).

26. Giorgio Agamben, *State of Exception*, 86.

27. For the case that Alan Dershowitz has made for the United States to

torture people with full legal immunity see chapter 4 of his *Why Terrorism Works* (New Haven, CT: Yale University Press, 2002). For the endorsement of this hallmark of American concern for the cause of human rights around the world see Michael Ignatieff's equally horrid *The Lesser Evil: Political Ethics in an Age of Terror* (Princeton, NJ: Princeton University Press, 2004).

28. I have examined the inevitable globalization of Iranian art in general and cinema in particular, a corollary consequence of its domestic censorship, in my "Artists Without Borders: On Contemporary Iranian Art," in Octavio Zaya, ed., *Contemporary Iranian Artists: Since the Revolution* (San Sebastian, Spain: Museum of Contemporary Art, 2005). In English, Spanish, and Catalan. In the United States no one has done more to promote Iranian cinema—indeed, world cinema in general—than the distinguished director of the New York Film Festival, Richard Peña.

29. For more on the impact of the Islamic Revolution on Iranian cinema see Hamid Naficy's *Cinema and National Identity: A Social History of the Iranian Cinema* and my *Close Up: Iranian Cinema, Past, Present, Future.*

30. For more on Shirin Ebadi see her memoir, *Iran Awakening: A Memoir of Revolution and Hope* (New York: Random House, 2006). The selection of Azadeh Moaveni, the author of *Lipstick Jihad: A Memoir of Growing Up Iranian in America and American in Iran* (New York: Public Affairs, 2005), as the translator and co-author of Shirin Ebadi's memoir is a particularly unfortunate choice. An infinitely better choice as translator and co-author of Ebadi's memoir would have been the distinguished scholar Nasrin Rahimieh. But apparently her impeccable scholarship, superior command of English, moral integrity, and above all her not having jumped on the bandwagon of Lipstick Jihadists like Moaveni and Roya Hakakian disqualified her for the task. For my take on this band of career opportunists see my "Lipstick Jihadists: Books That Will Misguide You!" *Publio*, Winter 2006.

31. For a critical assessment of the Vietnam Syndrome in the United States and its global consequences see Geoff Simons, *Vietnam Syndrome: The Impact on US Foreign Policy* (London: Palgrave Macmillan, 1998).

32. Giorgio Agamben, *State of Exception*, 86.

7. The End of Islamic Ideology

1. With the fiasco that the U.S. neocons have now visited upon the world, Francis Fukuyama is jumping ship and seems to be the first high-profile figure among them to defect after the terror that the United States has perpetrated in Iraq. See his *America at the Crossroads: Democracy, Power, and the Neoconservative Legacy* (New Haven, CT: Yale University Press, 2006). For a cogent review and exposure of the continued fault lines of his new positions, effectively seeking to correct the course of the Bush administration that has not done exactly as he has said, see the excellent review by Perry Anderson, "Inside Man," in *The Nation* April, 24, 2006.

2. In my *Authority in Islam* I have given a detailed account of this argument about Islam in general, as I have in my essay "The End of Islamic Ideology" about Shi'ism in particular.

3. I have made the first case in considerable historical detail in my *Truth and Narrative*, and the latter in the new introduction to my *Theology of Discontent*.

4. For a cogent account of social conditions in Iran during the reform movement see Fariba Adelkhah's *Being Modern in Iran* (New York: Columbia University Press, 2000).

5. I take much of my data here and elsewhere from a diverse set of Persian dailies published in Tehran during the presidential election of 2005. I have checked and balanced the leading reformist paper *Sharq* with the staunchly conservative *Keyhan* and corroborated the facts and figures of the election with such official news organizations as the ISNA and the IRNA.

6. The most significant component of the opposition movement outside Iran is the Mojahedin-e Khalq organization, entirely discredited inside Iran since its active collaboration with Saddam Hussein during the Iran-Iraq War. Then comes the late shah's son, Reza Pahlavi, wasting his royal funds on useless, self-promoting propaganda, engineered by the U.S. neocons. To read an excellent report on Reza Pahlavi's treacheries with the neocons see Iraj Pakravan, "Pahlavi Pulling a Rajavi?" *The Iranian*, February 10, 2003, at http://www.iranian.com/Opinion/2003/February/Pahlavi/2.html (retrieved on May 30, 2006). Particularly revealing in Iraj Pakravan's article are the two pictures showing Reza Pahlavi in the fitting company of Eleana Benador, the director of the infamous neocon operation Benador Associates. After the Mojahedin and Reza Pahlavi come a number of disgraceful treacheries, such as Abbas Milani and Larry Diamond's West Coast neocon joint venture called the Iran Democracy Project at the Hoover Institution. None of these chicaneries has any grassroots basis inside Iran; all of them are wasting the U.S. taxpayers' precious money—for without exception, any contact between these charlatans and the legitimate opposition will discredit those heroic efforts and perpetuate the illegitimate reign of the Islamic Republic. For a comprehensive essay on the U.S.-based Iranian opposition see Connie Bruck's "Exiles: How Iran's Expatriates Are Gaming the Nuclear Threat," *New Yorker*, March 6, 2006.

7. Abbas Kiarostami's public letter to Mahmoud Ahmadinejad was published a few days before the second round of the election on June 24, 2005, on a variety of Web sites including the following: *Khabgard*, http://www .khabgard.com/?id=1980137215 (accessed June 20, 2005).

8. In an opinion piece that Roya Hakakian wrote for the *Washington Post* ("In Iran, Listen for the Metaphor," *Washington Post*, June 19, 2005) between the first and second rounds of the presidential election, she too argued that the age of idealism in Iran was over and that an era of pragmatism was upon us. The key word in Hakakian's essay is "pragmatism," a word that in her judgment "offers evidence of an Iran that is growing less idealistic and more realistic." One cannot of course abuse one's perspective of hindsight and fault Hakakian's rather ludicrous prediction that this particular presidential election in June 2005 would be a sign of Iranians "struggling to shed the fundamentalism of the last quarter-century." Even astute political observers failed to predict a landslide victory for the most notorious fundamentalist among all the candidates. But one can wonder what in the world the

young, Connecticut-based Iranian meant by describing her homeland as "a country where the primary mode of expression for most of its history has been the romanticized, ambiguous language of poetry." Is that why over the last two hundred years alone scores of Iranian poets have been viciously tortured and murdered—because they had a "romanticized and ambiguous" language? Reza Shah's torturers used to sew the mouths of poets such as Farrokhi Yazdi; his son Mohammad Reza Shah's secret police used to piss in the mouths of writers critical of his regime and cold-bloodedly execute poets such as Khosrow Golsorkhi; Khomeini had poets such as Said Soltanpour shot dead on the spot; and the most distinguished living Iranian poet, Esmail Khoi, cannot even set foot in his homeland. Are these punishments meted out because their victims all speak in the "romanticized, ambiguous language of poetry"?

9. BBC News, World Edition, June 25, 00:31 GMT. Retrieved on that day. The most reliable statistics of the election, facilitating an assessment of the electorates, came from the Islamic Students News Agency (ISNA), which reported that a total of 27,959,253 votes were cast, of which 17,248,782 favored Mahmoud Ahmadinejad, 10,046,701 went to Hashemi Rafsanjani, and 663,770 were declared void and invalid. The newspaper *Sharq* provided the following statistics: first round, 6,159,453 for Rafsanjani and 5,710,354 Ahmadinejad; second round, 27,959,253 total votes cast, 10,710,971 for Rafsanjani (37 percent), and 17,248,282 for Ahmadinejad (63 percent).

10. The obsequious servitude of some leading expatriate Iranian intellectuals to European Enlightenment modernity, corroborating the false dichotomy of "Islam" and the "West" and consistently defending the primacy of one over the backwardness of the other, has now resulted in a bizarre character called Aramesh Dustdar and a sheer act of lunacy he calls "The Impossibility of Thinking in a Religious Culture." His argument is that Iranians and Muslims have not produced a single thinker worthy of this man's approval. The problem with tempests in teacups such as Dustdar is that although they physically live in Europe, they have remained miraculously parasitical and entirely ghettoized inside a hermetic seal of mind-boggling limitation. Frightfully ignorant of the snowstorm of groundbreaking debates over the last half century, bulldozing the European intellectual history from top to bottom and then attacking Iranian and Islamic cultures in their entirety from the vantage point of an outlandish Eurocentrism of the time of Ernest Renan and his generation of racialized theories of culture, people such as Aramesh Dustdar have infested the Weblogestan, as they call it, with an avalanche of nonsense such as "The Impossibility of Thinking in a Religious Culture."

11. For a fuller discussion of Mohsen Makhmalbaf's *The Marriage of the Blessed* see Eric Egan, *Films of Makhmalbaf: Cinema, Politics and Culture in Iran.*

12. For a fuller discussion of Jafar Panahi's *Crimson Gold* see my forthcoming book *Masters and Masterpieces of Iranian Cinema*, chapter 12.

13. For a more detailed discussion of the relationship between fact and fantasy in Kiarostami's cinema, definitive to this scene in Panahi's *Crimson Gold*, see the chapter on Kiarostami in my *Close Up: Iranian Cinema, Past,*

Present, Future. See also the excellent work of Alberto Elena, *The Cinema of Abbas Kiarostami* (London: Saqi Books, 2005).

14. Among the many signs of this Islamic populism was the heavily publicized letter that President Ahmadinejad wrote to President Bush in early May 2006, in a highly flamboyant language reminiscent of the putative letters that the Prophet Muhammad wrote to the Sassanid king and the Roman emperor inviting them to join Islam. For the official text of the letter see the Web site of the ISNA at http://www.isna.ir/Main/NewsView.aspx?ID=News-713360&Lang=P (accessed May 9, 2006). The admonitory letter—taking significant issue with U.S. imperial hubris around the globe, yet in a rhetorical and entirely useless tone—was dismissed by Bush's administration, and in fact backfired when a few Iranian dissidents in and out of their country used its occasion to write scathing letters back to Ahmadinejad rightly accusing him of precisely the sorts of atrocities with which he had charged President Bush. Among such letters was one written by Mohsen Sazegara, once a Muslim revolutionary turned opposition figure inside Iran, who subsequently joined forces with one of the most retrograde neocon ventures in Washington, D.C., the Washington Institute for Near East Policy. With the same blinded zealotry that fanatic catechumens such as Sazegara sought to destroy the cosmopolitan disposition of Iranian political culture to facilitate an exclusively Islamist takeover of its ideals and aspirations, they now join forces with the most fascist elements within the neocon camp—all of course in the Orwellian name of fighting for democracy in Iran. People like Mohsen Sazegara were instrumental in stealing the hopes and betraying the aspirations of a nation and causing a beautiful and cosmopolitan revolution to degenerate into a horrid Islamic theocracy. They have now run away from that theocracy and joined forces with the functional equivalents of the selfsame clerical criminals, though this time around they are clean-shaven and properly attired in suits and ties. If people (like Mohsen Sazegara) who are constitutionally ignorant of the struggles we face here in the United States are not carefully monitored and countered, they will help turn this republic toward the same fascism they created in Iran. Given the criminal record of the Islamic Republic and the theoretical bankruptcy and historical ignorance of the so-called reformists, we must expect even more of these born-again "seculars" coming to the United States. That they have been arrested, incarcerated, or even tortured by their former comrades in the Islamic Republic does not generate an iota of credibility for these career opportunists. For the imminent danger of a rising theocracy in the United States, see an extraordinary book by Kevin Phillips, *American Theocracy: The Peril and Politics of Radical Religion, Oil, and Borrowed Money in the 21st Century* (New York: Viking, 2006).

15. Soon after the election of Mahmoud Ahmadinejad as president, a number of former U.S. hostages in Iran thought he looked like one of their captors. The press in Iran followed the allegation closely, and the leading members of the group that had occupied the American embassy—Abbas Abdi, Mohsen Mir Damadi, and Ma'sumeh Ebtekar—discredited such reports and verified that Ahmadinejad was not one of them. Later Said Hajjarian, a leading reformist who survived an assassination attempt in 1999,

confirmed that the person in the picture who was misidentified as Mahmoud Ahmadinejad was in fact a person named Taqi Mohammadi, who later become an opponent of the Islamic Republic, was arrested, and subsequently committed suicide in prison. (This according to a detailed report in *Sharq*, July 4, 2005.) For the most recent account of the U.S. hostage crisis see Mark Bowden's *Guests of the Ayatollah: The First Battle in America's War with Militant Islam* (New York: Atlantic Monthly Press, 2006).

16. For an excellent essay on the relationship between populism, militarism, and Shi'ism see the insightful essay by Kazem Alamdari, "The Power Structure of the Islamic Republic of Iran: Transition from Populism to Clientelism, and Militarization of the Government, *Third World Quarterly* 26, no. 8 (December 2005).

17. For a full discussion of their economic ideas see their respective chapters in my *Theology of Discontent*.

18. For the promise that Hugo Chávez holds for Latin America and perhaps for the world at large see the forthcoming book by Tariq Ali, *Pirates of the Caribbean* (London and New York: Verso, 2006).

19. The height of the U.S.-Iran standoff on nuclear technology reached a crescendo with the publication of Seymour Hersh's article "The Iran Plans," *New Yorker*, April 17, 2006, in which he revealed a Pentagon plan to invade Iran. This article marked the height of a global concern for yet another disastrous U.S. military adventure in the region.

20. The publication of Abbas Milani's "Can Iran Become a Democracy?" *Hoover Digest*, no. 2 (2003) could be read as a clear indication that by 2003, the same year that Azar Nafisi published her *Reading Lolita in Tehran* while at the SAIS in Washington, D.C., the West Coast neocons were already in competition with their East Coast counterparts. Between Nafisi telling her American readers that her teaching of the "Western classics" had ensured a pro-American constituency in Iran, and Milani telling them that the Iranian middle class was the fifth column of U.S. imperial designs in the region, the East Coast and West Coast neocons had bracketed the discourse and concluded that Iran was quite figured out. For more on Milani's services to the U.S. neocons, see Ervand Abrahamian, "Empire Strikes Back: Iran in U.S. Sights," in *Inventing the Axis of Evil: The Truth About North Korea, Iran, and Syria*, chapter 2. The recruiting patterns of such neocon operations as the SAIS and the Hoover Institution need a more thorough examination. For a preliminary assessment, see my "Native Informers and the Making of the American Empire," *Al-Ahram*, June 1–17, 2006.

21. During the second term of George W. Bush's presidency, Secretary of State Condoleezza Rice declared the allocation of millions more dollars to topple the Iranian regime (aka to "promote democracy in Iran"). Among the expatriate Iranian neocon operations accepting money from this fund, wasting our tax money, while lending legitimacy to the Bush administration as an arbiter of human rights abuses, at a time that the whole world was indignant at U.S. human rights abuses around the globe—in Iraq, Afghanistan, Cuba, and an entire labyrinth of torture chambers in Europe, in particular—was a Connecticut-based outlet called the Iran Human Rights Documentation Center, which openly declared that it received money from the U.S. State

Department to engage in its activities. The systematic abuse of human rights by the Islamic Republic was thus inoculated against any kind of criticism by this treacherous act of pretending to defend human rights in Iran while effectively lending legitimacy to U.S. imperial warmongering around the globe. The board of directors of this center includes Ramin Ahmadi, Roya Hakakian, and Roya Boroumand. For more details see their Web site at http://www .iranhrdc.org.

22. For a principled refutation of Michael Ignatieff's work see Conor Gearty's "Legitimising Torture—with a Little Help," *Index on Censorship: Torture—A User's Manual*, January 2006, available at http://www .indexonline.org/en/news/articles/2005/1/international-legitimising-torture-with-a-li.shtml (accessed May 23, 2006). "The 'enormous moral hazard' identified by Ignatieff," Gearty concludes, "is unlikely to have kept . . . the Rumsfeldians, Donald himself, awake at night. But what probably helped him sleep soundly was the knowledge that a coterie of idealistic, well-meaning liberal intellectuals and human rights lawyers have handed him the intellectual tools with which to justify his government's expansionism, just as they now allow his cronies to parade their abuse of human dignity as evidence of their moral superiority."

23. At the height of the nuclear standoff between the Islamic Republic and the Bush administration, a fugitive Iranian journalist named Amir Taheri published an article in the Canadian daily the *National Post* in which he fabricated a story that the Islamic Republic was about to force its Jewish citizens to wear something like the Star of David Jews had to wear in Nazi Germany, thus provoking legitimate international outrage. The *National Post* had to retract the story and apologize to its readers. For more details of the event see Jim Lobe's "Yellow Journalism and Chicken Hawks," *Asia Times*, May 25, 2006. The basis of this fabricated news was a piece of legislation in the Islamic parliament mandating the specifics of "Islamic clothing," targeted particularly against Iranian women, a no less totalitarian and atrocious act of the Islamic Republic that was entirely ignored once it became clear that the Iranian Jewish community was not its target.

24. For more on the rise and demise of liberation theology in Latin America see Gustavo Gutierrez, *A Theology of Liberation: History, Politics and Salvation* (New York: Orbis Books, 1988).

Postscript

1. This reading of modern world economic history is very much indebted to and largely in line with Immanuel Wallerstein's argument in *The Modern World System: Capitalist Agriculture and the Origins of the European World Economy in the Sixteenth Century* (New York: Academic Press, 1974). But to me the beneficiaries of this world system were not just the European capitalists but also the comprador bourgeoisie that came to facilitate the plundering of their native lands; nor indeed were those disenfranchised by the system exclusively non-European, for the European working class and peasantry were very much at the mercy of the same abusive system, and thus shared

the destiny of the poor and the powerless around the world. Thus, I have concluded that colonialism is in fact nothing but the abuse of labor by capital writ large and globalized, which conclusion leads me to believe that capitalism at its very inception has always been already global, with colonialism not accidental but in fact definitive to it, as definitive as the working class, the cheap labor it provides, and the raw material it transforms into manufactured and sellable goods. The evidence of this position we can see as much in economic as in semiotic terms: all the bourgeoisie around the world look the same—they all think they are white; while all the working classes and the peasantries around the globe also look the same—they are racialized into abused minorities, while in fact they are the majority, ruled over by a white-washed minority that thinks and projects itself as the normative majority. It is a bizarre paradox, but that is how it is. Next time you watch Akira Kurosawa's magnificent film *The Seven Samurai* (1954), see it with this idea in mind, and you'll see my point. And if you don't have access to *The Seven Samurai*, then just see John Sturges's *The Magnificent Seven* (1960), or better yet see John Lasseter and Andrew Stanton's *A Bug's Life* (1998)—they are both nicked and cloned from Kurosawa.

2. Again I refer you to the very last part of Immanuel Kant's *Observations on the Feeling of the Beautiful and Sublime*, 109ff.

3. There is a vast and growing body of literature on the notion of colonial modernity. Most immediately useful is Frederick Cooper's *Colonialism in Question: Theory, Knowledge, History* (Berkeley: University of California Press, 2005), in which he seeks to generate a syncopated synthesis among all previous articulations of colonial modernities and posits the notion of colonial modernity as a merely "claim-making device" (146). Before Cooper, David Scott in his *Refashioning Futures* (Princeton, NJ: Princeton University Press, 1999) had extensively demonstrated the effect of European modernity on the political manufacturing of the colonial subject. Meanwhile, Antoinette Burton's "Introduction: The Unfinished Business of Colonial Modernities," in Antoinette Burton, ed., *Gender, Sexuality, and Colonial Modernities* (London: Routledge, 1999), traced a similar colonial formation on the modernized colonial body. Equally important readings of the notion of colonial modernities in their African and Asian contexts are articulated by Achille Mbembe in his "On the Power of the False," *Public Culture* 14 (2002); by Nicholas Dirks, in his pioneering study, "Colonialism Is What Modernity Was All About," *Public Culture* (1990); by Partha Chatterjee in his "Two Poets and Death: On Civil and Political Society in the Non-Christian World," in Timothy Mitchell, ed., *Questions of Modernity* (Minneapolis: University of Minnesota Press, 2000); by Saurabh Dube's "Colonialism, Modernity, Colonial Modernities," in *Nepantla: Views from the South* 3, no. 2 (2000); and by a number of other postcolonial theorists in Tani E. Barlow, ed., *Formations of Colonial Modernities in East Asia* (Durham, NC: Duke University Press, 1997). The notion of an *anticolonial modernity*, which I have suggested in this book, seeks to shift the emphasis away from *the impact* of European modernity on the colonized world and toward *the responses* of the colonial world to their colonial occupiers by way of producing *effective* (not alterna-

tive) modernities. On the notion of "alternative modernities" see Björn Wittrock, "Modernity: One, None, or Many? European Origins and Modernity as a Global Condition," *Daedalus* 129, no. 1 (2000), and John D. Kelly, "Alternative Modernities or an Alternative to 'Modernity': Getting Out of the Modernist Sublime," in Bruce M. Knauft, ed., *Critically Modern: Alternatives, Alterities, Anthropologies* (Bloomington: Indiana University Press, 2000).

4. For this reason I categorically disagree with the argument put forward by Dipesh Chakrabarty in his *Provincializing Europe: Postcolonial Thought and Historical Difference* (Princeton, NJ: Princeton University Press, 2000), 3–26, that the European Enlightenment is a universal project. It is not. It is not, not because the world does not want it, but because European philosophers and theorists of Enlightenment modernity specifically dismissed the rest of humanity from partaking in it—for the world was the object of European knowledge for Kant, and as such was a plaything not a humanity, and as such it lacked agency, autonomy, primacy. The exclusion of the non-European was definitive and integral to the very notion of European modernity. If the world enters it, it is no longer either European or European modernity.

5. I have discussed this Kantian-Hegelian writing of "the Oriental" out of history, in a dialogue with the distinguished Indian subalternist Ranajit Guha, in some detail in my "No soy subalternista," in Ileana Rodriguez, ed., *Convergencia de tiempos: Estudios subalternos / contextos latinoamericanos estado, cultura, subalternidad* (Atlanta: Editions Rodopi b.v., 2001), 49–59.

6. For the initial statement of Jürgen Habermas on modernity see his *The Philosophical Discourse of Modernity: Twelve Lectures* (Cambridge, MA: MIT Press, 1990). For a comprehensive discussion of Habermas's defense of modernity see Maurizio Passerin d'Entrèves and Seyla Benhabib, eds., *Habermas and the Unfinished Project of Modernity: Critical Essays on the Philosophical Discourse of Modernity* (Cambridge, MA: MIT Press, 1997). See in particular Maurizio Passerin d'Entrèves's introduction, pages 1–37, for more on Habermas's distinction between *societal* and *cultural* modernities.

7. Theodore Adorno and Max Horkheimer's *Dialectic of Enlightenment: Philosophical Fragments* (Palo Alto, CA: Stanford University Press, 2002) is the inaugural text that ushered in the beginning of the end of modernity for Europe.

8. This is so far as the substance of contemporary Iranian political scene is concerned. When it comes to the scholarly representation of Iranian political culture, chiefly responsible for the systematic breakdown of the evident cosmopolitanism of Iranian culture, and that of its regional countries at large, first and foremost is the bloated legacy of Orientalism, and after that the area studies' pathological reduction of cultures and the complexity of their multifaceted dimensions to security issues at major U.S. and European academic institutions. (For an updating of Edward Said's critique of Orientalism see my introduction, "Ignaz Goldziher and the Question Concerning Orientalism," in the new edition of Ignaz Goldziher's *Muslim Studies* [New Brunswick, NJ: Transaction, 2006]). Particularly notorious after the heyday of Orientalism and simultaneous with the political scientism of area studies has been the discipline of anthropology, which in fact prides itself on being

illiterate, and thus chiefly responsible for anthropologizing—rendering living and thriving cultures premodern, native, nativist, and primordial. In the field of Iranian studies in particular, from the generation of Michael Fischer and Bill Beeman to that of Ziba Mir Hosseini, this definitive illiteracy of the anthropologist about the Iranian cosmopolitan culture has resulted in categorical provincialization of a political culture that the anthropologist has had no clue which way to read. Not one anthropologist of the Iranian scene has a blasted clue about the flowering achievements of Iranian literary and artistic modernities. (Michel Fischer categorically reduces them to objects of anthropological, entirely meaningless, observation and comes up with useless insights.) See for example Michael M.J. Fischer, *Mute Dreams, Blind Owls, and Dispersed Knowledges: Persian Poesis in the Transnational Circuitry* (Durham, NC: Duke University Press, 2004) for a set of quite curious, but entirely vacuous and useless, observations about Iranian cinema. The anthropologist, as a rule, is far more at home in Qom (or any other remote town or small village) than in Tehran, is far more conversant with a half-literate mullah than with a multilingual poet, novelist, or filmmaker—and this is so far less because of the pathological monolingualism of the cultural anthropologist (who can scarcely ask for a glass of water in "the native's language" without the help of the native informer) than because of fundamental epistemic limitations as to how the integrated complexity of a living culture operates. Furthermore, there is a pathological relation of power operative between a white European or American male anthropologist and the provincial or rural setup of his anthropological observations that feeds into the active primitivization of a living culture. This is not to deny or denounce or dismiss the extraordinary significance of provincial or rural lives in countries such as Iran, but (quite to the contrary) to mark the epistemic reduction of the totality of a culture that includes such sites but is not normatively limited to or defined by them. Jalal Al-Ahmad, Gholamhossein Saedi, Bahman Ibrahim Beigi, and scores of other Iranians have done vastly informative studies of Iranian rural and provincial and tribal lives—but they have never reduced the totality or organicity of the Iranian cosmopolitan culture to such sites, as European and American anthropologists have habitually done. The history of European and American anthropology in Iran over the last half century clearly indicates that if you place a juridical text of some significance in front of the anthropologist, she or he can (with, of course, the help of a native, as anthropologists call them) read and decipher a page or two and run away theorizing the people they thus believe they have understood. But place a poem by Ahmad Shamlu, or a film by Abbas Kiarostami, or a novel by Shahrnoush Parsipour, or a picture by Shirin Neshat in front of them, and they have no blasted clue which way to run for cover. They will have not the faintest idea what to do, for example, with the literary audacity of Shahrnoush Parsipour, the poetic mesmerism of Sohrab Sepehri, the sinuous camera work of Amir Naderi, or the tendentious eroticism of a Shirin Neshat video installation. So they keep going back to some obscure mullah in some back alley of Qom for a chat or two and then coming back with a theory or two about Iranian culture or the future of democracy in Iran. It is quite a scandal. For the most recent example of this sort of anthropological complicity in misrepresenting the cosmopolitan complexity of Iranian culture, effectively reducing it to the medieval mandates of Shi'i jurisprudence, see Ziba Mir-Hosseini and Richard Tapper, *Islam and Democracy in Iran: Eshkevari and the Quest for Reform*. For a groundbreaking critique of the whole discipline of anthropology see Edward Said's "Representing the Colonized: Anthropology's Interlocutors," *Critical Inquiry* 15, no. 2 (Winter 1989): 205–25.

9. For more on Gianni Vattimo's notion of *il pensiero debole* see his *The End of Modernity: Nihilism and Hermeneutics in Postmodern Culture* (Baltimore: Johns Hopkins University Press, 1991).

10. For more on the antimetaphysical articulation of a morality against ethics see the miraculous works of John D. Caputo, particularly his *Against Ethics* (Bloomingdale: Indiana University Press, 1993).

11. However, on occasion I have ventured to theorize aspects of that emancipatory eroticism. See for example my "Shirin Neshat: Transcending the Boundaries of an Imaginative Geography," in Octavio Zaya, ed., *The Last Word* (San Sebastian, Spain: Museum of Modern Art, 2005). In English and Spanish.

12. An emerging body of criticism, fully conscious of grassroots and Third World feminism, has begun to tackle the all too necessary assessment of the court-initiated imperial feminism that defined the discourse of the women's rights movement during the Pahlavi period. As evident in such monarchist historiography as that of Mahnaz Afkhami's "Women in Post-Revolutionary Iran: A Feminist Perspective" (in Mahnaz Afkhami and Erika Friedl, eds., *In the Eye of the Storm: Women in Post-Revolutionary Iran* [Syracuse, NY: Syracuse University Press, 1994], 5–18), a considerable part of the feminist literature conducted within the domain of Iranian studies proper has an entirely sanguine reading of the status of Iranian women during the Pahlavi dynasty—a kind of feminism that was sponsored by the Pahlavi court under the auspices of Ashraf Pahlavi, the late shah's twin sister, and her WOI (Women's Organization of Iran). For a more critical assessment of Iranian women's history during both the Pahlavis and under the Islamic Republic see the seminal work of Parvin Paidar, *Women and the Political Process in Twentieth-Century Iran* (Cambridge, UK: Cambridge University Press, 1995) and Valentine M. Moghadam, "Gender Inequality in the Islamic Republic of Iran: A Sociodemoghraphy," in Myron Weiner and Ali Banuazizi, eds., *The Politics of Social Transformation in Afghanistan, Iran, and Pakistan* (Syracuse, NY: Syracuse University Press, 1994). For a more comparative assessment of women's movements in the region see Valentine M. Moghadam, *Modernizing Women: Gender and Social Change in the Middle East*, 2nd ed. (New York: L. Rienner Publishers; 2003.

13. For a groundbreaking discussion of anticolonial nationalism see Partha Chatterjee's *The Nation and Its Fragments*.

14. Contrary to Bernard Lewis's treacherous suggestion that countries such as Iran are susceptible to balkanization, by which he means the age-old British trump card of fabricating ethnic unrest in such provinces as Khuzestan, Kurdistan, or Azerbaijan to facilitate their own colonial control, the pervasive and powerful cosmopolitan culture that underlies many potential ethnic or sectarian divisions within countries such as Iran speaks to

an entirely different historical experience. The problem with mercenary Orientalists such as Lewis is that they are so off the mark and lost in reading the cosmopolitan disposition of any culture that they invariably reduce it to their own perturbed imagination of what and where it is.

15. Equally flawed is this repeated nonsense about Islam now experiencing its Reformation, the most recent proponent of which is a precocious graduate student named Reza Aslan in a book called *No god but God: The Origins, Evolution, and Future of Islam*. Why should the world follow the periodization of the social and political history of Europe—or anywhere else for that matter? If Christianity experienced a Reformation, so must Islam? Who decided that European Reformation and Enlightenment, filled with their own complicated causes and calamitous consequences, and in terms domestic to European history, must be repeated anywhere else in the world? The same European history that witnessed the Reformation also produced pogroms, genocides, and holocausts. So should Islamic history repeat or emulate those few items as well—and why, by what authority, and on the basis of what scholarship can a person be given a podium to make such high-falutin proclamations? Under the catalytic and global impact of European colonialism, much of the world has had to recast its social and intellectual history in dialogical terms that have thus modified the rest of world history. No sane person can think in such retrograde terms and see the world in such regurgitated mantras. The social and intellectual history of Islam, subject of a vast body of scholarship, of which these neocon artists are blissfully ignorant, has followed a pattern and a periodization domestic to its own civilizational, cultural, and political terms. Assimilating one civilization to the manufactured periodization of another is the supreme sign of a colonized and whitewashed mind that cannot think except in terms acceptable and familiar to the presumed white audience. "In democratic times," wrote Alexis de Tocqueville in *Democracy in America*, "the public frequently treat authors as kings do their courtiers; they enrich and despise them. What more is needed by the venal souls who are born in courts or are worthy to live there." His prophetic soul! For the details of Tocqueville's take on "the Trade of Literature" in the United States see his *Democracy in America* (New York: Vintage, 1945), vol. 2, 64.

16. For a comprehensive examination of the institution of Adab in Islamic context see the magisterial work of the late George Makdisi, *The Rise of Humanism in Classical Islam and the Christian West: With Special Reference to Scholasticism* (Edinburgh: Edinburgh University Press, 1990).

17. Toward the end of his life, Edward Said had become increasingly interested in the varieties of literary humanism by way of rescuing European humanism from its inherent blind spots. See his first posthumous book, *Humanism and Democratic Criticism* (New York: Columbia University Press, 2004), which makes specific references to literary humanism in Arabic, through the work of George Makdisi.

18. This particular piece of jewelry is also the work of the Iranian neocon at the Hoover Institution Abbas Milani. See his *Lost Wisdom: Rethinking Modernity in Iran* (Washington, DC: Mage, 2004). The argument of this book, that over that last one thousand years, no less, Iran has been caught

between a search for modernity and a belligerent "religious obscurantism," is the singular sign of illiteracy in three adjacent areas: (1) Islamic intellectual history and the dialectical vicissitudes of its varied discourses (all the subject of a massive body of scholarship, of which this neocon is blissfully ignorant); (2) the specifically European disposition of a colonial kind of modernity in the philosophical grounding of whose Enlightenment humanity at large was effectively written out of its emancipatory project (equally the subject of an expanded scholarly and theoretical literature); and (3) Third World encounters with colonial modernity and the emancipatory movements and anticolonial modernities they have engendered.

19. For a cogent set of reflections on multiple modernities see S.N. Eisenstadt, *Comparative Civilizations and Multiple Modernities*, 2 vols. (Leiden, Netherlands: Brill Academic Publishers, 2003).

20. For more on the widespread significance of Weblogs in Iran see Nasrin Alavi, *We Are Iran: The Persian Blogs* (London: Portobello Books, 2005). In another piece, Nasrin Alavi gives some extraordinary statistics worth noting here. "Those who lived through the Iranian revolution of 1979," she correctly observes, "are now a minority. In the post-revolution baby-boom, Iran's population has more than doubled to almost 70 million, of whom 70% are under 30 years old. At the same time, literacy is well over 90%, even in rural areas; and in 2005 more than 65% of students entering university were women. This demographic shift means that young people dominate Iranian society and that educated young voices speak most clearly and sharply in the Iranian blogosphere. They have experienced the limitations of a theocracy in the restrictive absurdities imposed upon their daily lives, and they see radical Islam more as a problem than as a universal remedy. For them, Ahmadinejad is not the champion of political Islamism around the world but at best a figure of fun." From Nasrin Alavi, "Iran: The Elite Against the People," *Open Democracy*, at http://www.opendemocracy.net/democracy-iran_war/elite_fears_3571.jsp (retrieved on May 23, 2006). The critical question of Iranian bloggers is now the subject of a forthcoming PhD dissertation at Stanford by Sima Shakhsari.

Index

terror, 217; and Iranian sense of displacement, 4–6; and meaning of land, 48; paradoxes of, 24–25, 27–30, 45–50, 58–59, 98–99, 249–53, 251n3. *See also* anticolonial modernity; colonial modernity, dawn of
colonial modernity, dawn of, 32–66; and Babism, 56–58; and colonial incursions, 32–36, 74, 75; and court reformists, 50–55, 73–74, 77; and expat intellectuals, 47, 49–50, 59–65; and historical self-awareness, 44; and idea of nation-state, 47, 49–50; Mirza Saleh's meeting with D'Arcy, 32–36, 41–42; Mirza Saleh's travelogue, 40–45; paradoxes of colonial modernity, 45–50, 58–59; and parliamentary democracy, 45; Persian language and prose, 36–45, 54, 59–66; Persian literary modernism, 39–40, 54, 59–66; printing technology, 43; and Qajar court, 32–41, 50–60; revolutionary movements, 56–59; and Shi'i clerical establishment, 52–53; and Shi'i scholasticism, 36–37; Tobacco Revolt, 58, 75, 274n24; translation movement, 43–44, 51–52, 64. *See also* Qajar dynasty (1789–1926) and colonial modernity
colonialism, European, 23–24; Constitutional period and economic imperialism, 71–72, 75–78, 80–82, 84; and Qajar dynasty, 32–36, 71–72, 74, 75–76, 77
communication technology, Islamic Revolution period, 140–42
Conrad, Joseph, 107; *Heart of Darkness*, 107, 253
Constitutional Revolution (1906–11), 67–104; and American figures, 83–84; as anticolonial movement, 71–73, 76–78, 85; assassination of Nasir al-din Shah, 67–70; and the British, 75, 80–82; and colonial economic imperialism, 71–72, 75–78, 80–82, 84; and Islamist ideology, 85; and nascent bourgeoisie, 76–78, 86, 88; and new constitution (1906), 70–71, 73, 79; and Qajar dynasty, 67–80; and the Russians, 75, 79–82, 84; and Shi'i clerical establishment, 74–75, 77, 78–80, 276–77n6; and social democratic ideas, 85. *See also* Constitutional period (1906–11)
Constitutional period (1906–11): anticolonial modernity and literature, 90, 98–99; educational reforms, 90–91; free press, 87, 91–94; and global capitalism, 85–88; influence of world revolutionary movements, 87; and literary modernism/humanism, 89–104; modernist cinema, 104; modernist fiction and drama, 103–4; and pan-Islamism, 87–88; Persian poetry, 99–103, 104; satirical prose and

poetry, 94–97; urban intellectuals in politics, 87; women poets, 100–101; women's rights and emancipation, 87, 91–92
Contras, 171–72
cosmopolitanism, 29–30, 248–63, 307–8n9; and antiracism, 256–57, 258–59; and feminism, 257–58; and Iranian cinema, 29–30, 262; and Islamic culture, 29–30, 254–56, 259–61; and nationalism, 258–59; and Orientalists, 299n22, 307–9n9, 309–10n14. *See also* anticolonial modernity
Cuban Revolution (1959), 128
cultural modernity: cinema, 104, 114–15, 132, 135, 154, 180, 195, 207–10; Constitutional period, 89–104; and expat intellectuals, 59–65; fiction, 103–4, 114, 116–17, 122, 129–30, 132, 208; and Islamic Revolution, 174–75, 179–81, 208; literary (Constitutional period), 89–104; literary (Pahlavi period), 114, 116–17, 118–20, 122, 129; literary (Persian), 39–45, 54, 59–66; Pahlavi period, 114–20, 122, 128–30, 132, 133–36; poetry, 114, 118–20, 122, 129, 132, 174–75, 208; post-Khomeini period, 207–10; and Western literature, 30, 133–35
Cushman, Thomas, *A Matter of Principle*, 8
Cyrus the Great, 23, 132, 133, 147, 155

Daneshvar, Simin, 130, 132, 174, 292–93n47; *Savushan*, 132
Dar al-Fonun, 51, 90, 121
D'Arcy, Joseph, 32–36, 41–42, 46
D'Arcy, William Knox, 82
Darwin, Charles, *The Origin of Species*, 52
Darwish, Mahmoud, 30, 135
Davis, Angela, 134
Dehkhoda, Mirza Ali Akbar, 92, 96, 97–98, 100; *Amthal-o-Hikam*, 97; *Charand-o-Parand (Gibberish)*, 97; *Loghat-nameh*, 97
Delbanco, Andrew, 291n38
demographics: Islamic Revolution period, 137, 149; religious, 149, 204; youth population, 137, 311n20
Dershowitz, Alan, 206
Descartes, René, *Discourse on Reason*, 51–52
Dialectic of Enlightenment (Adorno and Horkheimer), 206
Dickens, Charles, 134
Dolatabadi, Mahmoud, 130
Dostoyevsky, Fyodor, 30, 108, 134
Du Bois, W.E.B., 134
Dustdar, Aramesh, 302n10

East India Act (1784), 35
Ebadi, Shirin, 209–10, 238, 300n30